Praise for papers in this collection:

'Don Markwell's rich discussion of transformational leadership reflects his own deep experience as a transformative leader in both the global Rhodes community and the University of Western Australia. In this very thoughtful collection, Markwell engages head-on with the significant challenges and opportunities of the current century, including the rapid rise of Asia and the need for world-class education.'

Dominic Barton

Managing Director, McKinsey & Company
Rhodes Trustee

'In our fast changing and globalising world, the tasks to ensure peace and prosperity become ever more daunting. By combining thoughts on leadership and education, Don Markwell provides many valuable insights in how great leaders and great institutions have brought about the necessary change, often in very challenging circumstances. Especially in times of growing scepticism in the world, he shows us many paths of how to get things done.'

Dr Hans-Paul Buerkner

Chairman of The Boston Consulting Group
Chairman of the Association of German Rhodes Scholars

'Don Markwell brings to the pages of this collection his striking qualities of depth of vision and enthusiasm of purpose – but, above all, his passionate belief in the importance of individual agency and leadership. His essays, seeded throughout with self-effacing wit, are thought-provoking, often profound and informative, but above all hopeful in their belief in our own capacity to make a difference to the world we live in.'

Justice Edwin Cameron

Judge of the Constitutional Court of South Africa
General Secretary to the Rhodes Trust for Southern Africa

About the author

Born in the outback of Queensland, Australia, and Rhodes Scholar for Queensland for 1981, Donald Markwell became the first Rhodes Scholar to serve as Warden of Rhodes House, Oxford, responsible for the Rhodes Scholarships around the world (2009-12).

He came to this role from serving as Deputy Vice-Chancellor (Education) at the University of Western Australia (2007-09).

Dr Markwell was previously Warden of Trinity College at the University of Melbourne (1997-2007), and Fellow & Tutor in Politics at Merton College, Oxford (1986-97).

He has served as Executive Director of the Menzies Research Centre, an Australian public policy think tank, since 2012.

Other books by Donald Markwell

State of the Nation: aspects of Australian public policy
(edited with Rachael Thompson & Julian Leeser, 2013)
'A large and liberal education': higher education for the 21st century
(2007)
John Maynard Keynes and International Relations: Economic Paths to War and Peace (2006)
Liberals face the future: essays on Australian liberalism
(edited with George Brandis & Tom Harley, 1984)

*

Also extensive involvement in the preparation of
A Public Life: The Memoirs of Zelman Cowen (2006)

'Instincts to lead':
on leadership, peace, and education

Donald Markwell

with a preface by Elliot F Gerson
American Secretary of the Rhodes Trust

Connor Court Publishing
Australia

Published in 2013 by Connor Court Publishing Pty Ltd

Connor Court Publishing Pty Ltd.
PO Box 224W
Ballarat Vic 3350 Australia
sales@connorcourt.com
www.connorcourt.com

ISBN: 978-1-922168-702(pbk.)

Cover design: M. Giordano. Cover photograph by Paul Gray, of Rachel Paterson,
Dustin Stuart, Jackie McArthur, and Vinay Menon at Rhodes House, Oxford,
June 2013.

Printed in Australia

For Claire, Andrew, and Elizabeth,

for Gill Williams (Lady Williams)
a dear friend to many, and a woman of elegance and grace

and in memory of
Mrs Jinny Fletcher
(29 April 1922-21 July 2010)
whose generous hospitality meant so much

and of
Dr Clarita von Trott zu Solz
(19 September 1917-28 March 2013)
who showed that love is stronger than death

Contents

Acknowledgements

The photograph on the front cover of this book – showing current Rhodes Scholars from the University of Western Australia at Rhodes House, Oxford – reflects my gratitude to both institutions, and the fact that the speeches and writings in this book derive mainly from my years as Deputy Vice-Chancellor (Education) at the University of Western Australia (2007-09) and as Warden of Rhodes House (2009-12). The photograph was taken by a Charlie Perkins Scholar, Paul Gray, and I am very grateful to him and to the Rhodes Scholars photographed – Rachel Paterson, Dustin Stuart, Jackie McArthur, and Vinay Menon. The greatest reward from educational leadership is working with and for students, and this has very much been my own experience.

As well as to so many students, I owe a great deal to very many colleagues both at UWA and at Rhodes House and in the wider Rhodes community, and I am deeply grateful to them. For particular assistance at Rhodes House related to this volume, I especially thank Dr Andrew Graham, Charles Conn, Mary Eaton, Shelley Nicholls, Kate Tilley, and, at an earlier time, Ben Lundin. At the University of Western Australia, I especially thank Professor Ian Reid, Dr Carolyn Daniel, Janice Moffett, Sandy Johnston, Ambelin Kwaymullina, and Simon Kidd.

Elliot Gerson, American Secretary of the Rhodes Trust and Executive Vice President of The Aspen Institute, has written a very generous Preface, and I am profoundly grateful to him for this and for his warm collegiality and friendship. For comments on papers in this collection, I am also deeply appreciative to Dominic Barton, Dr Hans-Paul Buerkner, Justice Edwin Cameron, Justice Eileen Gillese, Professor Andrew Hamilton, Dr Kopano Matlwa Mabaso, Professor Alan Robson, Prashant Sarin, Very Revd Dr Jane Shaw, and Professor Thomas H B Symons.

The editing of this book has been very ably managed by Emma Yabsley, whom I thank most warmly for her astute judgement, technical skills, collegiality, gentle prompts, and much else: without her valiant and invaluable efforts, this book would not exist. Professor Amin Saikal in Canberra and Katy Hansen in Oxford kindly checked key facts for me, and I am very grateful to them, and also to Liam Brennan, Adam Bextream, and Rachael Thompson for their most valuable assistance. Michael Gilchrist has undertaken the type-setting and layout of this book, and Andrew Markwell has prepared the Index, and I warmly thank them for all they have done with much-valued diligence and care. Dr Anthony Cappello of Connor Court has been most encouraging and supportive. My heartfelt appreciation to him, M. Giordano, and McPherson's Printing Group for their crucial roles in the publication of this volume.

Some of the work for this book was undertaken while I was a visiting professor in the School of Political Science and International Studies at the University of Queensland, and a visiting scholar in the Centre for Leadership, King's College, University of Queensland. Both the School and the College made me extremely welcome, and I am very much in their debt.

Several of the pieces in this book have been published elsewhere, and I thank: *Pacifica* for permission to republish my book review published here as 'Leadership in churches: the challenge of creative leadership'; the Lowy Institute for International Policy for permission to republish my commentaries on Mrs Thatcher and on the Schwarzman Scholarships, which both first appeared on Lowy's *The Interpreter* site; *The Times* for permission to republish my obituary of David Alexander, first published in *The Times* on 12 August 2010, and reprinted anonymously in *The American Oxonian*, Fall 2010; *The Round Table: The Commonwealth Journal of International Affairs* and Taylor & Francis for permission to republish my December 2011 eulogy for Sir Zelman Cowen, which was published in *The Round Table;* Oxford University Press for permission to republish extracts from my book *John Maynard Keynes and International Relations: Economic Paths to War and Peace* (Oxford University Press, 2006); *The Independent* for permission to republish my obituary of Sir Keith Hancock, first published in *The Independent* on 24 August 1988; and Palgrave Macmillan for permission to republish my eulogy of Hedley Bull, which was first published as 'Hedley Bull as a teacher' in Robert O'Neill & David N Schwartz (eds), *Hedley Bull on Arms Control*, Macmillan Press in association with the International Institute for Strategic Studies (IISS), 1987.

Several of my speeches as Warden of Rhodes House, Oxford, were previously published in *The American Oxonian*, and I am most grateful to its editor, Dr Todd Breyfogle, for his support for their republication here, and his encouragement, and that of many others, in the purposes – of promoting civic-minded leadership, international understanding, and liberal education – which are so central to this book.

Preface

The Rhodes Scholarships are the most famous award for graduate study in the world, bringing outstanding young scholars every year from five continents to the University of Oxford, and then forever changing their lives. Their renown though has less to do with the Scholars' subsequent academic distinctions, as formidable as they are, than with their remarkable record of leadership in almost all fields of human endeavour, but especially in service to others. Donald Markwell was the first Rhodes Scholar to become Warden of Rhodes House. His wisdom and insights about leadership and higher education made him an ideal choice to run the Rhodes Scholarships at a pivotal time in their century-plus history. He brought to Rhodes House extraordinary warmth, much charm and good humour, and passionate dedication to student welfare. And his vision for a close global community of Rhodes Scholars will be a legacy forever shaping the Rhodes Trust.

Now, this wonderful book will be a resource and inspiration for a much broader audience, and fittingly at a time of near-universal yearning for far more enlightened leadership of our most important institutions, public and private alike.

Don Markwell is the rare student of leadership who is himself a true leader. In addition to his acute observations of transformative leaders, and his sophisticated understanding of the theory of leadership, he brings his own wide practical leadership experience to bear. While I was witness to his leadership to the Rhodes Trust, I know from countless others how he has brought hard and positive change to the other institutions to which he has also been entrusted. For example, amongst other initiatives, he championed a complete overhaul of the academic courses for the University of Western Australia. Curriculum reform is a pressing issue worldwide, and many lessons can be drawn from Don's description of the consultative process he so ably led.

There are many things that distinguish this book from myriad others on leadership. For one, Don's international perspectives and experiences are especially enriching. Examples abound from Africa, Asia, North America, and Europe, as well of course from his native Australia. And as a prominent scholar of international relations, he is especially insightful about the development and encouragement of leaders with the values and visions to advance the causes of peace, tolerance, and mutual understanding. Indeed, at Rhodes House, he brought unprecedented attention to the aspiration of Cecil Rhodes that his Scholarships could prevent future wars. Of course, they didn't – but in time they and similar ones modelled on them could. Markwell compellingly suggests how strengthened links among nations, especially those forged by their young and future leaders during shared educational experiences, can now reach scale and breadth to have profound implications.

Finally, the book is infused with wisdom about the importance of the classical values of liberal education, and of the indispensable role of the university to human progress. In a time when too much of the world's focus is limited to the extrinsic value of education to prepare people for jobs, it is welcome indeed to be reminded so eloquently of how collegiate education should serve as the foundation for inspired leadership, as the cultivator of 'instincts to lead', and as the crucible in which future leaders develop and fine tune their moral compasses and chart their ambitions against the world's greatest challenges.

Elliot F Gerson
American Secretary of the Rhodes Trust
Executive Vice President, The Aspen Institute

Introduction

On his death in 1902, Cecil John Rhodes left a will and codicils that set out a great vision of an international scholarship program. It had essentially two fundamental purposes. The first was to broaden the horizons and promote a spirit of public service among outstanding young people with 'instincts to lead'. The second was to create a network of friendship between the major powers so as to 'render war impossible'; in Rhodes's view, 'educational relations make the strongest tie' between nations. These purposes were to be achieved through bringing these outstanding young people of many countries – chosen on criteria of excellence in intellect, character, leadership capacity, and commitment to service – into the broadening and supportive collegiate environment of the University of Oxford, to engage with each other and with fellow students from Britain and other countries, and to maintain connections throughout their lives beyond. The brilliant efforts of many people have given effect to this vision over the decades since Rhodes's death.

For some three-plus years, from 2009 to 2012, it was my exciting privilege and demanding responsibility to serve as Warden of Rhodes House, Oxford. This meant having responsibility, under the Rhodes Trustees and working with colleagues in Oxford and in many countries, for running the Rhodes Scholarships around the world. I would like to record my gratitude to all those people – at Rhodes House in Oxford, and in many countries – who contributed to what was achieved in this time.

It was necessary in those years to try to strengthen the sense of international, inter-disciplinary, and inter-generational community among Rhodes Scholars (embracing alumni and current Scholars) within Oxford and globally, to engage Rhodes Scholars in consultation about the best future for the Rhodes Scholarships in the 21st century, to enrich further the experience of Rhodes Scholars in Oxford, to refresh and open up the governance of the Rhodes Trust, and to encourage philanthropic support for the Scholarships (such support had not been sought before the pioneering efforts of my distinguished predecessor, Sir Colin Lucas). The encouragement of philanthropic support was both to sustain the existing Scholarships in the face of the financial volatility of the present century, and to make possible an expansion of the Scholarships to give the best effect to Cecil Rhodes's vision in the geopolitical realities of the 21st century (including, in time, amongst other initiatives, to create Rhodes Scholarships to bring outstanding Chinese students, chosen on the Rhodes criteria, to Oxford).

I came to that role in the Rhodes community after a career in university teaching, research, and academic leadership, most recently from 2007 to 2009 as Deputy Vice-Chancellor (Education) of the University of Western Australia (UWA). At UWA, my role was to help to shape strategy and policy on all aspects of enhancing the student learning experience within one of the finest universities in Australia. This included leading a consultative review of the University's course structures which led to the radical reform of course structures and curriculum. This initiative and others (such as outreach to potential students from disadvantaged backgrounds, and to enrich the campus experience of students, including to promote residence on or near campus) arose in the context of the aspiration of the University of Western Australia to become, by mid-century, genuinely one of the 'top 50' universities in the world.

Many of my speeches as Warden of Rhodes House discussed aspects of the great purposes of the Rhodes Scholarships – the nurturing of 'instincts to lead' into effective civic-minded leadership, and the promotion of peace between nations – and the educational philosophy reflected in Rhodes's vision: in particular, the importance of 'breadth' and liberal education, and the value of collegiate education and of student engagement in extra-curricular activities. At the University of Western Australia and before, many of my speeches also discussed these and other issues in education.

This volume presents a selection of speeches and writings on these various topics in my successive roles, especially at UWA and Rhodes House, since 2007. It is in some sense a sequel to the volume on educational issues from my time as Warden of Trinity College, University of Melbourne, from 1997 to 2007, published as *'A large and liberal education': higher education for the 21st century.*[*]

Each of the pieces in this book was, of course, prepared for a specific occasion, and the texts reflect that. For example, many use the identifiers that specify a Rhodes Scholar by the constituency for which they were elected, their Oxford college, and year of commencement in Oxford. Some pieces may reflect the spirit of the times and immediate circumstances more than others. Some were prepared before 2007, but have been included because they may add something to the theme being developed – themes of leadership, discussions of individual leaders, peace and the promotion of international understanding, and various aspects of university education. Some limited editing of pieces in this book has been done, most especially to reduce repetition, and the unevenness of footnoting between different speeches remains.

The recurrent emphasis on Africa reflects the origins of the Rhodes Scholarships in southern Africa, where Cecil Rhodes made his home and fortune, and the continuing commitment of the Rhodes Trust to Africa. The Rhodes Trust has always provided considerable support to educational and other activities in Africa. At the time of the centenary of the Rhodes Scholarships in 2003, under the leadership of Lord (William) Waldegrave as Chair of the Trustees and Dr John Rowett as Warden of Rhodes House, it entered into a partnership with Nelson Mandela to create a leadership program for Africa, the

---

[*] Australian Scholarly Publishing & Trinity College, University of Melbourne, 2007.

Mandela Rhodes Foundation, based in Cape Town (of which I had the honour to be a Trustee from 2009 to 2012). One of my activities as Warden of Rhodes House was also to seek support for additional Rhodes Scholarships for Africa, as well as to seek to secure those currently in existence, as a means of promoting high-quality civic-minded leadership in Africa.

The pieces in this book 'On leadership' reflect, inter alia, the transformative potential of good leadership, the differing styles of leadership that may be needed in different contexts, and the challenges for leaders arising from resistance to change. It may be that my own thinking about leadership and leaders is too focussed on transformation; but the work of many of the leaders discussed in these pages – Nelson Mandela, F W de Klerk, Margaret Thatcher, and many others – shows that in many situations transformation is not too much to hope for.

My own more modest experience of leadership roles at UWA and in the Rhodes community over recent years has involved sustained processes of consultation – at UWA to review and, as a result, to work to reform curriculum and course structures, and in the Rhodes community, to engage powerful minds and grateful and generous spirits around the world in shaping (and helping to resource) the best possible future for the Rhodes Scholarships. While more directive and less consultative forms of leadership are sometimes needed, this experience – some of which is reflected in this volume – has affirmed my conviction that such processes of consultation can often both engender good ideas and engage great support far beyond what could otherwise be achieved.

My own observation and experience of leadership leads me to emphasise the potential impact for good of setting clear and ambitious goals (what Jim Collins and Jerry Porras called BHAGs – 'big hairy audacious goals")* and of using those clear and ambitious fundamental purposes to shape everything the

---

* Jim Collins and Jerry I Porras, *Built to Last: Successful Habits of Visionary Companies*, HarperCollins, 1994.

organisation does. All key decisions are thus made by going back to the core question: what are we fundamentally trying to achieve? Some of the papers in this book reflect the core goals of the two institutions I tried to serve in these years: the goal of the University of Western Australia to become in time one of the 'top 50' universities in the world, and the goal of the Rhodes Scholarships to be refreshed and resourced to make the greatest impact for good that is possible in the new realities of the 21st century. Some of the papers also reflect the great potential value of finding in the founding principles of an organisation, and in its history, pointers to what its core contemporary and future purposes should be, and how best to achieve those goals. Some also reflect the benefits that can flow from encouraging wide-ranging conversation about how best to achieve the fundamental purposes of the organisation in the changing context of today and tomorrow.

In this rapidly-changing world, leaders often have the task of managing change in their organisation, even their country. Such 'change management' typically requires clarity of purpose, effective communications, engaging support for those purposes, identifying the actions needed, engendering the appropriate sense of urgency about them (as against complacency on one hand, or panic on the other*), sustained focus on implementing change, and following through with resolve. The political skills – the inspiration, the diplomacy, the carrots, and sometimes the sticks – needed to overcome often subterranean resistance to necessary change are among the recurring themes of leadership literature. Significant and rapid change is often needed, but often creates fear, insecurity, and anxiety; and one of the challenges to leaders is how to carry with them those who experience that stress and fear of change. Sometimes even the resisters do not understand or acknowledge their own resistance or the reasons for it. The politics of change can be very difficult both within countries and within organisations, and it requires of leaders

---

* John P Kotter, *A sense of urgency*, Harvard Business Press, 2008.

such qualities (amongst others) as clarity of purpose, skills of persuasion, generosity of spirit, and 'grace under pressure'.* (Needless to say, I do not pretend to be myself a paragon of all the virtues I have identified as being desirable, nor to have succeeded in all the tasks I suggest are needed.)

Different contexts can require different styles of leadership, and one of the forms of intelligence or judgement needed of good leaders is the ability to discern which style the context requires. It is sometimes said that there are gender differences in leadership styles. It is certainly my conviction that one of the enduring challenges of leadership in many places is to be fully inclusive, and to promote gender equity. The encouragement of women's leadership has been central to my own work for many years, and this too is reflected in this book (though less than I would like).

The section of the book 'On leaders' contains tributes to or assessments of diverse individuals which were prepared for specific contexts. These include speeches to welcome or introduce individuals on particular occasions, or to pay tribute to, or mourn, them on their passing. The choice of leader is thus eclectic, reflecting circumstances; but I hope this kaleidoscopic selection of pieces nonetheless suggests valuable lessons for leadership. They reflect leadership in different contexts, but especially leadership in politics (domestic and international), education, culture, and intellectual thought. There is more on educational leadership in other sections of the book, especially 'On education'.

It was for me an exciting discovery as Warden of Rhodes House to learn how much Cecil Rhodes himself had thought about the importance of promoting peace between nations, and the means to do this. In the context of his own day, he saw the growth of the British Empire as a means towards this, and came

---

* The aspirational phrase 'grace under pressure' was Ernest Hemingway's definition of courage, cited by John F Kennedy in his *Profiles in Courage,* for which he won the Pulitzer Prize in 1957.

to see the development of understanding (or 'an understanding') between the great powers (at the turn of the 20th century, the British Empire, the United States, and Germany) as the key to this – and the development of educational relations between countries as the key to such understanding. This aspect of Cecil Rhodes's vision was more strongly emphasised and better known in the first half of the 20th century than it was subsequently. Rhodes's remarkably idealistic vision of peace being promoted through international scholarships is set out in the section of this book 'On peace'. A number of pieces then discuss this vision specifically in the 20th century context of the German Rhodes Scholarships (including the ultimate sacrifices made by some for the international friendship they worked to promote), and then look ahead to its further embodiment in the 21st century, most especially in developing scholarship links between China and the rest of the world (especially but far from only the United States). More or new Rhodes Scholarships for Africa, India, Pakistan, and many other countries and regions around the world also have great potential and are worthy of strenuous efforts and generous support.

If the re-emphasis of Cecil Rhodes's peace purpose for the Rhodes Scholarships helps to shape thinking about the Rhodes Scholarships in the 21st century, and helps to encourage and shape other scholarship programs (such as the Schwarzman Scholarships and the New Colombo Plan), then in my view that is all to the good: faithful to Cecil Rhodes's intentions, and much needed in our own time.* If the Rhodes Scholarships did not

----

* One of my current tasks as Executive Director of the Menzies Research Centre, a public policy think tank, has been to contribute to shaping the 'New Colombo Plan' – a plan for encouraging Australian students to study abroad in universities in the Asia-Pacific region. The vision of the New Colombo Plan is also imbued with Cecil Rhodes's vision of promoting international understanding and harmony through student mobility. This link was explicitly made by Tony Abbott MP (himself an Australian Rhodes Scholar) in a speech in Oxford on 14 December 2012. That same spirit was reflected in 2013 in the creation of the Schwarzman Scholarships to China, an exciting new initiative with similarities and differences with the Rhodes Scholarships. The Schwarzman Scholarships are discussed in the section of this book 'On peace'.

prevent world war in the 20th century (which, idealistic though it was, was Cecil Rhodes's goal), they nonetheless did and can do much to promote international understanding. Two examples of this that seem clear to me are that they have contributed to Anglo-American friendship, and to understanding of Africa (always important for the Rhodes Trust) among the US foreign policy 'elite'. The section of this book on the German Rhodes Scholarships reflects some of the noble efforts of Rhodes Scholars to promote Anglo-German friendship. A world always at risk of international conflict needs more such efforts at promoting international understanding. One important development has been that, as well as 'elite' programs, of which the Rhodes Scholarship was the progenitor, there have increasingly been other programs to promote people-to-people relations, including through large-scale student mobility, and more.

The section 'On peace' also touches on some of the alternative approaches to war and peace with which I have been concerned: John Maynard Keynes's emphasis on economic factors making for war or peace, the Commonwealth as an element of solidarity and cooperation in a world of conflict, and the Anglo-Australian tradition of thinking about international relations (reflected in the writings and teaching of Sir Keith Hancock, Hedley Bull, R J Vincent, and Geoffrey Jukes) which has helped to shape my own approach. This section reflects the fact that one of my own long-standing research interests has been in the history of thought about the causes of war and the means of promoting peace. While greatly influenced by 'realist' thinkers who emphasised the importance of a balance of power and of effective deterrence, I have more often written on 'idealist' thinkers, especially those who, in the first half of the 20th century, believed that the conflictual nature of international politics could be changed to a more harmonious one, and so peace promoted. Such idealist writers, thinkers, and actors as Norman Angell, Gilbert Murray, Melian Stawell, Alfred Zimmern, and John Maynard Keynes –

and now Cecil Rhodes – have caught my eye. The means which they and others proposed to achieve peace included the creation of a rule of law in international politics, perhaps enforced or encouraged through international organisations such as the League of Nations or the United Nations; economic means, such as the promotion of free trade, benign 'globalisation', or good governance of the international economy; through the creation of other webs of interdependence and of transnational solidarity of one form or another between peoples (e.g. people-to-people relations within the British Empire and Commonwealth); through the promotion of democracy; and others.

Cecil Rhodes believed that 'educational relations make the strongest tie', and believed (as Stephen Schwarzman appears to believe today) that the prospects for war and peace could be significantly influenced, if not determined, by what happens in a university. This is remarkable testimony to the importance of universities. Moreover, as already mentioned, Rhodes's will embodied an educational philosophy that emphasised the importance of what Rhodes called 'breadth to [students'] views', the value of extra-curricular activities (including in which 'moral force of character' or 'instincts to lead' could be seen and encouraged), and the value of colleges. It is no wonder that the Rhodes Scholarships have for 110 years been closely connected in various ways with liberal education and colleges.

These topics – including the roles of universities, and attributes of the world's best – naturally then form part of my discussion, both at UWA and at Rhodes House, on educational issues. It is evident from his will that Rhodes was concerned with the quality of experience Rhodes Scholars would have in Oxford, and in their staying connected as alumni* (though he did not seem to foresee the need or desirability of their replenishing

---

* One of the generally neglected clauses in Cecil Rhodes's will (section 34) says that he wanted 'scholars past and present [to] have opportunities of meeting and discussing their experiences and prospects'. He provided for an annual dinner for this purpose; clearly now, with thousands of Rhodes Scholars dispersed around the world, much more than an annual dinner is needed.

the funds he left in his remarkable but not wholly inexhaustible bequest). As Sir Anthony Kenny has pointed out, one of the impacts of the Rhodes Scholarships was to promote the internationalisation of Oxford University in the 20th century.[*] Indeed, they have clearly contributed and contribute still to the wider and continuing internationalisation of universities around the world. Various of the pieces in this book reflect the diverse links between Oxford and many people and organisations in many countries. One of my recurring themes has been what can be learnt from examining the attributes of the best education and the best educational institutions and systems that can be identified around the world.

Rhodes wanted to offer educational opportunities that would transform the lives and outlooks of outstanding young people. The creation of life-changing opportunities for individuals of potential, regardless of their background or financial need, is or should be one of the central purposes of any educational institution. The creation of such opportunities, including opportunities for intellectual breadth and engagement in enriching campus life for students from all backgrounds, has been one of the great motivations of my whole professional life.

Both the founder of the Rhodes Scholarships, Cecil Rhodes, and the founder of the University of Western Australia, John Winthrop Hackett, were 19th century British men who made fortunes and wielded great power in distant colonies, and used or left most of their wealth to promote noble and enduring purposes. Whatever else may be said about them, they are exceptional exemplars of philanthropy – something much needed today.

I hope that some of the pieces in the section 'On education' will be useful prompts to thought about the role and desirable spirit of universities today and for the future, and of how their great purposes in teaching, research, and service can best be

---

[*] Anthony Kenny (ed.), *The History of the Rhodes Trust*, Oxford University Press, 2001, pp. 520-21.

pursued – applying enduring values in rapidly changing and often challenging contexts. These pieces will be open to various criticisms, one of which is that they do not give enough attention to how rapid changes in technology and in its use are, or may be, changing the university world. While something is said of this here, it is an important topic for fuller discussion elsewhere, and one that seems to have grown in significance quite rapidly and recently.

One of the arts of leadership is, of course, often (if not always) to apply enduring values in changing contexts, and to balance tradition and innovation in the way best suited to the needs of the time. Many of the values we most need in the 21st century were well expressed by great thinkers and actors of the 19th, of whom John Stuart Mill, John Henry Newman, and Cecil John Rhodes are for me among the most compelling. Nurturing leadership that engages effectively with the great (often fast-changing and global) challenges of the 21st century, while holding fast to unchanging values, is central to this book. Those challenges include issues of peace and security, and of economic, environmental, and other problems, in a context where power is increasingly dispersed, and traditional modes of leadership seem less effective than once they were. Part of the challenge is for international cooperation in a globalised world in which there is a significant shift of power from West to East (especially to Asia) and from North to South. The pieces in this book do not, of course, provide a full answer to all this, but I hope they help us to glimpse and grasp at least some of what is needed.

One of the pieces in this book, a speech given at an Oxford-Cambridge dinner in Chicago, mentions that Cambridge and Oxford do much to promote Anglo-American friendship, which is a cornerstone of 'liberty and liberality'. David Alexander expressed the values of liberal education as 'the quest for an open mind in an open society'; it has often been said that liberal education is education for the wise exercise of freedom. Sir Zelman Cowen, whose spirit endures, stood for the values of individual liberty under law, rational discourse, and civility in a free society. Many others mentioned in this book have also fought for the values of a free society, and the generous-spirited celebration of the individual in a diverse and tolerant community. I hope it will be evident that these values are amongst those that I personally consider most important in public affairs.

Part I: On leadership

'Instincts to lead': leadership for Africa's and the world's future

Welcome for the Archbishop Tutu Leadership Program
Rhodes House, Oxford, 1 September 2010

It is a great pleasure for me as Warden to welcome you to Rhodes House, the home of Scholarships which, like the Archbishop Tutu Leadership Program, aim to nurture leaders for the future – leaders for Africa's future, and leaders for the world's future.

In doing this, I am, on behalf of the Vice-Chancellor, warmly welcoming you to the University of Oxford – a university which has done its fair share of nurturing leaders for so many countries around the world, including in Africa, as well as, for example, 26 British Prime Ministers and over a third of the current British cabinet. Amongst the African leaders nurtured by Oxford, I think, to give just one example, of Festus Mogae, for a decade President of Botswana, one of only two recipients of the Mo Ibrahim award for African leaders who govern well and then retire, honorary fellow of Oxford's University College, and someone who himself has worked in this room as a Trustee of the Rhodes Trust since earlier this year.

The Rhodes Scholarships, like the Archbishop Tutu Leadership Program, have their origins in Africa, and aim to contribute, not least, to the future of Africa as well as to the wider world. It is not surprising, I think, that development of the African Leadership Institute, which initiated the Archbishop Tutu Leadership Program, owes so much to the work of three African Rhodes Scholars: Peter Wilson, Michael Stone, and the late Norman Swanepoel – 'Swanie' – to whose memory it is fitting that we pay tribute today.

It is also fitting that we should meet in the Beit Room, named for Cecil Rhodes's business partner and Trustee, Alfred Beit, himself an enduring benefactor of educational opportunities for Africans through the Beit Trust. It is in this room that, at the Oxford launch of the Mandela Rhodes Foundation several years ago, Nelson Mandela was photographed sitting in a chair carved with Cecil Rhodes's initials, seated here beside this white marble bust of Alfred Beit. That symbolic photograph hangs in this building, just around the corner in the Milner Hall – named for another figure significant in the history of southern Africa and of the Rhodes Trust. It also hangs in the Mandela Rhodes Building in Cape Town, which I visited just last week, and which is the home of the Mandela Rhodes Scholarships, another program working hard and well to promote exceptional leadership for Africa.

It is hardly possible to visit Africa, as I have just done – visiting Zambia, Zimbabwe, and South Africa over the last two weeks, and following a trip last November to Kenya – without being struck by the fact that the quality of leadership is literally a matter of life and death for millions of people, whether from disease such as HIV/AIDS, or from civil conflict, even genocide, or from political oppression, or from malnutrition and starvation. The difference between the impact of high-quality leadership and the impact of low-grade leadership is immense, and the contrast of leadership quality between places and between times is stark. We see this, for example, in the impact of leadership on the chances of fragmented societies somehow over time being made whole, on the prospects for achieving or sustaining democracy with a free media and the rule of law, on the likelihood of corruption and even kleptocracy, on the prospects for private or public sector action to alleviate poverty and gross inequality, including through creating a climate favourable to business and other private action that will help raise living standards, and more. As you know better than I do, all these are live issues in many African countries, including – avoidably – in South Africa today.

While the examples I have given seem to relate especially to political leadership, it is important to stress that the world needs – Africa needs – exemplary leaders in all walks of life: purposeful leadership in service to the public good is possible, indeed needed, in all sections of a society, polity, and economy. Archbishop Tutu is himself an example of this, leading in and from the church with great social impact. One question for many African countries is what constructive role church leaders will play in securing the future.

We like to say that the Rhodes Scholarships, aiming to nurture 'leaders for the world's future', seek young people of exceptional intellect, character, capacity for leadership, and commitment to service. In his will, setting out the criteria for selection for his scholarships, Cecil Rhodes said that he wanted young people who exhibited 'moral force of character' and 'instincts to lead', and who would come 'to esteem the performance of public duties as [their] highest aim'. What are 'instincts to lead'? How do we recognise them? How do we nurture and develop them in others, and in ourselves?

What, indeed, is leadership? Of the many definitions available, I like especially the one that regards good leadership as inspiring, challenging, pushing, perhaps even compelling, a community of people or an organisation to deal effectively with their real issues.

If good leadership is about dealing effectively with a community's real issues, then it follows that it is not simply about the holding of office – being elected or chosen to be president of this, or chair of that – though holding office can be a necessary but not sufficient condition for exercising some forms of leadership, and election or selection by others can be a pointer to capacity for leadership. Leadership is more than holding a position; it is about being an agent for real improvement. Alas, too many holders of office are not agents for real improvement, not exercisers of what I think truly qualifies as good leadership.

Conversely, leadership can be exercised by people who do not hold formal office – for example, the asker of the hard questions, the gadfly, the proposer of ways forward, the pourer of oil on troubled waters (if one can use this image today, given BP's troubles in the Gulf of Mexico), the active citizen, the civil dissenter who refuses to comply with oppression, the whistle-blower: the person who, from any position or none, acts as an agent or catalyst of positive action in dealing with the issues that matter most. In saying this, I cannot help but think of the work of a Nigerian Rhodes Scholar, Tajudeen Abdul-Raheem, whose life was tragically cut short last year by a car accident in Kenya, and whose book of African 'postcards', written from the perspective of the pan-African activist he was and published posthumously under the title *Speaking Truth to Power*, was launched here at Rhodes House just weeks ago. Speaking truth to power is a form of leadership. And I think also of Bram Fischer, who sacrificed his privileged Afrikaner life to defend Nelson Mandela and others on trial for their lives, who himself died not long after his own release from prison under the apartheid regime, and who is remembered in Oxford with an annual memorial lecture. This lecture will be given in 2011 by another of Nelson Mandela's lawyers, Advocate George Bizos.[*]

It is widely believed that the nature of leadership has changed over recent decades. One person who has publicly espoused this view is, like you, a sometime visitor to Rhodes House, whose photograph, like Nelson Mandela's, hangs here: Her Majesty the Queen. In early July, the Queen spoke at the United Nations in New York for the first time, she thought she recalled, since 1957.[†] She said that, since then, she had 'travelled widely and met many leaders … from around the world'. She continued:

> I have also witnessed great change, much of it for the better, particularly in science and technology, and in social attitudes.

---

[*] See 'Nelson Mandela, Bram Fischer, and George Bizos: the courage to resist' in the section of this book 'On leaders'.

[†] The Queen's speech at the United Nations General Assembly, New York, on 6 July 2010.

Remarkably, many of these sweeping advances have come about not because of governments, committee resolutions, or central directives – although all these have played a part – but instead because millions of people around the world have wanted them.

Referring further to what she called 'these subtle yet significant changes in people's approach to leadership and power', the Queen said:

> It has perhaps always been the case that the waging of peace is the hardest form of leadership of all. I know of no single formula for success, but over the years I have observed that some attributes of leadership are universal, and are often about finding ways of encouraging people to combine their efforts, their talents, their insights, their enthusiasm and their inspiration, to work together.

In saying this, it seems to me that the Queen – drawing on her own extraordinary vantage point for the observation of leadership – was very much agreeing with those analysts of leadership who say that, by comparison with decades ago, it is today in many (though certainly not all) contexts more about influencing and less about instructing others to act as you wish them to act; more about 'soft power' and less about 'hard power'; more than before about consultation, consensus-building, communication, and co-operation; and more about active listening as well as active signal-sending. We can all readily think of exceptions and qualifications to this; and yet there is a real point.

The scholar of leadership and power, Joseph Nye – also an Oxonian and Rhodes Scholar – has said that what he calls the 'big man' view of leadership, so powerful in earlier generations, is increasingly out-dated in the information age, in which networks replace hierarchies, and it is important to think of leaders being, in his words, 'in the centre of a circle rather than at the top of a mountain'.[*]

---

[*]   Joseph S Nye, Jnr, *The Powers to Lead*, Oxford University Press, 2008.

It is, Nye has argued, increasingly important for leaders to exercise 'soft power' – the exercise of attraction – rather than the giving of orders. This may be especially so given the challenge and opportunity of leading inclusively in culturally diverse environments today, when perhaps more than ever before it is recognised that the contributions of women and men of all backgrounds need to be engaged for optimal or even sustainable solutions to problems.

If there is truth in all of this, it has important implications for how each of us should exercise leadership ourselves, and how we might identify and encourage 'instincts to lead' in others.

There is an important gender aspect to this. Joe Nye believes that women are, in general, intuitively better at exercising 'soft power' than men. Whether that is true or not, it is widely agreed that, in general, women exercise leadership differently from men, and that those whose task it is to identify and nurture leadership should be open to the gender differences in leadership styles, as well as to other diverse forms of leadership – as Amanda Sinclair has put it, of 'doing leadership differently'.* You hardly need me to remind you how important the pursuit of gender equality is for the future of Africa; Nick Kristof and Sheryl WuDunn have indeed described it as the great moral challenge of this century, as well as a key to development and much more.[†]

In the days (now, happily for them, long gone) when I used to inflict speeches on audiences of school children and undergraduates, I thought it important to stress that leadership, for example student leadership, though of course it needs very much to take account of the views of others, is not about the pursuit of popularity, and that it is far better to do what you believe to be right and to seek to persuade others to share your view, even at the risk of unpopularity, than to engage in the

---

* Amanda Sinclair, *Doing Leadership Differently: Gender, Power and Sexuality in a Changing Business Culture*, Melbourne University Press, 1998 & 2005.

† Nicholas D Kristof & Sheryl WuDunn, *Half the Sky: Turning Oppression into Opportunity for Women Worldwide*, Alfred A. Knopf, New York, 2009.

ultimately self-defeating pursuit of popularity, which will often result only in being brought into contempt. Today, when my job includes inflicting speeches on postgraduate students and distinguished mid-career professionals such as you, I prefer to say that it is important that leadership be based on values, on character, on integrity, on principles, on the selfless pursuit of the public good and not the selfish striving for private gain. Again, it is hardly possible to visit many countries in Africa today without being struck by the importance of this – the blessing of the presence of such leadership and the calamity of its absence – and it is hard to imagine that leaders inspired, as I am sure we all are, by the extraordinary example of Cape Town's Archbishop Tutu would not seek to base their leadership – your leadership – on ethics and integrity. Please forgive me from again quoting an earlier Capetonian, Cecil Rhodes, who sought Scholars who, in his words, exhibited qualities of 'truth, courage, devotion to duty, sympathy for and protection of the weak, kindliness, unselfishness, and fellowship'.

Yet in all this there are paradoxes and pitfalls to watch out for. How do we combine these qualities of unselfishness with the ambition and drive necessary for most effective leadership? One form of answer to that is, of course, what Jim Collins, author of such books as *Built to Last, Good to Great*, and *How the Mighty Fall*, calls 'level 5 leadership"* – the combination of personal humility with resolute professional focus and will – and what others have called the combining of *meaning* in our work, the pursuit of noble goals which motivate us and others, with remorseless discipline in their execution.† How do we encourage people, such as (I suspect) many in this room, who have only ever really known success in their activities to be willing to run the risk of failure? Willingness to run, even seek, risk is essential to real leadership.

----

* Jim Collins, *Good to Great: Why Some Companies Make the Leap...and Others Don't*, Random House Business Books, 2001, ch. 2.

† I am grateful to Michael Rennie for his emphasis on this.

Archbishop Tutu is well familiar with the biblical injunction to be as 'wise as a serpent and gentle as a dove'. The wisdom of a serpent is what we might call political skill; and political skills are ordinarily essential to the effective exercise of leadership. I commend to you a superb book on this, Ronald Heifetz and Marty Linsky's *Leadership on the Line: Staying Alive Through the Dangers of Leading*.* It shows us that because leadership is about change, it is bound to provoke resistance from those who fear the risks of change. Avoiding or overcoming such resistance requires political skills of a high order, as well as courage.

In his book *The Powers to Lead*, Joe Nye, whom I mentioned earlier, presents Machiavellian political skills as one of the six critical skills needed for leaders. He presents these skills as what he calls the 'soft power' skills of emotional intelligence, vision, and communication; the 'hard power' skills of organisation (including organising information flows well), and the Machiavellian political skills I have just mentioned; and the 'smart power' skill of 'contextual intelligence', the ability intuitively to identify a strategy that will work in the context. The form of leadership most likely to be effective depends highly on the context, Professor Nye argues, and part of the skill is in identifying the best forms for the context and issues faced. It is not for nothing that Richard Stengel in *Mandela's Way: Lessons on Life* entitles one chapter 'Lead from the Front' and the next chapter 'Lead from the Back'.†

However the tactics may vary, at the heart of the most effective leadership, I believe, is clear focus on the core purposes a leader wishes to achieve, and approaching problems with a view to transforming them from negatives to the greatest positive that is possible. In leadership, it is crucial continually to ask such questions as: what are we fundamentally trying to achieve? What are the key elements of our strategy toward that goal? What are the most significant obstacles, and how shall we deal with them?

---

* Harvard Business Press, 2002.

† Richard Stengel, *Mandela's Way: Lessons on Life*, Virgin Books, 2010.

What are the most important sources of support, and how can we deploy them to greatest effect? Above all, we need continually to sharpen our focus on, and refresh our thinking about, what our fundamental goals are, and how everything we do moves us closer to those goals. We need to see opportunity where others see only problems; to identify the potential for something wholly new or better, and to make the most of that potential. We need to step back from the immediate details and take in the whole landscape in order to understand the environment in which we are operating, and what the big strategic needs and opportunities are.

Yet there is no escaping the fact that such creative leadership is hard, often thankless and lonely, almost unavoidably conflictual, and frequently even overwhelming. It can be helped by having mentors and coaches to turn to for disinterested discussion and even advice, as well as having other refuges from the storm – perhaps in music, exercise, religion, or meditation. It requires some focus on self-preservation as a person, and on refreshing yourself – intellectually, physically, emotionally, and spiritually. It requires the development of positive psychology while being honest, at least with yourself and in supportive contexts with others, about your own insecurities. It requires a commitment to continual learning and renewal, such as you have reflected in your participation in this leadership program; on the strategic use of time; and on stepping outside the immediacy and busy-ness of the day-to-day to focus afresh on long-term goals and the things that matter most for your organisation and in your own life. It requires self-discipline.

It can be helpful in all this to have likeminded people with whom you can talk candidly, and I hope that you will find staying involved with the African Leadership Institute and the alumni community of the Archbishop Tutu Leadership Program will help you in this.

Much can be learnt about leadership from the examples – the successes and failures – of significant leaders. I am struck and delighted by fact that some of the most important writing about Nelson Mandela has been done by Oxonians and indeed by Rhodes Scholars: for example, Richard Stengel, whom I have already mentioned, who collaborated with Madiba on *Long Walk to Freedom*, has more recently published *Mandela's Way*, which has much to teach us about leadership; Oxford's Professor Elleke Boehmer has published her own analysis of Mr Mandela*; and Shaun Johnson, now director of the Mandela Rhodes Foundation, is the author, amongst much else, of *Strange Days Indeed*, which Madiba has described as 'a unique, vivid, eyewitness diary of the rebirth of a country' from apartheid to democracy.[†]

When Nelson Mandela came to Rhodes House, and was photographed in this room, he also signed our visitors' book. So too have many other leaders of note – Mahatma Ghandi, the Dalai Lama, Margaret Thatcher, Bill Clinton and Hillary Rodham Clinton, and many more. In welcoming you to Oxford and to Rhodes House this afternoon, may I ask that, at an appropriate time later today, you join them in our visitors' book, signing the page that will record for posterity your presence here as a participant in this Archbishop Tutu Leadership Program?

You could not be more welcome, and I wish you well for the discussions to come, and for your contribution today and over the years ahead to meeting Africa's, and the world's, urgent and sustained need for excellent and ethical leadership.

Your continent needs you!

---

*   Elleke Boehmer, *Nelson Mandela: A Very Short Introduction*, Oxford University Press, 2008.

†   Shaun Johnson, *Strange Days Indeed: South Africa from Insurrection to Post-Election*, Bantam Books, 1994, p. 1.

Developing leaders for a world of global forces and rapid change

University of Oxford alumni reception
Auckland, New Zealand
6 August 2011

It is a remarkable thing that, just as elsewhere in this city the All Blacks are about to play the Wallabies, you are kindly enduring listening to an Australian. Thank you!*

It is, in fact, a great pleasure for me, as Warden of Rhodes House, to be with you here in Auckland, and to speak about, and I hope stimulate discussion of, one of the greatest ways in which Oxford, including through the Rhodes Scholarships, can contribute to New Zealand and to the wider world: through developing leaders for a world of global forces and rapid change.

The rugby is of course highly relevant to this. Sport is one of the crucibles in which leadership and teamwork are evident, and in which leadership capacity and an aptitude for teamwork are developed. I think, for example, of the leadership by the New Zealand Rhodes Scholar David Kirk of the All Blacks in 1986-87, including when the All Blacks won the inaugural World Cup. If I mention that I was present in Soweto, South Africa, a year ago when the All Blacks defeated the Springboks in the hugely exciting last 15 minutes of the game, I hope you won't mind if I mention an All Blacks defeat – shown in the movie *Invictus*, which reflects the leadership of a remarkable kind which Nelson Mandela, in the context of the 1995 World Cup, displayed in helping to reconcile a divided and tense

---

* In the event, New Zealand's All Blacks defeated Australia's Wallabies in the rugby in Auckland that night, 30-14.

society: leadership for which South Africa and the wider world owe him so much. The 19th century poem *Invictus*˙, which Nelson Mandela knew so well, reminds us of the possibility and importance of personal self-mastery as an element of leadership. It concludes with the lines:

> I am the master of my fate:
> I am the captain of my soul.

I mentioned David Kirk, captain of the All Blacks when they first won the World Cup, who has acted as an adviser to the New Zealand Prime Minister, and now has a trans-Tasman business career. He is one of many New Zealanders who have gone from this country, as Rhodes Scholars or in other ways, to Oxford, and returned to contribute to New Zealand society, or played leadership roles in other ways around the world. It is invidious to name individuals, but you might forgive me for naming a few such Rhodes Scholars: our chair, Jane Harding, Deputy Vice-Chancellor (Research) at the University of Auckland; Arthur Porritt, Lord Porritt, the Olympian who became Governor-General of New Zealand; John Hood, who – like Sir Colin Maiden before him – became Vice-Chancellor of the University of Auckland, and who then contributed so much to Oxford as its Vice-Chancellor, and who this December will become Chair of the Rhodes Trustees; Professor Ngaire Woods, also a Rhodes Trustee, who has been leading the creation of the Blavatnik School of Government in Oxford. I also wish to pay a tribute to one Rhodes Scholar who died this year, Denis McLean, Deputy High Commissioner for New Zealand in London, Secretary of Defence, and Ambassador to Washington in complex times.

2011 has been a year of great lessons in leadership. The Arab Spring has reminded us that leaders who wish to conserve must in fact reform, and that to some extent their fate has been in

---

* By William Ernest Henley (1849-1903), a contemporary of Cecil Rhodes's.

their own hands; and it shows us again the power of people whose ideas of freedom are encouraged through modern media, and who can now organise through social media. The News Corporation phone hacking scandal has reminded us that leaders set the tone for what happens in an organisation, and that the culture created or condoned by leaders will shape what people in an organisation or community will believe is acceptable. Events in the United States – from the shootings in Arizona that nearly killed Congresswoman Gabrielle Giffords, to the avoidable and self-destructive crisis of the debt ceiling – show (amongst other things) how much damage rancour and the encouragement of ill-will can do. Responses to disasters – from the earthquakes in Christchurch to those in Japan, to the floods in my native Queensland, to the famine in East Africa, and many more – show the need for leadership in the face of disasters, natural and man-made. All these events have shown the difference that good or bad leadership can make, the challenges we face that require leaders, the possibility of leadership from people in all walks of life including active citizens who hold no formal office, and some of the constraints under which leaders operate.

The need for leadership to confront global, or at least international, challenges is daily brought into sharp relief: the need to respond effectively to environmental issues, including those related to climate change, population growth, water, energy and other resource 'security'; to respond effectively to economic crises, including the aftermath and risk of recurrence of the global financial crisis, the continuing recession or risk of double-dip in many countries, the successive crises of the Eurozone, and more; to respond to security issues, including terrorism, the wars in Afghanistan and Iraq, the need for post-war reconstruction in many places, the complexities of humanitarian intervention, such as in Libya but not in Syria; and much more. And all this while the global distribution of power, economic and political, has seemed to be shifting rapidly, increasing the need for, but complicating the process of, reform of what we might loosely call global governance.

The need for global solutions to many global issues has been evident, but the means of getting national, let alone global, solutions to them has seemed as elusive as ever, and the forces leading countries to be even more self-absorbed islands unto themselves have seemed stronger than for some time. A world that feels at times like white-water rapids cries out for leadership, leadership that is attuned to the real issues of our age, and that is effective in achieving outcomes. We need exemplary leadership in all walks of life, though my remarks this evening may seem to focus on leadership in public office.

As I have suggested, leaders today operate in a world that is marked by global forces – challenges that are international, and contexts for their solution that are international – and in a world of rapid change. One of the great drivers of this change is rapid development in information and communication technology. This gives leaders new ways of communicating quickly and widely, and new 24/7 demands and intrusions on them. It gives publics more information more quickly, and better capacity to organise themselves to question and challenge leaders. The fact that sources of information and opinion have become more diverse perhaps paradoxically allows people to live more in a world – of Fox versus CNN – where they obtain only the opinions they like – thus promoting division, not consensus, in society. The growth of the internet, email, and social media has contributed to undermining hierarchies in many places and organisations, and so contributed to the process by which leadership has become in many contexts even more than it has always been, a matter of consultation, consensus-building, and influencing other participants rather than just a matter of leaders deciding and instructing those they supposedly 'lead'. This has contributed to increasing the importance of what Joseph Nye has called 'soft power', and reduced, in some circumstances, the effectiveness of 'hard power'. It has highlighted the fact that leadership can be exercised in a diversity of ways: the dissidents who conjure up a regime-threatening demonstration through Twitter or Facebook may be exercising leadership as much as, perhaps more than, the president who contemplates using force against his own people.

The fact that leadership can be evident in many diverse ways presents both challenge and opportunity to those of us whose own roles are to provide educational leadership in identifying in young people what Cecil Rhodes called 'instincts to lead', and in helping to develop that leadership capacity and encouraging it to be applied to the great challenges that face individual institutions and countries, and the world as a whole. One aspect is recognising that leadership can be exercised differently by different people, including that there may be gender differences in leadership style, and not applying outdated stereotypes to what we recognise as leadership or to how we think that it is best exercised or developed. The works of Amanda Sinclair[*] and Nan Keohane[†], including the recent study of women's undergraduate leadership at Princeton[‡], remind us of this.

What are the qualities needed for leadership in the 21st century? Many are the same as ever; the flavour or importance of some has changed greatly. They include:

- clarity about the key purposes one is trying to achieve, and propensity always to refocus on core objectives, or ultimate purposes;

- the vision to see a better way, even a better world;

- the ability to identify the potential for improvement in any situation, and the determination to turn problems into opportunities for transformation;

---

[*] E.g. Amanda Sinclair, *Doing leadership differently*, Melbourne University Press, 1998 & 2005.

[†] Nannerl O Keohane, *Thinking about leadership*, Princeton University Press, 2010.

[‡] See http://www.princeton.edu/reports/2011/leadership/ – accessed 9 August 2011.

- the ability to think clearly and creatively;
- idealism about objectives, and realism about the context in which they are pursued and the means by which they must be pursued;
- the intellectual and broader personal flexibility or adaptability to respond to new and ever-changing questions or issues;
- the ability to understand the global or international nature of so many issues;
- the intellectual breadth and skills, in confronting issues that do not respect established disciplinary or other boundaries, to draw insights from different disciplines, and from people of different backgrounds;
- the ability to work across boundaries of nationality, ethnicity, culture, and faith, to find solutions to shared challenges;
- the ability and the inclination to communicate clearly, including creating persuasive, even inspiring, narratives of what is happening and why;
- the ability to engage others in seeking, finding, and implementing solutions;
- the ability to recognise which style of leadership is appropriate when – when consultation is the key, as against when leadership must be from the front;
- emotional intelligence, both understanding and mastering oneself, and understanding others and being able to work effectively with them, in all their (and our) diverse human frailty and complexity;
- organisational skills, including the skills to organise information flows;
- remorseless focus on execution – on getting the job done, efficiently and effectively;
- a sense of service, and a commitment to promoting the public – the common – good and not simply private interest;

- what we might call 'centredness' – character that is marked by integrity, by courage, by humility and not by narcissism, by humanity and compassion, and by commitment to well-considered principles or values, with determination to do the right thing as best one can judge it, and not to pursue popularity for its own sake;

- a willingness to take risks, and to risk great and conspicuous failure, not caring too much what others think of you;

- wise judgement, including the political skills needed to navigate through the threatening shoals of leadership;

- the ability to find mental space for reflection away from the incessant demands for quick action, and addiction to our Blackberries; and

- the determination to 'see it through', and the personal resilience to do this in the face of pressures, criticisms, and opposition – the resilience to pick yourself up in the face of defeat or failure, and get back on with the job.

It is sometimes suggested that leadership capacity is innate, and cannot be taught – implying that it is an outcome of nature that cannot be nurtured to any significant extent. No doubt some is genetic: at least some of our intellectual capacity is a product of our genes. But if intellectual capacity cannot be nurtured, why on earth do we believe in education at all? Most, if not all, of the attributes I have mentioned are influenced by our environment, experiences, and education, not only by our genes, and can be significantly affected by shaping that environment, experience, and education. Important lessons can be learnt by people with innate leadership ability, including through reflecting on their experiences and by observing or reading about or otherwise learning about the experiences of others. Sometimes those who do not appear blessed with leadership capacity can emerge as significant leaders. It is often said that one of the greatest tools for learning about leadership is reading the biographies of effective leaders. It is also often said that many of the world's greatest leaders have benefited from a period in the wilderness, of defeat or failure or struggle against adversity that preceded their finest hour. Think of Churchill and his wilderness years, Roosevelt and polio, de Gaulle out of power for a dozen lonely years awaiting the call, Nelson Mandela in prison for 27 years. In Australia, the two longest-serving Prime Ministers were both removed from the leadership of their parties after early perceived failure, only to return after long reflection to sustained political success. All these leaders have learnt from experience, undoubtedly with the aid of comment, not infrequently critical and hostile, from others.

Oxford has a proud and unparalleled history of its graduates assuming leadership positions. Twenty-six British Prime Ministers, over a third of the current British cabinet, leaders in the British opposition, presidents and prime ministers of many countries (not yet, alas, New Zealand) have been Oxonians. And there have been Oxonians in leadership in business, academia, the professions, the public service, international organisations, NGOs and advocacy, churches and other centres of faith, the media, and much more. Is this all by chance? Is it all because Oxford is a selective institution that chooses public-minded people of talent, from whom leaders are most likely to emerge? While selection is important, it is only part of the story. Oxford's academic programs and its distinctive teaching methods encourage critical thinking and clear communication. They demand the ability to respond to the unexpected (sometimes very unexpected) and demanding questions and comments of tutors and supervisors. Some of Oxford's courses promote academic specialisation, while others promote breadth; some of the new offerings, such as the Masters of Public Policy being developed in the Blavatnik School of Government, will explicitly seek to develop leaders for tasks that demand breadth and the ability to draw on the specialist expertise of others as well as one's own. The life of Oxford's colleges is necessarily broadening, with students of different disciplines living, eating, talking, partying, and engaging in diverse extra-curricular activities together. They are environments that encourage the conversations that shape thought, values, and character. They are environments that provide great practical opportunities for developing both leadership and teamwork. Oxford is a place where the tradition of leadership encourages young people to believe that they can do it too. And Oxford is a remarkably *international* university – perhaps the most genuinely and deeply international of all the world's major universities.

It is an important historical fact that the internationalisation of Oxford, and indeed the internationalisation of higher education around the world, has been greatly encouraged by the Rhodes Scholarships – the first great international scholarship program in the world, and one that has inspired many others, including, for example, the great American program that bears the name of the Rhodes Scholar who initiated it, Senator J William Fulbright. It is also an important historical fact that the Rhodes Scholarships have, year after year for well over a century, brought to Oxford exceptional young people with an action-oriented focus on public issues. Their presence has necessarily helped to shape the character of Oxford. Many of them have stayed in Oxford, and three have become Vice-Chancellor of Oxford.*

The Rhodes Scholarship explicitly aims at nurturing 'leaders for the world's future'. How? We seek to do this in many ways.

First, the Rhodes Scholarship stands for certain values or ideals – of all-round excellence, of service in the public good, and of promoting international understanding and indeed peace through 'educational relations' between countries. The Rhodes ideal is one of excellence in intellect, character, leadership, and commitment to service. These are the values we declare, and

---

* The Very Reverend John Lowe (Ontario & Christ Church 1922) (Vice-Chancellor 1948-51). Sir Kenneth Wheare (Victoria & Oriel 1929) (Vice-Chancellor 1964-66). Dr John Hood (New Zealand & Worcester 1976) (Vice-Chancellor 2004-09).

the criteria on which Rhodes Scholars are chosen. The Rhodes Scholarship recognises and encourages desirable breadth, as well as appropriate specialisation; takes students to Oxford precisely because of the benefits of its collegiate educational environment; and is closely aligned to the basic philosophy of liberal education.

Like other students coming from overseas to Oxford, Rhodes Scholars chosen on the criteria I have mentioned obtain the benefits of international study and an Oxford education, not least the exposure to the wider world, learning to adjust to the unfamiliar, and gradually learning how to perform confidently and well on this wider stage. Rhodes Scholars enter into a tradition in which it is seen both as possible and as one's responsibility to be in some way a leader who promotes the public good. There are, of course, many ways to do this – in the private and so-called social sectors as well as in the public – and the Rhodes Scholarship is not prescriptive about the ways that Scholars should do this. While encouraging academic excellence (and the academic results of Rhodes Scholars today are extremely good), we encourage Rhodes Scholars to participate actively in their colleges and departments and in university activities, and this they do – from college and university sport to debating and drama and many other activities besides, to Middle or Graduate Common Room leadership roles around the University, to Junior Deans in many colleges, and more. Many of them also gain much from vacation travel in many countries.

Just as Rhodes Scholars, like other Oxford students, get to know fellow students of many countries in their colleges or departments, we at Rhodes House provide many opportunities for them to get to know Rhodes Scholars from other of the 14 different countries or regions around the world from which Rhodes Scholars come. We do this through social activities and through speaker events of various kinds which focus attention on world issues, and on life skills, including leadership, and career choices. Over the last year, for example, we have had – just to choose some interesting African examples – talks at Rhodes

House by George Bizos SC, who for over half a century has been Nelson Mandela's lawyer; the man who shared the Nobel Peace Prize with Mr Mandela, F W de Klerk, speaking on leadership in South Africa's transition; Mo Ibrahim, the Sudanese-born telecoms entrepreneur who has created the Ibrahim Prize to reward excellent leadership and good governance in Africa; and Elias Chipimo, Jnr, a Rhodes Scholar who is running for President of Zambia, and who stresses the importance of developing leadership capacity at all levels for Africa's future. Current Rhodes Scholars have also had opportunities to meet the Oxford-educated former President of Botswana, winner of the Ibrahim Prize, and Rhodes Trustee, Festus Mogae.

Through one-on-one mentoring meetings, email 'updates' from the Warden, and (for example) books on leadership in the Scholars' common room at Rhodes House, Rhodes Scholars are encouraged to reflect on their own passions and aptitudes, and what best use of their talents will give them a sense of purpose and meaning in their lives, and to reflect on the development of leadership, including on the qualities of character that it requires, and on the development of personal resilience.

Rhodes Scholars enter into a community which, like the broader Oxonian community, spans the generations. At the urging of current Rhodes Scholars, we are not only working to create more opportunities for Rhodes alumni to connect with each other across generations and countries, and to connect on issues they share interest in; but we are also working to create more opportunities for current Rhodes Scholars to connect more with our alumni, from whom they know they have much to learn, including about the responsibility, opportunity, challenge, and pitfalls of leadership in diverse fields and places. Having mentors and coaches can be hugely valuable: in the Rhodes community we create opportunities for such relationships to develop organically, as they often do, but do not seek any *formal* program of mentoring.

As we all know, the benefits of mixing in Oxford with

students of other countries are enormous. When in 1901, Cecil Rhodes provided for Rhodes Scholarships for Germany, in addition to those he had already provided for from the United States and much of the then British Empire, he said, 'The object is that an understanding between the three great powers will render war impossible and educational relations make the strongest tie'. Today, in sustained consultation in the Rhodes community, we have been asking – how should we think about this today? From what countries should Rhodes Scholars come in the 21st century? I am cautiously optimistic that, in time, this will (for example) lead to Rhodes Scholars from China, and from other countries, including several in Africa, not currently served by Rhodes Scholarships – at the same time as we work hard to raise the funds needed to fund the Rhodes Scholarships we currently offer, including three each year here in New Zealand.* By doing this, we can better develop a globally-connected network of exceptional young people who will become leaders in diverse fields in their various countries, better able to take on the problems of this century of hope and challenge.

Many of the challenges of leadership are great. Leadership in *public* office is generally badly paid by comparison with private sector leadership, all too rancorous, facing endless media and other criticism and intrusion, and remorseless in its public demands, which seem hard to reconcile with private life. Many people of civic commitment and idealism are deterred from pursuing public careers. But, of course, remorseless demands are a fact of life for leaders in perhaps all fields and sectors. In a world of constant change, there is little or no time that is steady state, no time of settlement or consolidation. The physical and emotional demands and stress on executives are great – from constant change, constant availability, global reach, and the need to manage ambiguity and anxiety, their own and others'. The risks of burnout are also great. Governance bodies that should

---

* The task of funding the three New Zealand Rhodes Scholarships has been greatly assisted by a generous benefaction from Mr Julian Roberston.

support their executives seem unable to identify effective ways of doing so. Not least, they must learn to do so by taking the long view, and not succumbing to short-termism, demanding apparent short-term successes that are not the best way to achieve the long-term objective.

The delegation that should enable leaders to cope is possible for some, and seemingly impossible for others. Learning to delegate and to manage others, to manage oneself to ensure self-preservation and renewal, to manage stress, to deal with ambiguity and uncertainty, and to manage change are all important skills for leaders to learn. One area for political leaders is how simultaneously to ride the bucking bronco of the 24/7 media cycle, and to transcend it, so that it does not overwhelm them.

It may be that the very scale of the challenges facing leaders today – issues which include the future of the planet! – discourages bright and civic-minded people from seeking leadership in public life. Yet it is the very scale of the challenges that makes it all the more important that good people be willing to face them. One of the roles for educational leaders, certainly one of the roles of those of us responsible for the Rhodes Scholarships, is to encourage young people who can make a difference to do what they can to do so, now and in the future.

Oxford has made an outstanding contribution to developing leaders for many countries in the past. I am confident that it will do so in the future, and your support will help it do so. New Zealand's links with Oxford are an important part of this legacy, and Oxford and New Zealand must play important roles in each other's futures.

Tonight, as the All Blacks take on the Wallabies – or is it the other way around? – we might think again of that 19th century poem, *Invictus*, with its reference to 'my unconquerable soul', and the verse that says:

In the fell clutch of circumstance I have not winced nor cried aloud.

Under the bludgeonings of chance my head is bloody, but unbowed.

Whether 'bloody' or not, may 'unbowed' be true tonight of the All Blacks, and of the Wallabies, and of the Oxford we all love, which helped to make us who we are, and which can do so much for future generations.

Leadership in colleges: 'Hermione Granger and the University of Macau'

Centre for Leadership, King's College, University of Queensland

*17 September 2012**

It is a great privilege to be with you tonight to open a discussion on leadership in colleges. I am grateful to King's College, so ably led by Greg Eddy, for such warm hospitality to us all tonight, and great kindness to me as a visiting scholar in the Centre for Leadership, which exists to promote leadership skills among the students of this college.

My aim tonight is to provoke your thinking by offering some perspectives on leadership in Australian university residential colleges. Colleges are sometimes associated with Hogwarts, introduced to all of us by the succession of Harry Potter books and movies – from *Harry Potter and the Philosopher's Stone* to *Harry Potter and the Deathly Hallows*. Many of the movie scenes at Hogwarts were shot in various parts of an Oxford college, Christ Church. By the time I have finished, you may think that the subtitle of this talk should – implausibly – be 'Hermione Granger and the University of Macau'. What on earth do Hermione Granger, of all people[†], and the University of Macau have in common? Wait and see!

Most people in this room have leadership roles in colleges, and I will value hearing your thoughts and questions in response to the perspectives I suggest. I owe the word 'perspectives' to my friend, the chair of the Council of Women's College, Sallyanne Atkinson, who makes the important point that there are many

---

* A version of this paper appeared in John A Moses (ed.), *Collegial Canon: A Celebration of John Morgan,* University of Queensland Press, 2013.

† Or wizards from the Harry Potter series.

approaches to leadership, and that the best one can hope to offer is perspectives, not prescriptions.

Though there are lessons to be learnt from successful leaders past and present, there is no single ideal model of leadership. There are many different styles of leadership, including gender and cultural differences in leadership styles. Different styles of leadership will be appropriate in different contexts. Some will require an emphasis on consultation, inclusion, consensus-building, and the exercise of influence rather than of direct power. Other contexts will place a greater premium on the decisive exercise of authority. One of the arts of a good leader is, while remaining authentic to themselves, deciding what style of leadership is appropriate to each context, and adapting accordingly.

Leaders matter. They make a difference. With so many challenges, the world and this country need excellent, ethical leaders. So do all organisations and institutions, including our colleges. The experience of providing leadership within a college can be, for student leaders, preparation for providing leadership in their later careers and in the wider community.

I am especially grateful that tonight we have leaders from various parts of several colleges – student leaders; leaders in the administration of colleges; leaders in the governance, the governing bodies, of colleges. Each and every one of these leaders has an important part to play in a college. Each should be motivated by the same purposes: to ensure that the college is as good as it can be, and that the education – the academic and the broader personal development of students – is as good as it can be. Colleges will work best, and students will gain most, if leaders at all levels – student leaders, administration leaders, governance leaders – work together, respectful of each other, towards a shared vision of their college as the best that it can be, in which students are encouraged and supported to be the best that they can be.

The American political philosopher and retired college and

university president Nan Keohane, in her book *Thinking about Leadership*, defines leadership this way: 'Leaders determine or clarify goals for a group of individuals and bring together the energies of members of that group to accomplish those goals."* Personally, I also rather like the definition of good leadership that it is about getting a group of people to deal effectively with their real issues. This latter definition highlights that holding a position, a title, does not make one a leader, or at least not a good leader; and that it is possible to be a real leader – to lead others, to be an agent for positive change, to challenge an organisation to deal effectively with its real issues – without holding formal office.

What does a leader in a college need to do to help ensure that her or his college deals effectively with their real issues? For me, an essential starting point of all good leadership is being clear about the purpose of the organisation, and asking – early and often – 'what are we fundamentally trying to achieve?'. So: what is the purpose of a college, and what are we in colleges fundamentally trying to achieve? In essence my answer is that a college is a residential academic community which aims to enrich the education – the academic and the all-round personal development – of its students. Let us dwell on this for a moment. This gets us a little closer to Hermione Granger and the University of Macau.

In the celebrations of this year's centenary of King's College, the President of the College Council, Justice Martin Daubney, spoke of the commitment of the College to excellence and to integrity. He spoke of the 'the goals of excellence in scholarship, [and] excellence in personal conduct, excellence in the facilities provided for the benefit of the students'. He spoke of the importance of the College's commitment to values, and said that 'when integrity … ceases to be the essence of our pursuits in this College, we will have ceased to be a place of higher learning

---

* Nannerl O Keohane, *Thinking about leadership*, p. 23.

and become nothing more than a secular provider of serviced accommodation.' So King's is a college which is 'a place of higher learning', committed to excellence and to integrity. It is not 'a secular provider of serviced accommodation' – or, as someone once said of another college, a 'hotel with attitude'. Justice Daubney did something I commend to all leaders in colleges – he went back to the founding vision of the college, early statements of its purposes, to identify what it is here for; and this, of course, expressed the kind of value-focused educational vision he articulated in his centenary address.

Last year, Professor Debbie Terry, now the Vice-Chancellor of this University, speaking at Duchesne College, said:

> Generations of students have now had the privilege of calling Duchesne home. Not only does the College provide a clear point of reference for students who are finding their way in a large and diverse institution, but it provides a rich and supportive environment in which academic success is valued and encouraged and future leaders are nurtured.

Professor Terry quoted the founding Chancellor of the University of Western Australia, Sir John Winthrop Hackett, as saying that 'universities would fail in their "perfect mission" unless they combined "in the largest and most pregnant sense" (an unusual turn of phrase) what he described as "the triple alliance of the lecture room, the examination hall and the college"'. Professor Terry went on to say that 'the role that colleges play in universities such as our own is as strong now as it was over 100 years ago when the university was first established'.

Professor Terry in her speech at Duchesne got right to the heart of some of the most important things about colleges: that they should be rich and supportive environments in which academic success is valued and encouraged, and in which future leaders are nurtured; and that they have a very important role to play in our universities, including but not only in helping students find their way in the large and diverse institution that is the university.

Professor Terry recognised the real nature and the value, for students and for the university, of colleges that live up to their calling to be true colleges. Some years ago, Professor John Hay, then Vice-Chancellor of the University of Queensland, said that the real life of a university today takes place in its colleges. His successor, Professor Paul Greenfield, was warmly and actively supportive of the role of the colleges of the University of Queensland, and I know that many people are grateful to him for that and much else.

Professor Terry's comments on colleges brought to mind another statement and endorsement of the collegiate ideal given at a Chapel service at St John's College here in the University of Queensland in 2006 by the then federal minister for education, Julie Bishop, now of course Deputy Leader of the Opposition.* Ms Bishop pointed out that residential college communities feature in most, if not all, of the world's finest undergraduate institutions. She commended colleges for their 'high degree of individual attention and interaction for students, the sense of intellectual engagement beyond the classroom and the focus on student welfare, character values and extracurricular activities'. Julie Bishop also pointed out that colleges tend to be magnets for philanthropy, and she encouraged the creation of additional and expanded colleges, with scholarship provision to help students take up college places. I cannot refrain from pointing out that the events at St John's College at which then-Minister Julie Bishop spoke were an example of an Australian college at its finest, promoting important debate on major issues, in that case the future of Australian universities. Those events were the brainchild of the Warden of St John's, the Revd Professor John Morgan, whose leadership in college has been invariably clear-headed and

---

* Hon. Julie Bishop MP, quoted from http://collegiateway.org/news/2006–australian–residential–colleges – accessed 5 September 2012, site no longer available.

warm-hearted, and an inspiration to so many.

When it is working well, a residential college enriches the education of its students, resident or in some cases non-resident, in many ways. Julie Bishop was right to point out that many of the world's greatest universities place very strong emphasis on students having the benefits of college life. Not only is this true of Cambridge and Oxford, and of Harvard, Yale, and Princeton, and of several other universities. But it is *increasingly* true even in some universities which have long had strong colleges: both Yale and Princeton, for example, have placed growing emphasis in recent years on their colleges, and have been working to refresh their college life. It is also the case that there has been a growth of colleges, or of emphasis on college life at its best, in many other universities around the world which seek to offer their students an education which is increasingly comparable with the best in the world.

In recent years, there has been growing recognition in many countries that in an 'information age' or a 'knowledge economy', and in a world of global competition, the success of economies and societies will be determined by the education of their people. So there has been, of course unevenly, growing focus on ensuring the highest quality of higher education. This is reflected in and accelerated by the growth of global rankings of universities, however spurious some of those rankings are. Universities aiming to offer the best education they can, and to be seen to do so, look at the attributes of the world's finest universities, and seek to emulate them.

In this context, many aspiring universities look at the world's best universities, observe the benefits of colleges to them and their students, and seek to emulate their college systems and to offer those collegiate benefits. This is true, for example, of some of the top universities in China, and in the two special administrative regions of China, Hong Kong and Macau. Hong Kong, as you well know, was a British colony on the South China Sea coast of China, and Macau was a Portuguese colony nearby, both returned to China as special administrative regions in the last 15 years.

Universities in both Hong Kong and Macau, as well as elsewhere in China and several other countries, are placing increased emphasis on colleges. The University of Macau illustrates this very well. It has a clear aim of becoming a truly world-class university. The University of Macau's website says that in recent years, as part of its efforts to improve undergraduate education, along with curriculum reform, it has been 'following the example of world-class universities and introducing a residential college system to implement whole-person education'. Colleges are central to its plans for the future:*

> To better support higher education development in Macau and to answer society's need for high-quality professionals, UM is building a new campus ... After moving to the new campus, ... UM will fully implement a system of residential colleges modelled upon top universities like Oxford, Cambridge and Yale. According to the preliminary plan, there will be between eight and ten residential colleges to complement the various faculties. Undergraduates of different majors and years of study will live in the same colleges. They will live and study together and will have ample opportunities to participate in various competitions and recreational activities organised by the colleges. It is hoped that through peer interaction and motivation enabled by such an arrangement, students can better acquire self-discipline, develop the ability to act independently, and realise whole-person growth.

A special University of Macau website on residential colleges spells out what is seen as their educational purpose, and seeks to set them in context. Under the heading 'Reforming Undergraduate Education through Residential Colleges', the

---

* University of Macau website – http://www.umac.mo/about_UM.html – accessed 5 September 2012.

University of Macau asks the question:[*]

> How to combine classroom learning with extracurricular life of students, how to let professors resume their genuine care for students and make a difference to their lives, and how to return to the goal of cultivating 'whole persons'? These [it says] are the major concerns behind the reform of undergraduate education in many universities.

The University of Macau website says that central to the answer is the traditional educational philosophy embodied in residential colleges, and refers to the colleges at Cambridge and Oxford; at Harvard and Yale and other US universities and liberal arts colleges; and at the Chinese University of Hong Kong; and refers to the growth in focus on colleges in recent years in the US, and in Asia, referring to Yonsei University in Korea, Tunghai University, National Chengchi University and National Tsing Chua University in Taiwan, and Fudan University in Shanghai, and developments towards liberal arts education and residential colleges at Peking University and the National University of Singapore. It says that this experience shows that 'the [Residential College] system can be implemented not only in resourceful and top private universities but also in general public universities.'

What is said by the University of Macau implicitly makes clear that they are not just talking about increasing the provision for students to live on or near campus. They are talking about creating colleges as, so far as possible, genuine residential academic communities. This distinction between a university with a high proportion of students living on or near campus and a university with real colleges was highlighted recently by Emma Watson, who – as you know – is the actor

---

[*] University of Macau website – http://www.umac.mo/rc/background.html – accessed 5 September 2012.

who played Hermione Granger in the Harry Potter movies. Emma Watson has spent part of her undergraduate years at Brown University, a leading American university which has a strong system of so-called 'residential life', with much student accommodation including what they call 'themed houses', but which does not have residential colleges. She has also spent a year at Oxford, which is a truly collegiate university, and where every student belongs to a college. In a recent interview with *The New York Times*, Emma Watson said that her first two years at Brown 'weren't easy' – quote – 'just because, you know, without the collegiate system…'* She seems to have meant that the sense of belonging to a community and the ready opportunities for friendship were much greater when living in a college, and that these mattered greatly to her. So there you have it: Hermione Granger, or at least Emma Watson, is – like the University of Macau – a champion of the collegiate system.

I have started this discussion of leadership in colleges by referring to the fundamental purposes of colleges. In my view, the most crucial aspect of leadership in colleges is shaping all you do in light of the fundamental purpose of the college: to be the best residential academic community that it can be, with all the benefits for students that flow from this. In doing this, there is so much to be gained from seeking to learn from the experience of other colleges, including from the best in the world, and from being ambitious for your own college. Perhaps the more we expose ourselves to the world's finest collegiate institutions and seek to learn from them and from other colleges elsewhere in Australia, the more self-confident we can be to be ambitious for our own. It has certainly been encouraging to see a kind of renaissance of the collegiate ideal in Australian universities, with many positive developments in their work to

---

* 'The Graduate', *The New York Times*, 17 August 2012.

enrich the all-round educational development of their students, curricular and extra-curricular.*

As well as enhancing the university education and all-round experience of their students, colleges also make it possible for students who could not otherwise come to university to do so. The role of colleges in promoting equity and access is especially important. It is important that they be centres of excellence within universities, and points of access to universities, rather than bastions of privilege.

So a college can provide a superb environment in which to be a university student. But this doesn't come about by chance. It takes leadership. It takes leadership partly because some of the natural pressures seem to work in the other direction. It is an unfortunate reality of life that colleges, which should be so uplifting, can in fact become places where conformism, sexism, sexual harassment and worse, racism, anti-intellectualism, and an over-emphasis on alcohol have damaged students. Some would argue that, like the Hobbesian state of nature or *Lord of the Flies* or *Animal House* or perhaps Slytherin, there is a natural tendency for such forces to emerge, and that an important part of the role of leaders at all levels in colleges is to stand firmly for the college as an educational community, and to stand firmly against those forces – I deliberately repeat them – of conformism, sexism, racism, anti-intellectualism, and over-emphasis on alcohol.

Sometimes the camaraderie, mutual support, and college spirit that many value goes too far and effectively demands that individuals conform to behaviour that they do not like and would not freely choose. It can effectively demand that they submerge their individual qualities and potential in seeming to be just like others, and make no place for fellow students from, say, diverse national or cultural backgrounds who do not share the same preferences. Colleges must be places where all

---

* See 'The value of university residential colleges' in the section of this book 'On education'.

students feel welcome and supported, a community in which each individual can both belong and be themselves.

It may be confronting, but it is important, to ask some blunt questions about your own college. Is your college a place where students who, for religious or other reasons, do not drink alcohol feel at home? Where students struggling with issues of sexual orientation feel able to be themselves? Where students from around Asia or beyond feel genuinely welcomed and invited in?

If your college is co-educational, is it an environment in which women students genuinely feel as much at home as men, and feel comfortable and encouraged to make as much of the opportunities? If your college is single-sex, does it promote positive and truly respectful gender relations, or does it reinforce demeaning stereotypes or prejudices? Emma Watson is quoted as saying of Hermione Granger: 'Hermione's not scared to be clever. I think sometimes really smart girls dumb themselves down a bit, and that's bad. … [There's] so much pressure to be beautiful. Hermione doesn't care what she looks like." This is sadly more relevant to popular culture, and to culture in some colleges, than it should be. The recent study, led by Nan Keohane, of undergraduate women's leadership at Princeton, which can be read on the Princeton website and which I commend to you, highlights the need for deliberate action, for leadership, to ensure genuine parity of opportunity for students of both genders.[†]

Is your college a place where students are encouraged, and expect themselves, to behave as adults – as men and women – or as 'kids', boys and girls in the last reckless gasp of childhood? Is it an environment, as it should be, in which students do truly learn to think considerately of others and respect each other's rights, including the right to sleep? Or is it an environment in which some feel entitled to have their desires, such as the desire

---

[*] Emma Watson, quoted from http://www.glamourvanity.com/emma–watson/ – accessed 14 September 2012, site no longer available.

[†] Princeton University, *Report of the Steering Committee on Undergraduate Women's Leadership*, 2011 – at http://www.princeton.edu/reports/2011/leadership/

to make noise in the early hours of the morning, override the legitimate rights of others?

Sometimes the important role of colleges as places of social activities which build community, friendships, and a sense of belonging goes too far, and an inappropriate emphasis on alcohol and sex leads to inappropriate behaviour which damages individuals, sometimes very severely.

Sometimes the need to integrate learning and living, with a very important role for extra-curricular activities, has the unintended effect that the college becomes so focused on the non-academic activities, important though they are, that it forgets its role as an academic institution. Colleges forget that part of their role is to help students *integrate* learning and living, to integrate their life in college and their life in the wider university, and instead act as if the college and the university are antithetical to each other, or at least highly distinct, rather than belonging integrated together.

In my experience, academic excellence, engaging and doing well in sport and in cultural and intellectual activities, the development of friendships, and much fun in social activities – all these things can come together in a positive way. These things are not opposed to each other: they are all attributes of all-round collegiate education. In a balanced community and individual life, all of these things can be combined. Not only that; they can reinforce each other, as people and colleges aiming for excellence in one area are likely to do better in many, if not all, areas.

What all this means is that, to be true to its core purposes as a college, leaders at all levels in a college need to be highly attentive to their culture, to the values that are enacted in reality in the life of the college, and to the need to stand firm for the best values, and to bring about cultural change where bad values have been allowed to prevail. Shaping and changing cultures is hard work, and requires strength of character and persistence. It requires that leaders articulate and embody a noble vision of the best the college can be. It requires that positive behaviours are encouraged, recognised, and rewarded, and that unacceptable behaviours are not accepted – that the intolerable is not tolerated.

It is widely accepted today, even more than ever before, that typically or usually the best leadership is collaborative, seeking input from others and engaging them in taking ownership of the solutions formed together to the real problems that exist. But we also know that collaborative leadership is not always possible, and that sometimes a leader, or a leadership team, needs simply to decide what will or will not happen, and to ensure that this is so. While it is ideal when a college culture represents a shared vision between all members of the college community, there are also times when the decisive exercise of authority is necessary to uphold the true values of the college; and leaders must be wise enough to know when to take such stands, and courageous enough to take them.

There is a crucial role for student leaders in upholding the best, and refusing to put up with the worst, in college life. Student leaders help to set the tone of college life, of what is celebrated and what is tolerated. Never is this truer than in orientation week, which – in setting the tone – can have a profound effect on the experience of students for the rest of the year. In the planning and running of orientation activities, student leaders working closely and honestly with leaders in the college administration can help to start each year on a note that rightly captures the values for which the college should stand, and to make all students – *all* students – welcome.

One of the most important lessons of leadership, in my view, is that leaders must do what they know is right, even when this risks unpopularity. It is a hard lesson for some people to learn, but trying to please everyone, presenting one face to some people and a different face to others, is the road to contempt rather than to popularity. Doing what you know is right is the road to being respected.

One of the great benefits of college life for many students is that it is a training ground for leaders, with many opportunities for leadership experience. An increasing number of colleges deliberately run leadership development programs or activities, even simply talks and discussions, which aim to develop students' leadership capacities.

The experience of being a student leader teaches important lessons for future leadership. These include lessons about:

- the need to combine courage and resolve with humility and integrity;
- as I just suggested, the need to risk unpopularity by doing what you know is right and needed;
- the need to develop your powers of wise judgement;
- the importance of understanding and monitoring the changing context in which you are working, to see the potential for improvement as well as possible pitfalls, and – while remaining authentic – adapting your actions to that context;
- the importance of communication, especially when there is change, something which many people will fear – even when they know that it is needed!
- the fact that everything that a person in authority does is noticed and so sends a signal, so it is crucial to embody the values of which you speak – to 'walk the talk', even 'be the change you want to see';
- the importance of developing emotional intelligence – of understanding yourself (with all your weaknesses, strengths, needs, stressors, and drivers), and of understanding others, and how best to engage and work with others;
- the importance of managing your time, which is a key to success in leadership roles as it is in your studies and later work;

- the risks of over-commitment, and the need to take steps to preserve your energy and to refresh yourself as a person;
- the importance of finding mentors – experienced and trusted people in whom you can confide and seek wisdom – as well as of being a mentor yourself; and
- the importance of learning from mistakes, your own as well as others', and of developing resilience to bounce back from your mistakes.

These are just some of the lessons which students – and their elders – can learn from their experience of leadership in college.

Such learning through reflection on experience is one of many ways in which college life enriches the university experience of college students, and thus in which the college contributes to the university. I think that one of the exciting opportunities for college leaders is to position colleges as important to the educational mission of the university. This can help to focus the attention of university leaders on what the elements of the best undergraduate education are, and can also lead to real benefits for colleges. In the case of the University of Western Australia, for example, recognition in the leadership of the University of the benefits of students being in college has led to funds – federal government and University funds – becoming available for over 1,000 additional college student rooms.

Strengthening the ability of colleges to enrich their students' education, including simply the ability to offer students accommodation, depends on financial resources as well as on clarity of vision and purpose. One of the important tasks for college leaders is to generate resources to enable each college to be the best that it can be. Increasingly important to this is engaging alumni and, importantly, other potential friends of the college, and gaining their philanthropic support for the college – for buildings, for scholarships, for other activities. One of the keys to this is creating a culture in which all members of the college understand, from the day they arrive and perhaps even earlier, that the opportunities they have were the product of the labours and generosity of those who have gone before, and that they should do all they can, as soon and as much as they can, to hand on these opportunities even better to generations who come after them.

As in so much else, this is an area where student leaders have much to contribute. Student leaders can help to welcome back and to engage alumni. Student leaders can also, for example, organise among students who are leaving the college at the end of the year a 'year giving' activity, in which all leaving students are encouraged by their fellow students to contribute something (it need not be much; $5 will do) to the college. This can help to create a sense that giving back to the college is something that you naturally do. This will ideally grow in time into sustained commitment to annual giving, and in time to major gifts and ultimately a bequest to the college.

It goes, I hope, almost without saying that if your college enriches the all-round education of students as much as it can, it will be well worthy of such support – and of the exercise of your leadership skills, now and over many years to come.

Leadership in churches: the challenge of creative leadership

Review of John Adair and John Nelson (eds), Creative Church
Leadership *(Canterbury Press, 2004)*
First published in Pacifica, *vol. 20, June 2007*

Real leadership, we are likely to agree, is different from management of the status quo. It is precisely because leadership is about change that it needs to be creative. No matter how clever or creative it is, it is bound to provoke resistance. Avoiding or overcoming such resistance requires political skills of a high order, as well as courage. While Daniel Goleman, whose writing on emotional intelligence has been so important, defines leadership as 'the art of persuading people to work towards a common goal"*, Marty Linsky (another of the most important contemporary students of leadership) defines it as 'disappointing your own people at a rate they can accept', and stresses the political skills leadership requires.†

To be creative, leaders need consciously to identify the core purposes they wish to achieve, and to approach problems with a view to *transforming* them from negatives to the greatest positive that is possible. In leadership it is crucial continually to ask such questions as: what are we trying to achieve? What are the key elements of our strategy towards that goal? For Christian leaders, as several chapters remind us, this requires keeping both eyes on 'the Kingdom of God' (however we define or consider this), while both feet are firmly planted on the ground.

The opportunity to exercise such leadership does not

---

* See Daniel Goleman, *Emotional Intelligence*, Bantam, 1995.
† See Ronald A Heifetz & Marty Linsky, *Leadership on the Line: Staying Alive Through the Dangers of Leading*, Harvard Business Press, 2002.

necessarily depend on holding formal office, but – sad to say – many who *do* hold formal office, in the church as elsewhere, are unable or unwilling to provide such transformative leadership. Leaders seeking popularity are unlikely to be able to bring those they seek to lead to confront in a truly creative way the fundamental issues before them.

As Malcolm Grundy refreshingly points out, given the centrality to the Christian faith of the Resurrection – of new life after death and despair – Christian leaders and Christians generally should be especially attuned to – indeed, enthusiastic for – the possibility of transformation, of new modes of life for individuals and for communities. What Grundy calls 'a lifelong commitment to redeem often hopeless situations' can and should be the essence of Christian leadership. Successful people are, as Charles Handy points out, 'the ones who see opportunity where others see problems'; and Peter Price helpfully reminds us that creative leadership requires the capacity to see the potential for something wholly new to be done or to come into being. As he points out, success can (at least sometimes) be achieved by acting as if the desired thing already exists. Bishop David Jenkins argues powerfully, even passionately, that God has not stopped being a creative agent of change in the world, and calls us to be part of this change. Jenkins advocates a new understanding between the three 'Scriptural' faiths of Judaism, Christianity, and Islam, and overcoming the tendency towards the selective, literalistic, and narrow readings of texts – readings that deny our common humanity under God. Bishop Jenkins ultimately raises the stakes as high as anyone: atheism is, in his view, a powerful alternative to the 'petty and self-centred quarrels of "the religious"'.

Gillian Stamp and Elizabeth Welch are among the writers who stress one aspect of leadership as being the ability to release the talents of others, to create conditions within which they are able to give of their best. Part of the challenge to creative leadership in the church is overcoming the resistance of those afraid of change, including those who, in the face of change, retreat to past certainties. This requires leadership that requires church members to confront, not to avoid, the real challenges (and therefore the opportunities) before them. A leader should insist that the real issues are dealt with, and repeatedly bring the discussion back to core concerns. As more than one contributor to this volume makes clear, this means that leaders can no longer profess 'to give ready-made answers to all questions of importance' (Todd), or pretend to know the will of God; but instead must challenge all those involved to confront the hard questions and together to seek answers. Sometimes top-down instruction will be appropriate, even essential; at other times the role of the leader is to get the group to face up to an issue. Part of the wisdom of true leadership is to know which approach is most appropriate and when.

Charles Handy argues that different kinds of organisation (variously focussed on mutual support, service delivery, or campaigning) require different kinds of leadership and management. Church organisations tend to blend all three functions, and care is needed in identifying the right kind of leader and leadership for particular organisations and situations. Handy's excellent chapter provides evidence for the powerful case made by Robin Gill and Derek Burke that the insights of strategic management, drawn from the study of other organisations in the business, public, and not-for-profit sectors, can be applied to the key challenges of many churches today (not least the Church of England), such as financial difficulties and declining attendances. Their emphasis on clear priorities and objectives, strategic planning, and 'strategic ownership' of issues shows that modern management can release energy, create shared vision, and build trust.

That the case still needs to be made for management and leadership education in the church shows how far from reality too many Christian leaders live. It also underlines the importance of the work of bodies such as MODEM*, the British ecumenical charity focused on management and organisational issues in ministry, under whose auspices this book was prepared. *Creative Church Leadership* contains a valuable guide to leadership literature which should help anyone interested in creative leadership to identify the literature that will be most useful to them in their challenges.

Dean Wesley Carr's thoughtful chapter, including his regrets about the downgrading of the special role of the clergy, helps us to understand how management and leadership can be exercised in the church (and how they should not be exercised). Sir Philip Mawer's short but powerful discussion of mutual confidence between the leader and the led, the leader's modest and realistic self-belief, and the leader's vocation and values points us, as do some other chapters, to Jesus's model of the servant leader. This provides the perfect example that, of the many diverse ways of leading, the 'macho' or 'hero' style of hierarchical leadership constitutes just one form, which is unlikely to be the best one. The work of Jim Collins, briefly mentioned in this book, suggests that what he calls 'level 5 leadership' – with its combination of personal humility and resolute professional focus and will – is what has enabled good companies to become and stay great: perhaps this is what churches also need.[†] A theme of this volume is the danger of too much emphasis on a single omniscient or omnipotent leader. It would have been helpful to see reference to the work of Amanda Sinclair and others on 'doing leadership differently'.[‡] Baroness Perry urges the church to learn from the secular world, including about the importance of emotional intelligence, of picking the right person for the job (especially

---

[*] Ministerial and Organisational [later Ontological] Disciplines for the Enhancement of Management.

[†] See Jim Collins, *Good to Great: Why Some Companies Make the Leap...and Others Don't*, HarperBusiness, New York, 2001. Jim Collins, *Good to Great and the Social Sector: Why Business Thinking is Not the Answer*, 2005.

[‡] Amanda Sinclair, *Doing Leadership Differently*, Melbourne University Press, 1998 & 2005.

when the quality of leadership is so often decisive for the success of an undertaking), and of the equality of contributions which women and men can make.

Several contributors, perhaps most powerfully Bishop David Jenkins, believe that one of the greatest challenges (and opportunities) of creative church leadership today involves helping people of different faiths live peacefully side by side. Church and political leaders, and other opinion leaders, can encourage inter-faith understanding, dialogue, and co-operation. This is an urgent challenge to leaders whose words and deeds should encourage inclusion and harmony between faiths, rather than underline differences and encourage conflict and alienation. There is more wisdom in the desire of the Prince of Wales to be 'Defender of Faiths', rather than 'Defender of the Faith', than even he knew when he first articulated that prescient thought. David Jenkins is not alone in lamenting the divisions in the Church of England on such issues as homosexuality and women bishops, and the dangerous retreat to fundamentalism among Christians and within some other faiths.

Because creative leadership requires passionate commitment, it also requires leaders to focus on self-preservation (including to prevent themselves being wholly consumed by the work) and on refreshing themselves – intellectually, physically, emotionally, and spiritually – on a regular basis. That this is easier said than done simply underlines its importance. Parker J Palmer is quoted as saying that 'a leader is a person who must take special responsibility for what's going on inside him or herself, lest the act of leadership create more harm than good'. Leaders and organisations not committed to continual learning and renewal, personal and institutional, will grow stale, and lose sight of their long-term goals. Leaders who do not think carefully about their use of time will find their strategic goals swamped by lesser demands, and ultimately perhaps suffer personal 'burnout'. In the church, perhaps more than anywhere else, it is essential for leaders to step outside the immediacy and busy-ness of the day-to-day and experience afresh something of the eternal and infinite.

Some chapters focus on theological training and its alleged defects. Bill Allen's research on what members of Christian groups see (rightly or otherwise) as the qualities of 'good' Christian ministers is, with some circularity and too many unquestioned assumptions, treated as a guide to what is required in Christian leadership preparation. He and some other writers, such as Martyn Percy, perhaps give too little regard to how the work of theological colleges in spiritual formation and academic theological education is a prerequisite for many of the other qualities sought. But the call for more research into the problems of the church (for example, why clergy leave ordained ministry) and for critical self-reflection within the church about its own problems and how to face them seems irresistible. Individual leaders, too, need to reflect on the lessons of their own failures, and need to be constructively supported in doing this.

Among the qualities identified as necessary for creative leadership – in addition to clarity, humanity, empathy, reflectiveness, self-understanding, and humour – is courage. As Norman Todd points out, the histories of prophets, saints and martyrs show that creative leaders should *expect* to be attacked. It may be, to use his distinction, safer to be a 'designated church leader' rather than a 'creative church leader', but it is crucially important that the designated also be creative. Creative leadership is hard. It often involves isolation and conflict, and can be unendurably demanding. To keep this in perspective and sustain oneself through the demands, the help of mentors and coaches can be crucial, as are other refuges from the storm – perhaps in prayer, meditation, exercise, music, or (say) gardening. It also requires political skills and personal survival skills, including the capacity to take in and reflect upon all that is happening around you while being yourself an active participant.

This volume helps us to see this problem. Perhaps, however, one does not expect a book written by church people for church people to be the definitive guide to the 'art of the possible' which many church people need. I therefore recommend that readers and practitioners of *Creative Church Leadership* also consider reading books such as Heifetz and Linsky's *Leadership on the Line*, most especially for its image of interspersing time 'on the dance floor' with trips up to the balcony to get an overview of all that is happening. Some may prefer their practical wisdom in more classical guise, such as Machiavelli's *The Prince*. There is no reason why the insights of practical realism should not be put to the purposes of God.

Ideas into action

Global Scholars' Symposium 2011
Rhodes House, Oxford
7 May 2011

After two days of inspiring and excellent talk, which we have been delighted to host here at Rhodes House, my guess is that the last thing you want is yet another speech. After all this constructive, engaging, and challenging discussion, the time has come to focus more sharply on turning ideas into action. Yesterday, in welcoming you to the Global Scholars' Symposium, Amol Verma said on behalf of the organisers – who have done an outstanding job – that 'not only do we hope to inspire questions but also to inspire action'. A number of groups this afternoon have raised ideas for action and proposed processes for refining ideas for the future.

Goodness knows that the world needs smart, globally aware, leaders of the future who are committed to action to deal with the challenges we face. Interestingly, almost all of the Scholarship programs represented here are named for people of action. Lord Clarendon, Cecil Rhodes, Winston Churchill, General George C Marshall, Senator J William Fulbright, Lord Weidenfeld, Bill and Melinda Gates – all were or are people of action, who all combined their bias for action with a real interest in ideas, and with a commitment in some way to promoting the public good as they saw it, either on a national or a global scale.

In seeking to turn ideas into action, one could do worse than learn from the examples, good and bad, of some of these people of action: their focus and their discipline; their ability to form and to express a clear vision; their ability to plan how to achieve that vision and to execute their plan; their capacity to build a team to pursue it; their powers of communication; their capacity to generate that necessary positive sense of urgency – the positive urgency that is sharply focussed on ensuring disciplined execution – 'action this day', as Churchill was wont to instruct; their resilience in the face of setbacks; and their resolve, again as Churchill put it, to 'never surrender'.

Instead of making a long speech, I would like today to leave you with five questions. First, what is the action *you* want to achieve – either now, or over the years ahead, or over the course of your career? It may be that there is a cause – perhaps more than one – which you are inspired to go from here now to pursue. I would be delighted to see immediate action emerging from your collective deliberation and your individual reflections. But I would also hope that you will come to see your own career as making the greatest contribution you can to helping to meet the world's great needs – if you like, making the greatest difference for good in the world that you can. Many Rhodes Scholars have heard me suggest that one way of thinking about your career is to identify the intersection of what you are passionate about, what you have a natural aptitude for, and what will give you a sense of meaning and purpose in your life. It is my hope that your sense of meaning and purpose will come from some objective or objectives which, in Cecil Rhodes's phrase, help to fight 'the world's fight'. What will your objectives be? What will your impact, your legacy, be?

My second question is: on the issue or issues you wish to impact, where does power lie, and how can you help to move the levers of power? Power – be it hard power, soft power, or smart power – comes in many changing forms, and leadership likewise comes in many forms. There is, for example, the power of ideas – and corresponding to that, there is thought leadership. The economist Keynes, one of the great 'thought leaders' of the 20th century, said that the power of ideas was vastly under-estimated compared to the power of interests. Indeed, he said, the world is ruled by little else than ideas. This may or may not have been right. Keynes himself, a person of great and diverse impact, illustrates the many different ways in which power, influence, and leadership can be exercised – for Keynes himself was an academic, author, journalist, broadcaster, an opinion leader, civil servant during both world wars, international negotiator, adviser to government, member of Parliament, businessman, and philanthropist. On each question he was concerned with, he sought to identify where power lay, and to influence its exercise. On the issues you are concerned with, how will you do the same? How will you mobilise ideas and interests, including ideas about interests, to achieve the goals you seek?

My third question is: if your issue or your proposed solution is not at present on the agenda for further debate and for decision, including for research, what will you do to get it on the agenda? It is sometimes harder to get an issue onto the agenda – to get it discussed, to get it recognised that discussion and decision are necessary – than it is to get a good outcome once it is on the agenda. Even if this is not the case, getting your issue addressed is likely to begin with getting it on the agenda for debate and discussion. A president or prime minister, a government or indeed any organisation, can only pursue so many objectives at once. How do you get your objectives onto their agenda for action? Those who through academic work begin to shape the agenda for research – the questions that are asked, the hypotheses that are tested, the paradigms that are shifted – can have a profound impact both on research and on the action that comes from it. How will you help to shape the agenda for discussion and for action on the things that you care about?

My fourth question is: how will you continue to prepare yourself for effective leadership for action on the world's challenges? How will you refine your existing skills of leadership – your capacity to get a group of people, from a small organisation or institution to a country or the international community, to confront its real issues? How will you adapt your leadership skills to different and changing contexts? How will you continue to refine your thinking about, your expertise on, the world's real issues? How will you continue to develop your global outlook, and your capacity for understanding, dialogue, and action that crosses, even transcends, boundaries of nations, cultures, and faiths – as CNN says, to 'go beyond borders', or in the theme of this conference, to 'Think Global'? Each of these questions warrants a long discussion in itself: but let me simply say that I hope that you will use your time studying in Britain to help you prepare yourself further for effective leadership for action on the world's challenges, and I hope that your participation in this Global Scholars' Symposium has contributed towards this for you.

My final question is: how will you prevent yourself from giving up? In any generation, there are many young people of talent, values, and vision who intend to make a major contribution to solving the world's problems who become diverted from their path – seduced by false gods, side-lined by private pursuits, discouraged by adversity, forgetting their original commitment, and making a lesser contribution, a lesser impact, than they could, and, it may be argued, than the world needs. How will you prevent this happening to you? What will you do to remind yourself, as I hope is true, that part of your life's purpose is to make the greatest difference for good you can in the world?

I hope that this Global Scholars' Symposium may have helped to precipitate immediate action for change, and that Scholars here will continue to collaborate and carry ideas forward towards action, including as you prepare for GSS 2012. One way that has been proposed has been through the new initiative arising from this symposium, 'Think Global Canada'. I hope your most immediate action will be to come back tonight, at 7 pm, for our Meet and Mingle party! I also hope that in years – in decades – to come you will look back on these two days as a time which helped to refresh, inform, and inspire your commitment to contribute, in deeds as well as words, to helping to solve a major challenge. What challenge will you tackle, I wonder? What impact will you have? And what legacy will you leave?

Part II: On leaders

Nelson Mandela, Bram Fischer, and George Bizos: the courage to resist

Welcome at the Bram Fischer Memorial Lecture
Rhodes House, Oxford, 24 February 2011

It is an immense pleasure and a profoundly moving privilege to welcome you most warmly to Rhodes House for this lecture in memory of an exceptional Rhodes Scholar, Bram Fischer, to be delivered by his friend and colleague Advocate George Bizos SC – a lecture in memory of one of the great lawyer heroes of the struggle against apartheid, to be given by another of the great lawyer heroes of that historic struggle for justice.

The names of George Bizos and Bram Fischer are, of course, unbreakably linked with each other and with that of Nelson Mandela, whose photographic portrait – taken in this building on one of his several visits here – adorns this Hall, and who is in turn also unbreakably linked with the Rhodes Trust through the Mandela Rhodes Foundation which supports African students undertaking postgraduate study in South Africa. In his autobiography, *Long Walk to Freedom*, Nelson Mandela wrote of his years as a law student at the University of the Witwatersrand: 'At Wits, I met many people who were to share with me the ups and downs of the liberation struggle, and without whom I would have accomplished little.'

After mentioning Joe Slovo and Ruth First, Mr Mandela wrote:

> … I began lifelong friendships with George Bizos and Bram Fischer. George, the child of Greek immigrants, was a man who combined a sympathetic nature with an incisive mind. Bram Fischer, a part-time lecturer, was the scion of a distinguished

Afrikaner family: his grandfather had been prime minister of the Orange River Colony and his father was judge-president of the Orange Free State. Although he could have been prime minister of South Africa, he became one of the bravest and staunchest friends of the freedom struggle that I have ever known.

Bram Fischer and George Bizos were, of course, to serve together in defending Nelson Mandela and others in the Treason Trial of 1956-61, and again when Mr Mandela and others faced the real possibility – indeed the likelihood – of the death sentence in the Rivonia Trial of 1963-64. Mr Mandela later wrote:

> Perhaps it is George's tactical skills in matters of the law for which he is best known. It was this skill that led Bram Fischer, the leader of our defence team in the Rivonia Trial, to include George in that landmark event. Indeed it was George Bizos who warned us at our first consultation after the Rivonia arrests that Verwoerd's government was preparing the ground for the death penalty to be imposed on all of those arrested.

Not long after the Rivonia Trial, George was to serve in the legal team that defended Bram Fischer himself when he was in turn on trial. It is fitting tonight also to mark the various contributions in those legal struggles of Joel Joffe – Lord Joffe, who is here tonight and indeed has helped to organise this lecture; of Sir Sydney Kentridge; and also of the Rhodes Scholar Rex Welsh, who for many years organised the Rhodes Scholarships in South Africa. His two successors in that role, Justices Laurie Ackermann and Edwin Cameron, have both also been Rhodes Scholar lawyers active in the fight against apartheid and in continuing efforts for human rights.

In late 1965, when Bram Fischer was on trial, an organising secretary from the Christian Action Defence and Aid Fund in London wrote to the Warden of Rhodes House, Sir Edgar Williams, seeking information about Bram Fischer's Oxford career for use in their materials to raise money for his defence. Sir Edgar Williams replied:

> Thank you for your letter about *my friend* Mr. Abram Fischer. He read first of all Jurisprudence and got a Third Class degree in 1933. He then took a third year to read for the Diploma of Economics which he passed in 1934. ... He played rugby football and lawn tennis for New College and he was President of the Ralegh Club, a Commonwealth Society which [the Warden wrote] still meets, as it did in his day, in the Beit Room of Rhodes House on Sunday evenings…[Emphasis added.]

Sir Edgar Williams's predecessor as Warden of Rhodes House, Sir Carleton Allen, who was Warden when Bram Fischer was in Oxford from Hilary term 1932 until the summer of 1934, also clearly regarded him as a friend. Warden Allen's admiration for Bram Fischer was clear in his annual Scholar reports. At the end of Bram Fischer's first year, Warden Allen wrote: 'A most attractive man, who shows not only qualities of great commonsense [sic] but of self-sacrificing kindness to others'.

At the end of his second year, Warden Allen wrote:

> In numerous ways he has derived great benefit from his time in England and in character, outlook, and disposition he is one of the most attractive Rhodes Scholars we have. …..I am certain that he will … be a man of mark and always of the most admirable personality…

And when Bram Fischer left Oxford in 1934, Warden Allen wrote:

> One of the most delightful of the Rhodes Scholars from any country, and a man who has won universal esteem and affection… after previous university training, he did not come to Oxford primarily for academic experience, and he has certainly derived the fullest and most judicious advantage from it in all other ways.

All who have been in touch with him view his departure with
real regret.

This high estimation of Bram Fischer was shared by the
Warden of New College, H A L Fisher, who was also a Rhodes
Trustee, and who wrote admiringly of his charm, character,
and ability. In Trinity term 1933, Warden Fisher wrote: 'One
of the nicest and most generally respected men in College.
Should exercise an admirable influence in the Free State.' That
Michaelmas term, the Warden of New College wrote that Bram
'Fischer has greatly gained in width of outlook [from] Oxford'.
And in the summer of 1934, simply: 'One of the best men in
College'.

In May 1948, just before the National Party came to power in
South Africa, Bram Fischer, in Johannesburg, completed a form
for Rhodes House giving an update on his activities. He wrote:

1. Married 1937 to Miss S.J. [Molly] Krige

2. 3 children

3. In active practice in Johannesburg as a member of the
   Transvaal Bar.

4. Principal Activity: Politics as a member of the Central
   Committee of the Communist Party of South Africa.

He enclosed this form with a letter to the Warden, in which
he wrote:

During the war the medical members of our army frustrated me
at every turn and I failed to get past them either by argument or
deceit. And so, as my form discloses, I turned to politics instead.
No doubt, my activity in this direction will come as somewhat of
a shock to you & Mrs. Allen. Nevertheless, it may be of interest,
as I doubt whether there is any other Rhodes Scholar yet who is
on the central committee of a Communist Party.

In fact, the Warden, who had no sympathy for communism, replied 'You are by no means the first Rhodes Scholar to have espoused the Communist cause. There are several quite prominently connected with it in Australia.'

Bram Fischer's letter had continued:

The set up in this country of course seems to lead one inevitably to socialism. With its race hatreds, prejudices, oppression & endemic fascism, S. Africa forces one to the conclusion that mere palliative measures will never succeed. In my life time I have seen the vote taken away from two large sections of the community – the Indians in Natal & the Natives in the Cape. Thus I took the plunge – one of the results being that I now appear in the police files as a man with a record – a number of us were convicted under our Riotous Assemblies Act of assisting in the "illegal" strike of African Mine workers in 1946. ... It's all somewhat Gilbertian of course. I still continue to be briefed by mining house[s] and other "capitalists" and my wife who called on you ... in 1937, continues to remain on good terms with her family – i.e. [her uncle] General Smuts!

Bram Fischer concluded his letter:

I would love to see you ... and Oxford again. At present there are no prospects, especially as our youngest is only 9 months old. However, we are determined to make a trip and so, some day, we shall turn up at Rhodes House and I shall be able to thank you & Mrs. Allen again for all you did for me ...

Today at Rhodes House we think with gratitude of all that Bram Fischer, at immense self-sacrifice, did for the rights of others. In remembering Bram Fischer's role in the struggle for human rights and a genuine and just rule of law in South Africa, we are immensely privileged to have George Bizos with us. When Bram Fischer first entered this Hall at Rhodes House nearly 80 years ago, George Bizos was a small boy in Greece.

When Bram Fischer tried to enlist to fight the Nazis in World War II, George's family perilously escaped the Nazi onslaught and ended up as refugees in South Africa. And then in the study and practice of law in South Africa, the lives of George Bizos, Bram Fischer, Nelson Mandela, and others struggling for freedom interlocked, and George became, not only Mr Mandela's lawyer serving him and his family on innumerable occasions over half a century and more, but also a legal colleague of and then a lawyer for Bram Fischer.

Nadine Gordimer, who in earlier years had written about why Bram Fischer chose jail, wrote this of George in the 1990s:

> The gales of war blew a 13-year-old Greek boy to our shores. He was to become a South African civil rights lawyer of international standing, a devastating cross-examiner of apartheid's authorised torturers and killers. Long before the Truth and Reconciliation Commission was visualised, George Bizos pursued the truth of what was being done to those who suffered under and had the courage to oppose a racist regime turned brutal tyrant. When George Bizos won a case, it was not just a professional victory – it was an imperative of a man whose deep humanity directs his life.

That deep humanity is reflected in George's memoirs, fittingly entitled *Odyssey to Freedom*, which I commend to you; and I am sure it will be evident in his Bram Fischer Memorial Lecture, and in his response to your questions afterwards.

In his powerful and moving foreword to *Odyssey to Freedom*, Nelson Mandela writes of George as his 'close friend', 'a wholly trusted confidant' through prison years and presidency and beyond, who 'is considered a member of our family' – 'Uncle George' to three generations of Mandelas – and 'a man whose contribution towards entrenching the human rights that lie at the heart of South Africa's constitutional values is impossible to overrate'.

Ladies and gentlemen – Advocate George Bizos SC.

F W de Klerk: the wisdom to reform

Welcome to lecture by Mr F W de Klerk
Rhodes House, Oxford, 17 May 2011

It is a great privilege to welcome you to Rhodes House today, and above all to welcome a leader who by an astute and visionary decision to embrace negotiations made possible South Africa's transition from apartheid to democracy, and who will today address us on a topic in which he played a unique role and which he knows uniquely well, 'leadership in South Africa's transition'.

The Nobel Peace Prize for 1993 was awarded jointly to Mr de Klerk, whom we are delighted is here, and to Nelson Mandela, whose photographic portrait taken on one of his many visits here is on this wall, and with whom the Rhodes Trust has joined in the Mandela Rhodes Foundation. I am aware, Mr de Klerk, from my fellow Rhodes Scholar Shaun Johnson, the director of the Mandela Rhodes Foundation, that you have given warm support to it from the outset, including a video endorsement, and we are very grateful; and I bring heartfelt greetings to you from Mandela Rhodes, where I have recently been.

Mr de Klerk and Mr Mandela were awarded the Nobel Prize 'for their work for the peaceful termination of the apartheid regime, and for laying the foundations for a new democratic South Africa'.

At the Nobel Prize Awards Ceremony in Oslo in December 1993, Mr Mandela said:

> Far from the rough and tumble of the politics of our own country, I would like to take this opportunity to join the Norwegian Nobel Committee and pay tribute to my joint laureate, Mr F.W. de Klerk. He had the courage to admit that a terrible wrong had been done to our country and people through the imposition

of the system of apartheid. He had the foresight to understand and accept that all the people of South Africa must through negotiations and as equal participants in the process, together determine what they want to make of their future.

In his speech on that occasion, focused on building a framework for peace, Mr de Klerk said:

Five years ago people would have seriously questioned the sanity of anyone who would have predicted that Mr Mandela and I would be joint recipients of the 1993 Nobel Peace Prize. The extraordinarily fortunate conjunction of two opposing leaders both committed to reconciliation and peace, and willing to take all the hard steps along the way, made this seemingly insane thought a reality.

As you may know, Mr de Klerk was born in Johannesburg in 1936, trained and practised as a lawyer, entered Parliament for the National Party in 1972, and held a succession of ministerial positions from Posts and Telecommunications to National Education and Planning. Having since 1982 led the National Party in the Transvaal, in February 1989 he was elected leader of the National Party and in September 1989 became State President of South Africa, immediately beginning the process which led, through the release of Nelson Mandela and much else, to the 'one person, one vote' elections of 1994, in which Mr Mandela succeeded him as President, and Mr de Klerk became, jointly with Thabo Mbeki, Deputy President of South Africa, a position he held until 1996.

Amongst his subsequent distinguished contributions to public life, Mr de Klerk is founder and chairman of the F W de Klerk Foundation, which works to uphold the constitution, promote peace and multi-racial harmony, and support disadvantaged children; and is chairman of the Global Leadership Foundation, which exists to improve the quality of political leadership and governance by enabling today's national leaders to benefit from the experience of former leaders.

By any reasonable definition of leadership, Mr de Klerk has played a truly historic leadership role, one that deserves widespread recognition and one from which we can all learn. One definition of good leadership is that it is about getting a group of people to deal effectively with their real issues. Mr de Klerk did this. The writer and teacher on leadership, Marty Linsky, has said that his 'favourite definition of leadership' is that 'leadership is about disappointing your own people at a rate they can absorb'.*

Mr de Klerk had the wisdom and the courage to do this – to lead his own people to confront realities so many did not wish to face, and by doing so – by pursuing a path of reconciliation and peace – actually achieved a manifestly far better outcome for South Africa than any likely alternative. It is of course an outcome – a constitutional democracy – that needs to be protected day by day, and in which many of the real issues of South Africa continue to need real leadership to resolve.

We are all deeply privileged to have Mr and Mrs de Klerk with us today, and I am delighted to call on Mr de Klerk to address us.

---

* Mr de Klerk made clear that he liked this formulation, which resonated with his own experience.

Margaret Thatcher: Conservative agent of international change

The Interpreter
Lowy Institute for International Policy
9 April 2013

As an Australian living in Britain for most of the Thatcher years, I watched at close hand the remarkable performance in foreign affairs, as in economic policy, of this transformative figure.[*] She stood shoulder to shoulder with US leaders, most obviously Ronald Reagan, in 'standing up' to the Soviet Union as – especially in the wake of the Soviet invasion of Afghanistan, the imposition of martial law in Poland, and other developments – the earlier spirit of détente had given way to what was often (I think wrongly) spoken of as 'the second Cold War'.

Just as Mrs Thatcher stood firmly against the miners in the miners' strike, she stood firmly against CND (the Campaign for Nuclear Disarmament) and others who opposed the refreshing of the Western nuclear arsenal in the early 1980s.

Yet perhaps Mrs Thatcher's most extraordinary accomplishment in relations with the Soviet Union was that she was one of the first to see that Gorbachev could himself be a transformative figure – someone she could 'do business with', and someone whose policies of perestroika, glasnost, and willingness to engage with the West should be encouraged and built upon.

Sovietologist colleagues of mine in the mid-1980s who were not natural allies of Mrs Thatcher's were nonetheless excited by her interest in, and perceptiveness about, this historic

---

[*] Margaret Thatcher (13 October 1925-8 April 2013). Prime Minister of the United Kingdom, 1979-90. This assessment was written the morning after her death.

opportunity, from which flowed the end of the Cold War and indeed the end of the Soviet Union.

It was also evident to me that her willingness to go to war with Argentina to reclaim the Falklands in 1982, a brilliantly successful show of defiance, courage, strength, and determination, led many to re-evaluate her (including her deeply controversial economic policies and her there-is-no-alternative approach) and to see strength where before they had only seen bloody-minded stubbornness. Many Commonwealth colleagues and observers saw only stubbornness in her resistance to sanctions against apartheid South Africa, though she had earlier played an important role in the transition to black majority rule in Zimbabwe.

The link between her economic and international approaches was, of course, evident in Mrs Thatcher's approach to Europe where, perhaps to over-simplify, she viewed the European Union as essentially a free trade union while many on the continent increasingly aimed towards a European federation. This was but one of many arenas in which she fought tooth and nail for what she saw as Britain's legitimate interests. Her scepticism about European monetary union strikes many now as prescient, of course.

Her resistance to the reunification of Germany, because of her fear of German dominance in Europe, was simply futile. Reunification was a necessary and, for most, a much-celebrated outcome of the collapse of the Soviet empire which she had sought, and the other consequences of which – such as the freeing of countries throughout central and eastern Europe – she warmly welcomed.

Mrs Thatcher also accepted that the expiry of the 99-year lease of Hong Kong from China could have no honourable outcome other than Hong Kong's return to China, and she negotiated what she thought were the best terms for this. She did so with a communist China that was bit by bit undergoing the kind of economic liberalisation that she warmly welcomed

– Thatcherism with Chinese characteristics, one might be tempted to say – and which, among other things, created opportunities for British business (something she seemed always keen to encourage, sometimes even controversially keen).

Although many factors contributed to the end of the Cold War and the collapse of the Soviet Union, and to other successes associated with her name, there is no doubt that Margaret Thatcher was in international affairs (as in economic policy and the relationship of the individual, market, and state) a figure of truly historic consequence and profound impact. The Iron Lady indeed.

Yvonne McComb King: 'if the trumpet give an uncertain sound ...'

80th Birthday Dinner
United Services Club, Brisbane
25 November 2000

I first met Yvonne* one morning around 6 a.m. on the driveway of Kevin Cairns's home at Clayfield during the campaign for the May 1974 federal election.† We had both gone there to volunteer to help hand out leaflets for Kevin to innocent commuters at railway stations around Lilley. Yvonne and her federal Liberal candidate were not altogether close, and Kevin cleverly solved the awkward problem of what to do with this over-enthusiastic 15-year-old schoolboy by sending Yvonne and me off together to Northgate railway station.

This was the beginning of a beautiful friendship. Over the next two years or so, I would often visit Yvonne after school at her office with the Royal Flying Doctor Service. As she was organising the Queen of the Outback competition, I would distract her with my thoughts on all manner of political and economic issues facing Australia under Whitlam. It was a little flattering, but also a little alarming, when Phillip Lynch, soon to become Treasurer of Australia, asked Yvonne, presumably after a federal executive meeting, who her new economic adviser was.

As the 1970s wore on, of course, our concerns increasingly focused on how to respond to the apparently growing misuse

---

* Yvonne McComb King (20 November 1920-9 August 2012). President, Liberal Party of Australia (Queensland Division), 1976-80. Also served as federal chair of Liberal Women's Council, and Federal Vice-President, Liberal Party of Australia. Liberal Senate candidate, Queensland, 1980.

† Kevin Cairns was the Liberal Member of Parliament for the Australian federal seat of Lilley, in Brisbane, Queensland, from 1963 to 1972, and from 1974 to 1980.

of power in Queensland under Premier Joh Bjelke-Petersen. For several months in 1980, Yvonne was still State President of the Liberal Party, and I was during that year President of the Young Liberals. Yvonne and I both believed that part of what the Liberal Party in Queensland needed to do was to run a Senate ticket separate from that of the National Party, and I was delighted that she finally agreed to the suggestion that she should stand as a candidate for the Senate on that Liberal ticket.

You may remember that in those days Princess Margaret developed a close friendship with a much younger man called Roddy Llewellyn. A friend of Yvonne's and of mine – I think it was Beryce Nelson – told me that the friendship between Yvonne and me was a matter of comment in some circles, and that the parallel was drawn with Princess Margaret and Roddy Llewellyn. Being young and innocent, it did not occur to me to assure Beryce that in its most important particular the parallel was entirely inaccurate. But from that moment Yvonne became to me 'Margaret' and, perhaps somewhat less enthusiastically, she acknowledged me as 'Roddy'. I do not know what the Special Branch officers who were tapping her telephone made of conversations between Princess Margaret and Roddy.

If the real Princess Margaret and Roddy were enjoying each other's company on Caribbean islands, this Margaret and Roddy were campaigning for the Senate through visiting country towns such as Roma and Chinchilla together – including giving a plug for the Romavilla winery – and country shows on the Darling Downs.

At the 1980 Liberal Party State Convention, Yvonne retired as State President of the Party to concentrate on the Senate campaign. In my tribute to her on her retirement, speaking as President of the Young Liberals as well as a friend, I quoted the passage from St Paul: '… if the trumpet give an uncertain sound, who shall prepare himself to the battle?'* I said, of course, that

---

* 1 Corinthians 14:8.

as a leader Yvonne gave no uncertain sound, and we prepared ourselves to the battle. Yvonne rang me later to say that this was one of her favourite verses from scripture. It seems to me to capture at least part of the spirit and calibre of the leadership of this happy warrior.

The mere fact that I went overseas in 1981 – for 15 years, as it turned out – did not in any way diminish our friendship. I remember when the telephone rang in my room in Oxford, and Yvonne said 'I have something to tell you'. For some inexplicable reason I heard myself say the words 'I smell a rat' – to which she replied 'He's a very nice rat'. And so he is! In fact, he's not a rat at all, but one of the most stimulating friends one could have. Yvonne and Malcolm* are, fortunately, great travellers, and we caught up over subsequent years in many different places, including, of course, here at home in Brisbane as well as at Kirribilli and elsewhere. I do not know what Princess Margaret thinks of a *ménage à trois*, but this one has been a very happy one.

And so, Yvonne, in celebrating this landmark birthday with you, I salute you for so many qualities – your commitment to the causes you believe in, your happy fighting spirit, your sense of service to the community, your wonderful optimism, your openness to ideas (even from 15-year-old schoolboys), your great sense of fun, and above all your brilliant capacity for friendship. The capacity for friendship is one of the greatest gifts there is, and Yvonne has it in abundance; and I, for one, am extremely grateful. God bless you.

---

* Yvonne married Malcolm King in 1984.

Sir Zelman Cowen: 'a touch of healing'

*State Funeral for Sir Zelman Cowen AK**

Temple Beth Israel, St Kilda, Melbourne

13 December 2011

In August 1940, George Paton, Professor of Jurisprudence at the University of Melbourne and a Rhodes Scholar for Victoria 14 years before, wrote a reference for a 20-year-old candidate for the Rhodes Scholarship who had dreamed since boyhood of going to Oxford:

> I have known Mr. Z. Cowen well for some years. His academic record…is one that has rarely been equalled. It is frequently the case that those who do brilliantly in Arts do not show quite the same aptitude for law, but Mr. Cowen shows the same skill in both fields. His mind is very keen and remarkably mature for one of his age. Very few could even attempt the task he is doing this year – finishing the law course and carrying a burden of University teaching as well. I have found his contributions in discussion classes very penetrating and interesting, and, although one is a poor student who can teach his mentors nothing, from Mr. Cowen I have learned a great deal.

> He has a rounded personality, broad interests and cultivated tastes. … He has great energy and that intellectual integrity which refuses to accept anything which has not been investigated. …

---

* Sir Zelman Cowen (7 October 1919-8 December 2011). There is more on Sir Zelman's life and career in the Sir Zelman Cowen Oration, 'Universities and contemporary society: civility in a free society', in the section of this book 'On education'. This December 2011 eulogy was first published as 'Sir Zelman Cowen: Educational Leader and Healing Governor-General', *The Round Table: The Commonwealth Journal of International Affairs*, February 2012, and is reproduced with permission by Routledge/ Taylor & Francis Group (www.tandfonline.com).

... He has the assured courtesy of a much older man, and, while he has no reticence in urging his own opinions, I have found him both respectful and willing to abandon his point of view, if its weakness could be shown. ...

In short, I feel he has that quality which would benefit most from a period at Oxford. I have written many of these testimonials for the Selection Committee, but this is the first time that I can write for a candidate who has exactly that intellectual flair of which great things can be predicted.

Zelman Cowen won the Rhodes Scholarship for Victoria that year, but was not able to take it up until 1945, after war-time service in the Navy. In Oxford, where he went with his young wife and life partner, Anna, he was appointed a permanent Fellow & Tutor in Law at Oriel College even before he topped the postgraduate Bachelor of Civil Law degree in 1947. From this base, he also did legal work in the post-war occupation of Germany, and had his first exciting exposure to law teaching in the United States.

In 1950, George Paton, as Dean of the University of Melbourne Law School, wrote to Zelman to see if he was interested in applying for the Professorship of Public Law there. He was; and the Warden of Rhodes House, Oxford, C K Allen, an under-stated but highly distinguished Australian lawyer, wrote from Oxford expressing 'both pleasure and confidence in supporting [Mr. Zelman Cowen's] application'. Noting his 'academic record, both in Australia and at Oxford', and that he had 'more than amply justified his election [as a Rhodes Scholar] on all grounds, both personal and scholastic', Warden Allen reported that 'since he was elected a Fellow of Oriel College I have ample evidence ... that he is a successful teacher who takes great trouble with his pupils, has a shrewd judgement of them, and is much appreciated by them. He is, in my opinion, a man not only of quick and extensive legal attainment, but of genuine scholarly interests.' He commended Zelman as a constitutional lawyer who would be a 'co-operative colleague ... efficient in ... administrative duties'. Oriel College, the Warden privately noted, would be 'very sorry to lose' this 'excellent tutor'.

Zelman Cowen was, of course, appointed to the Chair of Public Law, and as George Paton was almost simultaneously appointed Vice-Chancellor of the University of Melbourne, the 31-year-old Rhodes Scholar came home not only as Professor but also unexpectedly as Dean of the Melbourne Law School. Over the next 16 years, he truly transformed it into the modern law school, grounded in first-rate scholarship and teaching, and rich with international linkages, especially with the US universities he visited. His own inspiring teaching and encouraging mentoring are, I know, still remembered with gratitude by many law students of that time, now very senior in their profession. It was in these Melbourne years that Simon, Nick, Kate, and Ben were born. At the same time, Professor Zelman Cowen also emerged as a public figure, including through radio and later television commentaries on public and international issues, opposing the Communist Party dissolution referendum in 1951 and the Victorian hangings of the 1960s, and contributing internationally to the development of legal education and building up administrative talent in various Commonwealth countries and territories.

The early references I quoted from Sir George Paton and Sir Carleton Allen give insight into the qualities of intellect and character that led Zelman Cowen to so distinguished a career as legal scholar, author of many articles and several books, of which clearly one of his favourites was his biography of Sir Isaac Isaacs; pioneer in legal education; academic leader as Dean, and then Vice-Chancellor of the University of New England and then of the University of Queensland; tireless healing Governor-General of Australia; and then back at Oriel College, Oxford, as Provost, where he was proud to be the first Rhodes Scholar to be head of Cecil Rhodes's own college.

In his application for the Rhodes Scholarship in 1940, the 20-year-old Zelman Cowen wrote:

> The [teaching] work as a member of the University staff has entailed fair experience in public speaking. While at Scotch College, I was a member of the School debating team, and since that time have been keenly interested in public speaking. I have found that the work [teaching] in the [University] Extension Board particularly, together with invitations I have from time to time received to address bodies, such as Public Schools and clubs has afforded invaluable experience in this very interesting work.

It was indeed 'invaluable experience'. As a Vice-Chancellor and Governor-General, and in other public roles, Zelman Cowen was to find speeches a powerful instrument of leadership and healing. When, as a young Rhodes Scholar from Queensland with a shared interest in constitutional conventions, I came to know Sir Zelman in Oxford in the early 1980s, beginning one of the greatest friendships of my life, I was struck by how vividly etched, even scorched, in his mind was his speech to a large crowd in the Great Court at the University of Queensland, my much-loved alma mater, during the Springbok protests and University disruption of July 1971. For such a speech-maker to describe this as 'the speech of my life' reflects the tensions of those times. It also reflects that he was by nature a communicator. The late 1960s and early to mid-1970s were times of tumult and protest around the world, including at the University of Queensland, where the Vice-Chancellor had to steer the University between what was often abusive protest on the one hand and an overly assertive Premier on the other. During these troubles, Zelman and Anna Cowen showed 'grace under pressure' – which is a definition of courage.

Through 'the troubles' and beyond, Professor Cowen defended the rights and interests of students, and worked to build the University, engaging community support, including philanthropic support. Then, as before and later, he was an effective fundraiser. One important benefactor of the University of Queensland was a flamboyant grazier, Barney Joyce. When asked how he would like to be portrayed in the University's official portrait of him, Sir Zelman replied, somewhat cheekily: 'with my hand in Barney Joyce's pocket'. Her Excellency the Governor-General* has spoken of how, when she invited Vice-Chancellor Cowen at short notice to lecture to one of her law classes at UQ at that time, his was the best lecture she has ever heard, earning a standing ovation from the students.

Fulfilling his vision of the Vice-Chancellor as an 'independent public figure' as well as leader within the University community, in various public addresses in Australia and overseas Vice-Chancellor Cowen spoke of how the tearing of the social fabric in countries around the world was threatening the fragile consensus – the acceptance of shared values and rules – on which what he called a 'civil liberal society' depended.

The 1975 constitutional crisis and responses to it greatly strained the fragile consensus about crucial aspects of governance in this country. When in 1977 Sir John Kerr indicated his intention to resign as Governor-General, the Prime Minister, Malcolm Fraser, turned for his successor to a wholly non-partisan constitutional scholar and attractive public figure who, in thought and action, had grappled more profoundly than perhaps anyone else in this country with the issues of division, consensus, communication, and healing. In using Nehru's phrase 'a touch of healing' to describe what he hoped to bring to the office, Sir Zelman set the theme of his four and a half years as Governor-General. Above all, the healing was done through reaching out to community groups in all corners of the country, endless visits and countless speeches, reflecting careful research and what seemed like boundless energy. I first saw Sir Zelman Cowen, of whom of course I had known for years, when in 1978

---

* Ms Quentin Bryce AC.

he came back to the University of Queensland, where I was then an undergraduate, to give a major speech in the Mayne Hall, which he had been so determined and proud to build. His speeches aimed not least, in Sir Zelman's phrase, to 'interpret the nation to itself'. As we all know, this healing balm was a profound gift to the nation, for which we are right to remain grateful, and Sir Zelman's approach has been a model for a number of subsequent Governor-Generals.

On going back to Oriel College in 1982 as its Provost, Sir Zelman again brought healing – healing a college hurt by the sudden departure of its previous Provost, and presiding over the harmonious resolution of what had been the divisive issue of admitting women to Oriel, the last all-male college in Oxford. His speeches to rowdy undergraduates at dinners after rowing victories were legendary, showing his own depth of engagement in the full life of the College and enabling him humorously to encourage academic as well as sporting success. Sir Zelman combined the Provostship with other roles, including as chair of the British Press Council and of the Van Leer Jerusalem Institute, as well as speaking commitments around the world.

His extensive speech-making about the role of Governor-General and other Commonwealth issues reflected the fact that, although he had written on issues of monarchy and republic since the mid-1960s, he – along with most Australians – then believed that Australia had sufficiently achieved the substance of independence and had no need to change to a republic. But within five years of coming back to Australia in 1990, he believed that Australia's national journey and sense of itself now required that its head of state be, in words he liked, 'one of us' – unequivocally symbolising Australia itself. And so in the republican debate of the mid- to late 1990s, the constitutional lawyer who had brought healing to the nation in the position of Governor-General was advocating, including in speeches over which he laboured, an Australian president chosen by special majority in the Parliament.

By that time, with strong support from Victoria University, where he was a Distinguished Visiting Professor, Sir Zelman and his team were hard at work on his memoirs, *A Public Life*. They were launched by Justice Michael Kirby on Sir Zelman and Lady Cowen's 61st wedding anniversary, in June 2006. It is in these memoirs that one can read of many diverse interests that can barely be touched on today – music (especially Mozart), architecture, the press, his work on radio and television, adult education – and other aspects of his life, from the Jewish migrant experience of his forebears, his St Kilda boyhood and interest in ships and early aviation, and the joys of student days, through to his retirement work for Griffith Law School and the National Academy of Music, and for editorial independence at Fairfax newspapers, and much else besides. In recent days so many institutions and organisations have expressed their deep gratitude to him, and rightly so.

Both in his memoirs and in countless speeches and deeds over many decades are reflected the liberal values for which Sir Zelman Cowen was a beacon – individual liberty under law, including the rights to privacy and to free speech in a civil and tolerant society; the rule of reason, with a preference for moderation, collegial leadership and consensus-building, and even-tempered public and private discourse, with disagreement without rancour; uncompromising and scrupulous integrity; and education – in a college, a law school, or the wider university – that both broadens and sharpens the mind. In one such speech, he spoke of 'the study and reflective and speculative thinking which lies at the heart of good teaching' – something he exemplified, expected, and encouraged. Spending 34 of his 92 years leading educational institutions, while ceaselessly interested in broad public issues, he never lost his commitment to the interests of students, and was always delighted when any former student remembered his teaching or help that he had given.

George Paton in 1940 wrote of Zelman Cowen having 'exactly that intellectual flair of which great things can be predicted' – great things fulfilled beyond prediction, perhaps even beyond the prediction of his mother, who expected him to be a King's Counsel – and of his having 'that intellectual integrity which refuses to accept anything that has not been investigated'. For me, conversation with him was often a Socratic dialogue, an investigation – the pursuit of a topic beyond what I thought possible – marked by this experienced raconteur's sudden bursts of humour and an anecdote or three. He brought clarity of mind, charity of spirit, and civility of expression to all he did; erudition and elegance; wisdom in judgement; energy, single-minded determination, efficiency, and dignity in action; and a remarkable capacity for friendship – intensely loyal, warm and kind friendship, expressed in the most generous hospitality by him and Lady Cowen, in conversation that encouraged as well as stretched, and in correspondence that spanned the world.

Zelman Cowen was for me and for others, not only a truly exceptional academic and public figure at home and abroad, but a uniquely special friend and mentor, and a profound and wise influence on our lives. We remember him with love and gratitude, and we will miss him more than we can say.

Memorial Service
Oriel College Chapel, Oxford, 22 April 2012

It was in this Chapel in the spring of 1984, waiting for Evensong to commence, that I had one of my first important conversations with Sir Zelman Cowen – a conversation leading towards what became for me the most profoundly special friendship of my life.

I had known of Sir Zelman for many years. When my family was living in the 1950s and 1960s in the arid outback of Queensland, my mother had listened to radio commentaries on the news by Professor Zelman Cowen, who as a pioneering Dean of the Melbourne Law School from 1951 to 1966 was emerging as a significant public figure in Australia, often on radio and then television. A few years later in Brisbane, I knew that Professor Cowen was the father of Nick Cowen, an older boy who had befriended me at our secondary school; and I knew of his prominent role as Vice-Chancellor of the University of Queensland through the troubled days of left-wing student protest and right-wing state government assertiveness in Queensland in the early 1970s.

In 1977, my first year as a student at the University of Queensland, I was proud and excited that our Vice-Chancellor, by now *Sir* Zelman Cowen, was chosen to become Governor-General of Australia in succession to Sir John Kerr. This was in tumultuous times following Governor-General Kerr's intensely controversial exercise of the reserve powers of the Crown in dismissing the Prime Minister, Gough Whitlam, in the 1975 constitutional crisis arising from appropriations deadlock between the houses of Parliament. We young law students at the University of Queensland commented to each other that the new Governor-General had been, a decade before, the biographer of the first Australian-born and the first Jewish Governor-General of Australia, Sir Isaac Isaacs, and had published the second edition of one of the major works on the reserve powers of the Crown, H V Evatt's *The King and His Dominion Governors*. Mindful of the divisions in the Australian community, of Sir Zelman's courageous and calming stewardship as Vice-Chancellor, and of his public speeches as Vice-Chancellor on what he called 'the fragile consensus' on which a 'civil liberal society' depends, we watched with admiration as he brought exactly what he said, quoting Nehru, he hoped to bring as Governor-General – 'a touch of healing' – to a divided nation and polity.

In 1978, with another law student, now the Shadow

Attorney-General of Australia*, I had snuck in uninvited to the Mayne Hall of the University of Queensland, the building of which was one of Sir Zelman's proudest achievements as Vice-Chancellor, to hear him speak on his first return visit as Governor-General to our campus. And so I witnessed first-hand the brilliant, engaging, and tireless speech-making that was at the heart of his healing and, as he put it, of the role of the Governor-General in 'interpreting the nation to itself' in a very public way. Speech-making was also at the heart of his leadership in other roles, as a student leader at the University of the Melbourne from 1936 on, as Dean of the Melbourne Law School from 1951 to 1966, as Vice-Chancellor of the University of New England from 1967 to 1970, and of the University of Queensland from 1970 to 1977, and here at Oriel from 1982 to 1990.

I knew, soon after I came to Oxford as a Rhodes Scholar in 1981, that Sir Zelman and Lady Cowen were to return to Oriel – and it was just outside the Porters' Lodge of this College that I first met Sir Zelman and Lady Cowen late in 1982, within weeks of their arrival. Sir John Kerr, Sir Zelman's predecessor as Governor-General, had been in Oxford to give a speech to a dinner of Australian students; and the next day it was my unnerving duty to escort Sir John and Lady Kerr to see Sir Zelman and Lady Cowen, with whom they were to have lunch here at Oriel. And so for the first time I met Sir Zelman, of whom I had known since my Queensland boyhood. On subsequent encounters at dinners around Oxford, my fellow Australian students and I tried to get Sir Zelman to tell us what he thought of the dismissal of the Prime Minister by the Governor-General; but he maintained in private his public stance that no good could come from his commenting on that. And so in the spring of 1984, I sent Sir Zelman, somewhat audaciously, an article I had written on the 1975 constitutional crisis; and he contacted me, then a student at Trinity, and invited

---

* Senator the Hon. George Brandis QC.

me to dinner one Sunday evening here at Oriel to discuss it.

The evening began with a talk in the Provost's Lodgings – the first of very many – and then, what he regarded as integral to his role as Provost, Evensong in this Chapel. We discussed Australian constitutional history as we waited for the service to commence, and a comment he made just as the service was starting, about the history of Governor-Generals consulting High Court judges, spurred me to months of archival research on that topic.* This led on to several conversations on the 7 a.m. coach to London as he travelled to chair the Press Council, and I to do research at the Public Record Office at Kew on the early Governor-Generals and High Court judges of Australia.

And so began a deep friendship between us, bridging without difficulty an age difference of 40 years – reflecting, on Sir Zelman's part, a remarkable capacity for warm and generous friendship with people of all generations which was evident throughout his life. He became for me, as he did for others, a uniquely special friend and a uniquely special mentor.

The Choir commenced today's service with the beautiful words and music of Orlando Gibbons, 'The silver swan', which ends with those memorable words 'More geese than swans now live, more fools than wise'. I first heard that sung by the Choir of New College at a dinner there in December 1985 which Sir Zelman attended as an Honorary Fellow of New College – his first Oxford college – and which was presided over by his former student and then the new Warden of New College, Harvey McGregor QC. I was there as an equally new Junior Research Fellow of New College, secretly and anxiously wondering whether to apply for a tutorial fellowship at Merton. Seeking wisdom for this decision, I went to the one person I knew could give it, Sir Zelman Cowen. His encouragement, and indeed wholly unexpected offer to support me as a referee, was decisive,

---

* This unexpected conversation, initiated by Sir Zelman, ultimately resulted, inter alia, in my article, 'Griffith, Barton and the Early Governor-Generals: Aspects of Australia's Constitutional Development', *Public Law Review*, December 1999.

and without it I would not have committed the next decade of my life to that college around the corner – from which I came often to Oriel to talk with the Provost here, and from which we quite often walked round Christ Church meadow.

After Sir Zelman and Lady Cowen returned to Australia in 1990, Sir Zelman was offered and accepted many roles: his service as Chair of the British Press Council in the 1980s was followed by service as Chair of Fairfax, a major newspaper company in Australia, in the 1990s; he continued his work for the Van Leer Institute in Israel and as a Governor of the Hebrew University of Jerusalem; he helped to found and shape the law school at Griffith University in Brisbane; he chaired the board of Australia's new National Academy of Music; and he was a Distinguished Visiting Professor at Victoria University, based in Melbourne's less privileged western suburbs. He greatly enjoyed being close to Simon, Kate, and Ben, and their partners and families.

Having so brilliantly represented the Queen and restored the office of Governor-General of Australia from 1977 to 1982, by the mid-1990s Sir Zelman was convinced that the evolution of Australia's independent national identity now meant that Australia would be best served if its head of state was, in words he liked, 'one of us' – an Australian – and so he became an advocate of Australia's becoming a republic with a president chosen by special majority in both houses of Parliament.

I suspect it was at the Cowens' simple beach house at Caloundra, north of Brisbane, when I briefly visited in late 1994 or early 1995, that Sir Zelman asked me if I would be willing to come for a time from Merton to Victoria University in Melbourne as a visiting professor. The Vice-Chancellor of that University, Jarlath Ronayne, had a more specific idea: that I should come for a year to work with Sir Zelman on an oral history project on his life, which would contribute to the writing of his memoirs. And so I did; but a year led for me to over 13 years back in Australia. Sir Zelman's memoirs, *A Public Life*, were launched in Melbourne on 7 June 2006, the 61st wedding anniversary of Sir Zelman and the truly incomparable Lady Cowen.

In the dozens of hours of oral history interviews and in work on the memoirs, as in innumerable conversations before and since, always marked by humour, I learnt more of Sir Zelman's remarkable story: the experience of his Jewish immigrant forebears coming from Russia, on his father's side via England, to Australia; birth in St Kilda, Melbourne, in 1919, and his upbringing in the St Kilda Jewish community; his mother's aspiration that he become a King's Counsel; his childhood interest in ships and early aviation, and the beginnings of his lifelong passion for music, and of his loyalty to the St Kilda football club; and of his dream of going to Geelong Grammar School – then perhaps the Eton of Australia – and of his winning a scholarship to it, but of his being unable to go when at the last minute it emerged that attendance at Chapel was compulsory, which was not acceptable to his parents or to their Rabbi, Jacob Danglow.

The headmaster of Geelong Grammar School who offered that scholarship but also insisted on compulsory Chapel was an old member of Oriel, James Darling. As Provost of Oriel, over 50 years later, Sir Zelman Cowen was to telephone Sir James Darling to say that he – Darling – had been elected an Honorary Fellow of Oriel, which Darling described as 'the greatest day of my life'.

In endless hours of conversation, I learnt of young Zelman Cowen's going at the age of 16 to the University of Melbourne, where he excelled in arts and in law; threw himself into the extra-curricular life of the University; was the youngest ever tutor in the history of the University, at the age of 19; and was elected in 1940 as Rhodes Scholar for Victoria for 1941. More recently, as Warden of Rhodes House, I have learnt that one of his referees, Sir Kenneth Bailey, himself a Rhodes Scholar and

then Dean of the Melbourne Law School, wrote of the young
Zelman Cowen in August 1940:

His academic record [at Melbourne] is little less than
astonishing. ...His examination work in third-year Law last year
broke all records. ... Before I knew him well, I wondered whether
his success implied anything more than exceptional energy, wide
reading, a retentive memory, high powers of concentration,
and a fluent pen. These gifts are by no means inconsiderable in
themselves. But after seeing a lot of Cowen in small discussion
classes I am sure that he has also exceptional capacity for decisive
reasoning and for independent critical judgment. On any
showing, Cowen has a remarkable mind.

The Law School Dean continued:

Cowen has also a wide range of intellectual interests outside
the class room. He was one of the leaders in the newly-formed
Fine Arts Society, and it is an open secret now that for more
than a year he wrote a weekly article in the students' newspaper
"Farrago" under the general heading of "The Connoisseur's
Collation". He dealt most interestingly and energetically with
a wide range of books, musical and dramatic performances,
exhibitions of pictures and the like. I always find it difficult to
remember that he is still only 20.

Altogether I regard Cowen as possessing real distinction both
of intellect and character. I support his candidature without
reservation.

That candidature was of course successful, and so the vision
and munificence of a member of Oriel, Cecil Rhodes, made
possible the childhood dream of Zelman Cowen to come
to Oxford. A year before, however, on the outbreak of the
war in 1939, horrified by the advance of Hitler, Zelman had
immediately volunteered for service, and his coming to Oxford

was delayed by naval service – including during the ferocious Japanese bombing of Darwin – until 1945, when he came with his young wife, Anna, first to New College and then to Oriel.

In many conversations, I learnt from Zelman – and Anna – Cowen of those exciting, exacting years of BCL* study; of Warden and Mrs Allen at Rhodes House, the lively centre of the Rhodes community in Oxford; and of being elected a Fellow of Oriel even before winning the Vinerian Scholarship for topping the BCL in 1947. Sir Zelman will never have known of the reference that Warden Allen, who was Professor of Jurisprudence before going to Rhodes House, wrote for him for Oriel as early as April 1946 – 66 years ago tomorrow – after Zelman and Anna had been in Oxford only two terms:

> Dear Provost,
>
> ... Cowen is undoubtedly a very able lawyer, with a good practical knowledge and a scholarly approach. He has an enthusiasm for teaching... He is ... quick and industrious and extremely efficient in practical affairs. The same is to be said of his wife, who strikes me as a very capable young woman. Personally, Cowen is agreeable and tactful and I think would make a useful and co-operative colleague. I feel no doubt that he will make a mark in academic law, for he clearly means to do so, and is possessed of great determination. His range of legal knowledge is surprising for his age.

He was then 26.

After Zelman had great success as an Oriel tutor and an exciting term in Chicago in 1949, Warden Allen also supported him with a strong reference for the professorship of public law at the University of Melbourne, to which Zelman went in 1951, becoming also unexpectedly the Dean of the Law School at the age of 31.

---

* Bachelor of Civil Law, a highly demanding postgraduate law degree.

Sir Zelman and I talked of his work in building the modern law school in Melbourne, a model for others. It is not for nothing that the historian of the Melbourne Law School entitles the chapter spanning these years, 'Building the New Jerusalem'.* We talked of his crucial links with overseas law schools, especially his visiting professorships at Harvard and elsewhere; of his legal scholarship, writing on topics from evidence to federal jurisdiction in Australia to matrimonial jurisdiction to much more; of his anxious wait in 1967 and 1968 to see if his legal writings would be judged worthy of an Oxford Doctor of Civil Law, as of course they were; of his emerging role in public life in those years – opposing the referendum in 1951 seeking to ban the Communist Party, opposing the use of capital punishment in Victoria in the 1960s, his work in adult education, his many appearances on radio and then on television, commenting on diverse public issues; of his Boyer lectures – the equivalent of the Reith lectures – on privacy in 1969; of his interest in medico-legal and related ethical issues relevant to human tissue transplants, sparked by the early heart transplants by Dr Christiaan Barnard. Perhaps above all this I saw how touched he was by expressions of gratitude from former students, many now senior in the legal profession, who spoke of his impact on their lives and of their happy and grateful memories of his teaching and mentoring.

We talked of his unexpected move at the end of 1966 to take up the Vice-Chancellorship of the University of New England, a small rural university in northern New South Wales, where he had a vision, probably unrealistic, of building a national collegiate university, but which, despite many achievements and many happy times, he left in 1970 to take on the much larger metropolitan University of Queensland. He was to steer it courageously and in the face of outrageous provocation between

---

* John Waugh, *First Principles: The Melbourne Law School 1857-2007*, Melbourne University Press, 2007, ch. 4: 'Building the New Jerusalem: 1946-66'.

the threats to free speech and civil discourse on campus from abusive student protest, on the one hand, and threats to the autonomy of the University from state government, on the other. Throughout, he worked effectively to encourage community support for the University, and was a builder physically also, with 17 new buildings in seven and a half years as Vice-Chancellor, and displaying – as he had before and would later – great focus and effectiveness as a fundraiser, and keen interest in good architecture. Here, as before and after, his commitment to the welfare of students, and to the importance of teaching as well as of broader scholarship, was clear.

As an attractive and non-partisan public figure and constitutional lawyer who stood courageously for liberal values when they were challenged, who served as healer of a divided university, and who thought deeply about the issues of division and fragile consensus in wider societies facing the turbulence and strains of the 1960s and 1970s, Sir Zelman was the ideal, imaginative appointment as Governor-General of Australia in 1977; as he was the ideal appointment as Provost of this College in 1982, becoming – he was proud to say – the first Rhodes Scholar to be Provost of Rhodes's own college.

In Australia, Sir Zelman is remembered, with immense gratitude, admiration, and affection, as a healing Governor-General and an educational and community leader of wisdom and grace, one of the greatest of Australians, and one of the greatest of Australian Jews. It is impossible to overestimate his impact in the Australian Jewish community. His achievements and his very being gave it a sense of standards, expectation of itself, and confidence that no one had done since General Sir John Monash or Sir Isaac Isaacs.

Amongst at least a thousand mourners, including representatives of very many institutions and organisations he had supported, his state funeral in St Kilda, Melbourne, last December was attended by the current Governor-General and three of her predecessors, for all of whom he set a model;

by the current Prime Minister and three of her predecessors; and by current and previous Chief Justices and justices of the High Court of Australia; and it was broadcast live on national television. Both houses of the Australian Parliament have passed condolence motions in his memory, and the government has endowed scholarships to bear his name.

Today, again we remember a man who deeply loved his wife and his family; who loved and served his college, as he did other institutions to which he was devoted; who loved and served his country; and who loved his friends, to whom he showed innumerable acts of kindness, and who was in turn much loved by them. And we say 'thank you'.

Quentin Bryce and Amanda Bell: champions of women's leadership and of mentoring

Welcome to Their Excellencies Ms Quentin Bryce AC,
Governor-General of Australia, and Mr Michael Bryce AM AE
Rhodes House, Oxford, 28 April 2011

It is an immense privilege for all your fellow Australians here today to welcome Your Excellencies to Oxford, which has educated and is educating so many Australians, and specifically to welcome you to Rhodes House, the home of the Rhodes Scholarships. I am delighted that you have had the chance today to talk with so many outstanding Australian students and academics who will contribute, indeed in many cases are contributing, to the future of our country and the wider world, in diverse fields, as Australian Oxonians have been doing for generations.

Australian Oxonians who have done so – and indeed who have met, talked, partied, and dined, in this very Hall – in years past include Nobel Laureates Howard Florey and Sir John Eccles, public figures such as Sir Zelman Cowen – a dear friend of yours and of mine – and Bob Hawke, and countless others. Sir Zelman Cowen famously said that the role of the Governor-General is to represent the nation to itself, and, Your Excellency, your experience as law teacher and as a leader in collegiate education, as an advocate for women and for children, for human rights and equal opportunity, and as Governor of Queensland, have equipped you to play this role superbly.

To welcome you here is a particular personal pleasure for me. Governor-General, not only do you and I both hail from tiny towns in western or central western Queensland; but who would have imagined over 30 years ago, when you were my long-suffering tutor in administrative law at the University of Queensland, that I would one day welcome you here today? It is a great privilege and pleasure to do so, and all of us here in this Hall are delighted to welcome you and Mr Bryce. I am also glad to have this opportunity, as Warden of Rhodes House, to thank you for your much-valued contribution to the Rhodes Scholarships, as Governor of Queensland and as Governor-General.

You have today signed the visitors' book of Rhodes House, where you join diverse figures from Mahatma Gandhi to the elderly woman who as a little girl had been the inspiration for Alice in Wonderland, from Eleanor Roosevelt, Harry Truman, and Charles de Gaulle to Nelson Mandela, Bill and Hillary Clinton, and the Dalai Lama; and amongst Australians, from Sir John Latham to H V Evatt to your predecessors as Governor-General, Lord Casey and Michael Jeffrey.

We all greatly appreciate that you have come to Oxford to be with us today, and are grateful to you also for your exceptional service to our country.

The warmest of welcomes and the heartiest of thanks from all of us to you both.

From a talk prepared for Women's College,
University of Sydney, 22 May 2013

The reason I am here at Women's College tonight is because of the shared commitment of your Principal, Dr Amanda Bell, and myself – and of our shared inspiration, Ms Quentin Bryce – to the importance of women's leadership, and of mentoring.

The Rhodes Scholarships exist, in part, to identify outstanding young people with 'instincts to lead' and to encourage and help them combine their gifts of intellect, character, and leadership potential with a commitment to service, and so to be leaders for the world's future. Today, approximately half of all Rhodes Scholars elected around the world each year – sometimes more than half – are women. Ensuring that this would be so was one of the things I sought to achieve as Warden of Rhodes House, Oxford, from 2009 until last year.

This included through helping to open up previously all-male Scholarships in South Africa to women, drawing to the attention of Princeton University that it had not had a woman Rhodes Scholar for nearly a decade (a fact to which I will return), and encouraging a Rhodes constituency in a major country where a woman had not been elected as the Rhodes Scholar for that region for nearly a decade to review why this might have been so and what should be done about it. It also included encouraging women Rhodes Scholars in Oxford to think about how to develop their leadership potential, and hosting many events at which women of distinction spoke at Rhodes House about leadership, the skills and other attributes needed for it, and the difficulties that attend it.

Women's College exists to be an environment in which women students of the University of Sydney could develop through their university years to their fullest potential, including as leaders. You are very fortunate in the leaders you have had here. Professor Janet McCredie, Chair of your College Council for many years, is a dear friend of mine. It was a pleasure to visit Women's College previously when my friend Yvonne Rate was Principal. I was delighted last year when it was announced that Dr Amanda Bell, the Principal of Brisbane Girls Grammar School, was to become your Principal.

I had long admired Amanda Bell's purposeful and energetic leadership of BGGS, above all because the activities of the School seemed to focus squarely on an educational philosophy, and one to which I too am committed: liberal education. I was not deterred (though perhaps I should have been alarmed) that its materials occasionally quoted my own writings on education!

As part of this emphasis on educational breadth, I admired

the fact that Amanda Bell, with her background in fine arts, understood that an educational institution – a school, a college, or a university – is a cultural institution. A university, being a place where knowledge is conserved, transmitted, and expanded, is also a place where our cultural heritage is (or perhaps I should say our diverse cultural heritages are) conserved, transmitted, and expanded. This includes, among much else, being places where the performing and visual arts have always and should always have a treasured part.

When I went to visit Amanda at Brisbane Girls Grammar last year, we discussed such issues of educational philosophy, and the crucial role of colleges such as Women's College as residential academic communities. We also discussed the importance of promoting women's leadership, and the work of the review of undergraduate women's leadership at Princeton University, chaired by Nan Keohane.[*] That review had arisen in part from the realisation that Princeton, although producing Rhodes Scholars each year, had not had a woman Rhodes Scholar for nearly a decade. This may reflect the fact that even after many years of co-education, previously all-male institutions are often still (or again) dominated in important respects by men and a masculine culture. The work of Nan Keohane's committee, and the overhaul of scholarships mentoring at Princeton, seemed to change that, and in 2011 of the four Princetonians to win a Rhodes Scholarship, three were women. The President of Princeton, Shirley Tilghman, said to me that this turnaround was powerful evidence of the impact of mentoring. It appears to be the case that in many situations, women who are capable of achieving at a very high level are often more reluctant than men to put themselves forward for leadership positions, and benefit even more than men do from mentoring and encouragement – though Heaven knows that men need mentoring and encouragement also.

---

[*] Princeton University, *Report of the Steering Committee on Undergraduate Women's Leadership*, 2011 – at http://www.princeton.edu/reports/2011/leadership/

Amanda Bell is herself a committed mentor of other women, including of students, and is herself the beneficiary of the mentoring of a former Principal of Women's College, now the Governor-General of Australia, Her Excellency Ms Quentin Bryce. As it happens, Quentin Bryce was my tutor in administrative law at the University of Queensland in 1978, and has been a friend ever since. Quentin Bryce speaks with enthusiasm of the friendships she made with students of Women's College when she was Principal from 1997 to 2003, and it is evident that her continued mentoring of some of them means much to her and, I am sure, to them.

The Governor-General is, of course, a source of practical wisdom directly expressed. I am sure I will never forget my astonishment when, in a tutorial when I was a second-year undergraduate, she told our tutorial class that we were full-time students, that we should approach our studies like a job, that a full-time job was at least 40 hours a week of work, and that her subject was one quarter of our workload, so she expected at least 10 hours work a week on it. Though today this strikes me as obvious, it struck the 18-year-old me as extraordinarily demanding. There seemed so much else to do besides study!

Quentin Bryce has always been a person to befriend and mentor her students, and others. Like Amanda Bell, I am grateful for this – and I am grateful to Amanda for her own encouragement, support, and advice to me as we serve together on an academic advisory committee today. In that role, as in others, Amanda is quick – and right – to point out the important contributions that women can and should make. She, like Quentin Bryce, is a champion of women's leadership and of mentoring, and I salute both of them for this, and for much else.

David Alexander: the Rhodes ideal and liberal education

Obituary first printed in The Times, *12 August 2010, and reprinted anonymously in* The American Oxonian, *Fall 2010*

When, in May 1966, a 33-year-old Rhodes Scholar, Revd Dr David Alexander*, was formally inaugurated as president of the liberal arts college in Tennessee, Southwestern at Memphis, of which he was a graduate, the principal speaker was the Warden of Rhodes House, Oxford, Edgar (later Sir Edgar) Williams. Williams had come to admire and like Alexander when the young American had studied at Oxford a decade before, completing his doctorate in theology at Christ Church in 1957, and returning in 1960-61 to study Semitic languages.

Williams took as his theme the similarities of purpose of 'the residential English university', such as Oxford, and an American liberal arts college like Southwestern. It was these values – which David Alexander once expressed as 'the quest for an open mind in an open society' – that underpinned Alexander's outstandingly successful leadership of Southwestern at Memphis (later Rhodes College) and, from 1969 to 1991, as president of Pomona College in Claremont, California.

It was his commitment to these purposes, his love of Oxford, and his belief in the value of the Rhodes Scholarships in promoting international understanding and the public good that led Alexander to serve with great distinction from 1981 to 1998 as American Secretary to the Rhodes Trust. In this role, he oversaw the selection each year of 32 outstanding young American graduates to study at Oxford. It was above all for this service that he was appointed a Commander of the

---

* John David Alexander (18 October 1932-25 July 2010).

British Empire in 1998, and a Distinguished Friend of Oxford University in 2000.

One of his many areas of endeavour was encouraging women students to apply for the Rhodes Scholarships. Those chosen from the United States in his time included, for example, Susan Rice (now US Ambassador to the United Nations*), the social critic Naomi Wolf, and the media host Rachel Maddow.

The Rhodes Scholarships are not, in Cecil Rhodes's word, for 'bookworms', but for young people of exceptional intellect, character, leadership capacity, and commitment to service, reflected not least in intellectual and personal breadth. Rhodes wanted future leaders from many countries to mix with others and to gain the further broadening benefits of the collegiate environment of Oxford. The Rhodes ideal and the philosophies of liberal and residential collegiate education are closely akin, and David Alexander was the third Oxford-educated president of a US liberal arts college to run the Rhodes Scholarships in the US.[†]

In his masterly chapter on the American Rhodes Scholarships in Sir Anthony Kenny's *History of the Rhodes Trust* (2001), David Alexander reflected on the many US Rhodes Scholars who had contributed to educational (as well as other) leadership in the US, including through the values and methods in which they were inspired by their Oxford experience, and that 'Rhodes invented organised study abroad on a large scale'.

As president of Pomona, in 1980, Alexander advised graduates that 'your experience during your collegiate years should have taught you one lesson of transcendent value: temper your self-confidence with the assurance that there is more to learn, mitigate your certainties with the awareness of opposing points of view, and bolster your resolve to try always to improve

---

[*] Subsequently National Security Adviser to President Obama.

[†] Frank Aydelotte and Courtney Smith both served as President of Swarthmore College; William J (Bill) Barber was a professor at Wesleyan University, a liberal arts college; and Elliot Gerson is a great friend of liberal education.

yourself and to work for the improvement of the world around us. The summation of that transcendent lesson is openness: to be open to new and different ideas, to be open to the needs of others, and to be open to learn as much as your life can bring you.' It has rightly been said that he himself possessed these qualities.

In 1954, David Alexander had gone to Oxford from Southwestern at Memphis, and a year at Louisville Presbyterian Theological Seminary, 'in order to become a truly educated person'. He was commended by those who taught him for his 'genius' in languages, and his geniality. On his return from Oxford with his wife, Catharine, he was ordained in the Presbyterian Church, and taught biblical studies at San Francisco Theological Seminary from 1957 to 1964, before assuming the presidency first of Southwestern and then of Pomona.

During 22 years at Pomona, David Alexander led its development from a regional to a national liberal arts college, the enhancement of its educational reputation bolstered by a ten-fold increase in endowment. A Fellow of the American Academy of Arts and Sciences, he served on the boards of many educational, cultural, and other public bodies, including as President of the American Friends of the National Portrait Gallery, London. He is survived by his wife, Catharine, their three children, Kitty, Julia, and John, and by five grandchildren.

Alan Gilbert: the leader as story-teller and entrepreneur

Memorial event
University of Manchester
20 October 2010

By personality and by profession – as a historian, as a profoundly persuasive, inspiring and often mesmerising speaker, and as a leader of successive institutions – Alan Gilbert* was a story-teller, a teller of stories both about the past and about the future. He used the unexpected fact, the unexpected – even provocative – turn of phrase, the engaging way of looking at a problem and opportunities, to illustrate a theme and to draw us in, and to draw more out of us and of our universities than most of us believed possible. One of his attributes of leadership – helping to make him one of Australia's greatest modern Vice-Chancellors – was that, for each institution which he led, he had a narrative – a narrative of how a brilliant or at least a better future could be created that grew out of the institution's past and its present potential, and that met the challenges and opportunities of the future, which Prophet-like he foresaw with clarity, even when he wasn't always right.

It was my immense privilege to see these and other aspects of Alan's dazzling and at times almost ethereal personality and leadership when he was Vice-Chancellor of the University of Melbourne, from 1996 to 2004. I served as Warden of Trinity College within that University from 1997 until after Alan had left Melbourne to come here to Manchester. Alan was extraordinarily, inexplicably kind to me personally, and I am more grateful than I can say.

---

* Professor Alan Gilbert AO (11 September 1944-27 July 2010).

As perhaps you know, Alan was born on September 11, 1944, in Brisbane, Queensland – the city, though then more a large town, in which I grew up many years later. Educated in Canberra, Alan earned a Bachelor's and a Master's degree at the Australian National University. His Master's thesis in 1967 was concerned with Australia's Conscription Referenda of 1916-17, a rich and resonant topic. More importantly, in 1967, he married Ingrid, to whom – and to Michelle and Fiona – our hearts go out.

One of those who taught Alan at the Australian National University, one of Australia's best known if not best historians, Manning Clark, wrote in his memoir, *The Quest for Grace*, published in 1990, of the lively and stimulating students he had taught at ANU. He recalled Alan Gilbert as 'a young man of prodigious industry' and 'a shrewd observer of the human scene'.

Manning Clark also remembered Alan as a refugee from God. Like Clark himself, Alan had grown up in a deeply religious family. When I once asked Alan why he had specialised in the history of religion, he replied simply: 'comparative advantage'. When I looked puzzled, he explained that most historians had little understanding of religion, but he, given his highly religious upbringing, had an advantage. There could be few disciplines more rooted in the traditional humanities than the history of religion. Perhaps it says something about Alan that, even in explaining his choice of this as a career, he put it in the language of economics and strategy.

After lecturing for two years at the University of Papua New Guinea, Alan went on a scholarship to Nuffield College, Oxford, where in 1973 he completed his doctoral thesis on the growth and decline of Nonconformity in England and Wales in the early 19th century. His subsequent major publications made a significant contribution to the social history of British religious practice and secularisation, including using statistical analysis of religious practice in pioneering ways. He later also served as general editor of a series of volumes on Australians at different points in history.

From 1973 to 1991, Alan Gilbert made a distinguished career as a historian and, increasingly, as an academic leader in the University of New South Wales, including at the Australian Defence Force Academy in Canberra. In 1991, he became Vice-Chancellor of the University of Tasmania, and in 1996 Vice-Chancellor of the University of Melbourne.

In these positions, Alan Gilbert showed a remarkable capacity for visionary leadership, grounded in profoundly international, historical, and strategic perspectives; great resilience; and 'grace under pressure'. For a very painful and sustained stretch of months, he was being pummelled daily, and unfairly, in a Melbourne newspaper for one of his strategic initiatives, Melbourne University Private. Some of those working closely with him were amazed that he was able to put all this into strategic perspective – presenting it as a phase that had to be endured to achieve what had to be done to make private sources of revenue for leading universities as acceptable in Australia as in, for example, the United States. I said to him that I wondered how, in the face of all the pressure he was under, he maintained his equanimity. 'It's all acting', he said. A person of deep integrity, Alan was also a great actor – performing the theatre of leadership with apparent aplomb, concealing personal vulnerability in the interests of his institution. In all this, in good times and in bad, he was sustained by the love of his wife, Ingrid, and of his family – and, I always suspected, by his gruelling regimen of treadmill exercise.

At the University of Tasmania, amongst much else – from a new institutional structure, a new campus, new scholarships, and renewed alumni and community engagement – Alan successfully presided over the merger of the University and the Tasmanian State Institute of Technology. At the University of Melbourne, he developed a vision and a plan – the Melbourne Agenda – for making that university one of the finest universities in the world. These are easy words for Vice-Chancellors to utter, as so many do; but with Alan, you knew that he meant it, he knew what it meant, and he had the strategic plan to make the greatest strides possible towards that goal. For example, he knew that Melbourne needed to become a genuinely national – as well as local and international – university, and he initiated the brilliant Melbourne Scholarship program which has done so much to draw to Melbourne outstanding students from all parts of Australia. It will not surprise you that he also placed emphasis on recruiting Nobel Laureates. How poignant that he did not live to see Manchester's own announced.

Almost as soon as Alan had started at the University of Melbourne, major tightening of the public finances (somewhat like that announced in Britain today) commenced. Committed to a great future for the University and for universities, Alan responded – not by cutting the traditional heartland of the University, the arts and science faculties, as happened in many places – but by developing strategies for generating the revenue needed for sustained and in fact improved quality. Over many years, Alan had been and continued to be one of the clearest and most compelling advocates of policy reform and deregulation to enable Australia's universities to do this, including through student fees combined with loans and equity measures. This, he argued, was essential if any Australian universities were to be genuinely internationally competitive at the highest levels. He was unafraid to deploy market forces to promote high-quality education.

With many other colleagues, I worked closely with Alan on building up the contribution of international students to the revenue of the University, as well as to its intellectual capital, its international orientation, and its cultural diversity. We did not persuade Alan to give much emphasis to seeking philanthropic support for the University – though, for example, a major private benefaction made possible the landmark Bio21 development. Among more entrepreneurial strategies which Alan pioneered was the sale of educational services through a new entity, Melbourne University Private, which was later modified and, in changed circumstances, brought to an end. To encourage the international linkages and aspirations he knew were so crucial, Alan initiated a global network of high-calibre universities, Universitas 21, and through it U21 Global, a provider of online courses, as a revenue strategy based on optimism about the early growth of demand for what we were then starting to call e-education. To house some of his initiatives, Alan envisioned a massive building program, breaking out of the traditional confines of the campus and developing a truly impressive new precinct of buildings around the adjacent University Square. One of these buildings fittingly bears Alan's name.

While very much an entrepreneur, a future-oriented strategist, an innovator, a moderniser, a lateral thinker, an ambitious and focused benchmarker, a talent spotter, and a builder of the new, Alan was also a traditional scholar – and an educational leader who gave deep and creative thought to the problem of how to uphold traditional academic values and quality when the traditional campus-based university was seemingly being challenged by an 'information revolution', and at a time when public funding was clearly inadequate to provide for the highest standards of university education.

In a public lecture in 1997, Alan expressed his strong commitment to what he called 'the campus-based learning community' of personal interactions, informal as well as formal. But he also referred to the likely development of global 'virtual universities', offering high-quality online distance education, competing strongly with such traditional campus-based universities. He continued:

> To survive in such a world, traditional campus-based universities ... will have to offer students all the benefits that the best 'virtual' alternatives can muster – and much more besides! The so-called 'information super-highway' will have to run through the teaching and learning heart of every great campus, and the students will have to be as much at home in cyberspace as are

their counterparts in the 'virtual university'. ... Without that, no value-adding based on face-to-face, human interactions of a spatial learning community will be sufficient to save it from the emerging competition; with it, the intellectual, social and cultural rewards of campus life are likely still to create the best learning environment of all.

Not only was Alan committed to creating 'the best learning environment of all' and to high-quality teaching, he was himself by nature a teacher. The academic teaching his students in the university classroom became the academic leader teaching us all, teaching the university, the university and the community his classroom. Like so many others, I learnt so much from him. The lesson is sadly over, long before its time, but we are, I think, all of us still learning, and forever grateful.

John Hirst: historian, public intellectual, and active citizen

The University of Western Australia

10 July 2007

A very warm welcome to this public lecture by one of Australia's most distinguished historians, Dr John Hirst, entitled 'The Australians: Insiders and Outsiders on the National Character since 1770' – the title, you will not be surprised to learn, of John's most recent book.

In their book *The History Wars*, Stuart Macintyre and Anna Clark describe John Hirst as 'an accomplished and strikingly original historian working at La Trobe'. Elsewhere, as you may have read, Stuart Macintyre has described John as 'the gadfly of Australian history, stinging and provocative' and – to balance the ledger – Geoffrey Blainey has described him as 'one of the nation's most independent and original historians'.

Last year, John published a collection of essays under the title *Sense and Nonsense in Australian History*. The preface begins:

> For over twenty years I have been quarrelling in print with the standard left-liberal view of Australian history. I have also been puzzling over how best to write the history of societies that were colonies. The history of the mother country cannot be left behind; it remains the context in which colonial society forms and lives.

The preface continued:

> When Robert Manne invited me to assemble my essays for publication, I was pleased to find that they deal with important themes throughout our history since 1788, from

convict society to the republic. Taken together they provide
the interpretative framework for an alternative history of
Australia – which frees me from the obligation of writing it.

Indeed, John's published works are a substantial and
impressive contribution to our historical understanding –
including studies of convict society in early New South Wales,
through the birth of democracy in that colony in the mid- to late
19th century, the making of the Australian Commonwealth, and
more – including *The World of Albert Facey* and co-editing, with
Graeme Davison and Stuart Macintyre, *The Oxford Companion
to Australian History*.

Born in Adelaide 65 years ago yesterday – Happy Birthday,
John, and many happy returns of the day! – John was educated
at the University of Adelaide and, though grateful for his
historical training there, has written of his subsequent efforts to
escape some, at least, of the assumptions within it – including,
for example, an economic interpretation of Australian history
which disregarded the importance of ideals. And so, for example,
his history of federation, published just before the centenary
of federation, begins with the startling words – 'God wanted
Australia to be a nation', going on to show that this was indeed
the powerful belief of such federal leaders as Barton and Deakin.

Like various of his colleagues in that remarkable constellation
of humanities scholars at La Trobe University – such as Robert
Manne, Inga Clendinnen, John Carroll, and previously Claudio
Veliz – John Hirst may truly be characterised as a 'public
intellectual'. Unafraid of controversy, including on Indigenous
issues and on multiculturalism, he is both an academic historian
and an active citizen. Having in 1991 written in *Quadrant* –
in which he has published extensively – a piece entitled 'The
Conservative Case for an Australian Republic', John served
as a member of Prime Minister Keating's Republic Advisory
Committee, and in 1994 published his own book-length
Republican Manifesto. His advocacy of a republican future stands

alongside his resistance to what he has controversially called 'the blackening of our past'.

John has served, or serves, as chair of the Commonwealth Civics Education Group, as deputy chair of the Council of the National Museum of Australia, and as a member of the board of Film Australia. His teaching has spanned European as well as Australian history, and his writings extend to such topics as family law and the secret ballot. The link between John's historical work and his active citizenship is also perhaps reflected in the fact that this latest book, on the Australian national character, was commissioned by the National Australia Day Council.

It is a great pleasure to call on John Hirst to speak.

Rex Nettleford: leader in Caribbean culture and education

Memorial event
Jamaican High Commission, London
10 April 2010

When you come to Rhodes House, Oxford – the home of the Rhodes Scholarships – you will find in the main hall a portrait of Norman Manley, Rhodes Scholar for Jamaica for 1914 and later Prime Minister of Jamaica. Then, outside the entrance to the Rhodes House Library, the University of Oxford's Commonwealth library, you will find a large photographic portrait of Rex Nettleford*, Rhodes Scholar for Jamaica for 1957, widely admired and deeply mourned in the Rhodes Scholar community around the world. I am honoured to be joined here today by current Rhodes Scholars from Jamaica, worthy successors of Rex Nettleford, who maintain the distinguished standard of Jamaican Scholars in Oxford.

When Rex Nettleford was given the life-changing opportunity, at the age of 23, to come to Oxford, it was recorded: 'mother a domestic servant and doubtful if boy knows his father'. The undergraduate academic success of this scholarship boy (I speak as a scholarship boy), with a strong interest in West Indian history and government, combined with wide extra-curricular interests, sporting and cultural, and his lively personality and leadership capacity made him seem a natural Rhodes Scholar. The notes on his selection record:

---

* Professor the Hon. Rex Nettleford, OM (3 February 1933-2 February 2010). Vice-Chancellor of the University of the West Indies, founder of the National Dance Theatre Company (NDTC) of Jamaica, writer, and dancer.

Most willing to help others from his poor surroundings – real Jamaican interest in dance and drama – [directs] plays etc – Tireless organiser and lighthanded firmness with unruly choruses of small boys. Incorporated his learning with his dancing.

Undertaking postgraduate study in Politics, and a member of Oriel College, young Rex prospered in Oxford. At the end of his second term, his supervisor, the Commonwealth historian A F (Freddie) Madden, reported:

Rex has been immersed in his B.Phil. work this term, especially in Government; but that has not prevented him from communicating something of his zest and enthusiasm to the Ballet Club and to invigorating Oriel. ... our paths have crossed weekly in the class which has been drafting the British Constitution where he has been a useful member.

Rex himself wrote graciously to the Warden of Rhodes House, Mr (later Sir Edgar) Williams, at the end of his first term, in December 1957. Writing from London, where he planned to spend the Christmas vacation doing academic study, Rex enclosed a card which was a print of 'a lino-cut by Albert Huie, one of Jamaica's leading artists'. Sending best wishes for Christmas, the young Jamaican wrote: 'I shall do my best with the cold, smoggy bleak of London.'

At the end of his third term the next summer, Dr Madden wrote that he had 'very little contact' with Rex that term as he was doing 'other work for his B.Phil.' He might also have mentioned Rex's extensive extra-curricular activities during term. 'However', Dr Madden continued, 'my ignorance of his progress is now being remedied, as he has decided that we can have weekly tutorials during this summer vac. in his special paper on Comparative Colonial Government.' After that series of tutorials during the long summer vacation which Rex charmed his supervisor into giving him, Dr Madden wrote:

Rex did a number of essays for me during the Long Vacation and impressed me with his ability, his maturity and his sense of proportion. He has considerable capacity for work – particularly the facility of getting hold of the essential facts and arguments in long government white papers and constitutions. But his presentation of them is not pedestrian: he is no earthworm. His personality is impressed upon his writing: the judgments he makes are his own.

The Dean of Oriel College, also a scholar of politics and history, Christopher Seton-Watson, wrote in that summer of 1958: 'Mr Nettleford has made a considerable impact on the College during his first year, through his energy and vitality, sociability and varied talents. He has been a great asset to the life of the College.' A year later, in the term in which Rex Nettleford passed his degree where several others were failed, a Fellow of Oriel, Dr J W Gough, reported: 'I hear nothing but good of the part he plays in the life of the college.'

He had also found time to be a choreographer and producer of Oxford operatic and theatrical productions, including one that went to the Edinburgh Festival in the summer of 1959, just before Rex returned home to Jamaica to be Resident Tutor in the Department of Extra Mural Studies at the University College of the West Indies, a capacity in which he had temporarily served just before coming up to Oxford two years before.

Those qualities of intellect and character, those passions and that personality, those deep interests in culture, the Caribbean, constitutional citizenship, and the Commonwealth, which were so evident in his years as a Rhodes Scholar in Oxford, greatly helped to shaped Rex Nettleford's remarkable life and career over the half-century since, until the grim news of this last February.

Rex maintained links with successive Wardens of Rhodes House – his file at Rhodes House contains many lively letters from him, over the decades from the 1950s to the 2000s – and he was an active participant in the Rhodes affairs of Jamaica and the Commonwealth Caribbean, serving for many years on the Rhodes Scholar selection committee in Jamaica.

After Norman Manley died in 1969, Rex Nettleford wrote to the Warden of Rhodes House in September 1970 saying that he was editing a volume of Norman Manley's speeches from 1938 to 1968, and also mentioning the imminent publication of a book of his own dealing with 'identity, race and protest in Jamaica', and the publication the previous year of *Roots and Rhythms, the story of the Jamaica National Dance Theatre Company*. In a later letter discussing Rhodes Trust financial support for the Norman Manley book, Rex wrote: 'I am making the contribution because of my own belief in what Manley did for Jamaica and his contribution to the political literature of decolonization.'

Over subsequent decades, the widespread and warm admiration which Rex earned around the world was evident in many ways. In 2002, he gave a 'brilliant' Commonwealth Day lecture at Rhodes House. The Jamaica and Commonwealth Caribbean Secretary to the Rhodes Trust, Peter Goldson, and his wife Suzanne were there, and they recall that 'it was truly remarkable for us to observe the warmth and respect with which he was greeted by old friends and prominent academics from around the Commonwealth'. My own link with Rex Nettleford was initially through our shared involvement with Commonwealth affairs. In 2003, the centenary year of the Rhodes Scholarships, when the University of Oxford conferred honorary degrees on four prominent Rhodes Scholars from around the world – one of them former Australian Prime Minister Bob Hawke – Rex Nettleford was one of the chosen four. The citation described him as 'a Vice-Chancellor, a man of the greatest versatility: effective in action, outstanding in erudition, and most supple in the dance'.

The following year, the Rhodes Trust established the Rex Nettleford Fellowship in Cultural Studies, not least 'to honour Rex's distinguished contribution to higher education and the cultural life of the Caribbean'. One of my first acts as Warden of Rhodes House last July was to confirm that a Rex Nettleford Fellowship could be awarded in 2010.

On his death this year, Peter Goldson wrote: 'The Rhodes community will forever remember Rex as a man who exhibited the best of Cecil Rhodes' aspirations of a scholar who was not a mere bookworm but one who valiantly and colourfully engaged in the world's fight.'

In another warm remembrance of Rex, a Canadian Rhodes Scholar of the 1950s who became a Canadian Vice-Chancellor, Ian Macdonald, wrote:

> The one practice for which I did not share Rex's enthusiasm was his penchant for breakfast meetings. Nevertheless, I cherish my last such occasion with him on the Mona Campus of the University of the West Indies on March 7, 2007 when he was as sparkling as the morning sun.

On this sparkling and celebratory but also sad morning, I am sure that for so many people, Rex Nettleford will truly remain in cherished memory, as he was in life, 'as sparkling as the morning sun'.

David Hatendi: the gift of charm

Welcome to Rhodes House, Oxford
after the Memorial Service for Dr David Hatendi
22 May 2012

Thank you for being here this afternoon to remember with thanksgiving and celebration the life of our dear and immensely charming friend, David Hatendi.* People have come from far corners of the globe, including from Africa and North America, as well as from various corners of this country, and we are all very grateful.

On your behalf and on behalf of the Rhodes Trust, I would like to join Nyasha Hatendi in thanking the Chaplains, past and present, of University College for today's service, and the Master and Fellows of Univ. We are very grateful, as we are to everyone who has contributed to such a beautiful and moving service, to these refreshments, including the flowers – which both here and in the Univ Chapel come from the Rhodes House garden – and to featuring David prominently on the Rhodes House website this week.

Your presence here today reflects the remarkable personal impression that David made on people. Xan Smiley spoke warmly of this. Let me briefly say just a little more about this, drawing on David's experience as a Rhodes Scholar at Univ.

When David was applying for the Rhodes Scholarship from Rhodesia, as it then was, in 1976, the Head of Psychology at the University of Rhodesia wrote in his reference for David:

---

* Dr David Tapuwa Hatendi (22 May 1953-12 March 2012). First black Rhodes Scholar for Rhodesia (later Zimbabwe) (Rhodesia & University College 1977). Worked at the World Bank and in private finance. National Secretary to the Rhodes Trust for Zimbabwe (2009-12).

I would particularly like to comment upon his interpersonal relationships which always seem to be very good. He is the kind of person who ... gets on well with everybody. ... I have little doubt that he will go on to make an important contribution in the business area and will reach a high position of responsibility.

From his first term in Oxford, David was receiving reports that confirmed this view. At the end of his first term, in December 1977, the Dean of Graduates at Univ reported:

... he seems to have fitted in and is very well liked. He appeared at the Servants' Party last week with one or two other graduates and confirmed that he is at home in just about any social situation. His tutors have reported favourably...

At the end of David's first year in Oxford, 1977-78, the Warden of Rhodes House, Sir Edgar Williams, wrote of him:

A very nice man indeed. If you shut your eyes and go on listening you are left with the impression that you may have been at School together. He is universally popular, agreeable in temperament, does his best to work hard and has played off and on for the Authentics [cricket team].

In the summer of 1979, his report from Univ said:

David Hatendi continues to be a most popular member of the College – he has, for instance, been elected as the President of the Shakespeare Club, which is the main dining club in Univ. these days. He is working well...

And six months later, in December 1979, the Dean of Graduates reported:

A good term judged both by his supervisor's report and his effectiveness within the College. His forthcoming marriage will make the term even more memorable. A delightful man of whom we are all very fond.

As we all are.

At the end of David's time in Oxford, in the summer of 1980, the Warden of Rhodes House, Sir Edgar Williams, described him as 'a very attractive fellow and very popular in his College', who had married Angelina 'in a very crowded College Chapel'.

After David and Angela's wedding in the Univ Chapel in January 1980, David had written to Sir Edgar and Lady Williams, who were soon to retire:

> Seeing you both at the wedding gave me a tremendous sense of belonging. Thank you for coming and making it such a memorable occasion for us.
>
> We shall always treasure your wonderful present. For me it will always be a reminder of an Oxford that simply would not be right without you.
>
> Thank you very much for your wonderful spirit.
>
> Best wishes David & Angela

Today, we give thanks for the wonderful spirit of David Hatendi, who very much belonged here.

That wonderful spirit was evident, not least, in the enthusiasm, style, and discernment with which he conducted himself as National Secretary to the Rhodes Trust for Zimbabwe over the last three years, running the Rhodes Scholarships selection process there. It was through this that I had the immense pleasure of coming to know him and Angelina – including enjoying delightful dinners, prepared by them, here in my home and in theirs in Harare.

All of us at Rhodes House who had the joy and the privilege of coming to know David miss him very much indeed.

Our hearts go out to Angelina, Nyasha, Natasha, and Sarayi, and to all who loved David, and to all for whom he was so special – as the Dean of Graduates at Univ put it in 1979, 'a delightful man of whom we are all very fond'.

Would you please raise your tea cups or your glasses – whatever you have! – and join me in a toast to our dear, exuberant, unforgettable friend, David?

Noel Nannup: educator on Indigenous heritage

The University of Western Australia
13 May 2008

It is the tradition of the University of Western Australia to acknowledge that this University is situated on Noongar land, and that Noongar people remain the spiritual and cultural custodians of their land, and continue to practise their values, languages, beliefs and knowledge.

These words – with which significant University of Western Australia events customarily begin – seem especially fitting for this lecture, to be given by Noel Nannup on Aboriginal Spirituality, particularly that of the Noongar people – the spiritual and cultural custodians of this land.

Noel Nannup is a Noongar/Injabarndi man, born in Geraldton in 1948. His father was a Noongar man, and his mother was from the Pilbara. As he tells in his very moving chapter in the anthology *Speaking from the heart*, when he was a child his family lived first in old army tents on the edge of Geraldton, and then on a reserve. Leaving school on his 14th birthday, Noel worked in various roles – as a shearer, land-clearing for farmers (which his father told him was 'smashing our spirit'), in mining, and for a shire council. In 1978, sick of – as he put it – 'trying to be a white man', and seeking a new direction in his life, Noel became the first Aboriginal National Park Ranger, working for the WA Department of Conservation and Land Management (CALM), with which he worked for 26 years, until 2004.

Thus began Noel's role as a pioneering leader in education of tourists, students, and many others about the importance of

Aboriginal culture and of the natural environment with which it so intimately connects.

From 1978 to 1983, Noel worked in his mother's traditional homeland as a ranger at Millstream National Park in the Pilbara, and from 1983 to 1989 at the Geikie Gorge National Park in the Kimberley. Inspired by his time as a ranger, Noel studied Cultural Heritage at the University of Canberra, and then became CALM's Aboriginal expert in the southern part of this State, at Narrogin and then at Fremantle. His work included, for example, the mapping of ancient Noongar dreaming trails; the development of the Wagin Aboriginal Cultural Museum and the Aboriginal component of the Narrogin Heritage Park; the recording of oral histories of Aboriginal culture; developing teaching materials, such as 'Exploring the Woodlands with Nyoongars'; and the development of land management TAFE courses with an Indigenous focus.

As an educator about the rich cultural heritage of Aboriginal people, pioneer of Indigenous tourism, defender of the natural environment, heritage consultant, teller of stories, advocate of reconciliation, and much more, Noel Nannup has earned very widespread admiration and gratitude. This was reflected, for example, in 2004, when he was awarded an honorary doctorate – appropriately, a doctorate of Education – by Murdoch University. I am delighted to call on Noel Nannup to address us on the theme of Aboriginal Spirituality.

Nicholas Hasluck: leader in literature and law

Welcome at the Commonwealth Day Lecture
The University of Western Australia
10 March 2008

It is a great pleasure for me, as one of the Deputy Vice-Chancellors of this University, to welcome you to this 2008 Commonwealth Day Lecture, to be given by Justice Nicholas Hasluck AM QC, Chairman of the Commonwealth Writers' Prize Advisory Committee, on the topic 'Thought Crimes and Other Themes in Commonwealth Literature'.

In doing this, I wish to acknowledge on behalf of the University that this campus is situated on Noongar land, and that the Noongar people remain the spiritual and cultural custodians of their land, and continue to practise their values, languages, beliefs and knowledge. Indigenous issues are one of many issues which resonate in many countries of the Commonwealth.

In its 21 years, the Commonwealth Writers' Prize has become one of the world's leading literary prizes, being open to writers established and new in the 53 countries of the Commonwealth, and reflecting the vibrancy of literature around the diverse regions of the Commonwealth. Study of Commonwealth literature is one of the most dynamic aspects of Commonwealth studies today.

In recent years, a Commonwealth Lecture has been given annually in Australia – for example, in Melbourne in 2006 by the Secretary-General of the Commonwealth, Don McKinnon, and in Canberra last year by Malcolm Fraser. This Commonwealth Day, the University of Western Australia – with its many and long Commonwealth links – is honoured to be hosting the 2008 lecture in conjunction with the Commonwealth Round Table in Australia, and welcoming colleagues from other universities, the Australian Institute of International Affairs, and the Royal Commonwealth Society.

The Commonwealth Round Table in Australia is represented here tonight by Professor Geoffrey Bolton, who will propose the vote of thanks after the lecture and question time. Geoffrey Bolton is one of Australia's most eminent historians, and former Chancellor of Murdoch University. He is also writing a biography of the late Sir Paul Hasluck, federal minister for Territories, Defence, and External Affairs, and Governor-General, and father of our guest speaker.

Dame Alexandra Hasluck records in her autobiography that Nicholas Paul Hasluck was born in a Canberra hospital 'about 2 p.m. on 17 October 1942. I had a very nice room', she wrote, 'with a view across to Black Mountain, but I used to mutter to myself that I'd swap Black Mountain any day for a view of the Swan River from the windows of my house at Freshwater Bay.'

In the late 1930s, Alexandra and Paul Hasluck, both life-long writers, had created Freshwater Bay Press here in Perth; and some four decades later, Nicholas Hasluck revived the dormant press, because of his interest in the local publication of limited editions. It reflects what Max Harris called the Haslucks – 'a writing family', and one that is grounded in local community, but with international impact. Nick Hasluck has been published locally and globally, a prolific and prize-winning author of novels, poetry, short stories, essays, and drama – quite remarkably, written alongside a distinguished legal career, which culminated in his appointment in the year 2000 as a justice of the Supreme Court of Western Australia.

This combination of literature and law was evident in Nick's undergraduate studies here at UWA after his schooling in Perth and Canberra. He tells something of undergraduate days in a volume of recollections of UWA commissioned by the University for its 75th Anniversary in 1988. For example, he recalled unpredictable tutorials in English: 'The first tutor I had was Jeana Bradley. She used to keep a pair of white poodles in her room. They took an intelligent interest in our discussions, interposing a grunt occasionally or an eloquent sigh of despair.'

Nick's recollections are also of satirical writing for student revues; SAG (the Student Apathy Group), student politics, the Guild and Prosh; his presidency of the Blackstone Society; and debating alongside Robert Holmes a Court, with whom he later for a while practised law. This was after Nick returned to Perth – with his English wife, Sally Anne – after postgraduate legal study at Wadham College, Oxford, and work on Fleet Street. Nick's distinction in an evolving legal career saw him take silk in 1988, and he served as president of the WA Equal Opportunity Tribunal for a decade from 1990.

As he once put it: 'the legal Dr Jekyll or the literary Mr Hyde (or vice versa depending upon your viewpoint)' have been evident over several decades. Some, indeed, of his writing – both fictional works and non-fiction reflections on *The legal labyrinth* and *Offcuts from a legal literary life* – bring the two together. His many books include mystery thrillers and satire, writings inspired by his extensive international travel or historical settings (real or imagined) with contemporary resonance, from Egon Kisch to an imaginary French colony off Western Australia, and more. *The Bellarmine Jug* was winner of *The Age* Book of the Year Award in 1984, and *The Country Without Music* was joint winner – with Tim Winton's *Cloudstreet* – of the WA Premier's Book Award for fiction in 1991. Nick's writings have received the ultimate literary accolade – a PhD thesis, from Curtin University, entitled *The Conundrum of the West: Reading the Novels of Nicholas Hasluck,* which is available on the internet. Its most intriguing chapter heading is simply 'Foucault, Bentham and Hasluck'. You know you've made it when doctoral theses link your name with Foucault and Bentham! Another writer about Nick's work, Veronica Brady, has written of his commitment to what she calls 'the classical virtues of coherence and clarity'.

In a recent volume, referring specifically to his own father, Nick wrote: 'We are not bound by our fathers but it often happens that we act in accordance with their habits, and with their wishes, that being the way in which customs are handed downwards, independently of what the law prescribes.' Nick has edited two posthumous volumes of his father's writings – *Light that time has made*, which was launched by Fred Chaney, who is here tonight; and that classic of acute mid-20th century political portraits, *The chance of politics*.

Being committed, like his parents, to the encouragement and support of authors and the publication of their works, Nick has served as Deputy Chair of the Australia Council from 1978 to 1982, chair of the Literature Board of the Australia Council from 1998 to 2001, and as a member of the management committee of the Australian Society of Authors from 1990 to 1993. He has also served as Deputy Chair of the Western Australian Academy of Performing Arts (WAAPA). Since 2006, as I have mentioned, he has chaired the Advisory Committee for the Commonwealth Writers' Prize.

We are honoured and grateful that Justice Nicholas Hasluck has agreed to give the 2008 Commonwealth Day Lecture, and I am delighted to call on him to address us.

Part III: On peace

To 'render war impossible': the Rhodes Scholarships, educational relations between countries, and peace

'Sailing Dinner' of the Canadian Association of Rhodes Scholars
Ottawa, 24 September 2011

It is a real delight for me to be back in Ottawa with so many friends – old, new, and about to be made – and to greet Rhodes Scholars of different generations, including – why we are all here – the Canadian Rhodes Scholars of 2011, whom I have greatly enjoyed meeting today, and whom I look forward to welcoming to Rhodes House next Saturday. You will be joining a vibrant community of Rhodes Scholars in Oxford – a community of Scholars of high calibre like yourselves, and with many activities at Rhodes House as well as in your colleges and departments. Some of this is reflected in the 'Glimpses of Rhodes' video on the Rhodes House website.

Canadian Rhodes Scholars have a proud history of achievement in Oxford, and not only in ice hockey; and of subsequent leadership and service in many fields. It is not for nothing that, arising from the governance renewal of recent years, there are three Canadian Rhodes Scholars among our Rhodes Trustees – the Regius Professor of Medicine in Oxford, Sir John Bell (Alberta & Magdalen 1975); a highly successful businessman and philanthropist, John McCall MacBain (Quebec & Wadham 1980); and the global head of McKinsey, Dominic Barton (British Columbia & Brasenose 1984). Another Canadian, Professor Margaret MacMillan, the distinguished international historian and Warden of St Antony's College, Oxford, also serves as one of our Trustees. Other Canadians prominent in Oxford include

Rhodes Scholars such as the Dean of the Law Faculty, Timothy Endicott (Ontario & Corpus Christi 1983), and two professors of International Relations – Neil MacFarlane (Quebec & Balliol 1976) and Jennifer Welsh (Prairies & St Anne's 1987). Neil's chair is named for Lester Pearson, the Canadian winner of the Nobel Prize for Peace.

There being two Canadian Rhodes Scholar professors of International Relations in Oxford is entirely consistent with the strong contribution to international affairs of Canadian Rhodes Scholars over the decades and today. This is reflected in the careers of a number of people here tonight. Bob Rae, as you know, who was here earlier this evening, was opposition critic on foreign affairs before becoming leader of the Liberal Party, and has written extensively on international issues. In earlier times, a Canadian Rhodes Scholar, Arnold Smith, was the first Secretary-General of the Commonwealth, and two Canadian Rhodes Scholars, George Ignatieff and Yves Fortier, as Canadian diplomats, have been president of the UN Security Council. In his memoirs, *The Making of a Peacemonger*, George Ignatieff (Ontario & New College 1936) writes:[*]

> If it hadn't been for the Rhodes scholarship … I wouldn't have gone to Oxford, wouldn't have met Mike [that is, Lester] Pearson, and wouldn't have been persuaded by him to enter the External Affairs competition at Canada House in London.

Ignatieff doubted he would have become a diplomat, and also credits his travels in Europe as a Rhodes Scholar in the late 1930s with deepening his understanding of international realities that required an active policy for peace.

Mention of these Scholars reflects the fact that an important part of the proud history and present – and, I am sure, the

---

[*]   George Ignatieff, *The Making of a Peacemonger,* University of Toronto Press, 1982, p. 256.

proud future – of Canadian Rhodes Scholars has been their contribution to public life in Canada, including in politics and the public service. My own first visit to Ottawa, in 1985, saw me, a young Australian Rhodes Scholar, invited by Eugene Forsey (Quebec & Balliol 1926), one of the greatest experts on constitutional conventions in the Commonwealth, to his installation as a Privy Councillor by the Governor-General, Madame Sauvé, at Rideau Hall. Or, to go to an earlier time, in the late 1950s, for example, there were three Rhodes Scholar ministers in the Progressive Conservative government of John Diefenbaker, and the Speaker of the House of Commons was another Scholar, Roland Michener. A diversion: In 1967, as Roland Michener was about to become Governor-General of Canada, the Queen had him to lunch together with another Rhodes Scholar who was about to become Governor-General of New Zealand, Arthur Porritt (Lord Porritt).

In the late 1950s, as I mentioned, there were Rhodes Scholars prominent in the Canadian parliament and government, and four deputy ministers; the governor, deputy governor, and chief of research at the Bank of Canada; and in External Affairs, as it then was, there was an especially strong representation of Rhodes Scholars. At the one time, Rhodes Scholars 'held the posts of Under-Secretary and Assistant Under-Secretary and were heads of Canadian missions in the United States, West Germany, the USSR, Brazil, Egypt, and [last but not least] Australia ... H B O Robinson, the Department's representative in the Prime Minister's Office, had a particularly sensitive post, because [Prime Minister] John Diefenbaker was suspicious of the departmental establishment's ties to its former minister, Lester Pearson, now leader of the opposition'.* Basil Robinson, the Rhodes Scholar in Diefenbaker's office, later wrote a book, *Diefenbaker's World: A Populist in Foreign Affairs*, which draws

---

* Anthony Kenny (ed.), *The History of the Rhodes Trust*, Oxford University Press, 2001, pp. 236-37.

on his own diaries. Robinson writes of February 1962:*

> I also attended a Rhodes Scholars' lunch for the British High
> Commissioner, Lord Amory, at Carleton University. Amory
> made a wonderful speech. Rhodes Scholars were a sore point
> with the prime minister, one of whose greatest disappointments
> in life was not to have been selected for that scholarship. There
> were too many Rhodes Scholars around Ottawa for his taste.

This is, of course, a reminder of the importance of trying to
see ourselves as others see us, and of the importance of humility
and of diplomacy, and perhaps of avoiding self-important
cliquishness. But if there were 'too many Rhodes Scholars
around Ottawa' for the populist Diefenbaker's taste, I am sure
there were not too many for the taste of Cecil Rhodes. As we
all know, he created his Scholarships to bring outstanding
all-rounders into the broadening collegiate environment of
Oxford partly to encourage and to help prepare them, in a
phrase much used in recent decades, to fight 'the world's fight',
and he wanted them – us – in the words of his will, to come
'to esteem the performance of public duties as [their] highest
aim'.†

We need to be careful not to be narrowly prescriptive about
what this means. One of our Trustees, Julian Ogilvie Thompson,
told last year's Coming Up Dinner at Rhodes House:

> By public duty Rhodes did not mean purely political life. He
> understood public duty in a characteristically late Victorian
> manner, as involving a commitment, in whatever career a
> Scholar pursued, to the cultivation of civic virtue. His Scholars

---

* H Basil Robinson, *Diefenbaker's World: A Populist in Foreign Affairs,* University of
Toronto Press, 1989, p. 247.

† Quoted from 'Facsimile volume of MSS. Afr.t.1 (draft of wills, letter and other docs.
By Rhodes)', Bodleian Library of Commonwealth and African Studies, Rhodes House,
Oxford.

were not to be chosen from those committed merely to their own individual self advancement.

Julian Ogilvie Thompson continued:

Remember too that public duty can be pursued through a career in business, the primary calling, after all, of the Founder whose scholarship you hold. More than ever today, in the developed as in the developing world, we require men and women of civic virtue to make business their calling and an honourable calling.

At lunch today with the new Scholars, Brian Rolfes (Prairies & Wadham 1989) gave examples of contributing to the public good through work in the private sector. Whatever form it takes, I think there is a strong link between the notion of 'public duties' and 'service': Rhodes Scholars are encouraged to lead lives that somehow serve the public good and not merely their own private interests.

This emphasis on the Rhodes Scholarships as nurturing leaders committed to service, whose leadership is founded in good character, is of course an important part of what the Rhodes Scholarship is about. But Cecil Rhodes had another, related but distinct, purpose also, and it is increasingly clear to me that in the first half of the 20th century this other purpose was often, if not always, more prominent than service. Rhodes's other purpose was peace.

Rhodes wrote his first will in 1877, at the age of 24. We might be tempted to regard it as full of youthful naiveté; it certainly reflected a world and attitudes very different in many ways from our own. Rhodes wrote that he wanted, through the growth of the British Empire, including through the re-entry of the United States into it, to bring about 'the foundation of so great a power as to hereafter render wars impossible and promote the best interests of humanity'.[*] This was, if you like, a version of Pax Britannica. Fast forward 24 years to 1901. In a 1901 codicil to his 1899 will, Rhodes provided for the creation of Rhodes Scholarships from Germany to go alongside the Rhodes Scholarships he had provided for from various parts of what was then the British Empire and from the United States. He wrote: 'The object is that an understanding between the three great powers [the British Empire, the United States, and Germany] will render war impossible and educational relations make the strongest tie.'

Promoting bonds of sentiment within the Empire and between what he called 'the English-speaking peoples' generally – including, he hoped, the French-speaking peoples of Canada and the Afrikaans-speaking people of South Africa – remained central to Rhodes's vision. But he was in 1901 not seeing 'so great' a British Empire as the means to 'render wars impossible' as he had said in 1877, but was now seeing the creation of 'an understanding between the three great powers' as the means by which to 'render war impossible'. It is 'educational relations' nurtured by his Scholarships and perhaps others to come afterwards which will help make 'the strongest tie' in this. It seems that part, at least, of the means by which this will be achieved is through the mutual understanding and goodwill that Rhodes envisaged would be created through their experience in Oxford in the hearts and minds of exceptional young people who would become leaders and people of influence in their various countries.

Between Rhodes's 1877 desire to 'render wars impossible' and the almost exact 1901 echo – to 'render war impossible' – he had repeatedly expressed the same desire. In letters and statements relating to his intended legacy, he wrote of his desire for 'permanent peace in the world', 'the end of all wars', 'union with

---

[*] All quotations from the facsimile volume at Rhodes House cited above.

America and universal peace ... after 100 years', 'the discovery of an idea which ultimately leads to the cessation of all wars', and 'the peace of the world ... for all eternity'. Whatever we may make of his actions in his own life and times, these are Cecil Rhodes's words and declared goals.

If so-called realist thinkers about international relations believe that conflict is inevitable and inescapable, they stand in contrast to so-called idealist thinkers who believe that the conflictual nature of international relations can be overcome and more harmonious relations entrenched. This tradition is sometimes associated with the name of the philosopher Immanuel Kant, who – like Rhodes – dreamed of 'perpetual peace'. Idealist thinking about international relations was very significant in the late 19th and early 20th centuries, both before, during, and after World War I, 'the war to end all war'. Means of ensuring peace promoted by idealist thinkers have included, for example, the creation of a rule of law in international relations through, say, an effective League of Nations or United Nations; through the spread of democracy; through world government or world federation; through the influence of virtuous and powerful empires such as the British Empire was long thought by many to be; through the spread of free trade and other forms of economic interdependence; and through the spread of solidarity between peoples through various means. Needless to say – and I speak as someone much of whose academic work has been studying early 20th century idealist thinkers in international relations – there is a good deal to be said that is critical, or at least robustly sceptical, of much idealistic thinking; but its noble purposes would today command widespread support.

Cecil Rhodes's most substantial scholarly biographer, Robert Rotberg[*], spoke with Scholars at Rhodes House a few months ago, and I asked him whether Cecil Rhodes

---

[*] R I Rotberg, *The Founder: Cecil Rhodes and the Pursuit of Power*, Oxford University Press, New York, 1988.

was an idealist or a realist. He replied that beyond doubt he was an idealist. So he was seen by many who knew him well.

In 1907, speaking at the unveiling of a memorial to Cecil Rhodes's 'munificence' in the Examination Schools in Oxford, one of his original Trustees, Lord Rosebery, referred explicitly to Rhodes's vision of Scholars from 'two great Empires' – the British Empire and Germany – and 'from the mightiest Republic that has ever existed', the United States, who would 'take back' from Oxford 'to their homes and their communities a message of peace, civilization and good will'.*

Lord Grey, Governor-General of Canada from 1904 to 1911, and the man whose name adorns the Grey Cup, was another of Rhodes's original Trustees. Speaking at the opening of the Rhodes memorial monument in Cape Town in 1912, Grey described Rhodes as 'a practical idealist'. He said that what he called 'the unswerving aim of Rhodes's life' included 'establish[ing], so far as possible, permanent peace between the civilised nations of the world'. Grey said that 'The steps which were to lead to the realisation of [Rhodes's] splendid hopes were: (1) The unity of South Africa; (2) the unity of the British Empire; (3) the union of the Anglo-Saxon and Celtic peoples.' These latter 'steps' Grey described as Rhodes's 'means' towards his end, 'permanent peace'.†

In short, not only did Rhodes himself say that he wanted the Rhodes Scholarships to help 'render war impossible', but his first Trustees – people who knew him – saw and presented this as central to his vision and ideal.

In describing Rhodes as a 'practical idealist', Lord Grey was of course celebrating the fact that Rhodes had created something enduring and tangible in the form of the Scholarships he established as a means towards achieving

---

* Rosebery quoted from George R Parkin, *The Rhodes Scholarships*, Constable & Co, London, 1913, p. 236.

† Grey quoted from ibid., p. 82.

his ideal. Approaching the goal of peace through the route of education even today can seem innovative, and was truly ground-breaking over a century ago. This commitment to unprecedented and specific action to achieve noble goals, and to considering problems boldly from new angles, was part of what his contemporaries found so remarkable about Rhodes. The commitment to action meant that the Scholarships became a reality, and not merely a dream that Cecil Rhodes once had, long since lost.

When Rhodes died in 1902, his Trustees needed talented and energetic people to do the work of actually creating the Scholarships. Their first masterstroke was to turn for the so-called 'Organising Secretary' for the Scholarships to a Canadian, George Parkin, headmaster of Upper Canada College, an enthusiast for Imperial unity, friend of some of the Trustees from Oxford days, and a man of seemingly boundless energy and passion but also good practical judgement. (He was also, by the way, the grandfather of Alison Grant, who married George Ignatieff.) In the early years immediately after Rhodes's death, Parkin hurtled around the globe consulting and negotiating the arrangements by which the provisions of Rhodes's will would be given effect – for example, how Scholars would be selected. If Parkin had not done this brilliantly, we would not be here tonight. And had he not persuaded the Trustees very soon after Rhodes's death to increase the number of Rhodes Scholarships for Canada beyond the number provided by Rhodes, many people here tonight might otherwise be watching television at home this evening! Parkin richly deserves the naming of part of Rhodes House – the space between the rotunda and Milner Hall – as the 'Parkin vestibule', where his bust may be found. In the first two decades of the 20th century, Parkin was widely known, but is now too little remembered; a biography of him is understandably called *Parkin: Canada's Most Famous Forgotten Man*.[*]

In 1912-13, after nearly a decade of the Scholarships, Parkin completed a book, simply called *The Rhodes Scholarships*, which gave the background to the Scholarships. Parkin said that Rhodes's will 'embodies the thoughts of a man whose ideal of life was public service and who looked upon wealth as a trust to be used for the public good'. Rhodes's 1899 will, his final will, followed several others, going back to 1877. Parkin said that they 'were all inspired by the same central idea – the widening of Anglo-Saxon influence with a view to securing the peace of the world'.[†] After quoting the sentence in Rhodes's 1901 codicil about 'an understanding between the three great powers … render[ing] war impossible and educational relations mak[ing] the strongest tie', Parkin wrote:[‡]

> Such is the international scope of this remarkable testament – the contribution of a singularly original and powerful mind to the solution of the world's problems. It was arrived at in the mind of its Founder by a long process of evolution, the original motive of which was intense conviction – the moving spring a far-reaching idealism which gathered strength and direction as his outlook on the world widened.

It is an important point that Rhodes's thinking was continually evolving – his core purposes consistent, but his understanding of the context and his ideas on how to enact his purposes ever developing – and he clearly expected and empowered his Trustees to develop his program further to meet changing times and practical realities. Such remains their duty today.

---

[*] William Christian, *Parkin: Canada's Most Famous Forgotten Man*, Blue Butterfly, 2010.

[†] Parkin, op. cit., pp. 84-5.

[‡] Ibid., p. 98.

I am tonight stressing Rhodes's declared purpose of his Scholarships promoting peace through educational relations because this was clearly a major part of his purpose which was conspicuous for some decades but has been less conspicuous in recent decades, and should, in my view, again be given its intended centrality.

In 1946, the first and long-standing American Secretary to the Rhodes Trust, Frank Aydelotte, previously president of Swarthmore College and then director of the Institute for Advanced Study at Princeton, wrote a book published in the United States as *The American Rhodes Scholarships: A Review of the First Forty Years*, and published elsewhere under the title *The Vision of Cecil Rhodes*. Aydelotte, who worked very closely with the first two Wardens of Rhodes House, wrote:[*]

> In founding his system of scholarships Rhodes hoped to realise the great purpose of his life – the unity of the English-speaking peoples and the formation with Germany of so great a power as to make war impossible. He saw what generations of idealistic thinkers had seen before him and what two world wars have now taught the rest of mankind, the necessity of substituting law and order for the chaos of anarchy and force which has during the long history of the human race characterized relations between nations.

I think that Aydelotte thought that the fact that war had not yet been rendered impossible made it more, not less, important to keep on trying to contribute to that goal. And we might reasonably say that although the Rhodes Scholarships alone clearly cannot 'render war impossible', which is itself perhaps an impossible dream, they can nonetheless make some valuable contribution to international understanding and cooperation, and to increasing the prospects for peace.

---

[*] Frank Aydelotte, *The American Rhodes Scholarships: A Review of the First Forty Years*, Princeton University Press, 1946, p. 112.

One sign that the peace-through-educational-relations purpose of the Rhodes Scholarships was so conspicuous in the first half of the 20th century is that, when American Rhodes Scholars were believed by other Oxonians to be keeping too much to themselves and not mixing with students from Britain and other countries, they were accused of thwarting 'Mr. Rhodes's intentions'.[*]

Please let me give two illustrations of the peace purpose in action, associated with the German Adam von Trott and the American J William Fulbright. Adam von Trott was a German Rhodes Scholar for 1931. In 1937-38, he went on a long trip to 'America and the Far East', sending reports to Rhodes House. On the ship back to Germany in November 1938, he wrote to the Warden, C K Allen, saying that he hoped to visit him soon, and continued:[†]

> I wonder how Rhodes matters have been running in these turbulent times. The bad boys [that is, his fellow German Rhodes Scholars] haven't written me a word about it from Berlin. But this voyage and the sanity and vigour which I have found in the bonds to former Rhodes Scholars in so many places all over the globe has increased rather than diminished my interest even in the Berlin end of it. I think our own institution [the Rhodes Scholarships] should contribute something to solving the very problem which is facing our two countries now. Sorry to get rhetorical – but, don't you agree? Remember me to Mrs. Allen ...

Whatever Adam von Trott thought Rhodes Scholars could contribute to Anglo-German relations in late 1938, he was ultimately to be executed in the summer of 1944 for his role in the July 20 assassination attempt against Hitler. He is one of at least two German Rhodes Scholars executed by the Nazis

---

[*] Lord Elton (ed.), *The First Fifty Years of The Rhodes Trust and The Rhodes Scholarships 1903-1953*, Basil Blackwell, Oxford, 1956, p. 90. See also, e.g., 'Welcoming new Rhodes Scholars' in the 'On education' section of this present volume.

[†] Quoted from Adam von Trott file, Rhodes House, Oxford.

for their roles in resistance to Hitler. We are very proud of them.[*]

Later in 1944, an Arkansas Rhodes Scholar from 1925, J William Fulbright, was elected to the US Senate. When Warden Allen congratulated him, Fulbright replied – in a slightly odd expression, given that Cecil Rhodes had been dead over 40 years:[†]

> I confess that I feel it is quite an honor to be the first Rhodes Scholar to enter the Senate. I only hope that I may be able to make some contribution toward the peace and stability which Cecil Rhodes would like to see in this world.

Senator Fulbright was to become the longest-serving chair of the Senate Foreign Relations Committee. He championed US involvement in the UN, and condemned what he called 'the arrogance of power' reflected in its Vietnam entanglement. His name is best remembered for the Fulbright awards, whose purpose is 'to promote better understanding of the United States abroad and to increase mutual understanding between the people of the United States and of other countries'. Senator Fulbright wrote:[‡]

> My experience as a Rhodes Scholar was the dominant influence in the creation of the Fulbright awards. …That experience, together with the devastation of the Second World War and the existence of large uncollectable foreign credits, resulted in the Bill creating the scholarships. … The recipients of these awards may be considered as grandchildren of Cecil Rhodes, scattered throughout the world.

---

[*] See the section on 'The German Rhodes Scholarships: "an early peace movement"' in this book.

[†] Quoted from J William Fulbright file, Rhodes House, Oxford.

[‡] Quoted from Elton, op. cit., p. 212.

The Rhodes Scholarship as a progenitor of many other scholarships, and a pioneer of international student mobility and of the internationalisation of Oxford and of other universities, is an important story. If 'educational relations make the strongest tie', then one hopes that all of these forces contribute to the prospects of peace: the vision Fulbright inherited from Rhodes.

I have dwelt at such length on the peace purpose of the Rhodes Scholarships (on which, implausibly, even more could be said) because as we today work to give the best effect we can to the great ideals upon which the Rhodes Scholarships are founded, we need sufficient clarity about what those ideals are. It seems especially fitting to speak of this here in Ottawa – almost in the shadow of the Peace Tower; in a city which has, for example, given its name to a treaty banning landmines, a treaty that arose (like the Rhodes Scholarships) from private initiative and active citizenship; here in Ottawa, where so many Rhodes Scholars have worked to promote good international relations, and where more might again.

The Rhodes Scholarship is in important ways unprescriptive and unprogrammatic. We identify, invest in, and engage exceptional young people, and support them in what seems to them the best use of their talents. We do not prescribe courses of study, fields of activity, or – Heaven forbid! – opinions. But the cumulative effect of the Scholarships, in the warp and weft of real life, should be to promote certain things, importantly including service and international understanding.

Some of this will be through Scholars who specifically devote themselves to the goal of promoting international harmony. Just as Scholars in earlier generations have sought to do this – I have mentioned figures from Adam von Trott to George Ignatieff to J William Fulbright – so I have no doubt that many Scholars today are working to improve international relations in a diversity of ways, some more controversial than others. For example, in the United States, Republican Senator

Lugar is the ranking member of the Senate Foreign Relations Committee, and Susan Rice, a Democrat, is Ambassador to the United Nations. There have been and are many Rhodes Scholar diplomats and writers on international affairs, and many whose studies and careers are in fields, including in healthcare, development, trade, and much more that relate directly or indirectly to the prospects of peace. Many are active in NGO work and in international organisations. To illustrate the diversity let me simply embarrass two people who are here tonight – Adriaan De Hoog and Roxanne Joyal. While Roxanne works for Free the Children, Adriaan has followed his diplomatic career with writing novels of diplomacy; his website tells us that in his third, just-about-to-be-launched novel, *Natalia's Peace*, 'forces pushing for a more enlightened world order are pitted against ones that profit from armed conflict, as the novel examines what the international community could do to end senseless killing'.* Just as there are many ways in which Rhodes Scholars can live lives of service, so there are very many ways in which they can contribute to international understanding, cooperation, and peace. I know that many Scholars are today contributing in diverse ways, and I have no doubt many more will in the future.

There are some obvious and important implications for the Rhodes Scholarships of clear focus on the peace and international understanding purpose of Rhodes. The first is for the experience of current Scholars – the need to encourage them to get to know Scholars and other students of other countries, not just their own, and to think about and engage with international issues. Encouragingly, when on the day I became Warden I emailed the then-current Scholars and asked them for ideas on how to improve the Scholarship, the most important theme of their answers was the desire for more opportunities to get to know Scholars from other countries. This has been an important theme of our social and other activities at Rhodes House. Similarly, we have had

---

* http://www.adriandehoog.com/– accessed 24 September 2011.

several speakers at Rhodes House on international issues, and Canadian Rhodes Scholars (some here tonight) earlier this year led the organisation at Rhodes House of the so-called Global Scholars' Symposium, bringing together overseas postgraduate students in Britain on major scholarships, to discuss world challenges.[*]

A second possible implication is that the more we are focused on international understanding and cooperation, the more we should try to give reality to the global community of Rhodes Scholars – through all the means we have of communication and events spanning national boundaries – such as the lively global Rhodes events we had at Rhodes House on the Oxford Alumni Weekend last weekend, or the 2012 events I recently mentioned in an email and which are on the Rhodes House website. It is often forgotten that Cecil Rhodes in his will encouraged what we would call alumni relations, including connection between current Scholars and alumni[†] – something our annual survey of current Scholars shows many of them are keen to have more of. The desire for increased opportunities for Scholars of all generations to connect with Rhodes House and with each other has been clearly reflected in the consultation of the last two years, and we are doing our best to facilitate such opportunities.

The notion of a global community of Rhodes Scholars is not a recent one. For example, in a volume entitled *The First Fifty Years of The Rhodes Trust and The Rhodes Scholarships 1903-1953*, Lord Elton discussed ideas of how, in his words, 'to maintain a viable Rhodes community not only within each constituency but throughout the world'. He mentioned events, such as the reunion on the 50th anniversary that he was marking; publications such as what he called 'the Warden's sprightly and informative annual Christmas letter'; the overseas travels of officers of the Trust; and more. He wrote that 'the

---

[*] See also 'Ideas into action' in the section 'On leadership' in this book.

[†] Section 34 of Cecil Rhodes's 1899 will, quoted on p. 9n of this book.

time may come when the need will be felt of a periodical, and conceivably an Association, to do throughout the world what is already being done for the national constituencies." Today, we are together refreshing our thinking about what is best done at local, national, and global levels, including working in time towards a global online community; and I would like to thank officers and members of the Canadian Association of Rhodes Scholars and the Canadian Rhodes Scholars Foundation for your leadership in this. I urge all Rhodes Scholars of all generations to participate fully in the evolving life of the global community of Rhodes Scholars.

A third possible implication of having Rhodes's focus on peace clearly in mind is in our thinking about what countries Rhodes Scholars should come from in the 21st century. In the consultation of Scholars around the world over the last two years, asking from what countries there should be Rhodes Scholars, there has been considerable support for seeking the additional resources needed to increase Rhodes Scholarships from India and Africa, to reinstate them in some places where they have been cut, and in time, with proper safeguards and great care, to create Rhodes Scholarships from China and perhaps other parts of the world. Input from Scholars is helping the Trustees towards a strategic vision of the best geographic footprint for the Rhodes Scholarships so that they have the greatest relevance and positive impact possible in the world of the 21st century. It is early days, but I am quietly confident that in time good will come. Throughout, of course, we will protect the criteria, selection process, quality assurance, and reputation of the Rhodes Scholarships.

I said that any expansion opportunities would require additional resources – additional to the £100+ million we need to raise over the course of this decade simply to secure and improve upon our existing Scholarships. So far

---

* Elton, op. cit., pp. 46-7.

we have raised in pledges or cash some £20.4 million – an encouraging start. The exciting news is that, as of this month, we formally have tax deductibility in Canada for donations to the Rhodes Trust, fully recognised by the Canada Revenue Agency. The long, frustrating wait is over, and Canadian Scholars can now commence fundraising in earnest! Expect to hear before long from your fellow Canadian Scholars about this. Thanks to the generosity of some Scholars, a Canadian development director will be appointed, working from Toronto, to support the Canadian Rhodes fundraising effort. I would also commend the generosity of the Scholar who will pay for 'reverse Rhodes' students coming from Oxford to Canada over the next decade while the Canadian Rhodes Scholars Foundation discontinues its fundraising so as to ensure total focus on fundraising to secure the Rhodes Scholarships.

The participation of all of us in this effort – according to our capacity – in annual giving, bequests, and if we have the capacity, major gifts – is extremely important. The participation of all of us will maximise support, will encourage Scholars capable of major gifts to give fully to their capacity, and will be important as we go to non-Scholars, corporations, and foundations. Our lives were transformed by the incredible gift of a Rhodes Scholarship, and we should do everything we can to secure and improve it for future generations.

It is for the sake of future generations that Cecil Rhodes created the Rhodes Scholarships – to recognise and nurture excellence in intellect, character, leadership, and service, for the good of communities in many countries; and, as I have stressed tonight, to promote understanding and peace between countries. His aim was to 'render war impossible' through 'educational relations'. What will be our contribution to this in the realities of our time? This requires careful thought and determined action, and I know that Canadian Rhodes Scholars can be counted on fully to play their part – to play your part – in this.

The German Rhodes Scholarships:
'an early peace movement'

Dinner of the Oxford European Reunion, Berlin
7 November 2009

We are here in Berlin to mark the 20th anniversary of the coming down of the Berlin Wall, contributing to the end of the Cold War and the reunion of a divided city, country, and continent – one of the great transformations of the 20th century. In celebrating that reunification, tonight's Oxford alumni reunion also marks the long-lived bonds between this city, this country, and this continent with Oxford. I would like to talk briefly about some aspects of those links that go back long before 1989.

One of the many important elements of the Oxford-German bond has been for over a century and remains the German Rhodes Scholarships, which remind us that the links between Oxford and Germany have spanned many generations and have been of profound importance.

Cecil Rhodes, who died in 1902, through his will and codicils created scholarships to bring outstanding all-rounders from the United States, many countries of the British Empire as it was, now the Commonwealth, and Germany to Oxford to gain the benefits of collegiate education there, and to be encouraged to promote the public good.

The codicil to Rhodes's will that created the German Scholarships was very short. It was signed in January 1901:

> I note the German Emperor has made instruction in English compulsory in German schools. I leave five yearly scholarships at Oxford of £250 per ann. to students of German birth the scholars to be nominated by the German Emperor for the time being

... The object is that an understanding between the three great powers will render war impossible and educational relations make the strongest tie.

C. J. Rhodes

Since the first German Rhodes Scholars arrived in Oxford in 1903, twice interrupted by war and twice renewed, German Rhodes Scholars, like other German Oxonians, have contributed much to Oxford, to Germany, and to the wider world.

This year, as well as being the 20th anniversary of the fall of the Berlin Wall, is a special anniversary for two German Oxonians who came to Oxford as Rhodes Scholars, two people about whom 'it is difficult to speak, and impossible to be silent'. 2009 is the centenary of the birth of Adam von Trott zu Solz, who came to Oxford briefly in 1929 to Mansfield College, and back to Oxford, to Balliol, in 1931 as a Rhodes Scholar. This year is also the centenary of the selection as a Rhodes Scholar and the coming to Oxford, to Trinity, of Albrecht von Bernstorff.

Both Adam von Trott and Albrecht von Bernstorff were executed in this city in 1944 and 1945, respectively, for their roles in the resistance to Hitler and assassination efforts against him.

Both their names, together with the names of the Rhodes Scholars from Germany and all other countries who were killed in the world wars, are inscribed in Oxford in the rotunda at Rhodes House, where this week, which includes Remembrance Sunday, there is a wreath of poppies in their memory.

The links between Oxford and Germany are reflected in the lives, and the deaths, of Albrecht von Bernstorff and Adam von Trott. Count Bernstorff had been at Oxford before the First World War. In 1926, after one of the many Rhodes reunion dinners he attended in Oxford, he wrote to the first Warden of Rhodes House, Sir Francis Wylie:

> I feel that I owe you a word of thanks on behalf of Mandt [his fellow German Rhodes Scholar] and myself to tell you how

very happy we were to be able to attend the Dinner at Oxford again this year. For me personally I must say that it has greatly impressed me to be in touch again with the great and growing community of the Rhodes Trustees and the Rhodes Scholars after all the unfortunate events that have separated us during the years of the war and after. Mandt and I, and I feel sure that a very large section of the former German Rhodes Scholars will agree with us, greatly appreciate [the welcome we received] ..., and for me personally I can only say that I shall more than ever try to live up to the ideas which prompted Cecil Rhodes in making his will.

Bernstorff, who was an outspoken liberal, sat on the Rhodes selection committee that chose Adam von Trott as one of the German Rhodes Scholars for 1931. The stepson of another of the 1931 German Rhodes Scholars is here tonight – Thomas Böcking, the German National Secretary of the Rhodes Trust, and his wife, Silvia Böcking. We are enormously grateful for their outstanding contribution for over 30 years to the ties between Germany and Oxford, principally, but not only, through the Rhodes Scholarships.

Adam von Trott was at Balliol from 1931 to 1933. In November 1938, he wrote to the Warden of Rhodes House, C K Allen, from a trip that took him to the US and China:

> I wonder how Rhodes matters have been running in these turbulent times. The bad boys haven't written me a word about it from Berlin. But this voyage and the sanity and vigour which I have found in the bond to former Rhodes Scholars in so many places all over the globe has increased rather than diminished my interest even in the Berlin end of it. I think our own institution should contribute something to the very problem which is facing our two countries now. Sorry to get rhetorical – but, don't you agree?

Adam von Trott took part in the July 1944 assassination attempt against Hitler and was hanged in this city in August 1944, at the age of 35.

Just over a week ago, Mansfield College, where he had first been in Oxford, hosted the fourth Adam von Trott Memorial Lecture, and announced a new scholarship, for which they continue to seek funding, for a German student to study politics or international relations in Oxford at Mansfield College. For further information about the Adam von Trott Memorial Fund, please contact the Development Office at Mansfield College.

In September 1946, just over two years after his death, Adam von Trott's widow, Clarita von Trott, saw the Warden of Rhodes House and later wrote to him:

> I do want to tell you once more how grateful I was for the afternoon with you and that I could talk so freely with you about Adam and his and our fight and life. And it is wonderful to know that – if ever again in England – I could come to your house and find out many more details about Adam's life in Oxford – the time of his life which has determined the course of his later years.

Although mercifully in less dramatic ways, for many of us our years in Oxford have been 'the time of [our] life which has determined the course of [our] later years'.

As we remember the 20th anniversary of the breaching of the Berlin Wall, let us also remember German and other Oxonians of all the generations whose lives have been touched by Oxford, and who have contributed to Oxford and the wider world. Let us recall the noble, if incompletely realistic, vision for peace of Cecil Rhodes. And let us also celebrate those educational ties between Oxford, Germany, and the wider Europe, which go back so far and which mean so much for the future.

Reception, Rhodes House, Oxford
24 September 2010

It is a great honour for me as Warden of Rhodes House to welcome you to this, the home of the Rhodes Scholarships. We are here to mark the 40th anniversary of the reinstatement after World War II of the Rhodes Scholarships from Germany, and warmly to celebrate the outstanding contribution which Thomas and Silvia Böcking have made to the Rhodes Scholarships, especially since Thomas's appointment as German National Secretary to the Rhodes Trust in 1979, from which position he will retire at the end of this year.

In four months' time, it will be exactly one hundred and ten years since Cecil Rhodes added a codicil to his will which provided, in addition to the Scholarships Rhodes had already provided for exceptional all-round students from the United States and various parts of the British Empire, that the Kaiser could each year nominate five Scholars from Germany. Cecil Rhodes wrote, in words that echo through the years: 'The object is that an understanding between the three great powers will render war impossible and educational relations make the strongest ties.'

And so in 1903, before Rhodes Scholars from most other countries could be selected, the first German Rhodes Scholars arrived in Oxford. Many of the German Rhodes Scholars of the years before World War I were aristocrats. Very many read for the Diploma in Economics and were headed for the service of the state in Germany – precisely, I think, what Cecil Rhodes would have hoped, there to help encourage international friendship. One such Scholar was Count Albrecht von Bernstorff, the centenary of whose coming to Oxford in 1909 we marked last year. He was executed by the Gestapo in the early months of 1945 for his long-known opposition to Hitler, and his name is proud among the Rhodes Scholars, from Germany and other countries, whose sacrifices in the two world wars are remembered in the memorial in the Rhodes House rotunda.

In 1916, the Rhodes Trustees reluctantly accepted that circumstances required the abolition of these Scholarships, and this was done by act of the British Parliament. Thirteen years later, at a dinner in this building to mark its official opening, the former and future British Prime Minister, Stanley Baldwin, in his capacity as a Rhodes Trustee, announced that the Trustees, who had in fact been supporting other Anglo-German educational exchange for several years, were re-creating Rhodes Scholarships from Germany with effect from 1930. One of the 1930 Scholars was E F Schumacher, famous for his 'small is beautiful' philosophy, and the 1931 Scholars were Adam von Trott, who was to be executed in 1944 for his role in an assassination attempt against Hitler, and Adolf Schlepegrell, who later, under the Nazi regime, was unable to secure employment in Germany because of Jewish ancestry. In 1939, Adolf Schlepegrell found himself in Canada, and wrote from there 71 years ago this week to the Warden of Rhodes House, C K Allen: 'These are certainly very dark days for all of us… I was interested to hear that the Rhodes Scholarships have been temporarily suspended, and I naturally wonder whether we shall ever see German Rhodes Scholars again at Oxford.'

Little was he to anticipate that almost 30 years later, in March 1969, he would write to C K Allen's successor as Warden, Bill Williams:

Dear Warden

Thank you very much for your letter of 13th March telling me that the Trustees have created two Rhodes Scholarships for men from the Federal German Republic. It cannot have been an easy decision to rebuild that bridge for a second time but, as you say, I am glad that it was taken and hope that a good tradition will be lastingly resumed as the Founder would have wished it. I sometimes wonder what his reaction would be if he could see how his great idea has been adapted to 66 years of turbulent history.

And little was Adolf Schlepegrell to anticipate that a year later, in January 1970, he would receive from the Warden a telegram that read: 'Your stepson Thomas Bocking accepted by University College for 1970. Bill Williams'. In a letter of thanks, Adolf Schlepegrell wrote to the Warden: 'You can imagine how happy we are that the young man is following in his step-father's footsteps.'

Thomas was, of course, one of two German Scholars elected for 1970. I am delighted that his Rhodes classmate, Lippold von Klencke, who came up to St John's College in 1970, is also here today. It is very special that you are here.

In December 1970, Adolf Schlepegrell wrote to Warden Williams from Paris, after Thomas's and Lippold's first term in Oxford: 'Thomas came to see us on his way to Hamburg. My impression is confirmed that he is settling down well at Univ. despite his pre-marital preoccupations!'

With Thomas's mother, Adolf came in June 1971 to the Rhodes Trustees' dinner in this building, just weeks before Thomas and Silvia were to be married in Germany, and later wrote to thank the Warden:

> Back in Paris I still think a lot about our visit to Oxford. It was a splendid occasion which gave me particular pleasure as it brought up many memories of being a Rhodes Scholar 40 years ago and gave me a chance to see Rhodes Scholars to-day, including Thomas who appears to be entering into the spirit of the place rather well.

Thomas – and soon Silvia – had indeed entered 'into the spirit of the place rather well'. And so they have continued. And today, almost 40 years on, we are here, both to mark the reinstatement of the German Scholarships – a history shaped by many in this room – and to honour Thomas and Silvia Böcking, who have together served the Rhodes Scholarships – and the spirit of this place, including the spirit of fellowship and friendship – with great distinction. I am delighted that joining us in this celebration today is their son, Dr Felix Böcking, who in 1999 followed his father and his step-grandfather into University College, Oxford. It is a pleasure also to have the Master of University College and Lady Crewe with us here today.

In his letter of thanks to Warden Williams in June 1971, Adolf Schlepegrell wrote: 'We should like to thank you and Gillian again for receiving us so kindly and charmingly and for arranging everything so well.' Gill Williams, whose home this was for 28 years, friend to Thomas and Silvia for nearly 40 years, is also with us here, and is, as she always is, extremely welcome.

Until yesterday, it had been the plan of a member of the Rhodes selection committee that elected Lippold von Klencke and Thomas Böcking in 1969 to be with us here today; but illness has made this sadly impossible. This is Professor Sir Fritz Caspari, who was born in March 1914, before the start of the First World War; and was elected a Rhodes Scholar in December 1932, before Hitler came to power – in a selection in Berlin which the Warden of Rhodes House, C K Allen, attended and enthusiastically endorsed. Sir Fritz came up to St John's in 1933. I believe that Albrecht von Bernstorff, whom I mentioned earlier, served on the committee that elected him, and Sir Fritz also knew Adam von Trott. In a distinguished career as a scholar and a diplomat, Sir Fritz also served on the last Rhodes selection committee for Germany before World War II, and on the first Rhodes selection committee there after World War II. We are very sorry he cannot be with us, and he is very disappointed also.

An interview with Sir Fritz was recently filmed, and when edited will in some weeks' time be placed on the Rhodes House website, where I hope you will take the time to view it. In that interview with Fritz Caspari, as in the work of Thomas and Silvia Böcking, you will see reflected, amongst much else, the spirit of international understanding, including of Anglo-German friendship, which is a crucial part of what these Scholarships, continuing the vision of Cecil Rhodes, seek to nurture.

In his capacity as German National Secretary since 1979, Thomas has worked with six Wardens of Rhodes House. I am delighted that Sir Anthony and Nancy Kenny are here today, and Sir Colin Lucas sends his warmest wishes and regrets from abroad. Dr Robin Fletcher, Warden from 1980 to 1989, is in Orkney, from where he has sent this message:

> I am sorry not to be with you today. Among the duties which, as Warden, I enjoyed most was working with the Constituency Secretaries with the common aim of ensuring the smooth running of the Trust's activities in their various countries, particularly in the selection process. All were persons of some standing, prepared to give time and effort without remuneration. All were friendly and made visits a delight rather than a chore. The great majority had benefitted from the build up by their predecessors over an almost uninterrupted span of seventy-five years. Almost alone you faced the struggle to re-establish the Trust's position in Germany, make contact with the academic world there, and as far as the future can be certain, leave to your successor the fruits of your labour.
>
> One further but important point. While others had succeeded (was this the result of their Oxford experience?) in attracting the nicest ladies to marriage, Thomas had managed not only this but one who was prepared to add to the care of a young family an equal share of the business of the Trust. So it is very fitting that they should be honoured jointly.
>
> Bless you. Robin.

The high calibre of the German Rhodes Scholars, whose selection Thomas and Silvia have overseen with such skill, is testimony to all that they have done. One such German Rhodes Scholar is Professor Hannes Unberath, who in January will succeed Thomas as German National Secretary, and to whom we are very grateful indeed for all that lies ahead in that important responsibility. Hannes, who came to Worcester College in 1997, is an amazingly productive professor of law at the University of Bayreuth, with considerable experience already of the German Rhodes selection process.[*]

As a small token of our gratitude to Thomas and Silvia, we have some modest gifts that we hope will symbolise for them, now and always, their strong tie with Oxford, to which they have contributed so much.

Rhodes dinner, Munich, Germany
26 November 2010

We are here tonight to mark the 40th anniversary of the post-war Rhodes Scholarships from Germany, and to mark, with deep admiration and gratitude, the occasion of the retirement of Thomas Böcking after 31 years of committed and distinguished service as German National Secretary to the Rhodes Trust, and of his also committed and distinguished partner in that work (as in life generally), Silvia Böcking, to whom we are also deeply grateful.

As Warden of Rhodes House, I am delighted to welcome you tonight, and to express the hope that you will take part in future German Rhodes events, which I know some Scholars are keen to encourage – as well as coming to visit us back at Rhodes House when you can.

Tonight, after Thomas and I have spoken, Lippold von Klencke (Germany & St John's 1970) and Ambassador Peter von Butler – who has served with distinction as Chair of the German Selection Committee over several years – will say more. Among so many distinguished guests, I also want to acknowledge former Chairman of the Selection Committee, Professor Schweitzer, and Mrs Schweitzer, and this year's Chairman, Professor Reiner Krücken.

---

[*] Very sadly, Hannes Unberath passed away on 28 January 2013.

Many people who are not here tonight would have liked to be here. One has made a significant donation to the Rhodes Trust in honour of Thomas and Silvia. Another has written to me expressing 'deep gratitude [for] Thomas's work over all those years' – 'for his exemplary work as a modern German Rhodes Scholar and as the German secretary for the Trust'.

In the second half of 1969, months after the Rhodes Trust announced the re-creation of the German Rhodes Scholarships, the young Thomas Böcking did what he had planned to do since boyhood: he prepared – as most of us have done – an application for the Rhodes Scholarship. Thomas has given me permission to quote from his file. He wrote in his application for the Scholarship:

> I would like to go to Oxford to take a degree in Philosophy-Politics-and-Economics (PPE)... As long as I have not decided to specialise in any particular field of law I consider this combination of subjects, which to my knowledge can only be taken in Oxford, the best possible addition to the law course I have already finished. Such understanding is necessary for a lawyer in order to serve society as well as he can.

Thomas looked forward to the close contact with tutors in Oxford's tutorial system, and to working and living with, in his words, 'students from almost all the English-speaking countries coming from very different backgrounds'.

A few months later, in January 1970, having been elected – along with Lippold von Klencke, who is also here tonight – as one of the German Rhodes Scholars for 1970, Thomas received a letter from the Warden of Rhodes House, Sir Edgar (Bill) Williams. It began:

> You will be delighted to know that you have been accepted by Univ. to read (P.) P.E. I have told the Selection Committee

and also cabled your stepfather with the good news. I am not surprised but I am delighted.

Thomas's stepfather was Adolf Schlepegrell who, with Adam von Trott, had been Rhodes Scholar for Germany for 1931, and had also been at Univ.

The selection committee that selected Thomas and Lippold as the German Scholars for 1970 included Fritz Caspari (Germany & St John's 1933). As well as serving on the first selection committee after World War II, Fritz Caspari had served on the last selection committee *before* the Second World War, in 1938, and is living today at the age of 96 in Greenwich, London, where I visited him some months ago, and where an interview with him, about his remarkable life, was videoed a few weeks ago. It is good to think tonight of Professor Sir Fritz Caspari, and of all the German Rhodes Scholars since 1903 who have, in so many ways in so many different contexts, fought – and are fighting – the world's fight, and served and serve their country and the wider world with distinction.

When the German Rhodes Scholarships were re-created in 1969 for 1970, the Rhodes Trust appointed as the German National Secretary one of the first two German Rhodes Scholars who had been elected after World War I: William Koelle (Germany and Magdalen 1930). Herr Koelle's fellow Scholar of 1930 was the economist E F Schumacher, famous for his book *Small Is Beautiful*. William Koelle served as German National Secretary from 1969 to 1979. In 1978, the question arose as to who would succeed him, and the suggestion was made that it should be Thomas Böcking. In discussion of this, Thomas wrote to Warden Williams in September 1978:

Now I have left the Foreign Service and am very happily and I think usefully installed as a magistrate in Coburg. ... It was with great pleasure that I answered [Herr] Koelle's question, as to whether I would be interested in being considered as his successor as secretary to the German selection committee. ... I have received benefit and happiness from Oxford and it would be good if perhaps I could both pass some of it on and show gratitude in this way.

Tonight, Thomas and Silvia, it is we who express our gratitude to you for 31 years of service to Oxford and the Rhodes Trust.

Gratitude was the theme also of a letter Thomas wrote to Lady Williams in July 1980, after he and Silvia had seen Sir Edgar and Lady Williams in Oxford. Thomas wrote:

Let me say, however, that our gratitude to you both goes further than just this one occasion. Both when I was alone in Oxford and when Silvia came to join me there, you both showed great kindness, warmth and helpfulness, which was reassuring to me and was one of the corner stones of Silvia feeling so much at home and at ease in Oxford, and thus contributed to a time that was both very happy for us and formative. We are both grateful that these years were not just an episode but that they were rather the beginning of a firm link with Oxford and with England, where we still feel very much at home within a very short time... Moreover, I cannot omit to thank the Warden for the confidence he put in me in my present function as secretary.

After sending sincere gratitude and 'affectionate greetings', Thomas added:

P.S. I am just about to hang up the Founder's portrait in my study.

All Rhodes Scholars – perhaps all Oxonians – understand and share the sense of gratitude for the formative and usually happy time we spent as students in Oxford. Rhodes Scholars are, in particular, the beneficiaries of the extraordinary vision and generosity of the Founder of the Scholarship, Cecil Rhodes. His vision was that by bringing, from many countries around the world, outstanding young people into the collegiate environment of Oxford, they could be encouraged to promote the public good – to do something with their lives, with our lives, to make the world a better place. Rhodes's vision was also that the mixing of these Scholars from many countries with British and other students could promote international understanding and, indeed, peace.

This vision was, of course, not immediately realised, though many Rhodes Scholars did their best, sometimes very courageously and at high price, to promote it. But today we can affirm it, and affirm the role of educational ties, and of the Rhodes Scholarships specifically, in promoting international understanding and peace. Thomas last year said to me, at a dinner in Berlin, that the Rhodes Scholarships were an early peace movement: and so they were. Thomas and Silvia have both done much to contribute to the Anglo-German and indeed the wider international friendship to which our Scholarships aim to contribute.

I would also add that Thomas in his own work as a civil servant, public prosecutor, judge, and judicial administrator has also embodied Cecil Rhodes's hope that Rhodes Scholars would come 'to esteem the performance of public duties as [their] highest aim'.

And so tonight, we proudly celebrate the German Rhodes Scholarships – since 1903, since 1970, and under 31 years of conscientious, committed and distinguished oversight by Thomas and Silvia Böcking. We have tried this year to express our gratitude to Thomas and Silvia – including at a reception at Rhodes House in September, when I spoke of this history through the life and letters of Thomas's stepfather, Adolf Schlepegrell. At the dinner afterwards, the Chancellor of Oxford, Lord Patten, also paid tribute to Thomas's work, to the Rhodes Scholarships as – in his words – 'a jewel in the crown' for Oxford, and to the significance to Oxford of German students, academic staff, and alumni. A memorial booklet from the Rhodes House reception, listing all German Rhodes Scholars since 1903

– except the two elected today for 2011! – is on the table for you to take.

Tonight, as well as looking back with gratitude and pride, we also look forward. Thomas and Silvia have been very welcoming to the in-coming German National Secretary, Professor Hannes Unberath (Germany & Worcester 1997), who at the last minute was prevented by illness from coming here from Bayreuth. We look forward to the future confidently also with the two new German Rhodes Scholars elected here in Munich today: Katharina Behr and Timo Kauer. The calibre of Rhodes Scholars, globally and specifically from Germany, is very high. We look to a future also in which a number of Scholars are trying to organise future alumni connections – don't be surprised to hear from them!

For the Rhodes Scholarships generally, we look forward to doing all we can to give the best effect in the 21st century to the great ideals on which the Rhodes Scholarships are founded. There has never been a time when Rhodes Scholars have had greater opportunity than now to help to shape the future of the Scholarship which means so much to us, and there has never been greater need for us to contribute. Your support in so many ways will be important and deeply appreciated.

Tonight, to mark the 40th anniversary, to honour German Rhodes Scholars past, present and future, and to thank Thomas and Silvia, I would ask you to join me in two toasts: First – to Thomas and Silvia. And now – to the German Rhodes Scholars.

E F Schumacher

Event to mark the centenary of his birth
Rhodes House, Oxford, 16 September 2011

It is a very great pleasure for me, as Warden, to welcome you to Rhodes House, home of the Rhodes Scholarships, today for this session of the Oxford University Alumni Weekend to discuss the relevance of the ideas of a Rhodes Scholar of 1930-33, E F 'Fritz' Schumacher*, in this the centenary year of his birth.

We are delighted to welcome as speakers Fritz Schumacher's daughter and biographer, Barbara Wood; Simon Trace, the CEO of the group he founded, Practical Action; and Ann Pettifor, Executive Director of Advocacy International.

E F Schumacher was born in Bonn on 16 August 1911, and after brief studies at universities in Bonn and Berlin, came to New College, Oxford, in 1930 as a Rhodes Scholar from Germany. If you would like to see a photo from that time of the 19-year-old Fritz, there is one on the Rhodes House website from our News story on 16 August marking his centenary. Completing a Diploma in Economics in Oxford, he went on to read for a BLitt in Economics, both in Oxford and then, with the special support of the Rhodes Trust, in New York. Returning to Germany in 1934, the ascent of the Nazis made life there impossible, and he returned to England in 1937. Briefly interned early in the war as an 'enemy alien' and having to work as a farm labourer, he returned in 1943 to the Institute of Statistics here in Oxford, contributed to Beveridge's work on full employment policy, worked at *The Observer*, was naturalised as a British subject in 1946, and then from 1946 to 1950 worked in the Control Commission for Germany.

Then came the longest stretch of his career, as Economic Adviser and Director of Statistics for the National Coal Board from 1950 to 1970. His mind became focused on the energy crisis he foresaw, and the competing interests and problems of oil, nuclear, and coal power. Influential experiences in this time included serving as UN adviser on the economic development of Burma in 1955, contributing to the development of his ideas on appropriate or intermediate technology, which led to the creation of the Intermediate Technology Development Group, later Practical Action, and to his interest in 'Buddhist

---

* Ernst Friedrich ('Fritz') Schumacher (16 August 1911-4 September 1977).

economics'. He also, of course, developed an interest in organic farming and was a leader in the Soil Association.

It was in his retirement, after his confirmation into the Roman Catholic Church, and during the economic crisis of the 1970s with the dramatic interruption of post-war growth and the conspicuous emergence of energy and environmental crises, that Fritz Schumacher's influence and reputation reached a crescendo, with the publication in 1973 of *Small is beautiful – economics as if people mattered*, a massive best-seller, making Schumacher what has been called 'a hero of the alternative society' and a kind of rock-star economist, mobbed by student and other audiences of thousands. And then, just before the publication of his *A Guide for the Perplexed*, he died suddenly in Switzerland on 4 September 1977, and was deeply mourned.

Many groups and activities have honoured his work, and it is evident from the interest in today's session that he is also much remembered. Before handing over to our most interesting panel, who will discuss his economic and related ideas, let me briefly reveal some of the impressive and engaging personal story of Fritz Schumacher which emerges from his Rhodes Scholar file held in the basement of this building.

In 1901, Cecil Rhodes had provided for the creation of Rhodes Scholarships from Germany, to go with those from the United States and much of what was then the British Empire. Among the Rhodes Scholars who came from Germany before World War I was Count Albrecht von Bernstorff, a tireless worker for Anglo-German friendship, who became a mentor to Fritz Schumacher as to other Rhodes Scholars, and who was shot by the Gestapo just six days before Hitler committed suicide in 1945.

The original German Rhodes Scholarships were abolished by the British Parliament in 1916, and created anew by the Rhodes Trustees in 1929, with the first German Rhodes Scholars to come to Oxford in 1930. One of the two German Rhodes Scholars for 1930, the first since World War I, was E F

Schumacher. His file in this building reflects his time in Oxford, including his close bonds with the Warden of Rhodes House of his day, C K Allen, and the warm links with Rhodes House which he maintained till his death.

In 1931, Warden Allen wrote of E F Schumacher: 'he is entirely justifying his appointment to a Rhodes Scholarship'. In Trinity term 1932, a Rhodes Trustee, H A L Fisher, writing in his capacity as Warden of New College, reported on Fritz Schumacher that he 'has inaugurated the new series of German Rhodes Scholars with success. ... He is a nice well-mannered fellow who has made many friends and gained by Oxford.'

It was an exceptional thing that the Rhodes Trust supported Fritz Schumacher in spending a third year as a Rhodes Scholar researching banking issues in New York. On 30 January 1933, the day that Hitler was sworn in as Chancellor in Berlin, Fritz Schumacher – not knowing how influential that terrible appointment would be in the course of his own life and those of millions of others – wrote from New York to the Warden of Rhodes House reporting on his work on monetary research there:

> Before everything else I should like to give expression to my feelings of very sincerest thanks to the Rhodes Trustees. With the background of two years of study in Oxford my stay in New York so far has proved a most interesting time. New York's realism and eagerness for practical work is a fascinating experience after having learned to appreciate Oxford's love for tradition and deep thinking. They both together form an enviable background for any kind of study and make the problems of life appear in a new and altogether more penetrating light. My stay in England was of incalculable value to me, – besides acquainting me with England, – it helped me to understand Germany. America is helping me to understand Europe.

Back in Germany in September 1934, Fritz Schumacher wrote to Warden Allen, referring circumspectly to the difficulties of life in Nazi Germany, that he would 'for ever remain grateful to the Rhodes Trust for making ... possible' the experiences 'of utmost value' he had had. He served briefly on the Rhodes Scholarship selection committee for Germany before, as I have mentioned, returning to England.

Of the many further links between Fritz Schumacher and Rhodes House, let me mention only two. On 6 January 1940, just a few months after the outbreak of war, Fritz wrote from Weybridge, Surrey, to Warden Allen:

> Many thanks for your very kind letter of Jan. 2nd. My wife and I are both deeply appreciative that amidst all the burdens that rest on you these days you found time to enquire after our well-being.
>
> Although we are, as you say, in a rather difficult position, we are above everything else grateful for the fact that we can live here and have not been caught in the dreadful conflict of Ideals and Duty which is facing so many of our friends in Germany. But with nothing to do, although so much could be done, the feeling of frustration wears heavily upon me. The technicality of my being an 'Enemy Alien' – nothing could be more at variance with real facts – makes it extremely difficult to find new employment. I lost my previous job short[ly] after the outbreak of war.

In those difficult days, Warden Allen vouched for Fritz Schumacher – for example writing to one correspondent in March 1940: 'you may regard Mr Schumacher with every confidence, and any kindness which you can show him and his wife will be well spent.'

Needless to say, the Rhodes Scholarships which brought Fritz Schumacher and other outstanding Germans, such as Adam von Trott, to Oxford in the 1930s did not survive the outbreak of war in 1939. It was not until 1969 that the Rhodes Trustees made the decision again to create Rhodes Scholarships for Germany. When the then Warden of Rhodes House, Sir Edgar Williams, wrote to Fritz Schumacher to tell him of the re-creation of the

German Rhodes Scholarships, he enthusiastically replied, from Caterham, Surrey:

> What excellent news! I am delighted. Thank you for letting me know. If I can be of any help in any way, I am at your disposal.

Fritz Schumacher had been one of the first pair of German Rhodes Scholars elected after World War I. One of the first pair of German Rhodes Scholars elected after World War II, Thomas Böcking, is here today, and this evening will be recognised as a Distinguished Friend of Oxford. I am sure that Fritz Schumacher, whom Thomas met on family visits as a boy in the 1950s, would have been pleased.

I hope that these snippets from the life of E F Schumacher – connecting him so directly with this place and this community – are of interest as we turn now to consider his ideas on economics, intermediate technology, environment, energy, the limits to growth, food production, culture, and the human spirit – 'economics as if people mattered'.

Sir Fritz Caspari: 'a liberal from Heidelberg'

Service of thanksgiving for his life
St Mary's, Compton, West Sussex
20 December 2010

In late November, just five days before Fritz Caspari* died, the largest ever gathering of German Rhodes Scholars – a Rhodes dinner in Munich – heard warm tributes to Fritz from Lippold von Klencke and from me. Lippold was one of the first two German Rhodes Scholars elected after the Second World War, chosen in 1969 by a committee on which Fritz Caspari sat, as he

---

* Professor Sir Fritz Caspari (21 March 1914-1 December 2010). This eulogy was previously published in *The American Oxonian*, Winter 2011.

had also sat on the last German Rhodes Scholarship selection committee before the war, in 1938. Lippold von Klencke was also the nephew of Fritz's exact contemporary as Rhodes Scholar for Germany for 1933, Justus Carl von Ruperti. In Munich just over three weeks ago, Lippold paid tribute to Fritz as one of 'the outstanding personalities' of German Rhodes Scholars, and described him this way:

> Fritz Caspari, 1933, a liberal from Heidelberg who left Germany 1939 for the USA, returned 1954 for the reconstruction of Germany and became Ambassador to Portugal.

Fritz was born in Switzerland in 1914, and was taken by his parents to their native Germany before the outbreak of World War I. His father, an electrical engineer, was in fact on a business trip to Russia when war broke out, and Fritz did not see him again for three and a half years. Some of his earliest memories were of German soldiers returning across the Rhine at the end of the war. No doubt influenced by the strong background of his family in education, and by his mother's pacifism, he was encouraged to visit other European countries as he grew to manhood. Photographs of his European travels all seem to show him swimming.

After securing his Abitur at what he later translated as the 'Humanistic High School' or Gymnasium in Heidelberg, Fritz came in spring 1932 to London to study English and other subjects before returning to spend 1932-33 at the University of Heidelberg. In London he had met Count Albrecht von Bernstorff, a Rhodes Scholar from 1909, and a German liberal who since 1923 had served in the German Embassy in London seeking to promote Anglo-German friendship – precisely what Fritz would do from 1958 to 1963. Bernstorff encouraged Fritz to visit German Rhodes Scholars in Oxford, which he did, staying at Christ Church with G L von dem Knesebeck, a Rhodes Scholar from 1932 who, despite his closeness through Adam von Trott to those who planned the July 1944 assassination attempt against Hitler, survived the war, and whom Fritz visited for the last time on the day Knesebeck died in Lucerne in 1989. Albrecht von Bernstorff was executed by the Gestapo in April 1945, as Soviet forces were entering Berlin just two weeks before the final surrender.

In December 1932, Fritz Caspari was chosen with the aristocratic Justus Carl von Ruperti as one of the two German Rhodes Scholars for 1933. By the time he entered St John's College, Oxford, in October 1933, the Nazis – to whom he was irreconcilably opposed – had come to power in Germany, and the events of subsequent years led Fritz later to say that the Rhodes Scholarship not only shaped his life but saved his life. In Oxford, the charming, sociable and sporting, as well as academically excellent, Fritz impressed his tutors, his college, and the Warden of Rhodes House, and made many friends. These friends included such fellow Rhodes Scholars as Burke Knapp, from Oregon, who arrived at St John's on the same day as Fritz did and with whom he maintained a lifelong friendship until Burke's death in San Francisco in November last year, and C P 'Bill' Lee, from Arkansas, with whom he went to spend the year after Oxford, 1936-37, together teaching at Southwestern University in Memphis, Tennessee. Rowing for St John's, serving as Treasurer of its Archery Club – where women could be hosted – and serving as President of the College's Essay Society, and a member of Vincent's, the Oxford sportsmen's club, Fritz also found what he called 'a home' at Rhodes House, where he developed a close, warm, and enduring friendship with the Warden, C K Allen, and Dorothy Allen.

In his first year in Oxford, Fritz completed the Diploma of Economics, and then spent the academic years 1934 to 1936 researching and writing a BLitt thesis in Modern History on 'The Influence of the Renaissance on the English Conception of the State'. As Hitler was tightening his grip on Germany and increasingly challenging the international order embodied in the League of Nations, the young liberal from Heidelberg was sitting in Oxford writing on how the revival in the Renaissance of the classical Greek and Roman ideals of man and state and the humanistic conception of their relationship had, through the influence of Erasmus and English humanists such as Sir Thomas More and Sir Thomas Elyot, come to help shape the English conception of the state out of which democracy would be re-born and liberalism ultimately emerge. One part of the humanistic tradition was the notion, in Fritz's words of 1936, that 'the ideal gentleman is just, liberal, brave, wise, and temperate'. Was not Fritz himself as fine an example of such an 'ideal gentleman', as well as of a Renaissance man, as one could hope to find?

His 1936 Oxford study was always intended to form the basis of a German doctorate, and after teaching in 1936-37 in Tennessee, Fritz returned to Germany, choosing the young and hitherto un-Nazified University of Hamburg, where he could have a liberal doctoral supervisor, and where in January 1939, after a break of over two months when he was required to serve in the German army in Bavaria, he passed the examination for his doctorate on 'the humanistic influence on English political thought in the 16th century'. This topic was to remain central to his intellectual interests over subsequent decades, forming the basis of his book, *Humanism and the Social Order in Tudor England*, published by the University of Chicago Press in 1954 as he was leaving that University to join the Foreign Service of the fledgling Federal Republic of Germany. His book was reissued in paperback in 1968 in a 'Classics in Education' series from Columbia University, and published in German in 1988.

Renaissance humanism also formed the basis of the teaching he did over decades from 1955 as an Honorary Professor of English Intellectual History at the University of Cologne, and connected with many of the other academic articles and book reviews he published over the decades. One of these, strikingly, was a learned article published in 1946, very soon after the end of the war, on 'Sir Thomas More and Justum Bellum', or just war –

considering More's approval of what we might call humanitarian intervention to free a people from a tyrannical regime.

Fritz's book, *Humanism and the Social Order in Tudor England*, discussed many issues in the context of their day with which Fritz was concerned in the context of his: ideals of excellence of intellect and character, the importance of education and of scholarships in enabling social mobility for talented people not born into the aristocracy, and issues of statecraft. One 1950s reviewer, commending 'this scholarly and excellently written book', wrote:

> Professor Caspari is well aware of [the] dichotomy between the Humanistic and the 'Machiavellian' approach to political ethics. His book is so important because it attempts to show the practical side of Humanism and, hence, to demonstrate the balance which could be achieved between the ideal and the practical.

Fritz had long been committed both to the life of thought and the life of action. He said that he had gone to Oxford hoping to contribute later to the public life of Germany and to international understanding – precisely what Cecil Rhodes had hoped for in creating the scholarships that bear his name. But this was for Fritz not possible in Hitler's Germany. He said in an interview with James Fox decades later: 'The clash between what one might consider one's own liberal spirit and the Nazi spirit was inevitable and also difficult because of the way Hitler abused feelings of devotion to one's own country... and so I emigrated'. In 1939 Fritz went to Scripps College, a women's liberal arts college in Claremont, California, to teach German and history. Interned as an 'alien enemy' on the day after Pearl Harbour in December 1941, he was required to complete an 'alien enemy' questionnaire. Asked 'Why did you come to the United States?', he wrote: 'I found it impossible to live and work under the present regime in Germany, since my convictions prevented me from joining Nazi organisations. I accepted the offers of two American Colleges to come to this country and live and teach freely.'

Asked 'If you have never applied for naturalization [in the United States], state the reasons why', he wrote:

> I regarded myself as a voluntary political exile. I hoped that I might one day be able to aid in the restoration of liberty and decency in Germany and in the collaboration of such free Germany with the Anglo Saxon powers. Many of my English and American friends have urged me to retain my German citizenship for this reason, especially the men of the Rhodes Trust here and in England. If these conditions do not arise I most certainly hope that I may be allowed the privilege of becoming an American Citizen.

Fritz taught at Scripps College from 1939 to 1942, interrupted by being interned twice by over-zealous American authorities. One factor in the spurious case against him was his friendship with Adam von Trott, German Rhodes Scholar for 1931, who was under suspicion from US authorities when he and Fritz, quite unexpectedly to themselves, travelled on the same ship to the US in 1939. While Fritz stayed in the US, von Trott returned to Germany, where he was serving in the Foreign Ministry, and was executed in 1944 for his role in the July plot against Hitler.

When Fritz Caspari was interned in California during the war, gracefully enduring his frustration and displaying his efficiency and ingenuity as a chef in the internment camp, American Rhodes Scholars and other friends worked hard to have him released, writing warm personal commendations. One Rhodes Scholar, Stanley Pargellis, the Librarian of the Newberry Library in Chicago, enabled him to leave California in 1943 to work with him as a research scholar and librarian at the Newberry Library, an independent humanities library. Fritz's work there led to his appointment in 1946 at the University of Chicago as an instructor and then Assistant Professor in German and history, until 1954. During the war, Pargellis wrote of Fritz to the United States Attorney-General:

> I have seen a great deal of him… and know that he is as much a friend of freedom as that term is understood in this country as any American of my acquaintance.

Fritz himself had written to the US Attorney-General in 1942 of his 'fervent hope' that Hitler's 'government, and all the evil that goes with it, will be overthrown', and of his desire to help 'prepare for a better world order based on the "four freedoms"' of President Roosevelt.

No one had worked harder to help secure Fritz Caspari's release than Irving Miller Walker, President of the Board of Trustees of Scripps College, and a lawyer in Los Angeles. In February 1944, Fritz married his daughter, Elita Galdós Walker, and their partnership of 64 years produced four children and several grandchildren. In 1954, in the acknowledgements to his book, which he dedicated to her, Fritz wrote: 'My wife, Elita Walker Caspari, shared the labors of final revision and proofreading, and her judgment in matters of substance and style has been most valuable.' Elita is, as you know, buried in this churchyard.

Elita was committed to going with Fritz to Germany to take part in its restoration when the right opportunity came; and this it did in 1954, when Fritz joined the West German Foreign Service, first as deputy head of the North American Section, and then from 1955 – because he was one of few German diplomats untainted by Nazi association with real knowledge of Britain – as Head of the British, Commonwealth and Irish Section. When, like Albrecht von Bernstorff a generation earlier, Fritz went to the German Embassy in London as counsellor, his Oxford connections contributed to his efforts to nurture Anglo-German friendship.

From 1963 to 1968, Fritz served in the West German mission at the United Nations. It may have been while serving at the UN, or on other travels with him, that Fritz persuaded Willy Brandt not to resign from Kiesinger's grand coalition government of 1966 to 1969. Years later, Fritz and Elita's eldest child, Hans Michael, was to join the staff of the United Nations, during service to which Michael and his wife, Helen, died in a plane crash in Tanzania in 1980. Their funeral service was held in this church precisely 30 years ago today.

In 1968, Fritz and Elita returned to Bonn. Fritz at first had responsibility for German relations with the Third World and the UN, and from 1969 to 1974 served as deputy head and chief foreign affairs adviser in the office of the President of the Federal Republic, Gustav Heinemann, including accompanying him on trips as part of a campaign for reconciliation with countries invaded by Nazi Germany.

In 1974, soon after the so-called 'carnation revolution' in Portugal, Fritz went to Lisbon as German Ambassador. As Portugal teetered on the brink of civil war and with the real risk of terrorism and of communist seizure of power, Fritz – at risk to his own safety – played an important role in encouraging democratic parties; helping Portuguese democratic parties deepen links with German parties, trade unions, and other civil society bodies; facilitating Willy Brandt's reassuring early visit; encouraging other western powers not to give up on the infant democracy; resisting military exuberance while protecting democrats and would-be defectors; and much else. In a lecture he gave in retirement to the British Historical Society in Portugal, Fritz suggested that one reason Germans took such sympathetic interest in the Portuguese revolution which in 1974 peacefully overthrew a dictatorship was the failure 30 years before of the attempt within Germany itself to overthrow their much-worse dictatorship and the need for this to be done from outside.

Honoured in many countries, Fritz had already been elected an Honorary Fellow of St John's College, Oxford, and knighted by the Queen in 1972, and awarded the Grand Cross of the German Order of Merit in 1974. His contribution to the consolidation of democracy in Portugal earned him Portuguese recognition also. As you know, he and Elita continued to live in Portugal in retirement, with time in Germany and increasingly in England as the years went on.

Described in the 1930s by the Warden of Rhodes House as 'an excellent Rhodes Scholar', Fritz was always loyal and active in the Rhodes community, and – a superb correspondent – over the decades kept in close touch with Rhodes House and Rhodes alumni activities. Just this year, he was interviewed by two current German Rhodes Scholars, I visited him at Greenwich and only at the last minute did illness prevent him from coming to a reception at Rhodes House marking the 40th anniversary of the reinstated post-war German Rhodes Scholarships which he had helped to bring about, and we videoed interviews with him and with Conrad*, which will soon appear on the Rhodes House website as a documentary on aspects of Fritz's remarkable life.

In 1957, an update form from Rhodes House asked Rhodes Scholars for a 'short form of present occupation'. Fritz wrote: 'civil servant and professor'. So he was: Renaissance man, Renaissance historian, and man of action in the Renaissance of his own country and, unexpectedly, of another. Today, with gratitude and pride, we salute this 'liberal from Heidelberg' who balanced the practical and the ideal, and the 'ideal gentleman' – 'just, liberal, brave, wise, and temperate'. His own words of 1936 form, I think, a fitting epitaph to this remarkable man – widely admired, deeply loved, and an inspiration to us all.

---

* Conrad Caspari, Sir Fritz's son.

Scholarships for China

China Oxford Scholarships

Welcome to China Oxford Scholarship Fund Scholars
Rhodes House, Oxford
25 November 2011

It's a very great pleasure for me as the Warden of Rhodes House to join the Chancellor* in welcoming you to Rhodes House today. We are absolutely delighted that you are here.

Our links with China include, most recently, hosting in this room just a few weeks ago a lunch for the Chinese Vice-Premier for Economic Policy, Wang Qishan. It was a great privilege to have him here with the Ambassador and many other colleagues, as it is a very great privilege to have you here today.

Behind me you may have noticed this bust of Cecil Rhodes, for whom this building is named and for whom the Rhodes Scholarships are named. Cecil Rhodes, in the late 19th century and the beginning of the 20th century, had a vision of a scholarship program that would bring outstanding young people to Oxford. They would be chosen on much the same criteria, I think, as China Oxford Scholars are chosen: criteria of intellect, character, capacity for leadership, and commitment to service. Rhodes had a vision that such young people from many countries around the world would come into the collegiate environment of Oxford, and that here they would be encouraged and nurtured to be leaders for the future – people who would in their various countries make a difference for good, in the future of their profession, the future of their communities, the future of their country.

---

* Lord Patten of Barnes (Chris Patten), Chancellor of the University of Oxford and, inter alia, last Governor of Hong Kong.

Rhodes also aspired, through the mixing of students from many countries in Oxford, to encourage understanding between countries, and indeed to make a contribution to peace between nations. In 1901, he wrote that 'educational relations [between countries] make the strongest tie.' He believed that by bringing these exceptional young people together in the collegiate environment of Oxford, they'd get to know other future leaders from other countries here, and this would promote international understanding that would be conducive to harmony, cooperation, and peace between countries.

It seems to me that in 2011 that vision remains as vital and important as it was then. The China Oxford Scholarships serve a great purpose – as I cannot avoid believing the Rhodes Scholarships serve a great purpose – both in nurturing young people who will be leaders in the future, and encouraging connections between future leaders of many countries, which will promote international understanding and good relations between countries.

That only happens if the outstanding young people, such as yourselves, in coming to Oxford, get to know other students of other countries. It's important to get to know British students, and students of the other 144 countries that are represented amongst the student body of Oxford. As someone who came from overseas, in my case from Australia, as a student to Oxford, I know that that's sometimes easier said than done. You need to work at it. You need to keep on extending the hand of friendship yourself, seeking out every opportunity that you can to get to know students of other countries, students of other cultures, students of backgrounds different to your own. Oftentimes that's extremely hard work – but it's worth it. If you can achieve that, then as well as the benefit you gain from your academic studies, you will achieve something that is profoundly enriching for yourself personally, and you may make a major contribution to the future of your country, and its good future relations with other countries around the world.

It is in this spirit that I say again how welcome you are here today. If this is your first time here, I hope it is the first of many – and if you've been here before, please come again. China Oxford Scholars will always be warmly welcome here.

Rhodes Scholarships for China

In consultation with Rhodes Scholars around the world early in my time as Warden of Rhodes House, the idea of Rhodes Scholarships for China (and for a number of other countries) arose. These extracts from speeches reproduced earlier in this volume – the first in the section 'On leadership', the second in this section 'On peace' – reflect how the Rhodes Trust's thinking on this developed.

From 'Developing leaders for a world of global forces and
rapid change'
University of Oxford alumni reception
Auckland, New Zealand, 6 August 2011

As we all know, the benefits of mixing in Oxford with students of other countries are enormous. When in 1901, Cecil Rhodes provided for Rhodes Scholarships for Germany, in addition to those he had already provided for from the United States and much of the then British Empire, he said, 'The object is that an understanding between the three great powers will render war impossible and educational relations make the strongest tie'. Today, in sustained consultation in the Rhodes community, we have been asking – how should we think about this today? From what countries should Rhodes Scholars come in the 21st century? I am cautiously optimistic that, in time, this will (for example) lead to Rhodes Scholars from China, and from other countries, including several in Africa, not currently served by Rhodes Scholarships – at the same time as we work hard to raise the funds needed to fund the Rhodes Scholarships we currently offer, including three each year here in New Zealand.

By doing this, we can better develop a globally-connected network of exceptional young people who will become leaders in diverse fields in their various countries, better able to take on the problems of this century of hope and challenge.

From 'To "render war impossible": the Rhodes Scholarships, educational relations between countries, and peace' 'Sailing Dinner' of the Canadian Association of Rhodes Scholars Ottawa, 24 September 2011

A third possible implication of having Rhodes's focus on peace clearly in mind is in our thinking about what countries Rhodes Scholars should come from in the 21st century. In the consultation of Scholars around the world over the last two years, asking from what countries there should be Rhodes Scholars, there has been considerable support for seeking the additional resources needed to increase Rhodes Scholarships from India and Africa, to reinstate them in some places where they have been cut, and in time, with proper safeguards and great care, to create Rhodes Scholarships from China and perhaps other parts of the world. Input from Scholars is helping the Trustees towards a strategic vision of the best geographic footprint for the Rhodes Scholarships so that they have the greatest relevance and positive impact possible in the world of the 21st century. It is early days, but I am quietly confident that in time good will come. Throughout, of course, we will protect the criteria, selection process, quality assurance, and reputation of the Rhodes Scholarships.

The Schwarzman Scholarships: The Rhodes Scholarships of China?

The Interpreter
Lowy Institute for International Policy
22 April 2013

A flurry of well-orchestrated publicity yesterday heralded the exciting announcement in Beijing that American private equity billionaire Steve Schwarzman is leading the creation of a US$300 million scholarship fund to take students from the US and many other countries to undertake Masters degrees at Tsinghua University, Beijing.

The Schwarzman Scholarships represent the most significant educational philanthropy ever from the West towards China, and arguably one of the most striking acts of educational philanthropy in history.

The Schwarzman Scholarships are inspired by the Rhodes Scholarships, which since 1903 have taken exceptional students from many countries to the University of Oxford. They are clearly intended to be the Rhodes Scholarships of Asia. The core purposes of the Schwarzman and Rhodes Scholarships are the same: to promote international understanding and to help develop what Schwarzman calls 'future leaders' and the Rhodes Trust calls 'leaders for the world's future'.

Two hundred Schwarzman Scholars each year will be chosen from the US, China, and the 'rest of the world' on criteria similar to those for the Rhodes, expressed by Schwarzman as 'academic credentials, extracurricular interests and leadership potential'. They will go to Tsinghua University for a year to undertake one of four newly-designed Masters degrees, taught in English, and (it seems) will live in the Schwarzman College which is being created there.

There are queries and quibbles.

Why were African students excluded from the 'rest of the

world' eligibility for the scholarships? (It is said that this can be reviewed; it should be.) Wouldn't the impact of the Scholarship be greater if Schwarzman Scholars spent two or more years at Tsinghua, as Rhodes Scholars do in Oxford? Is it best for the Scholars all to be concentrated in a small number of courses and in one college? (Rhodes Scholars are dispersed across many courses and many colleges in Oxford.) Where will the remaining $100 million to make up the planned $300 million fund be sought? ($100 million has come from Steve Schwarzman, and $100 million from other donors, especially Western companies operating in China.)

Has the honorary advisory group been chosen for prestige or for real input? It includes, for example, three former US Secretaries of State (Kissinger, Powell, and Rice), three former Prime Ministers (Blair of Britain, Mulroney of Canada, and Rudd of Australia) and several other of the global 'great and good'. It has many Western members and only one Chinese; and, equally or even more surprisingly, there is only one woman.

The questions asked here do not detract from the likely profound significance of this initiative. If the Schwarzman Scholarships come anywhere near to fulfilling their goals, they will make an important contribution to answering in a positive way one of the most important questions of the 21st century: how will the rise of China and the use of growing Chinese power, and the response of the US and other states, affect the prospects for stability and peace in the international system?

The creation of the Schwarzman Scholarships at Tsinghua University reflects and will promote the rise of Chinese universities which aspire to being truly world class. They may also help to encourage efforts at liberal and collegiate education which have emerged in recent years in various Chinese and other Asian universities, including through the influence of Yale University, whose retiring President, Richard Levin, serves on the Schwarzman advisory group.

It is very much to be hoped that the creation of the

Schwarzman Scholarships will encourage the continuing development of a culture of educational philanthropy around the world, drawing on the US model of philanthropic generosity (and reflected recently in Australia in the outstanding $50 million gift to create the Tuckwell Scholarships at the Australian National University).

The unprecedented announcement, after his death in 1902, of Cecil Rhodes's vision of international scholarships and his massive bequest for them electrified much of the English-speaking and wider world. It is no surprise that the Schwarzman Scholarships are receiving major attention around the world today. They represent a breathtaking initiative that seems brilliantly fitted to the needs and opportunities of the 21st century. One can only hope the Schwarzman Scholarships will have as profound an impact for good as the Rhodes Scholarships have had and continue to have.

John Maynard Keynes: economic paths to war and peace

Keynes and international economic and political relations

Seminar on 'The Contemporary Relevance of John Maynard Keynes"

Trinity College, The University of Melbourne, 1 April 2009

It is a great pleasure to be back in the Sharwood Room, and at Trinity College, here in the University of Melbourne, for this seminar held under the auspices of the fund created with generosity and vision by my friend Bruce McComish to encourage revival of the study of economic history.

The current global economic turbulence is certainly encouraging aspects of such a revival, including a remarkable surge of interest in and indeed rehabilitation of the Cambridge economist John Maynard Keynes. If you seek evidence for this, just google the words 'John Maynard Keynes' and '2009', '2008', etc. But there is much more to Keynes than is captured in the proposition, widely shared but also much disputed, that this is a 'Keynesian moment' in economic history.

Marion Poynter in her magnificent 'life with letters' of Valentine Leeper, daughter of the first Warden of Trinity, quotes a letter to Valentine in 1922 from her brother Rex, who was in the British Foreign Office. Rex Leeper wrote: 'The present reparation arrangements are of course absurd. Keynes' books on this question are quite sound.'[†] Valentine Leeper's other brother in the Foreign Office, Allen Leeper, had, like Keynes,

---

* This paper was previously published under the same title, as Trinity Paper No. 33, by Trinity College, University of Melbourne.

† Marion Poynter, *Nobody's Valentine: Letters in the Life of Valentine Alexa Leeper, 1900–2001*, Miegunyah Press, Melbourne, 2008, p. 52.

been part of the British team at the Paris Peace Conference in 1919, Keynes as the principal Treasury representative until his resignation in June 1919, and Leeper as a member of the Foreign Office team.

This is not the only link between Keynes and members of this college and university. For example, Keynes's *Collected Writings* contain two letters from Keynes to a member of this college, Clive Latham Baillieu, Baron Baillieu as he became, in 1932 regarding depression policies in Australia and Britain.* A paper of mine on *Keynes and Australia* – written when I was working at the Reserve Bank under Peter Jonson and published by the Reserve Bank when I was Warden of Trinity – refers to this, and also to academics and academic visitors at the University of Melbourne, such as L F Giblin and W B Reddaway, who were important in bringing Keynes's *General Theory* to Australia in the 1930s.[†]

One of Keynes's letters to Baillieu spoke of the desirability in Australia of 'a program of public works for the reduction of unemployment'.[‡] It is precisely this – public works to reduce unemployment, or more generally fiscal stimulus to prevent or combat recession – that is most commonly associated with Keynes, and that many people seem to mean when they have said over the last six months or so that Keynesian policies are, or are not, needed in the global financial crisis (and now global recession) which we face. It is striking that this is the position, much resisted though it is, of the major international economic institutions, the IMF and World Bank, which Keynes helped create at Bretton Woods, and of the US and British governments, supported by Australia.

Although forecasts in the last 24 hours for growth, trade, and employment may strengthen the case for further stimulus

---

* *The Collected Writings of John Maynard Keynes* (hereafter CW), vol. 21, pp. 100-2, 112-13. On Trinity alumnus R G Casey, see CW, vol. 23, p. 321.

† Donald Markwell, *Keynes and Australia*, Reserve Bank of Australia, 2000.

‡ CW, vol. 21, p. 102.

in some countries, it seems to me that the task of working out Keynes's contemporary relevance is quite complex. Part of his genius is that his mind was endlessly moving. His voluminous, elegant and nuanced writings reflect the evolution of his thought and his ever-evolving responses to the circumstances of his day. It is not only that he was a classical economist before he became a Keynesian, and that this evolution took many years. He did not regard *The General Theory* as a final statement, and might well have produced yet another work of economic theory had he not been struck down by ill health and then consumed by the war effort. He made innumerable economic policy proposals, in many cases continually evolving to meet changing circumstances. This was as evident in his role in the planning during World War II for post-war international economic institutions and policy as it was during the Depression of the 1930s or in seeking the moderation of reparations demands against Germany from late in World War I until the end of reparations in the early 1930s. We can be confident that had Keynes miraculously lived on until the present day – he would have turned 125 last year! – his economic theory and policy proposals would have evolved considerably from where they were the day he died at the age of 62 in April 1946.

Shakespeare tells us that 'The devil can cite Scripture for his purpose'. As various misquotations and uncontextualised quotes from Keynes reflect, the devil can also cite Keynes for his purpose.

The word 'Keynesian' is itself problematic. Allan Meltzer, who wishes to depict Keynes as far less inclined to activist fiscal policy than the word 'Keynesian' was taken to mean, quotes Joan Robinson as writing in 1979:*

> In fact Maynard Keynes himself was somewhat sceptical about the possibility of achieving *permanent* full employment. When he

---

* Joan Robinson quoted from Allan H Meltzer, *Keynes's Monetary Theory: A Different Interpretation*, Cambridge University Press, 1988, p. 296.

dined in Washington with his converts, he told Austin Robinson next day: 'I was the only non-Keynesian there'. It was his British disciples, rather than he, who drafted the white paper in 1944 which proclaimed that it is the responsibility of government to maintain a high and stable level of employment. Keynes said: 'You can promise to be good but you cannot promise to be clever.'

I would say that Keynes was more concerned about the risks of inflation, less favourable to sustained deficit financing, less focussed on fiscal policy and more on monetary policy, more interested in keeping interest rates low, and more favourable to the use of free markets to allocate resources than was generally implied by the word 'Keynesian' as it came to be used by the 1960s and 1970s. In response to the excessively simplistic contrasting we sometimes see of Keynesian interventionist economics with the free market or laissez faire approaches associated most famously with Hayek and Friedman, it is worth recalling Keynes's letter to Hayek after reading *The Road to Serfdom* in 1944:[*]

> In my opinion it is a grand book. We all have the greatest reason to be grateful to you for saying so well what needs so much to be said.

Another of the problems of identifying the current relevance of Keynes is that we cannot be wholly confident we fully understand the nature and causes of the present crisis, including how long and deep it is likely to be.

Despite reservations about how we approach the contemporary relevance of Keynes and Keynesian ideas, I do believe that we can discern in Keynes's thought ideas which he clearly held to for sustained periods and which are highly relevant to our circumstances today. At the most general level, Keynes was one of the most influential advocates in history of

---

[*] CW, vol. 27, p. 385.

active economic management and of international cooperation in this. While the voices, including those of Barack Obama and Gordon Brown, have been loud and many for an active and coordinated international response to the current crisis, it has also been striking, not only how many critics there have been of major fiscal stimulus, but also how many commentators advocating Keynesian policies have argued for this essentially in the context of a single country only, neglecting the need for international cooperation. Even such sophisticated economists as Paul Krugman seem to me to have done this too often.

Keynes repeatedly recognised the need for US leadership in international economic cooperation, and it is likely he would advocate it today, combined (one might suspect) with encouraging the co-operation of other powers, such as China, whose actions in domestic stimulus and foreign lending are potentially of enormous international consequence.

As we meet here today at Trinity College, the leaders of the G20 countries are preparing to meet in London to discuss responses to the economic crisis. The *New York Times* columnist David Brooks recently wrote:[*]

> This is a global crisis, and a core lesson of the Great Depression is that a global crisis calls for a global response. As such, Tim Geithner and Larry Summers are preparing for the upcoming G20 summit with an agenda that has the merit of actually addressing the problem at hand: coordinate global stimulus, strengthen the International Monetary Fund, preserve open trade.

This, it seems to me, is the essence of the international relevance of Keynes today.

My understanding of Keynes and international economic and political relations is set out in my book, also published while I was Warden of this College, entitled *John Maynard Keynes*

---

[*] David Brooks, 'Perverse Cosmic Myopia', *The New York Times*, 19 March 2009.

and International Relations: Economic Paths to War and Peace.[*] It argues that Keynes should be considered as an idealist thinker about international relations who believed it 'possible to replace the conflictual international politics of the past with greater harmony and peace; that important in his particular form of idealism was the belief … that there are major economic causes of war, and that peace could be promoted by economic means; and that his evolving ideas about the economic determinants of war and peace were central to his contributions to planning and debating post-war reconstruction during and after both world wars'.[†] I might mention that another notable inter-war idealist thinker, from the extraordinary group of British scholars of classical Greece who became leading advocates of the League of Nations and a rule of law in international affairs, was a Trinity alumna, one of the first resident students of the Trinity Women's Hostel in the 1880s, Melian Stawell. Her portrait hangs behind the High Table in the College Dining Hall.[‡]

Keynes's contribution to post-war reconstruction reminds us that successful post-war reconstruction – such as today in Iraq and Afghanistan – generally requires effective measures to promote economic growth and prosperity. This economic emphasis underpins the Obama administration's recently-announced policy in Afghanistan and Pakistan.

Keynes's writings mentioned several economic factors which he believed could cause war, including impoverishment, population pressure, penetration by foreign capital, and the 'competitive struggle for markets'.[§] My book traces Keynes's thinking through four phases. First, as a classical liberal, brought up in the late 19th century with the classical liberal notion that free trade promotes

---

[*] Donald Markwell, *John Maynard Keynes and International Relations: Economic Paths to War and Peace*, Oxford University Press, 2006.

[†] Ibid., p. 3.

[‡] On Melian Stawell, see *'A large and liberal education': higher education for the 21st century*, pp. 105-8.

[§] Markwell, *Keynes and IR*, p. 3.

peace, something he believed through to the very early 1930s. 'Second, however, by 1919 he had concluded that internationally agreed state action was necessary to reconstruct and manage the international economy so that economic interdependence could work. This early liberal institutionalism' was evident in Keynes's approach at and after the Paris Peace Conference, including in *The Economic Consequences of the Peace* and subsequent proposals for the restoration of the European economy after the devastation of war and the further damage of the 1919 settlement. Keynes's approach then 'foreshadowed both his search for a middle way between laissez-faire and Marxian socialism, and [what I call] his mature liberal institutionalism of 1936-46. Before then, however, reflecting the protectionist and autarkic ideas of the Depression years, Keynes came temporarily to believe that a higher degree of economic isolation and national self-sufficiency might be more conducive to peace than economic internationalism was. This third view culminated in articles he wrote in 1933. Fourth, Keynes came to think that, if there were an international monetary system that did not pit the interests of countries against each other, and if states could and did pursue economic policies to promote full employment, then there would be no economic causes of war (other perhaps than population pressure). A high degree of freedom of trade would then be compatible with, and might promote, peace. This mature liberal institutionalism found expression in *The General Theory*, and underlay Keynes's attempts during the Second World War to build a suitable international monetary system and to promote the pursuit of Keynesian policies internationally."

As already suggested, it seems to me that the three key ideas that emerge from Keynes that are most relevant to international issues today are: first, the importance of international coordination of fiscal and monetary stimulus; secondly, the

---

* Ibid., pp. 3-4. (The only other discussion of which I am aware of the passages on war and peace in *The General Theory* is at Hyman Minsky, *John Maynard Keynes*, Columbia University Press, 1975, p. 159 .)

importance of global economic governance in the form of strong and effective international economic institutions such as the International Monetary Fund and the World Bank; and thirdly, the importance of resisting economic nationalism and protectionism, and of maintaining an open international economy. Each of these propositions requires elaboration that times does not permit; and – again – I do not pretend to know what Keynes himself would have thought in the circumstances of today.

For example, I am not confident to assert that Keynes would have seen stimulating demand as more important than restoring bank lending through the quarantining of toxic assets, or than improved financial regulation, domestic and international. Nor can we be confident how much or what kind of stimulus Keynes would think the present recession requires, or (though I think this unlikely) whether like some European leaders, such as Angela Merkel, he might think there has been enough for now. Nor can we be confident what he would have said of proposed or actual bailouts of banks, other financial institutions, and other companies, such as car companies.

I suspect Keynes would have been sympathetic to the proposal of World Bank President Robert Zoellick that a percentage of developed government fiscal stimulus be devoted to international development, and sympathetic also to the expansion of IMF resources widely expected to be discussed and agreed at the G20 in London. Keynes had a profound sense of the shifting of economic and political power, so I imagine he would have favoured reform of international institutions such as the IMF to reflect the rise of China and other powers; but the exact reforms he would favour it is not possible to say. Likewise, we can't know what he would have said of proposals, most recently renewed by the Chinese government, for an international reserve currency other than the US dollar – though this proposal is reminiscent of Keynes's own repeated proposals for an international currency such as bancor.

Some people hope, and others fear, that the current crisis means the end of modern capitalism and of globalisation. It is unlikely Keynes would have wished this, though he would no doubt have wished to reform modern capitalism and to make globalisation work better. Indeed, Keynesian economics was an attempt to save capitalism, domestically and internationally, by reforming and managing it. Keynes also believed, contrary to 1930s socialists who believed that capitalism caused war, that this need not be so, and that by managing capitalism well peace could be promoted.

It is important to recognise that Keynes had a brief period, in the early 1930s, as a protectionist. But for the vast majority of his life, both before and after, he favoured free trade, and believed it promoted peace. 'Keynes sometimes advocated free, or at least non-discriminatory, trade – for example, in 1903 and again in 1945 – because the alternative, exclusionist economic blocs, would cause friction and animosity. Sometimes it was the role of free trade in maintaining living standards, and hence domestic political order, that Keynes stressed; and sometimes a more nebulous hint that trade promoted international solidarity."* Like many other people, I am concerned that the professions by world leaders of commitment to free trade – commitments reflected in the World Trade Organisation, and reiterated in the current crisis at such meetings as the Asia-Europe meeting in Beijing last October, and the G20 in Washington and APEC meeting in Chile last November – are giving way in practice to capitulation to domestic protectionist pressures which risk leading to catastrophic economic nationalism.

We have already seen economic crisis in some countries, such as Iceland and Latvia, lead to domestic social and political instability; and the risk of this in some other countries, such as China, even from reduced growth is much talked about.

Keynes points us to the risk of economic nationalism leading

---

* Markwell, *Keynes and IR*, p. 270.

to international political conflict, including war. This, in my view, is a risk the avoidance of which requires concerted political leadership. Related potential economic causes of international conflict have been referred to in recent months. For example, last November the US National Intelligence Council in a report on global trends towards 2025 raised the prospect of international conflict over energy security.[*] In January this year, Hillary Clinton said:[†]

> … climate change is an unambiguous security threat. At the extreme it threatens our very existence, but well before that point, it could very well incite new wars of an old kind – over basic resources like food, water, and arable land. The world is in need of an urgent, coordinated response to climate change and, as [Barack] Obama has said, America must be a leader in developing and implementing it.

It is in this spirit, I think, that President Obama has recently arranged meetings for the 'major economies' on energy security and climate change. Efforts to combine economic stimulus with measures against climate change have given rise to the notion of a so-called 'Green New Deal'.

Recent discussions of economic causes of war are somewhat reminiscent of some of Keynes's discussions of economic causes of war. Not least, his work highlights the risk simply of economic depression leading to international political conflict – a powerful reason, if it be needed, for concerted domestic and international action to minimise the depth and length of the current global recession.

If this seems apocalyptic, perhaps it is as well to remember that recalling Keynes means to recall also a world in which the

---

[*] National Intelligence Council, *Global Trends 2025: A Transformed World*, November 2008, accessible at http://www.fas.org/irp/nic/2025.pdf

[†] Hillary Clinton, Nomination Hearing to be Secretary of State, 13 January 2009, quoted from http://www.state.gov/secretary/rm/2009a/01/115196.htm

great benign globalisation and growing interdependence of the late 19th and early 20th centuries gave way to two world wars interspersed with a great global depression. We cannot rest complacently on the assumption that this cannot happen in our time, with our own great globalisation so abruptly interrupted. We must work resolutely to ensure that it does not. It is my hope that the leaders now assembling in London will carry with them enough of the spirit of Keynes to take enough of the measures of international economic co-operation that are needed – and that this spirit is sustained through the many challenges of the long haul ahead.

Keynes and Germany, 1919

In May 2013, the historian Niall Ferguson provoked a storm of controversy with remarks suggesting that Keynes's economics were shaped by his being homosexual (he was bisexual) and childless. Being concerned for historical accuracy and the avoidance of prejudice, I pointed out that Ferguson had previously (in *The Spectator* in April 1995[*]) baselessly alleged that Keynes's approach to Germany in 1919 was shaped by a homosexual attraction to a German, Dr Carl Melchior. In apologising for his 'stupid' remarks of 2013, Ferguson nonetheless reiterated his view that 'The strong attraction he felt for the German banker Carl Melchior undoubtedly played a part in shaping Keynes' views on the Treaty of Versailles and its aftermath.'[†] Ferguson's claim, far from being 'undoubtedly' true, is very much open to doubt; indeed, I had sought to rebut what he had written in *The Spectator* in my book, *John Maynard Keynes and International Relations: Economic Paths to War and Peace*. The single most important point, amongst many, was that Keynes had formed his view on the key issues, including

---

[*] Niall Ferguson, 'Let Germany Keep Its Nerve', *The Spectator*, 22 April 1995, pp. 21-3.

[†] Niall Ferguson, 'An Open Letter to the Harvard Community', *The Harvard Crimson*, 7 May 2013 – http://www.thecrimson.com/article/2013/5/7/Ferguson-Apology-Keynes/

reparations, *before* he met Melchior at Treves in mid-January 1919, so that those views could not have been formed because of any attraction he felt to Melchior.

The following comprises extracts from my detailed discussion in *John Maynard Keynes and International Relations: Economic Paths to War and Peace* of Keynes's role and thinking on issues related to Germany before, during, and after the Paris Peace Conference of 1919.* Many dozens of footnote references to this section, most based on archival research, may be found in that book; it seemed redundant to reproduce them all here.

From John Maynard Keynes and International Relations: Economic Paths to War and Peace *(Oxford University Press, 2006).*

At the end of 1918, Keynes had a clear view of some of the elements of the post-war order he wished to see. His liberal-idealist faith in free trade, on which he had been brought up, was unshaken. He had urged the abandonment of inter-Allied debt, and Britain's forgoing her share of reparations, which he hoped would go to assist the new states. He had urged a moderate approach to reparations; and clearly wished the defeated powers to be treated so that they would not need assistance to avoid starvation, unemployment, anarchy, or perhaps Bolshevism. The fundamental views which underlay his actions at the peace conference, and which were expounded in *The Economic Consequences*, were already formed, and were shared by many others. But these views of the honourable, prudent, and practicable treatment of the defeated enemy, and what post-war arrangements would conduce to peace, were under fierce challenge within the British government. Which view would prevail would now be determined both by continuing struggle within the British government, and by the attitudes of the other powers, especially the USA, at Paris and after.

---

* Donald Markwell, *John Maynard Keynes and International Relations: Economic Paths to War and Peace,* Oxford University Press, 2006, pp. 53-63, 89-90. Reprinted by permission of Oxford University Press.

The Paris Peace Conference and the Need for International Action

From January to June 1919, Keynes was the principal British Treasury representative at the Paris Peace Conference (PPC). He was the Chancellor of the Exchequer's representative on the Supreme Economic Council (SEC) from its creation in February, and a member of its Finance Section (FS), and of various other committees. Keynes became an important, but by no means lone, advocate at Paris of the need for concerted international action to restart the European economy. He argued that relief must be provided to prevent starvation. War debts should, if possible, be forgiven. Reparations should be kept within Germany's moral obligation and capacity to pay. But the European economy, which was dependent on Germany, would not resume working if private enterprise were left unaided. Guarantees of credit, especially from the USA, were necessary. So, while Keynes wished there to be free trade and private enterprise, laissez-faire was not enough. He and others fought hard against those whose vision of the peace was more punitive than their own, especially those who saw continuing conflict with Germany as unavoidable and harmony impossible. In the event, Keynes so opposed the Treaty of Versailles that, in early June, he resigned from the Treasury in anger and exhaustion, and subsequently launched a great public assault on the Treaty.

For Keynes, the most important international relationship at Paris was the Anglo-American. He thought that the USA could forgive war debts, and lend to restart the European economy, and offered the greatest hope of moderating the reparation demands. Keynes believed that, in general, there were no necessary conflicts of policy between the USA and Britain, and strove to ensure Anglo-American cooperation at Paris. He worked closely with the US financial and economic experts, some of whom believed that US 'leadership' on such issues as relief was essential. But American power was not used as Keynes, and those American officials, believed necessary for European reconstruction. As Wilson and McAdoo had done during the war, some other US officials saw the economic dependence of Allied powers on the USA as creating the opportunity for the USA to exercise power over them.

[The chapter from which this is an excerpt] deals in turn with Keynes's activities during the peace conference concerning food supplies for Germany and Austria; seeking cancellation of war debts, and promoting a credit scheme for the rehabilitation of Europe; and concerning reparations, including his attempt to modify the draft Treaty. For brevity, the Allied and Associated Powers are referred to here as the Allies.

Feeding Germany and Austria

In the early months of 1919 Keynes was actively engaged in negotiations on relief to Germany and Austria, which, in the case of Germany, initially arose in the context of Armistice renewal talks. The blockade of Germany, imposed during the war, had been continued under the Armistice agreement. In January 1919, this agreement was due for renewal. Like many others, especially in the US team at Paris (including Wilson, Hoover, and others), Keynes feared the spread of Bolshevism in Germany unless relief were given immediately. Although Keynes had in late 1918 recognized the danger of Bolshevism in Germany, and was to do so repeatedly at Paris and after, he later wondered if some British anxiety over German food supplies had been exaggerated.

In January, Keynes was involved in discussing the 'financial constitution' of the Inter-Ally Supreme Council for Supply and Relief, including the shares that each state would carry of the financial burden of relief. Keynes favoured Britain's taking a 25 per cent share, more than Bonar Law wished, making an obligation of £12,500,000 (which Britain assumed). Britain was still both borrowing from the USA, and lending to other states. Keynes sought further British borrowing from the USA, arguing that without it Britain would not be able to take its part in the relief operation. The Treasury in Washington was strongly opposed to further lending, but Keynes found US Treasury officials in Paris, such as Norman Davis, more receptive. Britain's need for American help to provide relief was a recurrent issue (arising also, e.g., in Austrian relief).

Food for Germany

The Supreme Council for Supply and Relief, on which Keynes served under Lord Reading, decided on 12 January to supply the Germans with 270,000 tons of food (cereal, fats, and condensed milk). But the problem of how Germany would pay for these supplies divided the victorious powers (especially pitting France against Britain and the USA) and dominated a series of conferences between delegates of the Allies, including Keynes, and Germany: on 15-16 January, and again on 14-16 February at Treves; on 4-5 March at Spa; and on 13-14 March in Brussels. The food supplies agreed in January did not begin until after Brussels.

Dr Carl Melchior was a German spokesman in these and later meetings. Keynes was over time to develop a friendship with him that included correspondence and contact, intermittently, over many years. In 1921, Keynes wrote a moving, though incomplete and not invariably accurate, account of his dealings with Melchior.[*] Ferguson has suggested that Keynes's approach to Germany in 1919 was significantly influenced by a homosexual infatuation with Melchior.[†] Even if that is an accurate depiction of Keynes's attitude to Melchior, which is not certain, it is clear that Keynes, having been thinking about reparations since 1916, had formed his own views before any

---

[*] 'Dr Melchior', CW, vol. 10, pp. 389-429; for date, see vol. 30, p. 165.

[†] N Ferguson, 'Let Germany Keep Its Nerve', *The Spectator*, 22 April 1995, p. 21. Cf, N. Ferguson, *Paper and Iron* (Cambridge, 1995), pp. 211 ff, 226-8, 448, where some of the points made below are acknowledged. See also Ferguson, [*The Pity of War*, London, 1998], p. 400; Ferguson, 'Keynes and German Inflation', [*English Historical Review*, 1995], p. 369. Cf, MacMillan's robust approach ([Margaret MacMillan, *Peacemakers: The Paris Conference of 1919 and Its Attempt to End War]*, p. 193) with Keylor (in [M F Boemeke et al. (eds), *The Treaty of Versailles: A Reassessment after 75 Years*, Washington, DC & Cambridge, UK, 1998], p. 486) …

dealings with the Germans. Others in the British and American teams had formed the same views. Admiration for Melchior, far from being an idiosyncrasy of Keynes's, was expressed in April by Lloyd George and in May by Woodrow Wilson.

At the first Treves conference, Keynes saw as a very important concession that the Supreme War Council (SWC) had (as he had wished) authorized Germany to use her liquid resources to buy food, rather than keeping those resources to be taken as reparations. But the central practical problems for the British and the Americans, who wished to facilitate the supply of food to Germany, remained getting French agreement to Germany's paying with gold, and getting German agreement to hand over her shipping, all the while making clear to Germany that there could be no credits for food. Tensions between Britain and the USA, on one side, and France on the other, and between civilian and military authorities, were evident in Keynes's and Davis's recurrent tensions with Foch.

It has been suggested that 'the attraction Keynes felt for' Melchior in their first meetings on relief 'strongly influenced his judgment'.* If by this it is implied that the way Keynes handled the relief question reflected an infatuation with Melchior, or a bias in favour of Germany regardless of the merits of the case, then three points may be made against the claim. First, there were good reasons for Keynes to favour food relief in Germany: humanitarian concern, and the desire to avoid Bolshevism (or reaction) bred of hunger. At the time of the second Treves conference, for example, the situation was, or appeared to Keynes to be, that if Bolshevism were to be staved off, Germany's need for food supplies was urgent; the Germans insisted that their food supply should be assured before they surrendered their ships; the French refused to allow German gold to be used to buy food; the Germans did not have adequate other liquid resources; and no loan would be forthcoming from the Allies. After this February conference, Keynes was more than ever convinced that the only possible solution lay in allowing Germany to use her

---

* Ferguson, 'Nerve', p. 21.

gold to buy food. Immediately after the Brussels conference, Keynes's mother expressed the hope 'that you will be able to get some food into those hungry mouths before it is too late'.

Second, Keynes's concern, and impatience with what he perceived as French obstruction, was shared by others who (unlike many Frenchmen) had no reason to seek maximum reparations: most importantly, American officials such as Herbert Hoover and Norman Davis. On 19 January, Davis told Carter Glass, the US Treasury Secretary, that Treves had persuaded him that the German 'condition is graver than we thought'. Of course German officials sought to encourage this perception: but it was shared by British and American officials able to make independent judgements. On 20 January, Keynes sent Davis copies of two telegrams he had received on growing anarchy in Germany. At the time of the Spa conference in early March, Robert Lansing, the US Secretary of State, wrote that Germany was on the verge of 'Soviet Government', and that the situation could have been averted with food and raw materials two months before:

> We were ready to have the blockade lifted and the food and raw materials go in, but the Allies, particularly the military chiefs, opposed. Great Britain finally saw the menace and favored sending the articles in. France has now come to the same view but demands that we give Germany credit and that the Germans must not actually pay us as it would deplete the power of Germany to pay an indemnity. France says, 'You supply the goods and we will take the pay for them.' Of course we will do no such thing. Meanwhile the whole social structure of Germany is in flames and we sit and watch the conflagration.

Lansing feared Bolshevism from the Pacific to the Rhine, and perhaps beyond. But the US refusal to agree to credit for Germany to buy food was clear.

Third, Keynes's dealings with the German officials showed

a capacity for firmness as well as sympathy. At the first Treves meetings, Keynes insisted that, if Germany persisted in refusing to use her cash resources to pay for food, the world would see that it was Germany's fault that 'the offer to revictual Germany' had failed. Both then, and at the second Treves conference, when the Germans again insisted on their need for a credit for food, Keynes made the impossibility of this very clear. At the second meeting, the head of the German delegation, von Braun, replied with a formal statement, stressing the Armistice commitments to provide food for Germany, the need to lift the blockade so Germany could buy food from neutral powers such as Argentina, her need to keep her shipping so as to get food if she were not given credit, and the certainty of 'the inundation of all Europe by Bolshevism' if 'the means of assuring the nourishment of Germany' were not guaranteed immediately. The minutes record that 'By reason of its general character the Associated Delegates declared themselves unable to discuss the [von Braun] declaration, which would be submitted to their Governments.' Keynes wrote: 'we turned our trains towards Paris.'

In 'Dr Melchior', Keynes described the stand-off between Germany and the associated powers at the Spa conference, his private interview with Melchior to seek to resolve it, and the deliberately dramatic rupture of the conference. On 4 March, Keynes declared on behalf of the Allies that 'until the ships have been handed over it is not possible to consider additional supplies beyond 270,000 tons'. When von Braun reiterated that Germany would not hand over the ships until food supplies up to the harvest were assured, Rear Admiral Hope took Keynes's advice to abandon the conference, and advised the Germans that 'the Allied and Associated Delegates are leaving for Paris immediately to report to their Governments' – in the middle of the night of 5-6 March. This tactic was, in part, to bring to a head the division between the French and Anglo-American positions. The SEC on 7 March received resolutions proposed by the British, American, and French delegates, and, unable to agree, decided to submit them to the SWC. The British proposal involved releasing some food for some ships, not unlike the German suggestion at Spa. The American draft, stressing that 'Germany will collapse and peace be impossible if … assurance of food and productivity is not immediately given', made proposals in similar spirit. The French proposed delivering 'the 270,000 tons of food already agreed on' when Germany showed a 'genuine intention' to hand over 'the whole of her mercantile fleet forthwith'.

The SWC meeting on 8 March was colourfully depicted by Keynes in 'Dr Melchior'. The central problem was, as Clementel told the SWC, that 'on the advice of Mr. Hoover, 270,000 tons had been fixed as the amount of the first instalment of food-stuffs: But difficulties had arisen as regards the payment, so that nothing had as yet been sent.' Keynes encapsulated Lord Robert Cecil's proposals on behalf of the SEC:

> [T]hat Germany be informed that she is bound to deliver the ships, that we categorically undertake to furnish the food as soon as she begins to deliver the ships, that she be permitted to use her liquid assets, including gold, to pay for the food, and that the Blockade be raised to the extent of allowing Germany to export goods (with some exceptions) and to purchase food in neutral countries. He had to add that his French colleagues had not yet agreed to the use of the gold.

This SWC debate gives a sharp contrast between those who believed that Germany was at risk of revolution and needed to be helped, and those who believed that this threat was exaggerated, that Germany must be shown 'no signs of weakness', and that reparation to France must take priority over payment for food for Germany. As Keynes said, 'everything turned on the gold', which the French did not want used for food payment but for reparations. Keynes recounted how Lloyd George humiliated Klotz, and how, the threat of starvation and hence Bolshevism being stressed by Cecil, Hoover, and Lloyd George, it was agreed that 'the gold was to be used after all'. Keynes and Loucheur drafted the agreed text to provide the basis for negotiations with Germany in Brussels. Keynes also worked closely with US officials on how to mobilize other German resources, such as foreign securities, to pay for food.

At the Brussels conference of 13-14 March, Keynes (at Admiral Wemyss' instigation) saw Melchior privately, successfully seeking to ensure that the Germans made the declaration on surrendering their ships which, at French insistence, was necessary *'before* they were told our intentions about feeding them'. The German declaration made, Wemyss stated (in terms only slightly elaborating on what was agreed in the SWC on 8 March) the Allies' intentions on 'the revictualling of Germany'. Von Braun accepted them in principle, and technical details were sorted out in subcommittees on finance, food, and shipping. Brussels had concluded 'the arrangements for taking over the German merchant shipping and laying out a program for Germany's food supply until next harvest'. After Brussels, 'the food trains started for Germany'.

Some detailed business remained to be done with the German financial experts. So, as chairman of the Inter-Allied Financial Delegates in Armistice Negotiation with Germany, Keynes initiated the SEC's inviting Melchior and other German officials (unbeknownst to Foch) to France, where they stayed in Compiegne and then at Versailles. At Keynes's instigation, the SEC also approved invitations to neutral financiers for discussions regarding the future financial relations between Germany and neutral countries. Keynes boasted to his father: 'My latest deed has been to summon six Germans and also representatives of the Neutrals to Paris; and I am about to launch my scheme for the financial rehabilitation of Europe.' Keynes recalled in 1942 that the Germans and neutrals were called 'with a view to discussing a general project of international financial reconstruction, which, in the event, never came off. How much subsequent evil might have been avoided if only they had!'

Their presence gave the German delegates a direct means of communicating, not least to Keynes, their anxiety about the economic situation in Germany. It made it far easier for Allied officials to talk with both German representatives and neutral financiers on how to make possible Germany's paying for food imports, especially from the neutral powers. In April, the neutral financiers and German officials discussed with Keynes and other Allied representatives such issues as how Germany, with existing debts to neutrals and with her limited liquid assets not available, could secure further credits in neutral countries to revive her trade. The neutrals and Germany were trying to maintain or increase German buying capacity in the neutral countries in the face of the Allies' restrictions.

On 25 March, a report on 'Conditions in Germany' by a British official who had spent three weeks in Berlin was prepared for the Imperial War Cabinet. It spoke of worsening underfeeding, desperate unemployment, the weakness of the government, and the need for credit to restart industry. 'The most impressive fact in Berlin at present is the way in which everyone is reckoning with the probability or inevitability of Bolshevism ....Everybody is convinced that Bolshevism would inevitably spread from Germany to the rest of Europe.' There was a danger of 'the reactionaries' being strengthened. 'Democratic' circles believed the Armistice 'involved a compact to conclude peace on the basis of President Wilson's Fourteen Points'. Cecil wrote on his copy of this report: 'a terrific report – I do not see how Europe can be saved.' Keynes, too, saw this report. But he *did* see how Europe could be saved. On 25 March, the day 'Conditions in Germany' was prepared as a Cabinet paper, Keynes obtained FS approval for food supplies on the left bank of the Rhine which 'in effect involves the handing over of supplies to the Germans in anticipation of payment'. That same day he wrote the introduction to a proposed scheme for reparations that would not leave Germany in an impossible position. Within weeks, he had proposed a 'grand scheme for the rehabilitation of Europe'.

There was urgency in the efforts of the German delegation, neutral representatives, and others to make possible Germany's paying for food imports. For example, on 29 April, Hoover wrote that 'Germany is being fed from hand to mouth', and could not produce funds to cover food more than thirty days ahead of delivery. On 30 April, Keynes told the Financial Section that 'all the liquid resources of Germany would be required for the payment of food', and that, despite Germany's need for raw materials, no resources existed to pay for them. In dealings in the FS and with German officials in April-May, Keynes was seeking to ensure the supply of food and, if possible, raw materials to Germany; but he was impatient with the Germans over their slowness in surrendering assets in payment for supplies made to them.

In a joint meeting of the Food and Finance Sections on 8 May, it was agreed that the Allied commitments of supplies to Germany far exceeded the assets Germany was prepared to put forward.

> Mr Keynes said that the position ought once more to be put to the Germans very frankly. They still have substantial assets, such as their South American properties, and it is for them to choose whether they will provide the finance or go without the food. At present they did not propose even to begin the despatch of the next consignment of gold until May 15th.

In a meeting of the FS with the German officials on 12 May, Keynes 'pointed out that food had already been delivered to the full amount of the gold deposited at Brussels. He stated that unless the Germans could provide some further finance, Mr. Hoover would have to stop all shipments of food, and that in consequence there would be no deliveries of food in June.' Keynes foreshadowed a scheme to allow the sale of requisitioned securities in neutral markets. Having had to press the French earlier in the year to allow Germany to use its gold to buy food, Keynes was now pressing the Germans to do so to the necessary extent. It was not until 22 May, when Keynes told the Germans that 'food shipments had stopped, and would only be made as the corresponding amount of gold was deposited to the account of the Allies', that Germany declared itself 'ready to send 18 million pounds sterling to Amsterdam to the credit of the food account'. In April-May, Keynes was also involved in seeking the lifting of all blockade restrictions on the importation of food into enemy countries and the relaxation of financial restrictions on Germany. ...

Conclusion

... As we have seen, Keynes's principal ideas on the central economic issues of the [Paris Peace Conference] – relief, especially feeding Germany and Austria; war debts, and proposals for lending to restart the European economy; and reparations – were widely shared, though largely ineffective, at Paris. His resignation left him free to persuade a wider world of their urgency, and thus, he hoped, to give effect to them. They were already widely shared in liberal circles in Britain. But it was above all to the USA, whose economic power was essential to a satisfactory European settlement, that Keynes had appealed, unavailingly, in Paris, and to which he would appeal again in the coming months. ...

Within three weeks of leaving the peace conference, Keynes, encouraged by Smuts, had begun to write a book on the Treaty and the economic condition of Europe. He was uncertain whether he would persevere with it. Cecil and others encouraged him to do so, and *The Economic Consequences of the Peace* was published in December 1919. In the months of writing, Keynes was involved in a number of discussions of the needs of post-war reconstruction, including with a group of European and American financiers meeting in Amsterdam in October and November. ...

Keynes was a brilliant and influential expositor of ideas that many others shared. He aimed to shape public opinion, which he and other idealists believed supremely important. While he continued to believe that free trade promoted peace, he also continued to believe that post-war conditions required international action to restart the economic mechanism and thereby create the context in which free trade could promote peace: the laissez-faire doctrine of leaving economic reconstruction to private finance and private enterprise was not enough. ...

'A force for internationalism': why study the Commonwealth?

Opening dinner of the Association for
Commonwealth Studies conference
on 'Educating the Commonwealth about the Commonwealth'
Cumberland Lodge, Windsor Great Park, England
20 May 2007

What a remarkable achievement it is on the part of Tom Symons* that we are all here!

I would therefore like to begin by thanking and congratulating Tom on his leadership in the Association for Commonwealth Studies, which has made this conference possible. And I would like to acknowledge and thank all those others whose insights, labours, and generosity have made it possible for us all to be here.

An ideal after-dinner speech is often said to be short, simple, and funny – based on jokes or an amusing anecdote. I do not wish to disappoint you, but this seems strangely irrelevant to the opening dinner of a conference on 'Educating the Commonwealth about the Commonwealth'. I know of no jokes about the Commonwealth – other than perhaps Mark Twain's line about himself: 'rumours of my death have been greatly exaggerated!'

Rumours of the death of the Commonwealth have been greatly exaggerated for a very long time. Indeed, they have

---

* Professor Thomas H B Symons: amongst much else in a distinguished career of educational leadership and public service, founding President of Trent University, Canada (1963-72), and Chair of the Commission on Commonwealth Studies (1995-97). There is more on Tom in 'The value of university residential colleges' in the 'On education' section of this book.

accompanied almost every important step in its development. For example, they certainly accompanied the acceptance of India as a republic in 1949, while acknowledging the King as Head of the Commonwealth. From our current perspective, had this not happened the development of a modern Commonwealth would have been impossible. Predictions of the death of the Commonwealth accompanied many steps in the long and painful struggles against white rule in Zimbabwe and apartheid in South Africa – which also now seems to us, or at least to me, to show the importance, and not the impotence or the impending death, of the Commonwealth. Similarly, rumours in some quarters of the Commonwealth's terminal decline today seem to me exaggerated.

In 1959, the Australian scholar of International Relations, Hedley Bull, wrote an article entitled 'What is the Commonwealth?' to which question his answer was, in effect, 'not much'. Yet very nearly half a century later, in March this year, the current Australian Prime Minister – no less a political realist than Hedley Bull – could issue a Commonwealth Day message which said:

> Commonwealth Day is an opportunity to reflect on the shared commitment of Commonwealth nations to democratic principles, the rule of law, freedom of expression and the protection of human rights.
>
> The Commonwealth ... has strong historical connections, but is a contemporary body. Its decision in December 2006 to suspend the membership of Fiji from the Councils of the Commonwealth after the unlawful takeover of government in that country, demonstrates in our own region that it continues to speak strongly and with credibility on issues of democracy and openness in political affairs.
>
> This year, Commonwealth Day takes the theme of 'The Commonwealth: respecting difference, promoting understanding.' Australia supports this theme through our long-

standing and highly successful migration program, our relations with other nations, and through our overseas aid.

The Government looks forward to the Commonwealth Heads of Government Meeting to be held in Kampala, Uganda, at the end of the November 2007. This is the 37th such meeting of Commonwealth leaders.

Today, we are proud to reaffirm Australia's commitment to this unique association, and celebrate our common heritage and values.

Prime Minister Howard's reference to Fiji might just as readily have included reference to the Commonwealth's current work to promote democracy in countries from Bangladesh to Pakistan to Nigeria and beyond.

More generally, as we all know, experience around the Commonwealth, and most especially but not exclusively the developing countries of the Commonwealth, reflects its roles – both through international dialogue and consensus-building, and through practical co-operation – in such areas as promoting good governance, democracy, and human rights, including public sector capacity-building; desperately-needed sustainable development in its many aspects, including the promotion of trade and investment, debt relief, health, education, seeking to bridge the digital divide, environmental protection, and programs for youth and, crucially, to promote gender equality; and also in cultural diversity.

One area, of which we have not heard the last, is drawing attention to the need for action on climate change, not least because of the Commonwealth's many island micro-states and other territories at risk through rising sea levels – one of the vulnerabilities of small and other states with which the Commonwealth is concerned.

Even if, as some argue, the focus on terrorism and Iraq since 9/11 again reduced the Commonwealth's prominence, at least in some countries, simply to mention the issues I have just named seems to me to show that the Commonwealth is relevant – modestly and unevenly so, perhaps, but relevant – to very many, if not all, of the great challenges of our day. The *desirability* of its having impact is, if anything, greater, not less.

Canada's Stephen Harper has said:

> The international organisation of the Commonwealth exemplifies our commitment [to] collective action to address complex global challenges. As such, we welcome the opportunity to recognise the Commonwealth for the role it plays in facilitating dialogue and fostering consensus amongst the international community.

Who could doubt the importance today of encouraging just that?

The Commonwealth today is a polycentric association of fully independent states and of their peoples, with many webs of relationships at governmental and non-governmental levels which are bilateral or regional as well as Commonwealth-wide.

Although you will have heard this a thousand times before, it is worth reminding ourselves at the beginning of this conference that, in the words of the Commonwealth Secretary-General, Don McKinnon:

> The Commonwealth has become a truly global, multi-ethnic, multi-faith, multi-cultural, multi-national agglomeration of vastly-differing economies, societies and political realities; of equal member states. We have strength not only in our numbers but in our great diversity as well: 53 countries, 1.8 billion people, all the world's main religions, endless ethnicities, all the continents, from an enormous state like India, to tiny Tuvalu.

Although they said less than some of us might have wished, Commonwealth Education Ministers meeting in Cape Town last December reaffirmed their agreement 'to encourage education about the Commonwealth and its values, including human rights, in our systems of education' – in other words, to 'educating the Commonwealth about the Commonwealth', the theme of this conference.

Cumberland Lodge, where we are now meeting, has long played a special role in facilitating discussion within and about the Commonwealth. Speaking personally, having helped to organise conferences of The Round Table here in the early 1990s, I was last here in 1995, for early meetings of the Commission on Commonwealth Studies. That group, commissioned by the then Secretary-General, Emeka Anyaoku, and chaired by Tom Symons, produced the report *Learning from Each Other: Commonwealth Studies for the 21st Century* which recommended the creation of an Association of Commonwealth Studies as a central element of encouraging the study of the Commonwealth.

That report bears re-reading today, and what I want to say draws from it. While it specifically focussed on Commonwealth studies in higher education, it has much to say that is relevant to broader education about the Commonwealth – including in schools, and for the general public. *Learning from Each Other* helps us both to consider what 'Commonwealth studies' is, and to consider why it is important.

The Commission conceived of Commonwealth studies as 'the study of the Commonwealth as an association, and of the relationships and shared experience – present, future, and past – of its member states and peoples'. Embracing and drawing from many different disciplines, the Commission also argued that 'the designation of "Commonwealth Studies" should generally be reserved for those studies which have a Commonwealth context, which involve comparative study between Commonwealth countries, or which concern the relationship between the society under study and other Commonwealth countries, whether in a bilateral or multilateral Commonwealth framework or in a thematic context of issues'.

One of the points made by the Symons Commission is that the 'legitimacy and importance of Commonwealth studies has often been better understood in countries outside the Commonwealth than at universities in its member states'. Similarly, of course, while some member states within the Commonwealth seem at times complacent about their membership, one measure of the Commonwealth's continuing importance as an association is those sometimes surprising aspirants that express interest in joining. In recent years, Don McKinnon has said, these have included Palestine, Rwanda, Yemen, Algeria, and Israel.

There are many reasons for studying the Commonwealth, and I would like to suggest five.

The first is historical. 'The history of no Commonwealth country can be understood without knowledge and understanding of the history of the Commonwealth.' You cannot understand the modern world – say, the pattern of democracy, the end of apartheid, or the rise of India, or much else besides – without some understanding of the history of the Commonwealth and of the Empire – more accurately, empires – from which it evolved.

The second reason is the continuing contemporary importance of the Commonwealth as an association, a network and an actor in the world. In urging study of the Commonwealth, of course, no one is suggesting studying *only* the Commonwealth, or that the Commonwealth is more important than, say, American power, or the European Union, or the United Nations, or the emergence of China. But we are saying that the Commonwealth is of sufficient importance as an association to merit study alongside these and other phenomena. Academic study of it should, of course, include detached evaluation both of its weaknesses and of its strengths.

Studying the Commonwealth not only enables us to understand an important association of states and peoples, but – and this is my third reason for studying it – the wider the knowledge and understanding of it, the greater its capacity for good will be. In the words of the Commission on Commonwealth Studies:

> …the Commonwealth's capacity for service to the global community, through multi-lateral consensus-building, and to its own members, depends on a shared identity among the citizens and governments of member states. Commonwealth studies assist in creating a more informed understanding and recognition of the Commonwealth's role and potential.

In today's world, certainly no less than ever before, the existence both of the 'benign trans-national organisation' that is the Commonwealth and of some sense of solidarity between peoples of different Commonwealth countries can be useful elements promoting harmony and order in the face of all the age-old and resurgent forces of conflict and disorder. It is a force – not to be exaggerated, but also not to be ignored – for internationalism in an over-nationalistic world, and for multilateralism and for human dimensions in our evolving global governance.

Idealistic visions in earlier generations of the Commonwealth as a promoter, even guarantor, of global peace may now seem to have been exaggerated and proved to be illusory, and were political rather than purely academic projects. But this does not seem to me to be good reason for not encouraging understanding of the Commonwealth today, with all its diversity and limitations, as an element – one, perhaps modest, element – of order in what Hedley Bull described as 'the anarchical society' of states.

The Commonwealth experience of course includes instances of inter-faith hostility and violence, but – I think more importantly – it shows models of the promotion of inter-faith understanding, tolerance, and harmony – something for which the Commonwealth as an association has long stood. The importance of such understanding to the world's prospects for peace has arguably never been greater. This is a particularly acute instance of how the Commonwealth as a model for the celebration of diversity promotes, however imperfectly, values which the world desperately needs. The greater the understanding of the Commonwealth around the Commonwealth, the more likely will be the success of initiatives such as the Secretary-General's current one to promote interfaith understanding and respect.

Similarly, the greater the understanding of the Commonwealth around the Commonwealth, the greater will be the chances of success of its efforts in areas such as promoting democracy, including through election monitoring. To the extent that education about the Commonwealth includes education, as Ministers explicitly said, about its values – including democracy, human rights, and tolerance – then that education will clearly help to promote those values. Studying the Commonwealth should encourage that international outlook, even that sense of global citizenship, which seems to many of us essential for the 21st century.

Even if greater understanding of the Commonwealth simply encourages countries and regions to look out from their local preoccupations, and serves as a gateway from one region to another, it will do something worthwhile. I think, for example, that over some decades the Commonwealth has served this role through ensuring greater international attention to, or perhaps simply somewhat less neglect of, the problems of Africa than there would otherwise have been. If today this seems divisive and difficult, even hopeless, in regard to Zimbabwe, we have surely in recent years seen that it can make a positive difference on issues such as debt relief.

Some of the sense of solidarity between Commonwealth countries relates, of course, to the role of professional and non-government organisations and to the notions of civil society and 'the people's Commonwealth'. NGOs play an important, if in some cases contentious, role in the promotion of Commonwealth values.

My fourth reason for studying the Commonwealth is that the Commonwealth is a useful context within which to study – an important context within which to understand – many important phenomena. *Learning from Each Other* gave two disparate examples, and they remain relevant instances a decade later: the Commonwealth is a useful and appropriate context within which to study parliamentary systems of government in states old and new, and an important context for understanding diverse literatures in English. These words from the Commission's report continue to resonate for me – and not only because I have recently enjoyed reading the powerful novel *The Secret River*, for which Kate Grenville won last year's Commonwealth Writers' Prize:

> Contemporary writing is so vibrant in so many Commonwealth countries that the study of English literature would be incomplete without attention to the work of authors in different continents and regions. It is evident from study of the literary output of Commonwealth writers in different countries how they are drawing to a considerable extent on a store of common experiences and shared cultural forms.

It is good that publishing and literature will be important themes in this conference – just as the work of ACLALS, the Association for Commonwealth Literature and Language Studies, featured prominently in our report on Commonwealth studies a decade ago.

Literature is one element of what has been called the 'cultural Commonwealth'. 'Creative writing and literature, fine arts, performing arts including music, drama and dance, museums and conservation, and a variety of recreational pursuits [perhaps the most obvious are cricket and the Commonwealth Games, 'the friendly games'] are important threads in the fabric of the modern Commonwealth, and are in many cases subjects of study and research in universities and colleges.'

Kate Grenville's novel, *The Secret River*, to which I referred, is a harrowing and haunting account of convict settlement and the sometimes-peaceful but too often violent encounter of settlers with Indigenous people. Today, the Commonwealth remains a useful and appropriate context within which to compare, not only the history of such encounters in different countries, but also policies for seeking to advance the legitimate interests of Indigenous peoples, including the recognition of past wrongs and continuing to journey towards reconciliation.

This leads naturally to the fifth reason I want to urge for studying the Commonwealth – and this was perhaps the most powerful theme of *Learning from Each Other*. Please forgive me again for quoting from it. The Commission wrote:

> What has struck us most forcefully is the extraordinary and unprecedented opportunity that exists today for Commonwealth countries to learn from the rich experience of their Commonwealth partners in many fields.
>
> A significant degree of common heritage means that Commonwealth countries have important similarities (as well as instructive differences) in institutions, values and cultures, and to a large extent a shared language. The contemporary Commonwealth contains some of the most significant and creative societies and some of the most dynamic economies, as well as some of the most challenging and important problems, in the world community. Recent years have witnessed far-reaching innovations in many areas of public policy and in institutional forms. Commonwealth countries have been tackling, frequently in imaginative ways, what are often very similar challenges.

The Commission cited many instances – from economic liberalisation, democratisation and constitutional design, and many other fields of public administration and public policy, to environmental protection, greater opportunities for women, issues of national identity, conflict avoidance and resolution, and much else. The report continued:

> Because of the common heritage and the similar problems and experiences of Commonwealth countries in so many fields, comparative and co-operative studies of these experiences can yield insights of great practical and academic value. Such studies are in our view a legitimate, distinctive and important frame of reference for intellectual enquiry and policy analysis. By showing how institutions derived from a shared origin can adapt to different circumstances, they can provide policy-makers with options and object lessons which they may find it useful to consider. Whilst we warmly acknowledge the value of comparative studies with countries outside the Commonwealth, we believe that the value of comparative studies in a Commonwealth context has not been fully recognised. Practitioners and scholars will often find that more can be learnt from comparing Commonwealth countries with each other than can be learnt from studying other, more different systems, even when these other countries are geographically closer.

In the field of higher education, for example, with which I am personally most familiar, the extent and the ease of sharing ideas – both for government policy and for institutional practice – between Commonwealth countries is remarkable, and the impact of this sharing is profound – be it governments sharing experience on fees and student finance, or matching gift schemes to promote educational philanthropy; or sharing practices on schemes on research quality, teaching and learning, and quality assurance; or university leaders, under the auspices of the Association of Commonwealth Universities or bilaterally, sharing experiences and ideas. At the University of Western Australia in the last three months, we have hosted major visits from Pakistani, Malaysian, and British universities, and from the High Commissioners of Ghana, Bangladesh, and Britain.

Learning from each other is a reality – and much more can profitably be done.

The Commission on Commonwealth Studies cited the Grameen Bank in Bangladesh, which has since inspired a Nobel Prize, political reconciliation in southern Africa, some of which has sadly since soured but some of which remains strong, and social and public service reform in New Zealand as among instances of how Commonwealth studies can be 'a vehicle for enabling policy-makers in Commonwealth countries to extend the range of options they may wish to explore and to gain insights into the possible consequences of particular choices. In such ways such studies can contribute to the better management of social, economic, and political change.'

So, why study the Commonwealth?

- To understand the history which has shaped us all.

- To understand an association of governments and peoples of continuing relevance to today's and tomorrow's world.

- To enhance the capacity of that association to contribute to the welfare of its peoples and of the wider world, including to promote some elements of trans-national solidarity and values – especially of tolerance and even celebration of diversity – which are essential for a harmonious world.

- To understand phenomena – I have instanced parliamentary government and contemporary literature – in one of their most important contexts.

- And to compare the experiences, not least in diverse fields of public policy, of countries which are sufficiently similar for those comparisons to yield valuable academic insights and practical lessons.

There is, of course, much more that could be said, and some of it, I hope, will be said over the three days ahead of us.

I began by quoting Mark Twain. Let me also end with him.

Twain and US Senator Chauncey M Depew:

> ... once went abroad on the same ship. When the ship was a few days out they were both invited to a dinner. Speech-making time came. Mark Twain had the first chance. He spoke [for] twenty minutes and made a great hit. Then it was [Senator] Depew's turn.
>
> 'Mr. Toastmaster and Ladies and Gentlemen,' said [this] famous raconteur as he arose, 'Before this dinner Mark Twain and [I] made an agreement to trade speeches. He has just delivered *my* speech, and I thank you for the pleasant manner in which you received it. I regret to say that I have lost the notes of his speech and cannot remember anything he was to say.'
>
> Then he sat down. There was much laughter. Next day an Englishman who had been in the party came across Mark Twain in the smoking-room. ['Sir'], he said, 'I consider you were much imposed upon last night. I have always heard that [Senator] Depew is a clever man, but, really, that speech of his you made last night struck me as being the most infernal rot.'

Mr Chairman, this speech – though drawing deliberately on the Symons Report on Commonwealth Studies – is mine, and I hope that you will consider it a useful prompt to thinking about studying the Commonwealth, and *not* – I hope – as 'the most infernal rot'.

Some scholars of war and peace: Sir Keith Hancock, Hedley Bull, R J Vincent, Geoffrey Jukes

Sir Keith Hancock

Obituary
The Independent
24 August 1988

When, in 1934, Lionel Curtis, that indefatigable idealist of imperial unity, set out to persuade the young Australian historian Keith Hancock[*] to write a survey of the British Empire and Commonwealth, he was unwittingly performing both a great service to Commonwealth history and a considerable disservice to his own ideals.

Curtis's proposal (made with Arnold Toynbee) set Hancock firmly on the path of Commonwealth and, through that, economic history. Hancock's *Survey of British Commonwealth Affairs* is still a *locus classicus*, and it showed, with unmistakeable clarity, how ill-attuned Curtis's ideals were to an empire which, like all multi-national empires in this [20th] century, was subject to the great centrifugal force of nationalism.

Hancock's earlier work had also focused on nationalism. As an Australian Rhodes Scholar visiting Italy in 1922-23, he encountered the reality of Mussolini, and this led him back in time to study the growth of Italian nationalism in the 19th century. Returning to Australia as a youthful professor in Adelaide, Hancock (as he saw it) was sidetracked into writing his classical study, *Australia* (1930), which was, in part, both an

---

[*]   William Keith Hancock (26 June 1898-13 August 1988).

analysis of, and an enduring contribution to, the growing self-awareness of 'independent Australian Britons'.

But Hancock's passion was the study of war and peace. He sought to understand the endless struggle between the selfish pursuit of national interest and attempts to create a rule of law in international politics. Such work was better done in Britain than in Adelaide, and, confronting the tension between his calling as a historian and his love of his country, Hancock quit Adelaide in 1933 for Birmingham.

Though his mind recurred to these themes of order and conflict in international politics, the great work Hancock planned on this was never written, for it was at this point that Curtis and Toynbee proposed a British Empire Survey for Chatham House. Hancock insisted on full freedom to express his own point of view, and this he did, helping through his balanced, scholarly and realistic tone to defuse some of the Utopianism in discussion of the Commonwealth (and international politics generally) at that time.

Although the first volume of his *Survey* (1937) dealt with the constitutional and political problems of nationality, Hancock, unlike many Imperial historians, was not satisfied to study the Commonwealth without adequate attention to its economic development and difficulties, and he worked (and travelled) tirelessly to produce early in the war a second part, *Problems of Economic Policy, 1918-1939*. As David Fieldhouse put it, 'Imperial history was never the same again'. In moving the historians' spotlight from constitutional to economic issues in the Commonwealth, Hancock torpedoed both the notion of Imperial self-sufficiency which had triumphed at Ottawa in 1932, and the notion that free trade best helped the primary producing countries of (for example) West Africa.

But again Hancock changed direction. During the war, he agreed to serve in Whitehall as editor of the series on the civil history of the war – a series of 30 volumes, covering such topics as transport, food, fuel and social services. The editorship of this series (combined, during the war, with the night watch at St Paul's Cathedral in London) was a staggering achievement; and *British War Economy* (1949), the volume Hancock wrote himself with Professor Margaret Gowing, is a remarkable study of the mobilisation of the British economy for war.

In 1949, Hancock (now Professor of Economic History at Oxford) intended to return to Australia, to join the Australian National University being created in Canberra. But his Canberra plans collapsed, and instead he became Director of the new Institute of Commonwealth Studies in London. While building up the Institute, Hancock found the time to play a key role, in 1954, in a settlement intended to lay a stable basis for self-government in Uganda. But his mind was moving to South Africa, and he began work on the archives of Jan Smuts which culminated in the 1960s in the publication of two massive volumes of biography and of selections from Smut's papers. By this time Hancock was at last back in Australia, at the ANU.

He had already written an engaging and wise autobiography that traced the antipodean scholar's tension between *Country and Calling* (1954), and which ended on the surprisingly sour note of the collapse of his ANU plans in 1949. Though his arrival in Canberra was delayed for several years, Hancock's contribution there, both to the development of the university and to its intellectual life, was immense, and it continued virtually until his death.

His most important work after his 'retirement' was his 1972 study of man's impact on his environment in the Monaro uplands of New South Wales. At last he had the time to agitate against environmental vandalism and against US bases in Australia, and to write a second volume of autobiography. Hancock's twilight years were years of physical decline combined with extraordinary intellectual vigour, and, to the delight of his colleagues, he gave several scintillating seminars which belied his physical frailty.

Primarily a historian of the 20th century, Hancock's life was dominated by his major projects on the Commonwealth, the War, and Smuts; but his Canberra seminars, like his other published papers, reveal a diverse range of historical interests. He was dismissive of the frequent cry of historians that 'that's not my period', and was a strong exponent of the importance of perspective – of span – in history. He was a historian of great clarity and originality of insight, sceptical, realistic, and precise, who believed that a historian must 'get his boots muddy' in the subject he was studying.

Hancock was a quiet but definite man, a tireless and driven worker. He died in the knowledge that his admirers the world over had saluted, on his 90th birthday just weeks before, a great historian and a great Australian.

Hedley Bull as a teacher*

Memorial Service

University Church, Oxford

17 October 1985

When, as a graduate student of Hedley Bull's, I once suggested to him that someone should use the archives in the Bodleian Library to write a biography of Sir Alfred Zimmern, Oxford's first Montague Burton Professor of International Relations, his reply was characteristic, not at least in its self-deprecation: 'What is there to write a biography about? He didn't have an especially interesting life; he was only a professor.'

---

* Hedley Norman Bull (10 June 1932-18 May 1985). Professor of International Relations, Australian National University, 1967-77. Montague Burton Professor of International Relations, Oxford, 1977-85.

 This eulogy of Hedley at his memorial service in Oxford in October 1985 was published in Robert O'Neill & David N Schwartz (eds), *Hedley Bull on Arms Control*, Macmillan Press in association with the International Institute for Strategic Studies (IISS), 1987, and is reproduced with permission of Palgrave Macmillan.

Hedley Bull knew and exemplified the importance of being, as he self-mockingly put it, 'only a professor.'* Through the term before he died, under regular doses of morphine, he continued to lecture, and right to the end saw students at his home, because he thought this the most valuable thing he could do.

The tributes of tears of so many students, past and present, are testimony to our great sense of loss. The desire of so many to honour his memory and carry on his work has given impetus to the establishment of the Hedley Bull Memorial Appeal and, I hope, some comfort to Mrs Bull, whom all admire so much.

All the superlatives that say how fine a man and how great a teacher Hedley Bull was, do not begin to convey how much he meant to us. He was a magnet drawing graduate students to Oxford, and to the study of international relations. This was by no means confined to what Adam Roberts[†] called 'the Hedley Bull effect' – attracting students from the antipodes – though, of course, we Australians felt a special bond with him, and, I think, Australian students formed a link for him with Australia.

But he could be disconcerting. Soon after I arrived in Oxford as a graduate student, at a seminar in the lofty confines of the Old Library at All Souls to hear a distinguished professor from Princeton, he greeted me: 'G'day, cobber.' Rather taken aback, as he unmistakably intended I should be, I responded, much to my own embarrassment, 'How ya goin', mate?'

Or he might greet a newly arrived student with his half-sideways, sizing-up glance and, leaning forward at the shoulders, say, 'And what's your story?'

In supervisions, his half-smile, his long silences, his slow stroking of his chin and smoking of his pipe – all were apt to leave the awe-struck student, on the edge of his armchair, feeling

---

* This comment led, after Hedley's death, to my writing 'Sir Alfred Zimmern Revisited: Fifty Years On', *Review of International Studies*, October 1986, and (with help from Geoffrey Browne) 'Sir Alfred Zimmern', *Oxford Dictionary of National Biography*, Oxford University Press, 2004.

† See 'Sir Adam Roberts: man of peace in a world of conflict' in *'A large and liberal education': higher education for the 21st century*, pp. 308-11.

foolish. 'HB', as he signed his two-line letters in one's early days, clearly had no respect for the purveyors of nonsense; but his silences induced it. Into the chasm fell many a student.

On we would ramble, and he would say little. He would lean back in his easy chair, legs crossed, puffing on his pipe, occasionally acknowledging a point with a long drawn out 'ye-es'. The little that he did say said it all. He could see to the heart of the issue, and sent students away to confront alone, but not unaided, the fundamental and challenging, if not impossible, questions he posed.

Despite one's early unease, one came to realise that Hedley Bull took serious students seriously – not just in the sense, important though it is, of devoting much time and care to their work, but *listening* to them. Of course he was judgemental and dismissive; his standards were high, and he was rightly intolerant of the slipshod and the second-rate. But he was receptive to the ideas of his students, and open to persuasion by them. He was always accessible, and one came inevitably to develop warm, good-humoured relations. He was sensitive to the personal difficulties of students, and, though the references he wrote are said to be (like everything else he said or wrote) unflinchingly honest, he was solicitous of the future prospects of his students.

He devoted much time and thought to helping students find and refine thesis topics. His suggestions bore the distinctive stamp of his belief in the continuity of traditions of thought about international relations; one consequence was a series of studies of important thinkers previously neglected.

The first drafts of many chapters or papers were condemned; successive attempts would receive his careful attention. He once wrote on one student's draft: 'The wild advocacy of change at the end [of the paper], which is not supported by any argument, tells us more about you than about the subject.' Against the first four lines of another student's thesis draft, he wrote: 'An examiner would likely fail you for this, without reading any further.' Himself reading further, he wrote, 'In fact, this is sheer gobbledygook.' Where our liberated student had used the word 'spokespersons', he wrote, 'If you use this ghastly word I shall have you failed come Hell or High Water.'

The qualities that shone through in supervision meetings, and elsewhere, were his capacity to see the big picture and the central issue, to see the wood while we were not lost amongst the trees; and his commitment to academic inquiry, grounded in history and philosophy, seeking after the fundamentals of international relations – inquiry which, as he wrote, must be followed wherever it leads and not be perverted by the predisposition or the clamour for practical 'solutions'.

Hedley Bull taught, above all, by gentle guidance, undemonstrative example, and inspiration.

Men must be taught as if you taught them not;
And things unknown proposed as things forgot.*

This was Hedley Bull's way. He was singularly diffident about bringing his own writings to the attention of his students. He once gave me an offprint of an article saying, 'There's nothing in here you don't already know.' I read the article, not least to test this proposition, and found it to be entirely untrue, as of course he well knew it to be.

His own warm appreciations of teachers such as John Anderson and Martin Wight stressed the impact of their minds and their examples; and so it was with Hedley Bull himself. It was only later, I think, or away from his direct influence, that one realised just how great his impact was.

If in supervisions he asked big questions, it was in his writings and in his lectures that he gave big answers. He was an impressive, even dazzling, lecturer. He had presence, command, dignity. Here was the great man. Here revealed was his 'divine spark of creativity', and it sparked a sense of intellectual excitement in his audience.

---

* Alexander Pope, *An Essay on Criticism.*

Usually he lectured without reference to notes. He would often announce that he had five points to make, and proceed to expound them with great clarity. As with his written work, the structure was systematic; the content weighty and penetrating. Every so often, the hour would be up with only four of the promised five points made. Out he would go, gown flowing behind him. On such occasions, I sometimes wondered how many hard, thankless hours, late at night or in the early morning, went into each hour of easy, effortless brilliance.

Hedley Bull's lectures – like his writings, and his career – had a unity, a completeness. They told an ample story, but without disguising questions that remained.

I once suggested to him that he write up a particular set of lectures for publication. He said that he had thought of this, but went on, 'You will learn as time goes on that it's always good to have some lectures up your sleeve that your students haven't read.'

His lectures, like his writings, were sprinkled with memorable phrases, epigrams – many borrowed and many his own – and *ex cathedra* pronouncements. 'Thinking is also research'; 'professors do not make good policy-makers'; 'a high ratio of thought to publication'. He described John Anderson in terms one is tempted to use of 'HB' himself: 'a greater man than many who are more famous.' And, as in personal conversation so in lectures, his mischievous and irreverent sense of humour, of fun and even deliberate indiscretion was always there. Pity the poor Americans, recently arrived, whose revered professors' celebrated work was dismissed – with a twinkle and a smile – as 'cloudy and metaphysical.'

He was, of course, a master of demolition. Though not himself especially quick to respond on his feet to the unfamiliar or unexpected, it was in seminars and the question periods for guest lectures that he was most ruthless and most provocative. Here he wielded the broadsword. He was direct, forceful, iconoclastic. This 'happy warrior' was deliberately and engagingly provocative. One Rhodes Scholar had spent many months working on a Master's thesis under his supervision. Only weeks before the thesis was due, the student presented a seminar on it. Opening the discussion, 'HB', lighting up his pipe, announced, 'The real question is whether or not you have a thesis.'

Above all, Hedley Bull was honest, and he demanded intellectual honesty in others. It was a great privilege, and a great pleasure, to have studied under him, and to have come to regard him as mentor and friend. I hope he knew how much he was loved, and how much he would be missed.

R J Vincent

Memorial Service
University Church of Christ the King
Gordon Square, London, 13 March 1991

On 1 October 1973, John Vincent[*] opened a small school exercise book, and began a diary that he was to keep, on and off, for a decade. 'Have no delusions about going down in history,' he wrote, 'but seek to provide some future archaeologist with an account of everyday life in ancient England.' It was John's first day at the International Institute for Strategic Studies. He recorded that, after a talk with the Director,

> Went up to the LSE to join the library and looked at St Clement Dane's on the way. I like it; not too obviously heroic for a forces church, and the restoration fine.

Fifteen years later, as John waited for his interview for the Chair at LSE, it was to *this* church that he came, to sit and

---

[*] Raymond John Vincent (28 February 1943-2 November 1990). Graduate of the University College of Wales, Aberystwyth, and the Australian National University. Successively, Professor of International Relations, Keele University; Fellow of Nuffield College, Oxford; Montague Burton Professor of International Relations, London School of Economics.

ponder. Now, short years on, we are here to celebrate his life, and remember what he meant to us.

John's diary is a record of a man devoted to his wife and children, and of a fine young scholar finding his feet. Angela appears in almost every entry – her teaching; learning Greek on board ship – 'a floating Butlins', John called it – on the way to Australia; a trip home to Wales; her 'conversion to India' at the hands of Richard Attenborough. John's love and respect for her is unmistakeable.

On Geraint's 10th birthday, John listed his presents, which included a leather cricket ball. John recorded: he 'can in fact now bowl straight and quite fast – got me middle-stump first ball the other day, much to my disguised embarrassment.' Geraint, of course, is a footballer as well as a cricketer, and his passion is Liverpool. One summer holiday, John sent me a light-hearted postcard from Scotland which ended, 'Two of us are looking forward to returning to Oxford; one wants to go to Wales; one to Liverpool. Guess which.'

I first came to know John and his family in 1984-85, when we coincided for a year at Princeton. There, as elsewhere, John and Angela had lunch together every day they could, and they were generous together in their hospitality to students and colleagues. It was in Princeton that I came to know John's great capacity for friendship, his sense of the ridiculous, his complete lack of pretension, his irresistible cheerfulness, and his talent to amuse. The mild mockery, mixed with self-mockery; the willingness to risk making a clown of himself, though he never did; the capacity to make people feel at home, to make them feel that they belonged; the openness of personality and of mind – these were qualities he radiated to anyone who met him, or heard him speak.

John felt a special attachment to all the universities he worked in. I remember the time in Oxford when a Rhodes Scholar from Princeton came into the Social Studies buttery. John, of course, burst spontaneously into the Princeton song, complete with its exquisite arm movements. Typically, this was amusing and engaging, and not the least bit pejorative.

John took a real and sensitive personal interest in his students, and was unfailingly a source of wisdom, warm support, and – above all – encouragement. He was a gifted and inspiring teacher. Always approachable and always attentive, he invariably found the positives to emphasise, and helped even the most discouraged students find a road ahead. In seminars he was both incisive and kind. But he also had an inimitable skill for deflating the pretensions of students, or of others. After a long and pompous talk by a judge of the International Court of Justice on the gravity and importance of being a judge of the ICJ, John congratulated the speaker, and asked, on behalf of all present, 'How do we get the job?'

John engaged his audience in lectures and seminars, and brought his subject alive, with humour. He had a remarkable repertoire of accents and anecdotes, and often gently teased his audience. In the course of one lecture in Oxford, he managed to dismiss management consultants, politicians, and diplomats. A Canadian graduate student wrote him a note afterwards, saying that John had destroyed every career option he had ever had; did he have any other suggestions? John wrote back urging him to become an ice hockey announcer.

John was a master of colourful imagery. In *Human Rights and International Relations*, there is a strikingly irreverent egg-box image: international relations can be, alternatively, an egg-box, an omelette, or a fried egg, sunny side up.* John's 'arresting conclusion' to one lecture was the now-legendary phrase: 'if international relations is a jungle, don't be a zebra.'

John once organised a seminar series on 'neglected thinkers in international relations'; he joked that Hedley Bull had called it 'rightly neglected thinkers in international relations'. John presents us with the image of a relay team of scholars, the baton

---

* This passage was read at the service by Hidemi Suganami.

being passed from one runner to the next. On the day that Hedley died, John told me that he felt that a responsibility to run with the baton had been passed into his hands. Last year he wrote of the 17th century writer, Grotius, words that are poignant for our memories of John himself:

> ... even if we ... [see Grotius simply] as passing on the baton ... to Locke, it would still be useful to consult [him] not merely as a defunct publicist, someone who ran his lap some time ago, but as a scholar who has thought deeply about the tension between ... attachment to a local community and ... obligation to world society as a whole.

John, too, was a scholar who thought deeply. But he wore his scholarship lightly. He just got on with it. He had great self-discipline, and was able to lock himself away and write. It is extraordinary that a man who gave his time without limit to his colleagues and his students should also have left so great a published legacy, and been so distinguished an editor of the *Review of International Studies*. John's book on the principle of *Non-intervention* will undoubtedly long endure as a learned treatise – a classic work – on international order. And it was no coincidence that a man so just, and so optimistic, as John should have contributed increasingly to discussion of moral questions in world society – racial equality, subsistence rights, and, again, the dilemma of humanitarian intervention.

Yet it is not primarily as a colleague, a teacher, or as a scholar that I remember John. It is as a friend – someone it was always fun to be with; someone we could always turn to, whose response was always uplifting. I remember my last conversation with him, on the day he died, when – though it was clear something was terribly wrong – he appeared more concerned about *my* health and *my* future than his own, and joked – unrepeatably, I regret to say – about the medical tests he had undergone.

John did everything with a sense of humour and lightness.

He once left me a message, on the back of an old invoice, headed in large capitals – 'PANIC':

> Don, old mate,
>
> I have just mistakenly posted you a letter with no stamp on it that I meant to deliver by hand.
>
> Can you possibly babysit for us this evening ...
>
> [And here poking fun at the totally unearned Oxford degrees we had both been given:]
>
> It would be a great honour to have an M.A. (Oxon) sitting for us.

Who else would write: 'Looking forward to seeing you for Christmas. White tie at dinner?'

Last week I received from America a letter from a group of former Oxford students of John's. It concluded simply: We all 'remember John as a kind and gentle man. We miss him very much.' So do I; and so, I'm sure, do we all. It is hard to imagine a better teacher, a better colleague, a better friend, or a more profound inspiration to us all.

Geoffrey Jukes

Symposium for his 80th birthday
The University of Western Australia
15 August 2008

It is an unusual pleasure and, frankly, deeply moving honour for me to welcome you to this symposium on *Global and Regional Security: Contemporary Challenges* being held in honour of Mr Geoffrey Jukes* to mark his 80th birthday. This symposium is held under the auspices of the University of Western Australia

---

* Geoffrey Jukes (28 August 1928-20 March 2010).

– and specifically the Centre for Muslim States and Societies, and the discipline group of Political Science and International Relations – and of the WA Branch of the Australian Institute of International Affairs, of which I am proud to be a member. I am delighted that Geoff and Eunice Jukes are with us here at UWA today.

The personal pleasure and honour are not only because this is in the field of my own greatest professional interest, or that today's topic – challenges to security – is so timely, or that we have such distinguished speakers – though all this is true, and we are most grateful to all of the speakers. It is not only that Geoffrey Jukes was the supervisor of my colleagues Samina Yasmeen and Roderic Pitty, the joint convenors of today, to whom we are also most grateful. I would like to thank Roderic for his assistance with my preparing these remarks this morning.

I am especially honoured because of my own links with Geoffrey Jukes, including through two mutual friends (and mentors of mine), both of whom died long before their time, Hedley Bull and John Vincent.

In November 1988, I was two years into a permanent academic appointment in Oxford, and out of the blue came a letter obviously produced by a dot matrix printer on tractor-feed computer paper, signed 'G Jukes'. It began by pointing out that we had never met, but that our mutual friends John Vincent and Bob O'Neill thought we should, and going from there with engaging, astute, and ever so slightly conspiratorial commentary on academic politics. My file of letters between Geoff Jukes and me from the next few years shows that I replied – if you don't mind my quoting myself:

> Although we have not met, you are by no means a stranger! Mary Bull has spoken warmly of you in the past, not least of your support to Hedley at the end [meaning his death in 1985]. And I set a quote from you for discussion in a special prize examination here [in Oxford] just a few months ago.

And so the epistolary friendship took off. Although the visiting fellowship in the International Relations department at ANU that Geoff suggested did not eventuate because I fell ill, I remain enormously grateful to him for so many acts of kindness. And today I would like to try to repay some of his generosity of spirit by saying a little more about him.

Geoffrey Jukes was born in the UK in 1928, and worked for 14 years in the British Ministry of Defence and Foreign Office after graduating from Oxford in 1953. While he spent some time with British forces in Cyprus in 1956-57, his time in government service was mostly spent working on Russian and Soviet military history and strategy, and also contemporary arms control.

From 1959 until 1964 Geoff Jukes worked for the Director-General of British Intelligence in the Defence Intelligence Staff, first as deputy head of an overview section until 1962, then as its head until late 1964.

From the early 1960s until his departure to Australia, Geoff also advised Alastair Buchan, Director of the [International] Institute for Strategic Studies concerning details of *The Military Balance*, an annual review of strategic affairs, regarding Warsaw Pact military forces.

When the Wilson Labour Government was elected in Britain in late 1964, it set up a new section in the Foreign Office called the Disarmament and Arms Control Research Unit. Lord Chalfont [Alyn Gwyn-Jones] invited Hedley Bull to head this unit and Geoff to work with him. Their collaboration continued for many years, notwithstanding different views of the extent to which 'the Soviet threat' was based on evidence.

Before this appointment Geoff had applied for and been offered a post with Chatham House (the Royal Institute of International Affairs) as their Soviet specialist. While he did not accept that post due to Lord Chalfont's efforts, increasingly during the 1960s Geoff experienced an urge to express his opinions in public, particularly to counter what he saw as the exaggerations of Soviet military strength then current in the Western public domain.

In 1967 when Hedley Bull was appointed as Professor of International Relations at the Australian National University, he invited Geoff to come with him to Canberra. Geoff was duly appointed as a Fellow at ANU, specialising in Soviet affairs, and later a Senior Fellow.

A large number of research students from Australia, UK and other countries, especially in Asia, have benefitted from the fact that Geoff did not return to Britain, except occasionally for research, or to help with postgraduate teaching at Cambridge or Oxford, where he also had a role in guiding rowers to proficiency on the river.

Geoff has contributed significantly to the growth of an informed profession of International Relations experts in Australia and elsewhere. For example, he and Hedley Bull designed and set up the first taught Master of Arts in International Relations program in Australia in 1973-74. While Hedley gave general directions and piloted the program through the university boards, Geoff worked out the detailed design and ran the program until 1987. The program obtained three successive Ford Foundation grants, which provided scholarships for students from a range of Asian countries over a ten-year period. Altogether in its first 13 years the MA(IR) program attracted students from about 26 countries, including Indonesia, Singapore, Malaysia, Thailand, India, Pakistan, Bangladesh, and Sri Lanka, as well as from Britain, Japan, and elsewhere. In the early 1980s the program was extended to include some students from China.

As well as running the MA program for 13 years, Geoff supervised or advised PhD students researching a wide variety of topics in International Relations. At one time he was supervising 11 PhDs and 16 MAs concurrently. Since 1968 he has supervised or advised 57 PhD students and approximately

121 MAs to successful completion, including about ten since formally retiring at the end of 1993. He currently still advises four PhD students at ANU.

The MA established at ANU was taken into account in reform of the corresponding degrees at both Oxford and Cambridge after Hedley Bull went to the Oxford chair in International Relations, in succession to Alastair Buchan, in 1977. Kim Beazley, whom we are delighted to welcome here today, had undertaken the Oxford BPhil – the MPhil, as it became – in International Relations under Buchan, and I was to do it later under Hedley Bull, Adam Roberts, and others.

It is principally, but far from only, through supervision that Geoff Jukes has contributed to the development of many International Relations scholars in Australia and elsewhere. He occasionally delivers guest lectures. Thus he will be speaking to the National Institute of Defence Studies in Tokyo next month, about Russia's Prospects in the Asia-Pacific Region.

Geoff is a great academic traveller. He wrote to me in Oxford from Moscow in April 1991:

> My next visit to UK will be in late June. I shall be giving a paper on Stalin & Munich (Actually it's my article in the April *Journal of Contemporary History*) at a conference in Leeds, spending about ten days in UK, then going to Prague & Budapest before returning via giving a paper at a conference in Hokkaido. Hope to see you then.

Geoff has written extensively – in several books and articles – on Russian and Soviet foreign and security policy through various ages, including his book *The Soviet Union in Asia;* various aspects of the First and Second World Wars, with a particular focus on the Eastern Front, including the battles of Moscow, Stalingrad, and Kursk; the Russo-Japanese war of 1904-05, the Soviet-Japanese neutrality pact through most of World War II, and subsequent Russian approaches to Japan's 'Northern

Territories'; and much else. He has also, for example, co-edited a volume with Amin Saikal, who I am very pleased is here today, on prospects for settlement and stability in the Middle East, in which volume Samina Yasmeen has a chapter on women in politics in the Middle East.

Last week at the ANU the Prime Minister opened the Hedley Bull Centre in memory of one great Australian figure in the study of International Relations, and there was also published a volume – available online – entitled *Remembering Hedley*, in which Geoff rightly appears. Today here at the University of Western Australia, we friends and admirers of Geoffrey Jukes and people interested in this subject salute another major figure in this field; and we do it in one of the best ways we know how, in a symposium on a topic of importance to him and to all of us.

I am delighted to launch this symposium on challenges to security, and to celebrate the scholarship, the teaching, the collegiality and, perhaps above all, the friendship of Geoffrey Jukes.

Part IV: On education

'A large and liberal education'

Launch of 'A large and liberal education':
higher education for the 21st century*

The University of Western Australia, 3 August 2007

I would like to begin by acknowledging the Noongar people, on whose land this University sits – and also to say that one aspect of this book reflects the continuing need to create and enhance educational opportunities for Indigenous people throughout Australia, and also to make students, staff, and the wider community generally aware of Indigenous experience, wisdom, and knowledge.

Two or three weeks ago, a friend of mine who had an early copy of this book contacted me urgently. 'Great news', she said. 'I had the best sleep last night I've had in months.'

'That's terrific', I replied.

'Yes', she said. 'I was reading your book in bed.'

One such comment could be passed off lightly. But then on Sunday another friend told me that he had found reading the Acknowledgements of my book on the economist John Maynard Keynes very interesting – and three pages in, he too had fallen asleep.

Even I can begin to spot a pattern.

That second friend, the second one who reported finding my writings a great cure for insomnia, made an interesting comment – that Acknowledgements tell you a lot about a book and about its author and how they have worked. I would like to begin by reiterating the thanks I recorded in my Acknowledgements

---

* Donald Markwell, *'A large and liberal education': higher education for the 21st century*, Australian Scholarly Publishing & Trinity College, University of Melbourne, 2007.

to the many people who helped with it in so many ways – above all, the outstanding Research Assistants and colleagues, Geoffrey Browne and more recently Dr Carolyn Daniel, with whom I worked from 1996 until earlier this year, and the publishers, Australian Scholarly Publishing and the University of Melbourne's Trinity College.

To the thanks expressed in the Acknowledgements, I add my deep gratitude to Janet Holmes a Court, who is one of the great citizens of this state and this nation, whom I greatly admire, and who I am honoured has launched the book so generously. To Vice-Chancellor Professor Alan Robson, whose support in so many ways, including his kind words this afternoon, I greatly appreciate. My warm thanks to Terri-ann White and the Institute for Advanced Studies, for suggesting this launch, and for making it happen; to the Office of Development; the Co-op bookstore for providing you with this great opportunity to buy early for Christmas; and to you all for coming this afternoon. I appreciate your presence and support very much.

As you know, the pieces in this book principally come from my nine and a half years as Warden of Trinity College in the University of Melbourne. With over 1,700 students in all manner of programs, Trinity is today a unique tertiary educational institution – almost a mini-university, and in some ways more like an American liberal arts college than anything else I can think of.

Its links with UWA go back to the first Sub-Warden (or deputy head) of Trinity College, who held that position from 1876 to 1882 – John Winthrop Hackett – as you know, the founder, first Chancellor, and greatest benefactor of the University of Western Australia. Hackett had been close friends at Trinity College Dublin with the man who became the first Warden of Trinity College, Melbourne, Alexander Leeper. One of the three people to whom this book is dedicated is Leeper's daughter, Valentine, born in 1900. The section of this book called 'Exemplars', with pieces about individuals, includes short texts of mine from Valentine Leeper's installation as a Fellow of Trinity College in 1998, her 100th birthday two years later, her funeral in 2001, and then the interment of her ashes in a garden in the College in which she had played as a child in the early years of the previous century.

As it happens, Alan Robson was taught by Valentine Leeper's brother, Geoffrey Winthrop – Winthrop! – Leeper, the first professor of agricultural chemistry in the University of Melbourne.

One further linkage – of many – that seems fitting to mention given that we are here in this Prescott Room is that Sir Stanley Prescott, as he became, was – amongst much else – a tutor at Trinity College, Melbourne, and then Master of its neighbour, Ormond College, before coming to UWA as Vice-Chancellor in 1953.

Although most of what is in this book arose in the context of a particular and unique institution – Trinity College in the University of Melbourne – it is my hope that what it has to say is of wider interest, nationally and internationally.

As you may have gathered, the papers and speeches in this book focus on several themes, among them:

- the importance of aspiring to the highest standards of excellence in university education – what we here at UWA call 'achieving international excellence' – and the attributes of that international excellence;

- the desirability of students having an education that broadens as well as deepens them, and that equips them for a world of global forces and rapid change – which education comes in many forms, and this book seeks not to prescribe a form but more to diagnose a need;

- the importance of improving the quality of teaching and learning, including through increasing student engagement both within and outside the classroom, and the contribution that residential collegiate education can make to this and that colleges can make to the wider universities to which they belong;

- the importance of challenging students to aim to make a difference in the world, including their and our aiming – in the inspiring words of the motto of this University – to 'seek wisdom';

- the importance of passionate focus on equity and diversity, including the unfinished pursuit of gender equality;

- the importance of educational philanthropy for getting that 'margin for excellence' that world-class universities need, and to ensuring that talented students can get a fine education regardless of their financial means; and

- the need for Australian universities and colleges to engage with Asia and help our students develop that international, inter-cultural and inter-faith awareness that is so important for the future.

There is, as you may know, a genre of books of speeches by educational leaders, especially when they have left the leadership of a particular institution. Although the pitfalls of this genre are many, I have to confess that when the idea arose of this book, when it was announced that I was leaving Trinity to come to UWA, I did not resist. In the preparation of this book, my Research Assistant, Dr Carolyn Daniel, and I were repeatedly inspired and influenced by one other such book – a book called *Higher Ground: Ethics and Leadership in the Modern University*, which is a collection of speeches and papers by one of the most distinguished of living American educational leaders, Nan Keohane, who was successively president of Wellesley College and then of Duke University, and whose work for gender equality remains an inspiration.

Another person *soon* to retire from university leadership is the Vice-Chancellor of the University of Queensland, John Hay, an alumnus of UWA. John Hay recently said that one of the things he had learnt in his many years as a Vice-Chancellor was that there is a direct link between the level of applause for his speeches and their brevity.

With that lesson in mind, let me conclude simply by once again thanking you for your presence and contribution this afternoon. And should insomnia ever be a problem – remember that the remedy is '*A large and liberal education*'!

Working together to become 'world class' universities

ASEAN University Network Rectors' Conference
University of Brunei Darussalam, 29 January 2009

Increasingly, in the competitive global 'knowledge economy' of the 21st century, the economic and social prospects of countries depend on the quality of their 'human capital' – how well educated their people are. So the quality of educational institutions and systems at all levels of education, from pre-school to university and indeed lifelong learning opportunities beyond that, will significantly impact on a country's fortunes. In this context, countries and regions (such as the European Union and increasingly ASEAN[*]) wish to have 'world class universities' and 'world class university systems', and individual universities wish to be seen as 'world class'.[†] One of the many strategies used by institutions for achieving this competitive purpose is, perhaps paradoxically, to collaborate with others. And, perhaps also paradoxically, such collaboration can be seen as an indicator of the attainment of 'world class' status.

Taking a less instrumentalist view, Geoffrey Boulton and Colin Lucas have recently argued:[‡]

Academic scholars have maintained networks of international links since the early days of universities, long before the

---

[*] Association of South-East Asian Nations.

[†] See, e.g., Ka Ho Mok, 'Internationalising and International-benchmarking of Universities in East Asia: Producing World Class University or Reproducing Neo-Imperialism in Education', November 2007. See also, e.g., Wang Yibing, 'Realising the Global University – Some Roadmaps for Consideration by Universities in Developing World' [undated].

[‡] Geoffrey Boulton & Colin Lucas, *What are universities for?*, League of European Research Universities, September 2008, par 48.

phenomenon of globalisation ushered in by the recent communications revolution. That revolution has destroyed geographical barriers to communication and interaction, such that we now live in a novel world of virtual proximity, global perception and awareness … [I]rrespective of the outcome [of globalisation], the opportunity for universities to play an independent, mediating role in this changing world is clear. Internationally, they are located in different cultural milieus, but they share a common ethos that permits them to collaborate across cultural divides and to deepen in their students a sympathy for and understanding of the cultural assumptions and the complexities of the modern world. Over the last decade, universities have begun to develop international corporate links and networks that are increasingly used in structured ways to intensify dialogue, to articulate educational collaboration and to undertake joint research on major global problems. A convergent trend, that of increasing student mobility, should be seized on by them as the basis for the common task of educating the rising generation as global citizens, rather than merely as contributors to a university's finances or to the national workforce. These changes in behaviour, the rational and humane values that universities increasingly share, and the democratising force that they represent, also make it timely for them to find a common voice in intervening in international debate about global issues.

Within ASEAN, collaboration between ASEAN countries and universities has been clearly identified as important for human capital development. Whatever the motivation, a core question for this conference is what kinds of international collaborations – what kinds of collaborative activities, and with whom – will help universities within ASEAN countries to become increasingly 'world class'. This paper does not answer that question fully; it aims to stimulate thoughts which may assist ASEAN university leaders and others to reflect on it.

I am conscious, as you will be, of the wide diversity of

universities within ASEAN countries, and that the aspirations and opportunities that institutions have will vary enormously – between and, in many cases, within countries. Coming from a focus largely on research-intensive universities, some of what I have to say will seem relevant to some institutions and not to others. International collaboration may at first glance seem more relevant to research or student mobility than to the equity and access outreach activities of a university which is focussed primarily on social inclusion (e.g. on giving access to a university education to students who are the first in their family ever to go to university). But I would argue that there is much for institutions in one country to learn from how institutions in others handle issues of equity, access, and social inclusion. To give just one example: I was very interested to meet colleagues from two Vietnamese universities and the Vietnamese government recently visiting the University of Western Australia to discuss our activities in creating educational opportunities for Indigenous people – an issue of concern to them in their own context.

Before discussing international collaboration further, we need to consider what is meant by 'world class universities', how we know what a 'world class' university is, and what their attributes are.

What do we mean by 'world class universities'?

The term 'world class' is not completely clear. Does it mean 'among the best in the world'? If so, how high among 'the best' must it be? (Leave aside for the moment the questions of 'best at what', or how we identify what 'the best' are.) Or does 'world class' mean something more like 'what would be respectable enough in any country in the world'? Whatever it means, it implies some international standard of excellence, however high that standard might be, against which institutions are assessed (perhaps quantitatively measured).

As we all know, it is commonly said that the purpose of a university is the conservation, extension, and dissemination of knowledge. Put another way, it is commonly said that a university has three purposes, and academics within it have three fields of activity also: research, teaching, and service or community engagement (sometimes referred to as 'knowledge transfer'). But we also know that the purposes of universities vary considerably. Some are essentially teaching institutions only, with little, if any, focus on research. A smaller number are essentially research institutes with little, if any, focus on teaching. The extent and nature of the focus on service or community engagement varies greatly. The ways in which institutions balance their research, teaching, and service objectives varies over time. What it means to be 'world class' is necessarily related to the purposes or mission of the institution: '"world class" at what?' is the natural question.

There is clearly growing competition between universities to be seen as 'world class'. Just over three years ago, *The Economist* said that 'the most important recent development in the world of higher education has been the creation of a super-league of global universities that are now engaged in a battle for intellectual talent and academic prestige'.* All of my experience, before and since, suggests to me that *The Economist* is correct that there is such a battle. It is a battle in which institutions around the world, not simply those that are currently in 'a super-league', are competing for 'intellectual talent and academic prestige' and more – including competing for the talent of academic and general staff; the talent of students from undergraduates to doctoral students; prestige as teaching institutions; prestige as research institutions, including awards for staff, citations for research publications, and so on; prestige as institutions that engage and enrich the communities they serve; and resources from public and private sources, national and international.

----

* *The Economist*, 10 September 2005.

In the last five years or so, thinking about university quality has increasingly been dominated by reference to rankings of universities. The two most prominent, but not the only, international rankings are from the Shanghai Jiao Tong University (SJTU) and from *The Times Higher Education* (previously known as *The Times Higher Education Supplement*). The Shanghai Jiao Tong ranking is essentially a research ranking. *The Times Higher* ranking is an attempt to rank universities on a wider range of factors, including peer and employer review – but the methodology is even more questionable, and with an extraordinarily low response rate to the surveys on which the peer review is based, and with extraordinary volatility in ranking, is in my view not to be taken seriously as a ranking.

There have been rankings within individual countries for rather longer – most obviously, rankings such as the *US News and World Report* rankings within the United States. Here, too, methodology is questionable; the rankings rate universities on criteria which might or might not align with the actual purposes of the institutions being ranked; and, in part for that reason, there is evolution in the national rankings. In the United States, this includes the development of rankings, such as that of the *Washington Monthly*, based on very different criteria, and producing strikingly different results.

I do not think that any existing ranking adequately captures what it means to be a 'world class university'. I expect that we will see continuing evolution and development of rankings, so that those of a generation from now will be significantly different from what we have now.

The Shanghai Jiao Tong ranking was, in the words of its creators, developed 'in order to find out the gap between Chinese universities and world-class universities'.* As we know, the leading Chinese universities are committing immense resources, some of them provided by government, to rising rapidly through

---

* N C Liu & Y Cheng, 'Academic Rankings of World Universities – Methodologies and Problems', 2005, p. 1.

the global rankings. This appears a formidable phenomenon. We also know that other universities, including in North-East Asia and within ASEAN, are focussed on raising their international standing.

The University of Western Australia uses in all its materials the motto 'Achieving international excellence'. It does this, not only to describe what it thinks it is doing, but to focus itself on the need to do so. The University of Western Australia has an explicit goal of becoming one of the top 50 universities in the world within 50 years. By this, we do not mean being recognised on a particular ranking that currently exists, but by whatever are the generally accepted measures of that time. Our hope is that the rankings of universities then will give full weight to the range of desirable qualities of universities.

At UWA, we have undertaken three pieces of relevant research into the attributes of the world's 'top 50' universities: educational, research, and community engagement.* These papers are contributing to strategic and operational planning within the University, including to specific projects such as the University's Review of Course Structures, which has recently proposed significant reform of the University's undergraduate and postgraduate courses.† We are undertaking research on the trajectories by which some of the world's leading universities achieved that position, hoping to reveal more clearly the factors that make for success on that institutional journey.

The UWA studies of the educational, research, and community engagement attributes of the world's 'top 50' universities make use of the universities as identified in the currently existing rankings – in particular, the Shanghai Jiao Tong ranking – as being 'top 50'. But by identifying their

---

* *The educational attributes of some of the world's 'top 50' universities: a discussion paper,* by Dr Carolyn Daniel, The University of Western Australia, May 2008. The other papers were not made publicly available. A paper was subsequently done on finance also.

† *Education for tomorrow's world: courses of action,* Report of the Review of Course Structures, The University of Western Australia, September 2008.

attributes broadly – that is, identifying attributes of those universities which go beyond those on which they have been ranked – the UWA studies draw attention to the fact that there are desirable, even essential, attributes of universities which are not captured in those rankings.

It is often pointed out in Australia that there is a difference between a university being 'world class' and having 'a world class university system'. Some people have been thought to support policies that would lead to one university, or a small number of universities, being designated as the country's leading prospect(s) for 'world class' status, and being favoured with resources and perhaps with other policies that work to maximise their chances of 'world class' status. Others favour policies which encourage the development of 'world class' universities, but leave universities to compete as to which will achieve this, rather than having governments 'pick a winner' in advance. Others say that the focus on having one 'world class university' or a small number of such institutions is misconceived; that what will serve the country best is having a 'world class system' of universities, with the attributes of the collection of institutions being more important than the attributes of a single one or of a small number. Others respond to this that it is not possible to have a 'world class university system' without having at least one genuinely 'world class' university. This last is my own view. It seems to me that, now or later, this same issue arises for ASEAN countries.

In some of the discussions of becoming 'world class', it is sometimes implicitly assumed that what is meant is to be of the standard of the universities that are generally regarded as the *very* best in the world – the top ten or so, such as Harvard, Princeton, Yale, Oxford, Cambridge, Stanford, MIT, and others of that super-league. But this is too narrow a view of 'world class' – eliminating many very fine institutions, and frankly giving almost all institutions no chance of ever becoming, on this definition, 'world class'. Even when a university talks of becoming 'one of the top 50 in the world', or the 'top 30', or whatever it may be, there is a tendency for people to assume that what is meant is actually to be among the 'top 10'. This implicit assumption can lead people to think that the ambition is unrealistic, and should be abandoned. It is much easier and more realistic for an institution of high quality now to aspire to be in the top 30–50 universities than it is for it to aspire to be in the top, say, 15 or 20. Part of what we are doing at UWA is – as well as looking at the attributes of the top 10 or so universities – increasingly identifying attributes of universities in the range of 30 to 50, attributes which can help us to think about what distinctive attributes of excellence we will aspire to have, and how we will achieve the 'top 50' objective. We are also examining the resources available to the top 30-50 universities, to help us consider what resources we need to acquire to make our aspiration feasible.

What, then, are the characteristics of a 'world class' university?

I would like to consider the characteristics of a 'world class' university under the headings of education, research, and service or community engagement.

The educational attributes of a 'world class' university ultimately, it seems to me, come down to these: high quality of students, academic staff, courses, and teaching; a high degree of student engagement both in their studies and in the extra-curricular life of the university community; and a strong emphasis on equity, access, and diversity.

In previous papers, I have identified, as a sort of ideal type, the attributes that I identify in the finest undergraduate institutions in the world (such as the 'top 10' institutions I have previously named) – remembering, of course, that there is diversity among the leading institutions of the world, but recognising that the world's finest institutions also have many attributes in common.[*]

---

[*] This passage is adapted from *'A large and liberal education': higher education for the 21st century*, pp. 16-17.

They have concentrations of the very best students from around their country and indeed from around the world. Generally these students come together in a *residential* college community, usually in a campus of considerable beauty. Students benefit from individual mentoring or advising from senior academics. There is a high quality of academic tuition, with – because the best education is interactive – an emphasis on small group teaching and individual attention, by high-quality academic staff who – whether in research-intensive universities or the leading liberal arts colleges – work, sometimes with great difficulty and sometimes with great benefits, to combine research and teaching. At its best, this teaching stresses genuine mastery of material, independent thought, and clear communication. Face-to-face teaching is, of course, increasingly supplemented, but not replaced, by online provision. The focus is generally non-vocational at the undergraduate level, providing some form of liberal education.

In the 'top 10' (or so) institutions I am describing, there is a sense of engagement in a rich intellectual life and public debate outside the classroom, strong attention to student welfare and pastoral care, and concern for the development of character and values. There are rich opportunities for extra-curricular activities of a high quality – be they in sport, music, theatre, politics, religion, community service, or more – from which students gain much in their personal development. This is helped by the strong sense of cohort – of belonging to the Class of 2012, or whatever it may be – sharing its journey together through university years. All this generally takes place in a university or college of what would be widely considered only moderate size (smaller than very many other universities), and with a low ratio of students to academic staff.

What I have just described is, as I said, an ideal type of a 'top 10' undergraduate institution. Its value, I think, is to help us identify attributes we will, or will not, ourselves seek to develop. This 'ideal type' is, of course, of a campus university and puts emphasis on the ultimate immersive student experience on campus – the integration of living and learning in a residential environment. But we could adapt the ideal to describe a distance education institution, with students perhaps having their connection with it through learning materials passing through the mail, or in cyberspace. Or it could be a commuter rather than a residential university.

The research attributes of 'world class' universities are implicitly identified by the Shanghai Jiao Tong rankings.* The SJTU ranking is based on

1. alumni winning major international awards (i.e. Nobel Prizes and Fields Medals) – which, at a very high degree of abstraction, is said to be a proxy for the quality of education offered by the institution;

2. staff winning major international awards (i.e. Nobel Prizes and Fields Medals) – which, again at a very high degree of abstraction, is said to reflect the quality of academic staff;

3. highly cited researchers in 21 major research fields;

4. articles published in selected top journals (namely, *Nature* and *Science*);

5. articles indexed by major citation indexes (namely, Science Citation Index and Social Science Citation Index); and

6. research performance per capita.

You will detect that these criteria are meant to indicate (1) the quality of education offered, (2) the quality of academic staff, (3) the research output of the institution, and (4) the size of the institution. Other ways of measuring research quality include, for example, completions of Higher Degrees by Research (i.e. research Master and, especially, Doctoral degrees); publications by researchers – which may be raw numbers of publications, or of publications by category, including with ratings of journals;

---

* See, e.g., Liu & Cheng, op. cit. More generally, see http://www.arwu.org/

research income won in competitive grant processes; research income obtained from other sources – including internationally, from business, etc; recognition of researchers by national and international academies or other prestigious professional bodies; and patents gained, or other indicators of the potential application of research outputs.

Above all, then, the attribute being focussed on is quality of research output. Thought must be given to how to take account of the extent of research output and the relationship between quality and quantity, and its impact.

As well as the SJTU global research ranking, there are, of course, within various countries efforts to assess and even rank universities and departments within them on their research effort. Perhaps the best known is the British Research Assessment Exercise (RAE). Hong Kong has had its RAE. Australia has recently scrapped one such embryonic assessment exercise (RQF – Research Quality Framework) and is busily developing an alternative, ERA (the Excellence for Research in Australia initiative).

The service or community engagement attributes of 'world class' universities are less easily encapsulated. Such activities include activities which go under titles such as 'community outreach', 'knowledge transfer', 'community partnerships', and 'social inclusion'. This may include programs or activities which, for example, invite members of the wider community into the cultural and sporting offerings of the institution (e.g. its art galleries, museums, libraries, or concerts or theatrical performances, or sporting facilities and/or activities); involve members of the wider community in public lectures, conferences, or the like; offer teaching by university academic staff to people in the wider community (e.g. in continuing education programs); involve students and/or staff volunteering in community service activities; involve academic staff using their expertise to help solve community problems; and engage with businesses, assisting them with innovation and the solution of problems.

It is evident from the UWA study of the community engagement and educational attributes of the world's 'top 50' universities that such activities are extensively undertaken by such universities; that there are significant differences in the emphases they place on them and that these vary by country; that one area of variation is the extent to which student involvement in such activities is seen as important in the educational program of the university; and that some universities more than others use such activities as means of enhancing their local, national, and even international reputations.

Some issues for 'world class' universities

Before turning to how collaboration can help universities become 'world class', I think it may be helpful to identify several issues which the world's leading universities generally seem to confront. There are six I particularly wish to identify: the 'war for talent', the need for more resources, review of areas of teaching and research, enhancing the all-round student learning experience, equity and diversity, and internationalisation and globalisation. I will take these briefly in turn.[*]

First, there is what the management consultants McKinsey, controversially but I think without exaggeration, call 'the war for talent' – the competition to attract, develop, and retain the most outstanding faculty and academic leaders, and students, anywhere in the world, including increased recognition of family circumstances as a factor in career decisions, and renewed emphasis on developing one's own junior faculty members. The world's finest universities seek the very best people in the world, and invest in them. This is reflected in what I think of as 'the Harvard question': who is the very best person in the world in this field, and how do we get them?

Secondly, there is the need for ever-greater resources, which

---

[*] This section is drawn from *'A large and liberal education': higher education for the 21st century*, pp. 18-23.

governments are unlikely adequately to provide, and so need to be drawn increasingly from student fees, especially domestic student fees – wherever possible combined with scholarships and loans – and from major philanthropic support from actively-engaged alumni and other benefactors. Philanthropic support is proving increasingly important in universities in many countries, including in Europe, Asia, and Australia, and there are significant efforts, including by governments as well as universities themselves, to encourage it.

Thirdly, partly driven by developments in science, technology, and globalisation, there is review of the areas in which the university teaches and researches, most especially to ensure an inter- or multi-disciplinary approach where it is needed, as indeed it is from stem cell research to neuroscience to the study of global poverty to non-traditional security and beyond – all topics, and there are many others, that require expertise from across a range of sciences, and social sciences and humanities, including ethics. An interesting case is the need to understand various world religions if current international conflicts and cultural diversity within countries are to be understood, and the advantage in this to those institutions, such as several leading American and British universities, with strength in religious studies. How to balance the need for strong research within disciplines with the need to encourage and remove obstacles to multi-disciplinary research is demanding careful attention. How to refresh for the 21st century the traditional US vision of liberal undergraduate education, weakened by creeping vocationalism and other forces, is a major focus for many leading educators and institutions, many of whom believe that the need for such liberal education has never been greater than it is today, in a world of rapid change, global forces, polarisation of opinion and inadequate tolerance and humility, and pressures for instant action rather than sustained reflection. These and other concerns are reflected in reviews of curricula and course structures in many universities in many countries, including at the University of Western Australia and several other Australian universities.

Fourthly, partly in response to criticisms in the US – including from such figures as Derek Bok* – of the alleged decline in quality of university education, there has been renewed focus on the academic and broader student experience, be it through reducing student-to-staff ratios and class sizes, or curriculum reform, or improving students' writing skills, or re-strengthening out-of-classroom connections between faculty and students, or providing high-quality campus centres for students, or increasing online support, or increasing the emphasis on students engaging in community service, or encouraging student engagement in a variety of extra-curricular activities (including trying to achieve balance in what can be – should be – the very positive role of sport in universities), or enhancing the performing and visual arts in students' lives, or grappling – for the most part unsuccessfully, I think – with problems in student culture and behaviour. Harvard's January 2007 'A Compact to Enhance Teaching and Learning at Harvard' is just one noteworthy step in the increasingly global focus on enhancing teaching and learning, and the all-round student learning experience.†

Fifthly, there is in many 'world class' universities a strong emphasis on equity and diversity, including efforts, of uneven seriousness and success, to promote gender equality, ethnic and religious diversity, socio-economic diversity, and equal rights for LGBTs – the widely-used term for lesbians, gays, bisexuals and transgendered. Very many co-educational institutions retain essentially masculine cultures, and have not yet achieved the thorough transformation needed to have cultures of genuine equality. Some have embarked on wide-ranging programs

---

* E.g. Derek Bok, *Our Underachieving Colleges: A Candid Look at How Much Students Learn and Why They Should Be Learning More*, Princeton University Press, 2006.

† More generally, I especially recommend Richard Light, *Making the most of college: students speak their minds*, Harvard University Press, 2001, and papers by Alan Gilbert for the University of Manchester review of teaching, learning and the student experience.

of profound change. Reflecting concerns internationally for equity and social inclusion in higher education (which concerns have been increasingly prominent in Australia), there is also much concern in the US that, despite strenuous efforts and the expenditure of much money on scholarships and financial aid, top universities and colleges often remain too much, as the president of one of them has described his own to me, a 'rich people's place'. Efforts to increase the rate of participation of the relevant age cohort in higher education are important in ASEAN countries, as they are in the UK, Australia, and elsewhere.

Sixthly, there is in 'world class' universities a strong focus on internationalisation and globalisation, including seeking to develop a coherent strategy for all the rich dimensions of global engagement. Internationalisation increasingly means taking a global perspective on all matters and acting as an international (as well as a local, state, and national) institution, including setting high international standards in everything; encouraging international, inter-cultural and inter-faith awareness throughout the university community; ensuring a culture in which people of all backgrounds feel equally welcome; seeking faculty and students from around the world; encouraging language studies; encouraging international experience by students and staff alike; curriculum that genuinely reflects international experience and global issues; international community service projects; alumni activities around the world; and more. International collaborations of various kinds play an increasingly important part in such internationalisation. There is also much focus on the study and debate of issues related to globalisation, and also seeking to ensure that universities have expertise on all major regions of the world, including increasingly China, India, and the Middle East, and on major religions. While some universities are interested in teaching overseas, many are very cautious about overseas campuses.

There are, of course, other issues or trends in leading universities one could discuss. One is debate about the proper relationship between universities, the marketplace, and entrepreneurship. It is interesting how much attention some 'world class' universities are giving to their electronic presence and aggressive electronic projection, as part both of their focused communications strategies, and their thinking about how to use IT for external and internal projection as well as for enhancing education – for example, ensuring all faculty members and senior administrators have full CVs on their websites, with links to all their publications that are available electronically; using email for regular and attractive communications with alumni; ensuring their websites are of such quality and easy navigability as befits what is the university's most important publication by far; and using a portal within the institution as the electronic embodiment of the university's all-round educational offering to its students.*

Forms of international collaboration

If I have spent so much time discussing the nature and attributes of 'world class' universities, and issues before them, it is partly because I think that the path to becoming a 'world class' university, and for continuous improvement generally, depends upon the clear-minded and ambitious strategic and operational planning of each individual institution, and on the methodical and effective implementation of those plans – all this, of course, within the context in which that university operates.

As I have suggested already, one of the strategies for continuous improvement is international collaboration. There is a wide variety of multilateral and bilateral collaborations that are possible and increasingly prominent. These include:

---

* Obviously this was written some years before, for example, the development of Massive Open Online Courses (MOOCs).

- regional harmonisation programs – such as the work underway to develop a European Higher Education Area, of which the so-called Bologna process is the most famous part, and the idea of a 'higher education common space in Southeast Asia' which SEAMEO RIHED has been exploring[*];

- regional groupings of universities – such as the ASEAN University Network, or the League of European Research Universities;

- wider international alliances or groupings of universities – such as Universitas 21, or the Worldwide Universities Network, or the Association of Pacific Rim Universities, or – to take an older example – the Association of Commonwealth Universities;

- benchmarking activities – including the comparison of data to assess relative performance or to guide strategic deliberations (e.g. sharing student and staff evaluation survey data as a way of comparing the performance of universities);

- other collaboration in quality assurance – such as participation in review processes for other universities, such as reviews of parts of the university, or of degree programs (there is also collaboration between quality assurance agencies in different countries, including through the International Network for Quality Assurance Agencies in Higher Education);

- sharing ideas: arrangements involving exchanges of information and ideas, for example between university leaders with responsibility in many specific areas, to facilitate learning from each other's experience can be extremely valuable, including in strategic planning;

---

[*]   Southeast Asian Ministers of Education Organization – Regional Centre for Higher Education and Development.

- multilateral or bilateral research collaborations – for example, involving joint laboratories in two or more universities, or participation in projects such as, say, the human genome project;

- collaborations in research supervision – for example, involving cotutelle arrangements for PhDs leading to the award of the degree by both partner institutions at which the doctoral student is enrolled and supervised;

- collaboration in coursework teaching programs – such as the joint or dual degrees which are increasingly being offered by partner universities, with students spending part of their degree program in one university and part at the other, resulting in a degree that is jointly badged or in the award of two degrees, one from each institution*;

- collaborative e-learning – e.g. teaching using ICT so that classes conducted at one institution are made available to students at another or others;

- 'information networking' – such as the joint development of shared computing or other technological capacities, and inter-library collaboration (such as through AUNILO – ASEAN University Network Inter-Library Online);

- visiting scholar programs – including faculty exchange programs, both for research and teaching purposes;

- shared professional development activities for staff;

- study abroad and student exchange programs;

- collaboration in student extra-curricular activities – such as for sporting competitions, international community service activities, and so on;

- collaboration in service activities – such as when two universities partner together to assist a third university in its

---

* See, e.g., Jane Knight, 'Joint and Double Degree Programs: Vexing Questions and Issues', The Observatory on borderless higher education, London, September 2008.

capacity-building (increasingly suggested in collaborations between Chinese '985' universities and overseas universities, working to assist weaker regional Chinese universities);

- collaboration in money-making ventures – such as the development for revenue-generation purposes by Universitas 21 of U21 Global, the Singapore-based online graduate school; and

- collaboration in advocacy – including of the kind that Boulton and Lucas recommended, universities finding 'a common voice in intervening in international debate about global issues'.

Many of these types of collaboration are inter-connected, of course. Most obviously, some of the individually mentioned collaborative activities often take place within the regional or wider international groupings of universities also referred to. The collaborations can embrace any part of a university, including any academic discipline and any administrative function.

It might be added that there are further aspects of collaboration that are much more likely to take place between universities within a single country rather than internationally – including policy advocacy to their national government, shared marketing activities overseas or even locally (e.g. in outreach to under-represented sections of the community), and shared events overseas for the alumni of any of the country's universities. National collaboration between universities may well be differentiated by sector (e.g. research-intensive universities especially collaborating with each other, technological universities with each other, etc), as well as there being bilateral collaborations of all sorts and collaboration on some issues under a single national universities body (e.g. Universities UK, Universities Australia).

The forms of international collaboration are evolving. Jane Knight has identified the following aspects of internationalisation as a 'formidable force for change', many (though not all) of which relate directly to international collaborations:[*]

- the creation of new international networks and consortia;
- the growing numbers of students, professors, and researchers participating in academic mobility schemes;
- the increase in the number of courses, programs, and qualifications that focus on comparative and international themes;
- more emphasis on developing international/inter-cultural and global competencies;
- stronger interest in international themes and collaborative research;
- steep increase in cross-border delivery of academic programs;
- more interest and concern with international and regional rankings of universities;
- an increase in campus-based extra-curricular activities with an international or multicultural component;
- the investment in recruiting foreign students, and dependence on their income;
- the rise in the number of joint or double degrees;
- growth in the numbers and types of for-profit cross-border education providers;
- the expansion in partnerships, franchises, and branch campuses; and
- the establishment of new national, regional, and international organisations focused on international education.

---

[*] Jane Knight, 'The internationalization of higher education: are we on the right track?', *Academic Matters*, October-November 2008 (see www.academicmatters.ca).

Some benefits, problems, and lessons of collaboration

There are, of course, many benefits of international collaborative activities, and these will vary with the activity and context. Such benefits include:

- focussing the minds of institutional leaders and others – including staff at all levels, and members of governance bodies – on the international standards by which institutions need to operate, thus helping to raise institutional performance;

- exposing the institution to the refreshment of ideas from international collaborators about how to approach issues: the opportunity to discuss common issues frankly with colleagues from an overseas university can be highly stimulating, and can generate fresh approaches;

- the development of international, inter-cultural and, in some cases, inter-faith understanding by students and staff alike through their interactions (e.g. through study abroad, or studying or teaching in international collaborative teaching programs, or participation in visiting scholar programs);

- the sharing of research expertise, including in some cases research approaches which come at problems from different angles;

- more generally, enabling institutions to do together what they could not do, or could not do so well, separately – the standard argument for any cooperative activity;

- increasing the international recognition and reputation of qualifications offered by particular institutions and of their national or regional qualifications framework; and

- more generally, enhancement of the reputation and prestige of universities through their international connections.

In short, international collaborations can be important for building capacity, broadening perspectives, and raising profile and status. I would especially wish to draw attention to the benefits for universities of sharing ideas and information with international partners in the whole spectrum of activities within universities – from information resources to alumni relations and fundraising, from financial management to student services, from human resource policy and practice to curriculum reform, from research policy to residential colleges – as well as between experts in particular academic disciplines.

There are, however, also many problems with collaborations. These too will vary with the activity and context. For example, study abroad and student exchange can be hindered by incompatibilities in the academic calendars of institutions in different countries, making the timing of student exchanges hard to arrange; on the other hand, the differences between calendars can be an important factor enabling academic staff members from one institution to spend time in another.

Other factors that inhibit study abroad/student exchange may be mentioned to illustrate some of the problems of international collaborations. As well as calendar incompatibilities, such problems include:

- arranging credit transfer – the home institution being sufficiently familiar with and confident about both the academic content and the quality of the studies undertaken in the overseas university to grant credit towards the student's degree (in some cases, the structure of degrees prevents any credit, and in other cases the granting of credit is very readily handled, especially where credit transfer agreements exist);

- language – study abroad/exchange in a foreign language environment may only be practical for students of that language, or may further encourage the widespread use of English, including increasingly to teach programs within countries for which English is not an official language;

- cost – even when there are institutional and (as in Australia) government sources of financial support for study abroad, the cost can act as a deterrent to students;

- prestige – some students may be interested in study abroad/ exchange only at a limited range of institutions of high prestige.

The reference to issues in credit transfer highlights the fact that quality assurance issues are important in international collaborations. Institutions should want to ensure that the quality of the activities which are the subject of the collaboration is properly assured. They will be wise to be extremely cautious about any activity which risks their own quality, or the perception of their quality. One of the unresolved quality assurance (or perception of quality) issues in international collaborations is whether it is legitimate for students in international collaborative programs to receive two degrees, one from each of the partner universities, for work neither more advanced nor taking longer than would result in one degree if all of it was undertaken in a single university. As you know, there are moves towards an ASEAN quality assurance network, and there is other international collaboration between national quality assurance agencies.

A consequence of these and other difficulties can be that formal agreements between institutions for study abroad/ student exchange can be just that: formal agreements giving rise to very little real activity. This is a more general problem for international collaborations. It is far easier to sign Memorandums of Understanding than it is to give significant effect to them. Stories are told of institutions about to sign MOUs when they discover that they already have an MOU from some years before – to which so little effect has been given that no one in either institution is aware of its existence!

One of the principal reasons why efforts at collaboration often do not achieve their stated purposes is that they are purely 'top down' initiatives from the central administration of the university, and do not connect with the 'real work' that is undertaken within a university. Initiatives for research collaboration will only work if researchers within both institutions have good reasons to work together. While in some cases collaboration can be required, and there may be much to be said for offering incentives for it, its vitality will depend upon its connecting with the genuine research interests and needs of those undertaking the research. This is not always the case. Similarly, arrangements for student exchange or study abroad will only work if students actually wish to go to the other country and university. Again, there are agreements which do not lead to real activity because, for whatever reason, few students from one institution wish to go to the other.

Collaboration is costly of resources, including staff time and money. Like any activity, it has an opportunity cost. Coordination with colleagues at an overseas institution can be even harder to achieve in practice than coordination within one's home institution (which often seems hard enough). Resources are almost invariably scarcer than their potential uses, and it is necessary to prioritise. In practice, this can act as a drag on collaboration. The current global financial/economic crisis, with its adverse impact on the resources available to many institutions and individuals, heightens further the need for allocation of resources to be strategic – well judged to maximise positive outcomes for the resources available.

Strategies for successful international collaborations will vary. In research, for example, we may wish to identify universities for potential collaboration by such factors as numbers of highly cited researchers and highly cited papers, as well as other measures of research performance listed above. We know that the likelihood of citation of a scientific paper will be higher or lower depending on which combination of universities the co-authors are from. Having co-authors from leading UK or, most especially, US universities will increase the chances of citation, and having co-authors from both will increase them yet further. This may lead to a strategy of supporting collaborations likely to produce joint publications, and especially joint publications with high prospects of extensive citation. This may mean focussing on attracting visiting scholars from, and sending visiting scholars to, the centres of the most promising collaborations.

One might develop different strategies for collaboration in other fields than research. Wang Yibing has argued that experience shows 'that successful practices in cooperation in internationalisation of higher education would have at least' these features: 'clear focus on concrete substance, for example, curriculum development, faculty or students exchange program with clear purposes, collaborative research, etc., based on consensus reached by and mutual benefit for all parties involved'; 'Stable funding, such as the EU project called "The Asia-Link Program"'; and 'Sincerity, continuity and sustainability'.*

Some of the lessons for institutions concerning international collaborations would appear to include these:

1. develop collaborative arrangements which there is good reason to think will lead to real collaboration in practice because it is clearly in the interests of those 'on the ground' in both institutions to collaborate (even if they don't realise this yet);

2. select partners carefully and strategically, so as to maximise the chances of real collaboration happening;

3. promote collaborative opportunities (e.g. the opportunities for working with partner universities in an international network to which you belong) actively among staff and, as appropriate, students, making it as attractive and easy as possible for them to undertake the relevant collaborative activity;

4. when you enter into a collaborative arrangement that you hope will have significant benefits, work at it hard – as

---

* Wang Yibing, op. cit., p. 11.

with any activity, planning and implementing strategies to maximise the benefits, including identifying problems and their solutions, monitoring performance (possibly using targets), and reviewing plans and targets in the light of this;

5. consider what staffing will be needed to give effect to the collaborative arrangement, and provide it;

6. consider the extent of collaborative arrangements that will work – how many partnerships can actually be put into effect, and from which the institution will genuinely benefit. Some institutions seem to enter into innumerable collaborative arrangements for the sake of them, with no real chance of activity flowing from them, while some others seem insufficiently internationally engaged.

Another way of saying much of this is that the international collaborations chosen should form an integral part of the strategy of the institution, rather than an add-on.

There is, of course, more that can be said on each of these points. For example, from one perspective it makes sense for universities to enter into collaborations only with institutions that perform better than them, so as to be stretched and supported themselves to perform better. But a pairing cannot, obviously, be of two institutions which are both higher than the other in rankings. Institutions need to decide what characteristics – similarities, differences, levels of performance, reputation, ease of communication, and so on – matter in their selection of partners, and make selections that will best achieve their strategic purposes. The best collaborations will probably be between institutions which are sufficiently similar to have real grounds for collaboration (including mutual understanding), but sufficiently different for there to be joint gains from working together. Of course, it is also necessary to accept that institutions with which you may wish to partner might not, in careful analysis of their own strategic interests and in necessary selectivity about their collaborations, agree to collaboration with your university.

Several governments or, as in the case of Europe, regional bodies have taken many steps to encourage international collaborations between universities. This creates opportunities, incentives, and encouragement – for example, through scholarship programs that support student mobility, or programs supporting movement of academic staff. But the same problem can arise for nations as for universities – that unless what the government is wishing to promote connects with the real interests of the staff and students 'on the ground', it is unlikely to achieve its objectives. Moreover, the involvement of governments can run the risk of excessive control, and loss of that degree of autonomy which should be an inherent characteristic of a university (and which is, in my view, essential if a university is to become 'world class').

It may be that some governments of some other countries, keen to encourage collaboration between their universities and yours, will seek an undue degree of control. This seems to me to be a reason why ASEAN universities should seek diversity in the range of their international collaborations – collaborating within the ASEAN region, of course; collaborating with institutions in other major Asia-Pacific countries, such as (to mention them in alphabetical order) Australia, China, India, Japan, Korea, and New Zealand; collaborating with the United States, Canada, the United Kingdom, and continental Europe; and, as appropriate for particular purposes, with institutions elsewhere (the appointment of the President of the National University of Singapore to be the founding president of the King Abdullah University of Science and Technology in Saudi Arabia is an interesting case).

Conclusion

International collaboration is a strategy which many universities in many countries are using both to engage fully in internationalisation and globalisation, and as part of their strategies for raising themselves increasingly to 'world class' status, or simply to protect the position they already have. Significant international collaboration is necessary but not sufficient to achieve these purposes. It is hard today to imagine a 'world class' university which did not engage actively in a wide range of international collaborations: indeed, high-quality international collaborations might almost have become one of the defining characteristics of a 'world class' university. This is the case not least because one of the most important benefits of international collaboration is that it exposes us repeatedly to international standards, and exposes us to new ideas and possibilities for improving what we do.

Yet international collaborations alone will not enable a university to rise to 'world class' status; they need to be part of a wider strategy aimed at this. International collaborations are no panacea or instant recipe for this. Individual institutions need to develop, resource, implement, monitor, and refine their own individual strategies for 'world class' university status. Within this, international collaborations that are well chosen, well prepared, well executed, and wisely combined can make a valuable contribution to this strategy, and to raising the quality and performance of an institution in teaching, research, and service.

'The spirit of a university'

Farewell reception[*]
The University of Western Australia
14 May 2009

Thank you, Alan[†], very much indeed for your kind words; and thank you for the opportunity to serve with you, and to learn from you, over the last two and a quarter years.

It has been a privilege to work with you and with so many wonderful colleagues here in this University which I love. For me, UWA has been a very special place since I taught here for a few months in 1984. I was excited to return in January 2007, and I leave now with much sadness, and with gratitude to so many.

I came back to UWA in 2007 believing it to be one of the jewels in the crown of Australian higher education, and I leave knowing this.

My central goal has been to do all I can, working with colleagues throughout the University community, to continue improving the quality of the student learning experience at UWA, in all its dimensions both in and beyond the classroom, for all students including all international as well as Australian students. I am grateful to colleagues in all faculties and the School of Indigenous Studies, in all sections of the Registrar's Office and Finance and Resources, the Library and Information Management, the Guild (including the Postgraduate Students Association), the colleges which are a very important part of UWA, other parts of the UWA community, including members of the Senate, alumni and friends of the University, UWA

---

[*] On departing UWA to become Warden of Rhodes House, Oxford.

[†] Professor Alan Robson AO, Vice-Chancellor of the University of Western Australia (2004-12).

Extension, the Institute of Advanced Studies, and of course here in the Vice-Chancellery, and especially in my own office, for our work together towards this goal.

It has been a privilege to work with colleagues throughout the University, including with students, in the Review of Course Structures which led the University community to embark on the Future Framework* for degree courses – as I see it, a roadmap for the future of education at UWA. It has been a joy to work with so many colleagues in thinking about what is needed in UWA's educational activities for us to become genuinely one of the 'top 50' universities in the world by 2050, and in translating that thinking into plans for action, and into action. To achieve this important goal will require strategic focus and sustained determination, even a calm sense of urgency†, in the face of unavoidable financial constraint.

It has been inspirational to work with so many colleagues to seek, for example through the development of Aspire UWA, to make an outstanding UWA education available to students from far and wide on the basis only of merit, of potential, and not of privilege. It has been a pleasure to try to make a contribution, working with colleagues, in seeking to engage further support for UWA from the friends and potential friends of the University in the wider community.

It is invidious to name individuals, so I will not do so; but I can confidently say that I have reason, in many cases very much reason, to be grateful to every person in this room. So please let me say 'thank you'.

A few weeks ago, I suddenly and unexpectedly found that, while my back was turned and my mind was distracted with the busy-ness of life, I had reached the surprising age of 50, and as I reflected on this sobering fact I tried to learn a little about the year I was born, 1959. It was a time when, beneath conservative

---

* Later 'New Courses'.
† See, e.g., John P Kotter, *A sense of urgency*, Harvard Business Press, 2008.

rule in most western countries, cultural and political forces were quietly stirring that – fuelled by Vietnam, the pill, and much else – would lead to the youth revolt of the 1960s, with its unprecedented impact of popular youth culture on universities, in the aftermath of which revolt my fortunate generation came of age. Today I would like, with your indulgence, to say something about three – I think relevant – more sedate artefacts of 1959.

As some people will know, that was the year which saw the publication of *Kings in Grass Castles,* Mary Durack's account of the Duracks, Costellos, and Tullys as they pioneered and settled the far western plains of New South Wales and south-west Queensland and then the trek to the Kimberley. These were the 19th century white pioneers, with ambiguous relations with the Indigenous people, of the region of the Channel Country of outback Queensland in which I was born and was a small boy. Mary Durack paints a vivid portrait of what she calls 'the vast emptiness' of 'this pitiless country' – and I have childhood memories of looking out across the flat red plains, and of our pet kangaroo, and much else. There is, of course, much of Western Australia that is very similar, and I have often thought that my growing up in the outback of Queensland and then in Brisbane, which I think was then more like Perth than it is today, helped predispose me so much to like Western Australia and to like Western Australians.

As Mary Durack was publishing her family memoir of outback life, *Kings in Grass Castles,* the English physicist and novelist C P Snow was delivering the 1959 Rede Lecture on what he called 'the two cultures' – the culture of scientists and the culture of literary intellectuals. Snow belonged to both cultures and lamented the gulf between them. Some 50 years on, I too am struck by two cultures, two cultures within universities in many countries. These might be imperfectly characterised as the culture of the traditional autonomous academic as free agent, and the culture of academic management. Belonging myself to both cultures, I too lament the avoidable gulf we sometimes see between them. I believe that one of the challenges and opportunities of leaders at all levels in universities is to develop the healthiest synthesis or balance of the two. A university, being a large, complex, costly and generally under-funded organisation, must be efficiently led, managed, and administered if it is to achieve its aims of teaching, research, and service. Just as we need first-rate academics, so we need first-rate academic management. For this to be healthy, we need to ensure that everything that is done in a university – everything – is infused or at least consistent with the spirit of a university.

What is the spirit of a university? Sometimes the spirit of John Henry Newman, with his emphasis on liberal education, is contrasted with Wilhelm von Humboldt's emphasis on research. A paper last September by the current Warden of Rhodes House, Sir Colin Lucas, and the Vice-Principal of the University of Edinburgh, Geoffrey Boulton, entitled *What are universities for?* – worth finding through Google, I might say – argues that the spirit of the modern university embodies the complementary spirits both of Newman and Humboldt.[*]

Let us for a moment hear some other voices on the essence of a university. Robert Maynard Hutchins, who became president of the University of Chicago at the age of 30 in 1929 and led it for over 20 years, later wrote: 'The best definition of a university that I have been able to think of is that it is a centre of independent thought.' Hutchins depicted a university as 'an academic community. The aim of the community is independent thought. This requires the defence of the independence of its members.' Hutchins also wrote: 'True education is the improvement of [people] through helping them learn to think for themselves.'[†]

----

[*] Colin Lucas & Geoffrey Boulton, *What are universities for?*, League of European Research Universities, September 2008, p. 3.

[†] Robert M Hutchins, *Freedom, Education, and the Fund: Essays and Addresses: 1946-1956*, Meridian Books, New York, 1956, pp. 152, 161, 152.

Hutchins's Australian Vice-Chancellor contemporary, Sir John Medley, wrote in 1943: 'A university if it stands for anything stands for quality...'*

The philosopher Alfred North Whitehead wrote: 'the proper function of a university is the imaginative acquisition of knowledge. ... A university is imaginative or it is nothing – at least nothing useful.'†

The University of Newcastle in some of its materials has the statement: 'This is a place of opportunity.' As someone who started life as a poor boy in outback Queensland, I believe passionately in the life-transforming importance of education, and the importance of the university as a place of opportunity.

In June 1912, as the University of Western Australia was preparing to admit its first students and just three months before UWA's founding Senate wisely chose the motto 'Seek Wisdom', across the world the president of the University of Wisconsin – a geologist, Charles Richard Van Hise – gave a commencement address in Madison entitled 'The Spirit of a University'. He said that 'the essential spirit of a university, *which under no circumstances should it yield*' is 'freedom of thought, ... inquiry after truth for its own sake, ... adjustment of the knowledge of the past in the light of the newest facts and highest reason, ... the unalterable determination to follow wherever truth may lead regardless of preconceived notions or ideas'. What he called this 'uncompromising spirit of truth' made 'liberty' 'the vital thing in a university', and – he said – 'forever makes a university a center of [intellectual] conflict', marked by 'the eternal conflict of ideas'.‡

In reading – as one does – the National Academy of Sciences

---

* J D G Medley, *Education for Democracy*, Australian Council for Educational Research, 1943, p. 21.

† 'Universities and Their Function', quoted from Alfred North Whitehead, *The Aims of Education and Other Essays*, Williams and Norgate, London, 1955, p. 145.

‡ Charles Richard Van Hise, *The Spirit of a University*, Commencement Address, University of Wisconsin, Madison, 19 June 1912, pp. 4, 11, 5, 4, & 10. Original emphasis.

obituary of Charles Van Hise, which described his work both as a scientist and as a university president, I was struck by these words: 'His point of view was large and liberal, always incisive, often humorous.'* 'Large and liberal' – these are the words, borrowed in my case from a 19th century bishop and educational leader, James Moorhouse, which I had given to my own book, launched in this room by Janet Holmes a Court nearly two years ago, *A large and liberal education': higher education for the 21st century*. I have since learned that the phrase 'large and liberal education' was more commonly used in the 19th and early 20th centuries than I had known.

The idea of a university as an academic community has also been widespread, and – in the words of a paper from Villanova University just a few years ago – 'Collegiality is an essential element of the spirit of community in any academic institution'.† By collegiality, I think we should mean both an appropriately consultative approach to leadership and management – which consultation will often unavoidably need to be the prelude to decisive action by those entrusted with the task of decision and action – and also treating each other as colleagues, engaged together in a shared enterprise, acting towards each other with mutual respect, a presumption of goodwill, and wherever possible with friendliness.

All these words – academic community, independent thought, the uncompromising spirit of truth, quality, imagination, opportunity, large and liberal, collegiality – all these words convey, I think, important elements of the spirit of a university, and what I hope and expect always will be important elements of the spirit of this university.

I have dwelt so long on this because I think that it is a

---

* Thomas C Chamberlin, 'Biographical Memoir Charles Richard Van Hise 1857-1918', National Academy of Sciences, Presented to the Academy 1919, published in *Memoirs of the National Academy of Sciences*, Volume XVII, Government Printing Office, Washington, 1924, p. 149.

† http://www3.villanova.edu/facultycongress/docs/collegiality.pdf – accessed 9 May 2009.

necessary – a necessary but not in itself sufficient – condition of successfully synthesising the two cultures of academic autonomy and academic management that everything that is done in a university be compatible, or better still infused, with the spirit of a university. It must be, for example, a place of debate and not essentially of control; of efficiency and not officiousness; of not only tolerance but of celebration of diversity; of collegiality and mutual respect and goodwill.

If I were to pursue all this, I might dwell on the graduation address given by Leo Strauss at the University of Chicago in 1959 on 'What is liberal education?', or to take a different angle, for whose who want to understand the phenomenon of academic bureaucracy, the book *Parkinson's Law*, by C Northcote Parkinson, first published in 1958.

Also first published in 1958, and made into a movie in 1959, was the last book of that time I do want to mention – Graham Greene's novel, *Our Man in Havana*. Graham Greene called it 'a fair-story' and 'an entertainment'. In the movie comedy, Alec Guiness plays Jim Wormald, the British vacuum cleaner salesman who becomes an absurd spy in pre-Castro Cuba, sending back concocted reports to London from an imaginary network of agents who don't exist. One of his reports contains a fictitious diagram of what may be a (non-existent) weapons installation – a diagram based on the circuitry of a vacuum cleaner! I have never thought of myself as Alec Guiness, nor as a vacuum cleaner salesman, nor as a spy, let alone a fraudulent spy – so, Chief, I offer myself to be, not 'our man in Havana', but 'our man in Oxford'. If there is any way that from Rhodes House I can help the University of Western Australia over the years to come, with vacuum cleaner diagrams or in other ways, I will be delighted.

Thank you again for the privilege of serving with you in this fine University. I am enormously grateful to so many people, and wish you all the very best for the future.

Liberty and liberality: Oxford and Cambridge for a global future

Oxford-Cambridge Boat Race Dinner
University Club of Chicago
23 April 2010

It is an immense pleasure to be with you here in Chicago for this Oxford-Cambridge Boat Race Dinner. Not least, it gives me an opportunity to thank John Morrison for the truly outstanding contribution he has made through this Oxford-Cambridge Dinner and in so many other ways, including as a distinguished past President of the Association of American Rhodes Scholars. John, we are all in your debt, and we are very grateful to you and to Barbara.

Whatever rivalries we may feel, all of us here tonight are united in our gratitude to, affection for, and commitment to one or the other of two of the very finest universities in the world. Like most people here, I first went to one of them from far afield, and only because of the life-transforming opportunity created by a scholarship. While I went as a student to Oxford, I had earlier gone to Cambridge. In my last year of high school, 1976, I happened to win airfares from Australia to London. A former teacher from my high school[†] gave me a book to read that he said was the best introduction I could have to mid-1970s Britain. It was a biography of a Cambridge economist written by an Oxford economist – Roy Harrod's biography of John Maynard Keynes. As well as being one of the most influential economic thinkers and policy advocates of the last century, Keynes played key roles in the Anglo-American economic diplomacy that was so

---

* This speech was previously published as 'This great heritage', *The American Oxonian*, Spring 2010.

† Colin Charles Lamont (18 November 1941-7 July 2012).

important during and after both world wars. And so, influenced by reading Harrod on Keynes and drawn in part by the allure of Keynes and King's, just after Christmas 1976 I made my way for a day from London to Cambridge. Needless to say, it rained; but it was also beautiful and truly inspiring.

A little under four years later, I was awarded a scholarship that took me to Oxford, where as a student and then a don I wrote a thesis, later a book, on – yes – the Cambridge economist, John Maynard Keynes. I slightly hesitate to mention this in Chicago, the home for many decades of the most significant concentration in the world of anti-Keynesian economists; but I mention these instances of Oxford students of Cambridge thought to illustrate that we, graduates and friends of Cambridge and Oxford, are united in our commitment to scholarship and teaching of an exceptional and also a distinctive kind.

It is scholarship and teaching nurtured in a collegiate environment, in essentially residential academic communities in which each individual is valued; in which each has the real opportunity genuinely to belong to a community in which students of diverse subjects and backgrounds all belong and interact; in which teaching in tutorials and supervisions is, at its best, highly personal, both challenging and stretching, and also supportive; from where path-breaking research, including original thought and fierce debate, has impact around the world; where the life of the community is enriched and every student has the chance to be broadened by participation in extra-curricular activities, including sport such as the rowing we are reminded of tonight; in which our lives are enriched by deep friendships and enduring memories forged in places of exquisite beauty.

Most of us here tonight look back with gratitude and pride on this; others have this great adventure before them, and we wish them well.

The fact that an Oxford-Cambridge Boat Race Dinner is held in Chicago reflects also the fact that Cambridge and

Oxford are, while being British, also remarkably international – global – institutions. They have for a long time been, in the words used by my American alma mater, Princeton, 'in the nation's service and in the service of all nations'. Not least, Cambridge and Oxford have done much to promote Anglo-American friendship, which over the last century has been – and, who knows, perhaps over the next century will be – one of the cornerstones of liberty and liberality, or of what the American theologian Reinhold Niebuhr called 'peace and justice in a sinful world'.

Above all, however, I think of Cambridge and Oxford as examples of educational excellence, offering education that is genuinely among the finest in the world, and that I am sure will in the 21st century, as it did in the 20th century, educate leaders for the United States, as for other countries, who benefit immeasurably from the special, if sometimes mystifying, gifts only an Oxbridge education has to offer.

We are all part of this great heritage, and I hope and believe that we will do all we can to hand it on even better to those who come after us. Tonight, I am delighted to be with you here in Chicago to celebrate the heritage of which the Oxford-Cambridge Boat Race is such a fine expression.

Universities and contemporary society: civility in a free society

The inaugural Sir Zelman Cowen Oration
St John's College, University of Queensland, 1 March 2012

It is an immense pleasure to be with you here tonight, to be home in Brisbane and to be back at my alma mater, the University of Queensland, and here at St John's College; and it is a great honour to be invited to give the inaugural Sir Zelman Cowen Oration, in memory of an educational leader and healing Governor-General who was, for me, a close friend and mentor.

Thank you, Sir Llew*, for your generous introduction. In July 2010, I was delighted to be at the University's Centenary Dinner when you were recognised as Alumnus of the Year for your exceptional contribution to this University, above all as a much-loved Chancellor, and to this state, and it is a privilege to be able to acknowledge with gratitude your outstanding contribution. During your Chancellorship, under successive Vice-Chancellors, the progress of this University, which I have loved since my student days here over 30 years ago, has been exceptional, even astounding, most especially in its research intensity and capacity, and in the funding of this.

It is also a privilege to be here at St John's College as it celebrates its centenary. Just over 30 of its 100 years have been under the inspired, visionary, and indefatigable leadership of John Morgan. It is characteristically creative and constructive of John to initiate this Oration in memory of Sir Zelman Cowen,

---

* Sir Llewellyn Edwards, Chancellor of the University of Queensland (1993-2009). Llew's many other distinguished contributions to public life included serving as Queensland's Minister for Health (1974-78) and Treasurer (1978-83), and as Chairman and CEO of World Expo '88, held in Brisbane.

who, as you know, was the first Honorary Fellow of this College, the Vice-Chancellor of this University, and friend and advocate of the collegiate education for which this college stands. It is good to be able to say to John Morgan in this, the year of his retirement, how profoundly we all admire and appreciate all that he has done – including expressing gratitude for that great quality of friendship which he has brought to his leadership.

The capacity for friendship spanning the generations was one of the great gifts of Sir Zelman Cowen, and I count myself so fortunate to be among the many beneficiaries. I know too, Warden, how encouraged you were at early stages of your Wardenship by Sir Zelman, and how much this meant and means to you. Your story of his friendship and encouragement is shared by many, including by me from the time our deep friendship developed in the early 1980s when Sir Zelman and Lady Cowen had gone from Yarralumla to Oriel College, Oxford, and I was in Oxford as a Queensland Rhodes Scholar. It was striking to discover that there are more entries in the index to Sir Zelman's memoirs to 'Cowen, Sir Zelman ... friendships' than to anything else in the book.

As this is the inaugural Zelman Cowen Oration, I propose to devote a significant part of my remarks to the remarkable man this Oration exists to remember, and then to consider five themes relating universities and contemporary society now.

Sir Zelman Cowen, universities, and contemporary society

It is precisely 42 years ago today, on 1 March 1970, that Professor Zelman Cowen officially assumed the office of Vice-Chancellor of the University of Queensland. A few days before, he had already given a speech of welcome to the new students arriving at the University for Orientation Week. In that speech, he set out some of his vision for a university and for this University. He said that universities need 'to engage in a constant struggle to think progressively', and expressed hope that 'on this campus there will be the most vigorous discussion of the great issues of our times'. 'I stand', he said, 'for a self-critical, liberal, self-reforming campus which insists upon and asserts the value of free and searching enquiry and freedom of speech.' Speaking of the importance of defending 'the values of a free society', he said that all members of the University had a responsibility for maintenance of the University 'as a free society, in which all shall be heard, and no one shall be allowed to destroy'. He concluded by extending to the students his 'warmest good wishes for an exciting, uncomfortable, disturbing and greatly enriching life in the university. Go to it, boots and all.' As he wrote in his memoirs, he was 'taken at [his] word'.

Two years before, in 1968, Professor Cowen, then Vice-Chancellor of the University of New England, had given the inaugural Old Johnians' Lecture at this College, on the topic 'Australian Universities under Pressure: Betwixt Government and the Students'. These words precisely foreshadowed what would be a great theme of his own early years as Vice-Chancellor at this University. Here Sir Zelman steered a path betwixt the threat of government interference on the one hand and, on the other, the abuse by a minority of students of the right to protest, assailing the rights of others. Throughout, he showed a great commitment to the maintenance of freedom of discussion within the University in a spirit of civility, and to the autonomy of the University, free from government interference. This took clarity of commitment to the liberal values of a university, and the courage to see them through, including in the face of appalling personal abuse. These concerns were evident when, for example, in 1971 he wrote an article for *Argo*, the student magazine here at St John's College, encouraging members of this college to participate in the student affairs of the University. 'It would be wrong', he wrote, 'to withdraw within the walls of your College', but was important for 'the great middle' of the University to speak up for and with civility.

Throughout, he was deeply conscious of the connection of the University with contemporary society. It would not have been possible to lead the University through 'the troubles' of the early 1970s without reflecting on the way that the social turbulence of the late 1960s and early 1970s affected universities – including how this campus was affected by protests inspired by the international student protest movement, the Vietnam war – the first televised war – and here at home the heavy hand of certain elements of the state government, including during the Springbok tour of July 1971. And so it was that, in February 1973, Professor Cowen wrote to Sir Edgar Williams, one of my predecessors as Warden of Rhodes House, Oxford, who was coming to Brisbane a couple of months later. He wrote:

> Life here is very busy. As a large metropolitan University, it poses problems which are very different from those of New England. There have been tough times and there are plenty of problems ahead. I plan to be in Edinburgh for the [Association of Commonwealth Universities] meeting in August, and I have been picked out to give one of the plenary papers, of all things, on Contemporary Culture and the University. Pity me!

Far from needing pity, of course, Zelman Cowen excelled – and I think revelled – in such public addresses, and in discussing the links between universities and contemporary issues, culture, and society. In 1974, for example, he took as his title for the Sir Richard Stawell Oration in Melbourne, the title of a novel of Anthony Trollope which had been published precisely 100 years before – *The Way We Live Now*. Sir Zelman spoke with concern that a decade of extraordinary social change had produced crisis, tumult, violence, and uncertainty. In 1976, in the George Judah Cohen Memorial Lecture in Sydney, he expanded on these concerns under the title 'The fragile consensus', concerned that 'the security and integrity of liberal society and its values might not survive in an environment of extremism and polarisation'. In these addresses, always internationally minded, Sir Zelman addressed phenomena evident in many countries, helping to understand Australia in its international context.

In times of discontent, as Vice-Chancellor of this University, as Governor-General of Australia, and even in a less tumultuous context as Provost of Oriel College, Oxford, his most historic role was to bring, in the phrase of Nehru's which he quoted, 'a touch of healing'. His public speeches and actions are a great example of how academics can contribute to public debate and to public life, engaging deeply with contemporary society. Zelman Cowen engaged with contemporary issues throughout his career – opposing the Communist Party Dissolution referendum in 1951, campaigning against capital punishment in Victoria in the 1960s, supporting the Aboriginal referendum of 1967, opening out public debate in the late 1960s and in the 1970s on issues of privacy and on human tissue transplants in the wake of the first heart transplant.

Engaging with contemporary society was central to Sir Zelman's vision of the role of a university. In his dramatic speech in the Great Court in July 1971, he said, 'We serve the society in which we live by acting as its critic.' He went on, of course, to stress that this must be done constructively and with civility. 'Civility', he said, 'is a great virtue to be cherished and nurtured, especially in these troubled, sometimes tormented, days.'

One of the international leaders in higher education whom Sir Zelman admired, and indeed had brought to New England in 1969 to speak at a conference there on planning in higher education, was Clark Kerr, former President of the University of California system, then Chairman of the Carnegie Commission on the future of American higher education. Clark Kerr expressed the interplay, the mutual influence, between universities and society this way: 'As society goes, so goes the university; but, also, as the university goes, so goes society. The progress of knowledge [which is the business of the university] is so central to the progress of civilization.' I hope that my remarks will reflect examples both of universities shaped by society, and also of universities helping positively to shape society, sources of progress and shapers of trends, from science and technology to economic ideas, and more.

Sir Zelman brought to his thinking about the role of universities a lifetime of experience in them. He entered the University of Melbourne as an undergraduate at the age of 16, relishing the broad student life as well as excelling academically, and at the age of 19 was its youngest-ever tutor. Sir Zelman once said to me that if he were ever to erect a statue to anyone, it would be to the Master of Ormond College at the University of Melbourne, a mathematician called D K Picken, who at the start of his undergraduate studies had told him flat-out that he shouldn't study law by itself, which was his plan as he wished to go into the practice of law as soon as possible, but should study it alongside arts. The young Zelman came rapidly to see the enormous benefit of this broader study, and was throughout his life convinced of the importance of studying law in conjunction with other disciplines. He had also experienced the immense power of a mentor, and in this case the great influence for good which a college head could exercise. Although he was a non-resident student of Ormond College, Sir Zelman was also throughout the rest of his life conscious of the powerful educational influence which colleges could have.

In 1940, having completed his arts degree and while completing his law degree, Zelman Cowen was chosen as Rhodes Scholar for Victoria. Before taking up the Scholarship, he served in the Australian Navy during World War II, and in January 1945 wrote to the Warden of Rhodes House, Oxford: 'My plans, which have been slowly formed over four years in the Navy, are to remain in the academic world.'

There followed, of course, an academic career of immense distinction – as Fellow and Tutor in Law at Oriel College, Oxford, from 1947 to 1950; as Professor of Public Law and Dean of the Law School at the University of Melbourne from 1951 to 1966; as visiting professor at various US universities; as Vice-Chancellor of the University of New England from 1967 to 1970; as Vice-Chancellor of this University from 1970 to 1977; as Provost of Oriel College, Oxford, from 1982 to 1990;

and then as visiting professor and as supporter in many ways of various universities, including Victoria University in Melbourne and Griffith University here in Brisbane. Throughout this career, he combined great enthusiasm and effectiveness as a teacher, and as an innovator in education (most obviously as Dean of the Melbourne Law School, but also, for example, in the creation of a Teaching and Learning Institute here at UQ to investigate learning and teaching processes within the University); great commitment as a mentor and adviser to students, something too rare in our universities; and true distinction as a scholar and researcher, the author of many books and articles. One of these, a collection called *Sir John Latham and other papers*, emerged from the Macrossan Lectures which he gave at this University in 1965. In days before global university rankings and the arid language of 'world's best practice', Sir Zelman's understanding, borne of experience, of the attributes of the world's finest universities did not need to be expressed in such phrases; it was just part of him, and he brought this sensibility to all he did, and encouraged colleagues' linkages with leading universities abroad, the places with which he had bonds.

In his last years, few if any things, other than the profound love of his wife and family, moved Sir Zelman more than expressions of gratitude from former students of his teaching and his impact on their lives. Let me take this opportunity, belatedly, to say how grateful I am to those who taught me here at UQ in the 1970s and early 1980s, including such remarkable women as Quentin Bryce and Margaret White, who has so kindly agreed to propose a vote of thanks tonight.

As Vice-Chancellor of this University, Sir Zelman's concern for the welfare of students and his commitment to the importance of teaching and to the engagement of students in the community life of the University were evident. He worked to communicate within the University, including commencing the weekly *University News*. He reached out to the wider community, enthusiastically seeking to win support for the

University; he told me once that nothing was more rewarding than winning over a community. He overcame hostile media reporting by agreeing with the editor of *The Courier-Mail* that he would have access to put the University's view on issues of public controversy before the newspaper rushed to judgement. He was, as before and after, an adept fundraiser. He created an effective team for the leadership of the University. At the same time, he was a builder – with 17 buildings constructed in his time, including Mayne Hall (now the James and Mary Emelia Mayne Centre), and the cladding of the Great Court completed – and he contributed to beautifying the University grounds. Sir Zelman was rightly committed to honouring the philanthropy of the Mayne family. Please forgive an irrelevant aside: as reflected in Rosamond Siemon's gripping book, *The Mayne Inheritance*, the Mayne's home, near where the Wesley Hospital now is, was built on land purchased in 1881 from one of my ancestors, John Markwell, who with his extended family had arrived in Brisbane in 1849. I am delighted that Rosamond Siemon is here tonight; her tribute on the UQ website to Sir Zelman and especially his work with alumni is also excellent reading.

Vice-Chancellor Cowen promoted research, including that focused on Queensland's agricultural and mining industries. He also nurtured the arts – including music and the visual arts – within this campus, also seeing the campus as a cultural resource for the wider community. It is fitting that the trophy for the inter-collegiate arts competition among the University of Queensland colleges is called 'The Sir Zelman Cowen Cultural Award', and it is good to see that trophy on display tonight. In the earliest years of thinking about a cultural centre at South Bank, he encouraged this – and, Sir Llew, we are all deeply grateful for your historic role in subsequent developments there. Sir Zelman as Vice-Chancellor encouraged external studies, including initiating UQ study centres around the state. He grappled with the challenges of funding for research, teaching, and infrastructure in a time when government funding was always inadequate for UQ, and became more so with the economic thunderclouds of the mid-1970s. He sought to encourage inter-disciplinary and broader studies; he supported the contentious semesterisation of 1974 at least in part because it created greater possibilities for students to try out different subjects, and such was my own experience. All this was, of course, in circumstances very different from today, despite important continuities and similarities.

Speech-making was at the centre of Sir Zelman's leadership. A public intellectual *par excellence*, in public speeches as Vice-Chancellor he was fulfilling what he regarded as the role of a Vice-Chancellor as 'an independent public figure', a role perhaps less often played now than once it was. Sir Zelman had in fact emerged as a public figure during his period as Dean of the Melbourne Law School and Vice-Chancellor of New England. Through all this, as was said at his funeral, he became a beacon for liberal values: individual liberty under law, the rule of reason, and education – in a college, a law school, or the wider university – that both broadens and sharpens the mind. In times of apparent 'normality' and stability, such values may seem like platitudes; but we see the importance of standing clearly and firmly for them when they are tested in the crucible of crisis. In acts of courageous leadership, Zelman Cowen stood firmly for them at such times.

We live today in a society with many differences from that of the 1970s. And yet the way that Sir Zelman thought about the role of universities, and of this University, remains powerfully, profoundly, relevant. We must give effect in our time to the fundamental values and purposes of a university in the conservation, extension, and transmission of knowledge. How we do so will be influenced by, and will in turn influence, our contemporary society. There are many aspects of contemporary society to which we could refer. I would like tonight to mention – too briefly for thorough discussion – five aspects of the world as it is now and as it seems to be becoming.

An information age

The first is that we live in an information age. By this I mean two things – that this is an age in which there is more information, more knowledge, and more material purporting to be knowledge, much of it generated by university research, available than ever before; and secondly, that it is an age in which the competitive position, the comparative advantage, of economies and societies in the globally competitive knowledge economy and knowledge society will be determined by the knowledge, skill or expertise – and therefore the education – of their people.

The proliferation of information to which we have ready access means that, more than ever before, one of the great challenges for education is to equip students with the skills of discerning the good from the bad, and in developing a coherent and balanced picture – an information architecture – out of the immense proliferation. It is commonly said today, because it is true, that one of the problems for democracy today – most obviously to date in the United States – is the balkanisation of the media in this information age. People's ability to expose themselves only to the information and views they are comfortable with helps to polarise politics and promote distrust of others. Preparation for democratic citizenship, which must be one of the purposes of university education, depends upon students coming to have a broad understanding of the world around them, open to alternative understandings, and able to assess for accuracy and coherence the information and views they encounter.

The growth of information does not constitute the growth of processed knowledge worth having, and still less does it mean having wisdom. The seeking of wisdom remains something to which university education should contribute, including through encouraging the active – 'boots and all' – engagement of students in a rich extra-curricular life on campus, from which so much experience – and friendship – can be gained. Wisdom depends in part on having well-considered values and character, and on having a well-considered and informed analytical framework for viewing the world, while being open to alternative views. It is not possible fully to consider here the role of universities in this, but I have no doubt that Zelman Cowen regarded these things as crucial.

The growth and change of knowledge has entered a stage of unprecedented speed. We see this with the 'tsunami' of data in genetic analysis that has followed the human genome project; we will see it with the so-called 'data deluge' that will come from outer space with the Square Kilometre Array radio-telescope project. We see it with the extraordinary 'big data' that is generated by our use of the internet – data, for example, about what we read and what we buy. Data generated through this and other technologies is such that McKinsey say that 'big data' is 'the next frontier for innovation, competition, and productivity'. This is not only data for business. It has been said, for example, that the penetration of banking by mobile phone in Kenya is generating more and better data than ever before about the location of economic activity there, making it possible, for example, for government to have a much better dataset than ever for understanding infrastructure needs. The campaign to re-elect President Obama is investing heavily in the techniques of so-called 'knowledge discovery and data-mining', drawing on rapidly proliferating electronic data, including about individual tastes, to understand and influence voter behaviour – 'techniques that are frequently used by corporations wishing to crunch vast quantities of data in the search for interesting patterns about customers'. All this in an age in which privacy – a topic close to Zelman Cowen's heart – is perhaps more talked about than ever, despite (or perhaps because of) the fact that we reveal so much of ourselves through our electronic footprints, and of course so many in this Facebook age are willing to reveal so much about themselves.

In this emerging age of 'big data', the importance and potential for data analysis, long crucial in some fields of research, grows rapidly. This brings a need for more graduates to be specifically equipped in skills of data analysis. I would argue that it also creates a need for at least some rudimentary understanding of data analysis to be increasingly regarded as one of the core skills that a university education should provide to all graduates as part of its development of the skills of engaging critically with information, and of organising conceptually the massive amounts of information around us.

It is important to acknowledge that in some poor and misgoverned countries there remains a problem of data shortage, and of too little access by too few people to information; yet in much of the world, the increasing problem is understanding and managing the rapidly growing information to which we have such ready access.

The use of 'big data' to enhance competitiveness is one example of the much broader phenomenon that the competitive position of economies, as well as their strength as civilised societies, will be determined by how well they equip their peoples with the ability to compete in the knowledge economy and to engage in the knowledge society of the 21st century. So nations, companies, and other organisations today, more than ever before, develop talent strategies – strategies to attract and develop the most talented people they can, and to equip them to make the greatest contribution they can. Universities are crucial mechanisms for the identification, development, and acknowledging of talent; and wise leaders of government, business, and other parts of the community in many countries recognise this and promote the quality of university education, as well as research, in their countries accordingly.

A global world

The second aspect of the world today that I want to highlight is that today the local is global. That the talent strategies I just mentioned are for competing strongly in a global world reflects the profound importance today of international, even global, forces which shape or at least influence so many aspects of our lives. A significant proportion of graduates will work in contexts involving extensive international connection. It is a truth widely, if not universally, acknowledged that, in so international an age, education must equip students with international, inter-cultural, and inter-faith perspectives, understanding, and skills. The case for this seems to me overwhelming. Zelman Cowen, with his inherent understanding of the international nature of universities and, for example, of the importance of their international linkages, understood this before it was fashionable. He was the embodiment also of Jewish-Christian engagement, and his example should encourage wider inter-faith dialogue, which we so greatly need, and in which universities have a leadership role to play.

The emergent internationalism, even globalism, of a few years ago – when President Obama could be treated as stating the obvious when he said that global challenges require global solutions – has given way to a renewed nationalism in many countries – to forces of parochialism (including incipient protectionism), populism, and polarisation, in which countries beset by economic and other strife seem to be turning in on themselves, less interested in global solutions, and acting – in Nader Mousavizadeh's phrase – more as disconnected islands in 'an archipelago world' than as parts of the main. The shifting tectonic plates of economic, political, and military power in the world pose challenges and create opportunities for countries, companies, and universities to adapt to, to seize, and help to influence. This is evident, for example, in Australia's complex relationship with China – a relationship that is economically strong, strategically weak, and needing to be strengthened in people-to-people relationships, including through educational and research links.

Universities, being focused on the pursuit of truth and the outer reaches of knowledge, are of their nature part of a global enterprise. They must be places of broadening, not narrowing, horizons. Although global solutions to global problems may have entered a quiescent phase, international awareness on the part of graduates remains essential; and universities must continue to do all they can to encourage this. As Australian universities rightly seek to learn from and deepen links with the finest universities in the world, aspiring and working hard to become among their number, we need to build those links with the great universities of the world as they are, and as they are becoming – recognising that not only is there 'a super-league of global universities that are now engaged in a battle for intellectual talent and academic prestige', but that top universities, strongly backed by government, in many countries, especially in Asia, are determined to take their place in that super-league.

Change and innovation

The third aspect of contemporary society I wish to highlight is that we live today also in an age of rapid and seemingly endless change and innovation. Education must equip students to adapt to change, and to the change and growth of knowledge, and to make the most of it – as human beings coping personally with rapid change, as democratic citizens engaged in a society and world fast changing around them, and as workers whose economic contribution depends on adaptiveness and flexibility also, both within and increasingly as they change jobs. How best to do this is a matter for serious discussion in universities.

Sir Zelman enjoyed the statement by Robert Maynard Hutchins, the University of Chicago's great pioneer of general education, that in a world of rapid change, 'it now seems safe to say that the most practical education is the most theoretical one'. Sir Zelman quoted this in his 1970 Garran Oration, saying that it was 'perhaps a little extravagant'; but he was sympathetic to the general argument of Hutchins and others that specialised knowledge becomes out-of-date with ever-increasing speed, and so what is important to teach undergraduates, as a basis for a life of learning, is not specialised knowledge, but what we might refer to as the 'first principles' including a broad span of valuable knowledge and generic skills, including of critical thinking, problem-solving drawing on the expertise of others, and clear communication, which are transferable from one context to another.

Much of this change and innovation is driven by exciting developments in science and technology. University research is, of course, the source of much of this innovation, and must remain so – a powerful driver of innovation and improvement in so many fields with huge benefits in medicine, communication between people, economic performance, and more. That so many advances in science and technology emerge from within universities is a powerful example of how universities help to shape society, rather than simply being shaped by it. Universities must remain focussed on that 'endless frontier' of scientific discovery from which so much benefit has been derived, and so much remains to be derived. New frontiers – from the nano-est of nanotechnology, to the human brain, to still-unsolved diseases of the body, to issues of sustaining our planet, to the wide reaches of the universe – beckon us onwards. As we know, many of the most important discoveries have arisen from curiosity-driven research by scientists, the remarkable fruits of which show the utilitarian gains to be had from that noblest of callings, the pursuit of pure learning for its own sake.

In some parts of the world, science today faces a reaction from anti-scientific forces often associated with fundamentalist religion, and whether rightly or not sometimes characterised as 'denialism' – those who deny evolution, which is so strongly grounded in scientific observation, or those who straight-out reject the complex and important science of climate change. This anti-scientific spirit is perhaps most obvious in some parts of US public discourse today; but we must be wary of it here also. A healthier equilibrium between understandings of religion and science seems called for. This is not, of course, to deny the importance of careful thought about the ethics of research, something in which Sir Zelman took a keen interest.

It is no longer possible, if it ever was, to be a fully educated person without at least some basic knowledge of science and technology. This comes as no surprise to scientist advocates of liberal education, who point out that the classical liberal arts education included arithmetic, geometry, and astronomy, and that liberal education in the US today often has a strong scientific and mathematical focus.

Clearly universities must continue to give careful attention to how they can make best use of technological developments to enhance teaching, including to engage and educate students for whom so much of their lives is lived online. They must also give attention to how they can contribute to environmental sustainability, including through working to become sustainable campuses.

An inter-connected world

The fourth aspect of our times that I draw attention to is that everything is or may be connected. We are certainly more conscious now, I think, than for some considerable time, perhaps than ever, of the inter-connectedness of things. We now know that what happens in the environment of one part of the world can affect what happens in other parts of the world. New connections develop in field after field – between international security and religion, between music and computer science, between genetics and statistics, and much more. For example, it was possible on 10 September 2001 to think of international security without thinking of religion; on 12 September 2001 it was not.

As a result of the inter-connectedness of things, it has become a commonplace to say that the questions we need to grapple with are inter-disciplinary, and so we need to answer them in inter-disciplinary ways. I am struck by how much this call for inter-disciplinarity is voiced by leading scientists and engineers.

In recent weeks, I have read advocacy of inter-disciplinarity by Shirley Tilghman, the molecular biologist who is President of Princeton; by Charles Vest, the engineer who was president of the Massachusetts Institute of Technology; by Eric Lander, one of the pioneers of the human genome project; and others. Sir Zelman used to cite Charles Moorhouse, professor of engineering at the University of Melbourne. But for the most part this model of inter-disciplinarity is not how universities have traditionally organised themselves, and organising teaching and research to be truly and appropriately inter-disciplinary is more spoken of than achieved.

How to equip graduates for lives and careers in this inter-connected world presents great challenges to universities, many of which in diverse countries have approached it by reviewing the educational philosophy and objectives which underpin their courses. What combination of broad and specialist knowledge and what particular skills such as those of critical thinking, of communication, and of research – the skill of coming to an unfamiliar question and working out how to acquire the information needed to answer it – are matters that universities need to reflect on, as many are. Let me give just one example. Rick Levin, the President of Yale University, which has very strong ties in East Asia, especially in China and in Singapore (where it is working with the National University of Singapore to create a liberal arts college), argues that one of the most important developments in university education there has been that 'policy makers throughout Asia are currently focused on exposing their future leaders to the breadth and pedagogy of liberal education even as we worry about the rate at which Asian countries are training specialized engineers'. Universities around Asia, and in many other places, have been asking what education they can best offer their students to meet the needs of this century. A university that doesn't ask itself whether what it teaches is the best that it can offer its students for the world in which they will make their lives and careers is in danger of being left behind.

I note in passing that the green shoots of liberal education in some controlled societies in Asia, including China, pose real challenges and create exciting possibilities for the relationship between universities and society. To what extent does quality education and unfettered research depend upon its taking place in a free society? How can a university, as a free society in itself, operate properly within a controlled broader society? More positively, how can universities, as agents of debate and critics of society, help to generate positive change, including the liberalisation of controlled societies? These are important questions that will help to shape the future of Asia, and of our relations with it in this inter-connected world.

An 'unusually uncertain' age – and an age of indignation

The fifth aspect of contemporary society to which I draw attention is that uncertainty is the new certainty. At a personal level, the pace of change is for many people a cause of stress. One of the great paradoxes of our age, not for the first time, is the co-existence of material prosperity with widespread emotional anxiety and mental illness. Problems of substance abuse and suicide abound. This is something which universities must take account of in how they act as inclusive and supportive communities; in the services they offer to staff and students alike, including to promote a culture of wellness; in the education they offer to health professionals, educators, and others; and in the research they undertake, for example in such fields as mental health and psychology. Perhaps as they have always done, people search for meaning in their lives, and may currently be less often convinced than a few years ago that it lies in making money, powerful though that instinct remains.

We live in an age marked not only by endless change and innovation but by a renewed sense of instability – economic, social, and political. The global financial crisis and its aftermath have brought with them in many countries a profound and sustained sense of economic crisis and insecurity, and in several countries austerity which shows no sign of abating. It is to

Australia's great good fortune that this crisis has not been more evident here. In many countries, the statement of Ben Bernanke, Chairman of the US Federal Reserve, in July 2010 that the economic outlook was 'unusually uncertain' remains valid. The contrast between austerity in some parts of the world and continued, if uncertain, growth in others, especially in emerging countries, reflects and contributes to massive shifts of power, economic and political, from West to East, and from North to South.

For many weeks this year, London's *Financial Times* has been running a series entitled 'Capitalism in crisis'. Despite its apparent resilience in Australia, capitalism certainly has appeared to be 'in crisis' in many parts of the world, and the age-old clash of ideas about the nature of our economic and social systems, including debate about the best relationship of markets and state, has had renewed intensity, even ferocity. The Occupy movement, coming seemingly out of nowhere, has focussed more attention than for a very long time on issues of inequality, under-privilege, and fairness. In several countries, the debates between laissez-faire, Keynesian managed capitalism, social democracy, state capitalism in some countries, socialism, and more revolutionary ideas has taken on new edge.

Debates between competing visions of society and economic ideologies are increasingly fierce and rancorous, even violent, in many places. Universities must be places where facts can be sought, and interpretations, theories, and philosophies argued in a spirit of the rigorous, disinterested, non-partisan pursuit of truth, and – yes – in a spirit also of civility. It is an important example of the ways that universities help to shape society, as well as being shaped by it, that many of the great ideas that compete to shape the future of the world have been generated from within, and are certainly debated within, universities. Keynes, Hayek, and Friedman, for example, all wrote and argued from within universities, and their ideas have changed the world. The importance of universities as generators and debaters of social, political, and economic ideas, and as places where this should be pursued in a civil spirit of truth-seeking is never greater than in times of social stress, when the problems needing solution and the threats to the social fabric from fierce discord are greatest. Will our universities meet the test?

How uncertain economic forces play out will have an enormous impact on universities around the world, including in Australia. In some countries, such as the United States and the United Kingdom, major cutbacks in government funding for universities are underway – in the UK significantly but unevenly compensated for by increased but still constrained capacity on the part of universities to increase HECS-style fees paid by students.* In some countries, economic growth is being matched and in turn perhaps partially contributed to by major increases in government commitments to universities as central to the future of the country.

Although our circumstances today are different in many respects from those which Sir Zelman Cowen faced 40 years ago, the discontents of students and other young people are in many countries again one of the drivers of major protest movements. Some would argue that it is a sign of disengagement and complacency among students in many countries about the burning issues of our time that student protests are not *more* conspicuous among the recent waves of protests. Yet in country after country around the world it seems that we live in an age of indignation – an age of protest, of revolts against elites, or at least of simmering discontent and dissent. This comes in many forms – from the Arab spring, now better known by some as the Arab four-seasons; to the Occupy movement in many countries; to the very different spirit of protest reflected in the 'Tea Party' movement in the United States; to protests for diverse local

---

* HECS – for 'Higher Education Contribution Scheme' – is essentially an income-contingent loan program that enables Australian students to borrow from the government to pay their university fees, with later repayments made contingent on their reaching a minimum income level. It is now officially known as HELP, for 'Higher Education Loan Program'.

reasons in Russia, China, Chile, Israel, India, and elsewhere. In my own view, some – but not all – of these protest movements represent courageous and commendable responses to tyranny, corruption, bad leadership, and misconceived policies. Such protests give grounds for hope, even though the reality with which they engage is, like so much of human affairs, messy and murky.

Like some of the protests of the late 1960s and early 1970s, some of the protests of today represent a cry for popular participation. Technologies which enable people to know almost anything and to connect with almost anyone at the speed of light encourage impatience with lack of transparency and with hierarchy, and facilitate quick coordinated protest against them.

One of the many causes of discontent and indignation in some countries, such as the UK and the US, is a renewed grievance on the part of students and recent graduates about the cost of their education, and a desire that education as a creator of opportunity and a driver of social mobility not be lost. One of the great and growing challenges for policy-makers and educational leaders in many countries is how to balance the need for students to contribute to the cost of their own education and to pay appropriately for the private benefits that will flow to them from that education, on the one hand, with the need to preserve and promote the role of higher education in creating opportunity and enabling social mobility, and with recognising the substantial public benefits of education, on the other. In Australia, the invention of HECS was an enormous contribution to this, and it will be an important element in what will need to be continuing debate and action over the years ahead. How much of the cost of an education should be met from public, and how much from private, sources is in many countries a live issue. It is an unresolved question in this country. What is clear, I think, is that Australian universities are massively under-resourced to provide the education and research they should, and to be able to achieve and sustain the excellence that is needed if Australia is to hold its own internationally.

An age that is newly conscious of inequality and disadvantage is an age in which there are also renewed demands for focus on equity, access, and diversity – for social inclusion, if you like – in higher education. The Bradley Report and federal government focus on this are Australian manifestations of this, and there is much focus on these issues in some other countries also. I am not sure that all Australian universities have even now sufficiently accepted their responsibility for active outreach to seek to identify prospective students of potential from disadvantaged backgrounds, including Indigenous backgrounds, and help them fulfil that potential. In an old phrase, 'talent is everywhere, but opportunity is not'; and expanding opportunity for individuals, and making the demographic profile of the university student body more representative of society at large, is something which depends on vigorous action. This – including the creation and support of scholarships – is one of the many areas, of which research is another, in which philanthropy is increasingly important; and building a culture of philanthropy in Australia, and elsewhere, remains a crucial task for university leaders. Building focus on outreach with alumni, friends, and potential friends into all aspects of the work of a university is clearly essential to success.

The revolt against elites in many countries represents a real challenge to leadership. Citizens in most countries seem discontented and disillusioned with the quality of public leadership they have. The crises of recent years have seemed to highlight the weaknesses of established institutions, certainly including both government and business, and undermined confidence in leaders in those fields. While for much of the human race there is unprecedented prosperity and peace of a kind, nonetheless great challenges face the world – including environmental, economic, and security risks – and it often seems that neither local nor national nor international mechanisms can respond effectively to these real issues. National institutions seem dysfunctional and unable to deal effectively with national problems in many countries, and hope for the global solutions needed to global problems seems to recede into impossibility like a mirage. In this context, the skills of leaders must include the ability to develop new alliances to solve problems. Universities must necessarily focus on their role as educators of future leaders, and must give careful thought to what this needs. The nurturing of leaders for the future must be an educational philosophy and action, not simply a slogan. If we cannot count on scholars in universities to think about these issues, who will?

Conclusion

Tonight, in seeking to honour Sir Zelman Cowen's lifetime of connecting universities with contemporary society, I have of course chosen to identify and stress only some of the many aspects of the world today that I could have chosen – that we live in an information age, with profound and shifting international forces, of constant change and innovation, much of it driven by science and technology, with ever-changing inter-connections, currently facing much instability and uncertainty, to which many respond in a spirit of indignation.

We live, then, in complex and uncertain times. There are many causes for concern – more outside Australia than within – but also many causes for hope. In a world where we are often very conscious of problems, even crises, universities are – or should be – beacons of hope. Through the education they offer, the research they do, and the service they extend to their communities, universities help to develop the talent and the leadership, the discoveries and the innovations, and the means of connecting these to communities which provide hope for the future.

'We serve the society in which we live by acting as its critic.' These were the words of Vice-Chancellor Cowen in his famous speech in the Great Court of this University in July 1971 – what he regarded as 'the speech of my life'. Vice-Chancellor Cowen also urged his listeners to heed the words inscribed above the tower entrance to the Forgan Smith Building – the foundation stone of which, I might add, was laid 75 years ago next week. Sir Zelman didn't quote those words direct, instead urging his listeners to go and read them for themselves. The words are a quote from Disraeli, and speak of a university as a place 'of light, of liberty, and of learning'. Zelman Cowen undoubtedly regarded universities, including this fine University, as places 'of light, of liberty, and of learning'. As we consider the connection of universities and contemporary society in this time of anxiety, hope, and unusual uncertainty, the large and liberal spirit of Zelman Cowen can help to encourage, to guide, and to inspire us still.

The value of university residential colleges

The Ashley Lecture 2010
Trent University, Peterborough, Ontario
2 February 2010

It is an immense pleasure and privilege to be here with you at Trent University as Ashley Fellow for 2010, and to be invited to deliver the Ashley Lecture.[*]

In doing so, it is a pleasure to be able to pay a tribute to one in particular of the distinguished panelists who will respond mercilessly to this lecture, my friend of many years and the founding President of this University, Professor Thomas H B Symons – one of the great figures in higher education in the Commonwealth in the last half century, and someone of whom it may truly be said in this place, as of Sir Christopher Wren in London, 'if you seek his monument look around you'. And I join in my tribute to Tom the warmest and warmly merited recognition of Christine Symons.

The Ashley Fellowship at Trent was created with the bequest left on his death in 1974 by Professor Charles Allan Ashley. When Tom Symons was an undergraduate at Trinity College in the University of Toronto, Allan Ashley, professor of accounting, was also resident in that college. Through their interactions, Tom Symons learned much, including about the value of informal conversation in the collegiate environment. From their own experiences – including in Tom's case later as a student at Oriel College, Oxford, and at Harvard – both Allan Ashley and Tom Symons developed well-founded enthusiasm for colleges as a valuable component of student life at university. It is said that

---

[*] This Ashley Lecture was first published in Donald Markwell, *The need for breadth: On liberal education and the value of university residential colleges,* Trent University, 2010.

Allan Ashley was one of the few people whom Tom consulted when he was approached to consider taking up the task of founding Trent; and Allan Ashley contributed much to the early development of the University, including as a member of the Academic Planning Committee that shaped the founding of the University, and as a member of the University Senate in its early years.

Another of the early leaders of this University, whom I regarded as an exceptional human being and whom I was also deeply privileged to count as a friend, was Dr Eugene Forsey. Dr Forsey was the longtime research director of the Canadian Labour Congress and one of the Commonwealth's greatest authorities on constitutional conventions. He was also an early and longstanding member of Trent's Board of Governors and the second Chancellor of the University. The historian of the University, A O C Cole, writes: 'Forsey was universally respected and raised Trent's image wherever he went." Through shared interest in constitutional conventions, I came to know Dr Forsey, and in 1985, then a young Australian postgraduate student briefly visiting Canada, I was honoured to accompany him and another guest to Rideau Hall for his installation by the Governor-General as a Privy Councillor. When in 1991 I reviewed Dr Forsey's memoirs, *A life on the fringe*, soon after his death, my review was published in the journal *The Round Table* under the title 'Canada's best', amongst whom he certainly was.

Eugene Forsey, like Allan Ashley and Tom Symons, had real experience of the collegiate system at its best – in Eugene Forsey's case as a Rhodes Scholar for Quebec at Balliol College, Oxford. It is little wonder that they all supported the founding collegiate vision of Trent, expressed this way at the opening ceremonies for the University in October 1964 by Tom Symons, as its first President:[†]

---

* A O C Cole, *Trent: The Making of a University 1957-1987,* Trent University, 1992, p. 112.

† *Trent University Official Opening Ceremonies*, 1964, p. 16.

The philosophy which inspires Trent is based upon the conviction that education is, inescapably, an individual experience – individual to each student, to each teacher, and to every other scholar who may come to it. And this philosophy is reflected in the teaching methods of Trent University which seek to encourage each student to find a close and a direct contact with his teachers through the tutorial and seminar approach to instruction. ...

This philosophy of our University is also reflected in the decision that Trent should be a collegiate university – that is, that it should be made up of a number of smaller, sister colleges, which will be the fundamental units and the chief features of Trent University. Every student and every faculty member at Trent will belong to one or another of these colleges. In this way, through the colleges, members of the University may be helped to preserve a sense of individual identity as the University grows larger, and to find richer personal associations and a greater measure of academic assistance than would otherwise be the case.

A document prepared by current President Steven Franklin's Vision Renewal Review Committee stresses that 'We honour our legacy of commitment to the individual student...', and continues:*

Trent was founded on a vision of undergraduate education that saw each student as an individual who would flourish in an instructional environment of close interaction with faculty and their peers, in both formal and informal situations. Seminar teaching and college life are two hallmarks that have characterized that vision.

It is not for me, even if I were capable, to discuss that vision

---

* Vision Renewal Review Committee, 'Elements of Trent University Vision For Discussion'.

or the particular aspects of the colleges at Trent today. I have been asked to speak about the value of university residential colleges in the wider world of higher education, and I hope that what I can report from elsewhere may be of interest, or even of use, to you. Above all, I want to argue that, well run and under the right conditions, residential colleges can contribute enormously to the education of students, and so to achieving the core purposes of a university, and thus can contribute to the wider community.

I will do so under four broad headings – first, general observations about colleges and the value they can contribute; secondly, brief consideration of the collegiate ideal in history and especially the resurgence of interest in it in many places in recent times; thirdly, some recent empirical data from Australia on engagement through colleges; and finally, some food for thought on problems for colleges and the conditions needed for their success.

When I speak of a university residential college, I mean to speak, not of a building or set of buildings, but of a community – a group of people, not merely a physical facility. Quite simply, for me a residential college is a residential academic community, ideally a community bringing together students of diverse backgrounds and disciplines in close contact both with each other and with more senior scholars and teachers, also of diverse disciplines, and others who work to ensure that the college is a rich learning environment for its students.

In many instances, a residential college will also embrace in its community students as well as faculty and staff who are not actually resident in the college. This is in many cases a very important fact, highlighting for us that a college, if it is genuinely a college and not simply a boarding house, should be regarded as first and foremost a provider of education – at very least, a significant enricher of the all-round educational experience of its students – rather than as simply a provider of accommodation.

It follows inevitably, I think, from the nature of a residential academic community that each college will over time develop its own characteristics, culture, activities and offerings, and expectations of its members: and such diversity is in general to be welcomed. Expecting uniformity or standardisation between colleges will in general damage the very nature of the college as a welcoming and distinctive human community. Colleges necessarily imply some form of decentralisation and diversity.

Similarly, although the universities and colleges of many countries, certainly including Canada, the United States, and Australia, have developed from ideas originally imported, especially from Britain and in some cases 19th century Germany, and have many features in common, it is important to recognise that universities and colleges have evolved differently in different places, for reasons sometimes hidden in history. Most relevantly, residential colleges have developed differently in extent, shape, and impact in the countries I have mentioned, and features which seem natural to me – an Australian with collegiate experience in Britain, the United States, Australia, and only this last week in Canada – may seem very different to you or to others. Even the same words may mean different things.

Examples of this diversity include whether colleges are affiliated to or actually owned by the wider university and their degree of autonomy within the university, their governance, the extent and nature of their academic programs and the involvement of senior academic members, what proportions of students are undergraduates and what proportion postgraduate, whether they are religious foundations, and so on. I mention these examples of diversity to highlight that what I refer to in other places may be of greater or lesser relevance here, and I do not seek to prescribe what Canadian universities – and certainly not Trent – should do.

When it is working well, a residential college enriches the education of its students, resident or non-resident, in many ways:

- through giving them a sense, and a reality, of belonging to a community;

- through thus enabling a greater sense of identity and a lower risk of alienation as a member of a smaller unit than in the larger university of which the college is part;

- through academic tuition;

- through academic advising, and personal and professional mentoring;

- through academic support in other ways, from learning resources such as libraries to prizes and scholarships which encourage and acknowledge academic success;

- through pastoral care;

- through informal interactions between students, and between students, faculty members and staff – informal interactions which contribute to the social as well as intellectual development of students;

- in some cases, through interactions facilitated by the college between students and members of the wider community, including for example leaders in the professions and in public life;

- through opportunities to participate and excel in extra-curricular activities, such as sport, music, drama, the visual arts, debating, religious activities, political and advocacy activities, community service, and more – with all the benefits in personal development, such as in leadership development, and in community contribution which such activities can bring;

- through social activities;

- through the development of lifelong friendships; and

- through the encouragement of the values, such as living with integrity and respect for others, that should be nurtured through college life because they are essential to the success of college life.

The value of such collegiate experience for individual students can be immense, and with it the value for universities, including:

- as I have suggested, through integrating learning with living in ways that enrich education;
- through enhancing the attractiveness of the university to prospective students, perhaps most especially when it is used as a selling point, and so improving recruitment;
- through increasing student engagement within the university;
- through encouraging student retention;
- through encouraging alumni loyalty and support for the university;
- through providing a means of engaging faculty members more profoundly and enrichingly in the life of the university;
- through connecting members of the university with the wider community; and much more.

As already alluded to, it is often argued that residential colleges can be environments in which students and faculty members from diverse disciplines can come together to understand and solve issues which cannot be fully comprehended from the standpoint of a single discipline. The Cole history of Trent suggests that colleges here have been particularly important at some points in the development of inter-disciplinary programs.[*] This can be one of the ways – and there are others – that colleges can contribute positively to the research mission of a university.

It is often argued that colleges can, and ordinarily do, provide a particularly welcoming and supportive environment for students new to university, and especially for students from disadvantaged backgrounds and those who are the first in their family to come to university, for whom university can seem a very foreign experience. It is argued that colleges can, and ordinarily do, provide an especially good way in to university life for students

---

[*] Cole, op. cit., ch. 6.

from rural families, from distant parts of the country, and from overseas. In these and other ways, including through the provision of scholarships, it is argued that colleges can play crucial roles in the outreach, equity, and access agendas of universities, and in promoting the international, inter-cultural, and inter-faith understanding that is so crucial for the world's future. All this, of course, depends on colleges being such welcoming, and not alienating, environments: at which some colleges are better than others.

I give as one example that, at a number of Australian universities, colleges have played an important, even leading, role in the provision of support for Indigenous students. This includes providing a welcoming environment in which Indigenous students can feel at home; with Indigenous visiting fellows and others helping to promote wide understanding of Indigenous culture, experience, and knowledge; with summer schools and university preparatory programs for Indigenous students provided within the college; and with generous scholarships for Indigenous students, often provided by significant philanthropic support. I know of one case, and it might not be the only one, where the Chancellor of the University has said that a college has led the University in its work for Indigenous students.

It may be that provision for Indigenous students is in one or more cases an example of the wider phenomenon of colleges undertaking roles for the university which the larger university is, for whatever reason, less well able to undertake itself. To give another (I hope not too immodest) example: the college I used to head in Melbourne undertook several roles for the University of Melbourne which were said to be of great value to that University – roles such a providing a welfare safety net and excellent foundation studies for young overseas students, and providing a collegiate base within the university for visiting scholars such as the four Nobel Laureates who came for periods each year.

It is also the case that fundraising by colleges for scholarships and for other activities will be aided by the loyalty of many of their former college resident students. This is strongly evident in, for example, the loyalty of members of so many Oxford and Cambridge colleges to their college, loyalty reflected increasingly in philanthropic support. The potential of college loyalty to generate philanthropic support for activities within colleges which are of real benefit to the whole university will, I think, be reflected in some further examples I will mention later. Loyalty to a college may also contribute to loyalty to the wider university, with real potential for philanthropic support.

The collegiate ideal in education has, of course, been at the heart of the great universities of the world for hundreds of years – in Cambridge and Oxford since at least the 13th century. In the 19th century, John Henry Newman wrote of the need to combine what he called 'the system of Professors' with 'the system of Colleges and College tutors'. By a 'College' Newman meant 'a place of residence for the University student, who would there find himself under the guidance and instruction of Superiors and Tutors, bound to attend to his personal interests, moral and intellectual'. Newman insisted that colleges in this sense were essential to the 'wellbeing' and 'integrity' of a University.* This vision contributed to the creation of residential colleges in several mid- and late 19th and early 20th century universities in what were or became the dominions within the British Empire and Commonwealth.

As the person responsible for the running of the Rhodes Scholarships around the world, I am especially conscious that at the end of the 19th century Cecil Rhodes chose to give his scholarships to Oxford, rather than to Edinburgh, which he considered as the alternative, precisely because of the existence of residential colleges in Oxford.

Although in various ways, including in liberal arts colleges, it had long been fundamental in much of US higher education, the residential collegiate ideal reached its modern expression at Harvard, Yale, Princeton, and elsewhere only in the last century,

---

* Newman quoted from '*A large and liberal education': higher education for the 21st century*, p. 134.

most famously associated with the early initiatives of Woodrow Wilson at Princeton, the creation of the house system by President Lowell at Harvard, and the philanthropy of Edward B Harkness creating residential colleges at Yale.

But the classical ideal of collegiate education is by no means a thing of the past, or a matter for nostalgia. Quite the opposite.

In 2007-08, when I was Deputy Vice-Chancellor (Education) of the University of Western Australia, that University – aspiring to become by mid-century one of the world's top 50 universities – commissioned papers on the educational, research, and community engagement activities of the world's top 50 universities. The major paper researched by Dr Carolyn Daniel on *The educational attributes of some of the world's 'top 50' universities* concluded:[*]

> The majority of the top ten universities have over 90 per cent of their undergraduates living on campus; many more institutions have high percentages of students in residence or have students living in university-run accommodation very close to the campus.

Amongst other benefits identified, including some of those I have already mentioned, was that 'Colleges can be used to introduce innovative educational programs and to target particular segments of the potential student market'.

Dr Daniel concluded: 'There has been something of a renaissance in the college system in particular recently with many universities establishing, planning or expanding internal systems of residential colleges.'[†] Moreover, in many universities, steps have been taken to strengthen the role of existing residential colleges.

That there has been 'something of a renaissance in the college system' can be illustrated with examples from around the world – from Columbia, Princeton, and Yale in the US, to the National

---

[*] Carolyn Daniel, *The educational attributes of some of the world's 'top 50' universities: a discussion paper*, University of Western Australia, May 2008, p. 49.

[†] Ibid., p. 50

University of Singapore, to the Chinese University of Hong Kong, to Fudan University in Shanghai and Yuanpei Honors College at Peking University, to the Universities of Melbourne and Western Australia, and many, many more besides. The details of some of these may be found through the website collegiateway.org, which I recommend to you.

Part of the reason for this resurgence of interest in the college ideal in many countries today is that, in an intensifying global competition between economies and universities, universities in many countries are aspiring to become among the very best in the world, are looking at the attributes of the world's finest universities, are seeing that they are overwhelmingly residential universities, and are therefore seeking to adopt and adapt for themselves this key attribute of the world's best. Many have also noticed that some of the world's leading universities, with already strong residential college systems, are strengthening them further.

For example, Princeton has been one of the leaders of the so-called 'renaissance' in residential colleges, including with the opening in 2007 of Whitman College, made possible through, amongst other donations, a $30 million gift from eBay's Meg Whitman and her family. Please forgive me for quoting at some length from Princeton's own description of its residential colleges:[*]

> One of Princeton's most distinctive characteristics is its closeknit residential community. On-campus housing is guaranteed for undergraduates for all four years. The University's six residential colleges are the center of residential life and offer an array of academic and social programs that enhance the undergraduate experience.
>
> In fall 2007, with the opening of Whitman College, the University inaugurated an expanded residential college system

---

[*] http://www.princeton.edu/main/campuslife/housingdining/colleges/ – accessed 1 February 2010.

that provides more housing and dining opportunities for all undergraduates. The new system establishes three four-year colleges and pairs them with three two-year colleges, enabling juniors and seniors to remain linked to a residential college, regardless of whether they live there.

Each college has a faculty master, dean, director of studies and director of student life. Academic advising for freshmen and sophomores is centered at the colleges, and juniors and seniors also are encouraged to confer with their college advisers for nondepartmental academic advising throughout their undergraduate careers. Undergraduates also benefit from the guidance of residential college advisers, who are upperclassmen, and resident graduate students.

It is likely that Princeton's routine success in assessments of US undergraduate education is in no small part attributable to its residential college system.

In responding in February 2008 to a report he had commissioned and which recommended the creation of two new colleges at Yale, the President of Yale, Richard Levin, said:

> The residential college system is one of the glories of Yale, and it is a major reason why students choose to come to Yale and a major reason why Yale College students report greater satisfaction with their education than students at most peer institutions.

In June 2008, Levin announced that Yale would indeed proceed with creating two new residential colleges. Already $140 million had been donated for the purpose.[*] In September last year (2009), in responding again to the financial constraints arising from the global financial crisis, President Levin said that, while 'no major construction will proceed until funding is available from donor support or financial markets recover', Yale had 'secured donor support to continue the design of the new

---

* http://opa.yale.edu/news/article.aspx?id=5868 – accessed 1 February 2010.

residential colleges and to undertake site clearance, the first phase of which [would] occur [in the] fall'.

Last November, in marking the renovation of one of Yale's existing colleges (part of a long-term program of college renovation), President Levin 'affirmed Yale's unique residential college system as central to undergraduate life and excellent preparation for citizenship'. It serves, he said, as 'the locus of students' intellectual, social, and personal development, where they learn about community and working with others'.*

It is clear from these and other examples that could be given that, in the last ten to 15 years, many leading universities have been increasing their commitment to residential colleges. This is also evident further afield. Australia has seen a renewed focus in universities on residential colleges, and renewed efforts by several residential colleges to enhance the quality of the all-round educational experience that they offer. While I am conscious that there has in some universities been a retreat from autonomous colleges and from the collegiate ideal, quite a few Australian colleges have seen, in highly variable ways, such positive developments as:

- considerable increase in the extent and quality of their tutorial programs;
- the introduction of mentors for every student;
- the strengthening of their pastoral care or student welfare networks;
- an increased provision for postgraduate students;
- the development or expansion of programs to include non-resident students or 'associates' in the life of the residential college;
- renewal of the college's chapel life;

---

* http://yaletomorrow.yale.edu/news/calhoun.html – accessed 1 February 2010.

- increased support for extra-curricular activities such as sport, music, drama, and the visual arts;

- an increase in focus on community service activities and 'service learning';

- increased focus on leadership development, and on activities that lead students to look out to engage with the issues of the local, national, and international communities;

- greater emphasis on visiting scholars who enrich the life of the residential community;

- increased focus on prizes that recognise and reward academic as well as extra-curricular achievement and personal qualities; and

- increased scholarship support, including to make the benefits of college available to students of potential regardless of their means, and to diversify the student body for the benefit of all, including with real opportunities for Indigenous students.

Much of this has been done with growing philanthropic support from alumni and other friends of the colleges. Several colleges have strengthened positively their connections with the wider university with which they are affiliated, or to which they belong.[*]

For example, in the years 1997 to 2007, I was fortunate, as Warden of Trinity College within the University of Melbourne, to be a participant in developments at the University of Melbourne which I think observers would agree saw a significant enhancement of the contribution of the colleges to the life of the University. This enhancement has continued with the announcement in January 2010 of the offering by the colleges of non-resident places, with academic as well as extra-curricular and pastoral benefits, open to all students of the University – a

---

[*] This is elaborated at http://collegiateway.org/news/2008-markwell-naauc – accessed 1 February 2010.

very significant development in that context, and a further sign of the renaissance of colleges in one of Australia's leading universities. This is part of the University of Melbourne's wide-ranging and profound efforts to enhance the culture and student experience there, which also include major (if controversial) curriculum reform in the direction of broader undergraduate education leading into specialised or professional postgraduate education or training. One of the oldest of Melbourne's colleges has recently re-articulated its purpose as being 'to create a new generation of leaders through an unrivalled learning and living experience" – a noble goal, and the kind of clarity of purpose which, in my view, all institutions benefit from having.

Within the University of Western Australia, which is also undertaking major curriculum or course structures reform, many steps have been taken to strengthen the role and contribution of the residential colleges in the student experience, especially to encourage student engagement in a rich campus life. For example, the University has been providing financial assistance for further residential development within the colleges, and giving colleges access to funding for leadership development, mentoring, inter-cultural competence, and other enriching activities. Some of the University's major scholarships specifically cover college fees. The colleges are recognised in the University's key planning documents, and are contributing to the discussion of how the University can achieve its goal of becoming one of the 'top 50' universities in the world within 50 years.[†]

The Vice-Chancellor of the University of Melbourne from 1996 to 2004 was Alan Gilbert, now Vice-Chancellor of the University of Manchester.[‡] In his current role, from which he will

---

[*] Ormond College website – www.ormond.unimelb.edu.au – accessed 1 February 2010.

[†] More detail is at http://collegiateway.org/news/2008-markwell-naauc – accessed 1 February 2010.

[‡] Alan Gilbert sadly passed away a few months later, on 27 July 2010. My eulogy for him is in the section of this book 'On leaders'.

retire later this year, Alan Gilbert has led a review of teaching, learning, and the student experience at Manchester. In one of the discussion papers he authored to commence that process, he wrote:[*]

> ... the kinds of multi-layered, close-knit, highly-interactive learning communities that good university colleges and halls of residence create are likely to remain among the hallmarks of any great undergraduate educational experience.

The Manchester review, like developments at Melbourne and the University of Western Australia, reflects an increased focus in universities and colleges around the world over the last decade or so on the quality of education, including student experience. The increased focus on collegiate education in many places is part of the wider drive in many institutions to improve the educational experience of students, perhaps especially undergraduates, with increased attention to student engagement, out-of-classroom as well as in-classroom activities, the quality of teaching, greater student-faculty interaction, on-campus and virtual learning communities, curriculum reform, and so on.

Many advocates of collegiate education argue that its benefits have been evident over hundreds of years of experience. There have been empirical studies which have provided support for this. For example, in 1991, in their review of longitudinal studies of university impact, Pascarella and Terenzini noted that 'living on campus is perhaps the single most consistent within-college determinant of [university] impact'.[†]

Richard Light's bestselling book from 2001, *Making the most of college: students speak their minds*, based on detailed interviews with some 1600 undergraduates at Harvard and other leading

---

[*] Quoted from Daniel, op. cit., p. 51.

[†] Pascarella and Terezini quoted from *Engaging College Communities: The Impact of Residential Colleges in Australian Higher Education*, AUSSE Research Briefing, Volume 4, June 2009, p. 2

US colleges, provides evidence of what he calls 'the remarkable amount of learning that occurs in residential interactions' and the 'critical role of residential living arrangements" such as intermingling, rather than concentrating, students from diverse cultural, national, and other backgrounds. One of the most important findings of Light's study is that, when asked about their most profound learning experience, fully 80% of students quoted something that happened outside the classroom, including in many cases activities in their residential college or hall. This simple, striking fact helps to explain the renewed focus on student engagement outside as well as within the classroom, and including in residential settings.

Student opinion surveys in Australia tell a similar story. A June 2009 analysis by the Australian Council for Educational Research of data from the Australasian Survey of Student Engagement (AUSSE) compared the experience of students resident in colleges with students not resident in them.[†] It suggests, for example:

- that resident students are more engaged than non-resident students, including in active learning, student and staff interactions, and enriching educational experiences, and most significantly, in experiencing the university as a 'supportive learning environment';

- that these differences, what appear to be benefits, are actually greater for later-year undergraduates than they are for first-year undergraduates;

- that resident students are much more likely than non-resident students to plan to take part in such enriching experiences as practicums or internships, community service, and study abroad or student exchange;

- that resident students are more likely to find student, teacher

---

* Richard Light, *Making the most of college: students speak their minds,* Harvard University Press, 2001, p. 5.

† *Engaging College Communities,* AUSSE Research Briefing, Volume 4, op. cit.

and support relationships as friendly, helpful, and considerate than non-resident students do, and to experience much better relationships with other students;

- that resident students have greater overall satisfaction with their university experience; and
- that the greater benefits for resident over non-resident students are especially significant for international students.

These results provide strong evidence of the educational benefits of residential colleges, while also, as the authors of the research briefing argue, encouraging further research and thought on 'ways in which to further enhance the contribution that college communities make to higher education in Australia'.*

For all these positive perspectives on the renaissance of residential colleges, it is crucially important to acknowledge that many residential colleges face real challenges, and that obtaining the benefits of collegiate education requires a certain set of conditions. In some universities, colleges are in retreat rather than resurgence.

Some so-called 'colleges' lack the educational focus truly to merit that name. In some cases, unwisely led, colleges are bastions of privilege, not centres of excellence or points of access and inclusion. In some cases, the ability of the college to attract talented people with appropriate vision, values, and capacity for positions in governance and college leadership is unreliable. While some colleges have prospered financially, others have found it hard to implement a sustainable business model.

To give another example of a challenge and opportunity: colleges provide one of the best potential environments for encouraging mutually rewarding connection between students

---

* Ibid., p. 13.

from many different cultures and countries – but such positive interactions do not just happen by chance, and leadership within colleges is needed to encourage them and create good preconditions for them.

I quoted earlier from Professor Alan Gilbert saying – and it is worth repeating – that the rich 'learning communities that good university colleges and halls of residence create are likely to remain among the hallmarks of any great undergraduate educational experience.' Notice that Alan Gilbert spoke of 'good university colleges'. In 1998, then Vice-Chancellor of the University of Melbourne, he wrote an article for a college magazine that, drawing on his experience in several universities, began:

'College life! When it is good it is very, very good, but when it is bad ..."

He wrote of his 'considerable knowledge and experience of just how superb, and nurturing, and uplifting, life in a university college can be – and just how dehumanising, humiliating, abusive and tyrannical the "college experience" can become for sensitive individuals if shallow, chauvinistic or anti-intellectual values are allowed to emerge as the dominant culture.'

I am sure that Professor Gilbert had seen, as I have seen, where colleges, founded with noble ideals, have become places where conformism, sexism, racism, anti-intellectualism, and an over-emphasis on alcohol have damaged people – not enhanced their personal development, but subtracted from it.

Professor Gilbert had great hopes for what colleges could contribute to the development of students. But his warning about what he called 'the consequences of unbridled chauvinism, anti-intellectualism and invidious peer pressure' is not to be dismissed lightly. This warning was given not long after the

---

* Alan D Gilbert, 'The Challenge to Colleges – and Trinity's "formidable" contribution', *Trinity Today*, Trinity College, University of Melbourne, Summer 1998.

publication of a book by a former head of a college in another Australian university, under the title *Finishing School for Blokes*, which reflected offensive and vulgar behaviour which clearly negated the positive educational effect the college was meant to have. More recent alarming incidents in other colleges reinforce the grounds for real concern about the damage that can be done when values go askew, discipline is lax, and vulgar conformism replaces individual responsibility. It is part of the role of college leaders – including student leaders – to work to prevent this, and to ensure that the best and not the worst is brought out in students.

Some colleges have worked hard to nurture cultures of inclusion and respect, and genuine gender equality. My book '*A large and liberal education*' gives a brief account of such strenuous and at least partly successful efforts at Trinity College in the University of Melbourne.* Despite 30 years of co-education or coresidence, the culture of the institution remained male-dominated. This, I think, has been true in many other contexts: once all-male institutions, becoming co-educational, have continued for decades to have essentially masculine cultures. In such cases, gender equality does not arise spontaneously – a transformative process is required. I am pleased that the President of Princeton, Shirley Tilghman, has recently commissioned a committee chaired by Nan Keohane to review women's undergraduate leadership at Princeton: a study that I hope will contribute to understanding and action in universities and colleges far beyond Princeton.

Although I do not wish to be prescriptive for Trent or indeed any other university, perhaps I might, in conclusion, mention some of the conditions that I regard as important, even essential, for the best educational potential of colleges to be realised in the circumstances of the 21st century. They include these:

---

* '*A large and liberal education*': *higher education for the 21st century*, pp. 183-89.

- that colleges be inspired at all levels by a vision of themselves as educational institutions and not merely as accommodation providers;

- that they be diverse communities, with people drawn from many backgrounds – socio-economic, geographic, cultural, racial, and so on – but also that they take deliberate efforts to draw the greatest benefits from this diversity;

- that they be genuinely co-educational, with a real and energetic commitment to gender equality;

- that they embrace (as evenly as possible, in my view) students of all year levels, and not only or primarily first-years, and ideally including postgraduate as well as undergraduate students;

- that they be environments in which considerate and respectful behaviour is both expected and insisted upon – if you will permit the old-fashioned language I prefer in this instance, where there is discipline;

- that they be environments in which senior academics take an active, leading part, seeking deliberately to enhance the education of students and not simply providing a venue for parties;

- that this be reflected in programs of academic enrichment, ideally other programs for encouraging leadership, service and personal development, and the provision of pastoral care, as well as support for a rich array of high-quality extra-curricular activities; and

- that they be embraced by the leadership and administration of the university as respected and valued partners in enriching and supporting the education of students.

Where such conditions are met, the immense potential value of university residential colleges can be fully realised – value which is reflected in so many of the world's finest universities, and has been for centuries; and value which many universities and colleges around the world are working hard today to realise and increase. Doing so is, they rightly believe, of great benefit to their students, to their universities and colleges, and ultimately to the communities – local, national, and global – which they serve.

On 'breadth': liberal education for tomorrow's world

Forum on 'The end of liberal education'
Otonabee College, Trent University, Ontario
9 February 2010

The deliberately provocative title of tonight's discussion – 'the end of liberal education' – cannot go without challenge. While some in this university may believe that you have been witnessing 'the end of liberal education' here or elsewhere, in the world beyond there are signs in many places of a resurgence of interest in liberal education arising from fresh thinking about the changing world in which we live.

Far from being the end of liberal education, there is widespread interest in it internationally and, though they may be changing, the arguments for it are stronger than ever. Most significantly, there is a stronger emphasis evolving within it on the importance of including studies in science and technology, to which study of mathematics is often the necessary gateway.

First, what is liberal education? The expression 'liberal education' has various meanings, but at the core would normally be such elements as an emphasis on intellectual and personal breadth, including learning through wide reading and debate about a diverse range of human experience, the clash of great ideas, and the science and technology that help to shape our world; the encouragement, through such learning, of key intellectual skills such as a capacity to think for oneself, to express oneself clearly, and to interpret the nuances of words

---

* These remarks were first published in Donald Markwell, *The need for breadth: On liberal education and the value of university residential colleges,* Trent University, 2010. 'Breadth' was, of course, something Cecil Rhodes encouraged in his will.

and context; encouragement to be an active citizen in society, who has thought carefully about her or his values and beliefs, and who has wide and humane international and inter-cultural awareness and understanding; and a belief that such education should come before, or at very least accompany, purely vocational (career-specific) education.*

Contrary to some stereotypes, liberal education is not only or primarily about courses on great books, or only classics and history and other humanities. Modern liberal education at its fullest typically includes courses in the life and physical sciences, social sciences, history or other humanities, some study that relates to values and moral reasoning, some language, and so on. It will also typically include a strong emphasis on communication, most especially writing.

Liberal education will often be accompanied by focus on extra-curricular engagement as part of a student's all-round education. It is no accident that liberal education is often associated with – and in my view is most likely to be best accomplished in – residential colleges, in which students of diverse backgrounds are immersed together in an environment that brings together learning and living, provides rich extra-curricular opportunities, and formally or informally encourages sharing of insights from diverse disciplines.

Above all, the greatest purpose of a liberal education is to equip individuals for the wise and well-informed exercise of freedom. The phrase which I gave to the title of my book of papers on higher education, '*A large and liberal education*', was actually a phrase quite widely used in 19th century discussions of education: broad education that enlarges the individual.

The breadth of a liberal education will also usually be combined with a requirement that students do study at least one

---

* This is slightly adapted from '*A large and liberal education': higher education for the 21st century*, pp. 32-33. The adaptation underscores the importance of science and technology, a reflection of the needs of liberal education in our time. Various of the arguments in this speech have been adapted from that volume, esp. pp. 29-37, 67-9.

major or concentration in detail, alongside the range of other studies. It should also be stressed that liberal education does not mean that one does not get a specialised or vocational education at some point. Clearly very many people need that. But the argument for liberal education is that it should precede or at least accompany more specialised or vocational education, so that our graduates have breadth as well as whatever depth they get. It is important, I think, that the arguments for liberal education be made cogently to students who may be seeking what they think is the best (and quickest) way to prepare themselves for a job, and seek this through what is often misguided or premature specialisation.

In the United States, of course, there has long been a strong emphasis on liberal education at the undergraduate level often leading into professional postgraduate education. Though there are real challenges to it, recent years have also seen, in many US colleges and universities, a review and refreshing of liberal education for the new century. Let me give just two examples.

At Harvard, a long curriculum review has resulted in the current Harvard first-year class being the first class to undertake a new Program in General Education, which replaces a set of core courses that had been in place for more than three decades.[*] 'Gen Ed' requires students to take one course in each of eight broad categories of learning: Aesthetic and interpretive understanding; Culture and belief; Empirical and mathematical reasoning; Ethical reasoning; Science of living systems; Science of the physical universe; Societies of the world; and the United States in the world. At least one course must involve a substantial study of the past.

By contrast, at Brown University, a major review of the curriculum led to a restatement of Brown's liberal education goals, in which students are not required to undertake a particular core curriculum but are challenged to build their own,

---

[*] See, e.g., Corydon Ireland, 'Welcoming Gen Ed', *Harvard Gazette*, 4 September 2009.

bearing in mind various goals.* These goals are worth quoting, as they reflect the goals of liberal education: Work on your speaking and writing; Understand differences among cultures; Evaluate human behaviour; Learn what it means to study the past; Experience scientific inquiry; Develop a facility with symbolic language; Expand your reading skills; Enhance your aesthetic sensibility; Embrace Diversity; Collaborate fully; Apply what you have learned.

The refreshing of liberal education in many US institutions has been matched by a surge of interest in it in many other countries. In Australia, the most conspicuous but not the only examples are the decisions by the University of Melbourne and the University of Western Australia to move most of their professional courses from undergraduate entry to graduate-only entry, and to introduce requirements that undergraduates undertake some proportion of their studies outside their area of concentration. At the University of Melbourne, this is known as 'the Melbourne Model', and a similar (but in important respects different) approach is known at the University of Western Australia, with equal alliteration, as 'the Future Framework'.[†] At the University of Western Australia, I was responsible for leading the consultative and research-based process by which over two years that university, starting with the question 'what is the best education we can offer our students for the 21st century?', came to embrace this broad approach, with requirements of undergraduate degrees that, as well as breadth, include work focused on communication skills, work that will develop research skills, and engagement in community service.

Although the results may be less obvious, there has also been growing interest in such curriculum reform in the direction of liberal education in some British universities. When he

---

* 'Liberal learning at Brown' –http://brown.edu/Administration/Dean_of_the_College/ curriculum/downloads/Lib_Learning_Goals.pdf – accessed 25 February 2010.

† Later 'New Courses'. See 'A consultation process for curriculum reform: the Review of Course Structures at UWA', next in this section of this book.

commissioned a full review of teaching, learning, and the student experience at the University of Manchester, Vice-Chancellor Alan Gilbert asked the relevant review committee to 'consider and make recommendations in relation to the objective of ensuring that the University provides all its graduates, irrespective of particular program of professional orientation, with a *broad and liberal education* providing opportunities for personal, moral, social and cultural development'.* 'The University of Aberdeen has already detailed a new curriculum that offers undergraduates the opportunity to study a wider range of disciplines, while the Vice-Chancellor of the University of Warwick is taking soundings on a new general education program.'†

But such interest is not confined to western universities. Last week, the president of Yale, Richard Levin, gave a major address in London on 'The rise of Asia's universities', with particular focus on China and India. It is worth quoting him at some length:‡

Asian leaders are increasingly attracted to the American model of undergraduate curriculum, which typically provides students with two years to explore a variety of subjects before choosing a single subject on which to concentrate during their final two years. There are two principal rationales for this approach. First, significant exposure to multiple disciplines gives students alternative perspectives on the world, which both allows them to function more effectively in their chosen field and better prepares them to encounter new and unexpected problems. The second rationale is that students are in a better position to choose a specialization at age twenty than at age eighteen. ... At its best,

---

* http://www.manchester.ac.uk/medialibrary/staffnet/briefing_paper_ug_education.pdf – accessed 25 February 2010. Emphasis added.

† Hannah Fearn, 'Extreme Makeover', *Times Higher Education*, 4 February 2010.

‡ Richard Levin, 'The rise of Asia's universities', speech at Royal Society, London, 1 February 2010.

[the American model] produces strong results by effectively broadening the perspective of graduates.

... In today's knowledge economy, no less than in the nineteenth century when the philosophy of liberal education was articulated by Cardinal Newman, it is not subject-specific knowledge, but the ability to assimilate new information and solve problems [that] is the most important characteristic of a well-educated person. The Yale Report of 1828, a document with enormous influence on American undergraduate education, distinguished between the "discipline" and the "furniture" of the mind. Mastering a specific body of knowledge – acquiring the "furniture" – is of little permanent value in a rapidly changing world. Students who aspire to be leaders in business, or medicine, or law, or government, or in the academy need the "discipline" of mind – the ability to adapt to constantly changing circumstances, confront new facts, and find creative ways to solve problems.

Professor Levin continued:

In Asia's quest to build world-class universities, there has already been dramatic movement in the direction of developing an American-style curriculum. Peking University introduced Yuanpei Honors College in 2001, a pilot program that immerses a select group of the most gifted Chinese students in a liberal arts environment. These students live together and sample a wide variety of subjects for two years before choosing a major field of study. Yonsei University in South Korea has opened a liberal arts college with a similar curriculum on its campus, and the National University of Singapore has created a University Scholars program in which students do extensive work outside their disciplinary or professional specialisation.

For the past six years, the presidents, vice presidents, and [Communist] party secretaries of China's top universities, those singled out for special support by the government, have met annually with Yale faculty and administrators in a weeklong workshop to learn about the practices of American institutions and share their own experiences with the reform of curriculum, faculty recruitment, and pedagogy. Although I do not claim a direct causal linkage, their progress toward curricular reform has been astonishing. At Fudan University, all students now take a common, multidisciplinary curriculum during their first year before proceeding with the study of their chosen discipline or profession. At Nanjing University, students are no longer required to choose a subject when they apply for admission; they may instead choose among more than 60 general education courses in their first year before deciding on a specialization.

To the Asian examples which Richard Levin mentioned, I would add these:

- in Singapore, in addition to the University Scholars program he mentioned, a new American-style liberal arts college affiliated with the National University of Singapore is being developed, and NUS itself has course requirements 'designed to foster breadth of learning' so that, in its words, NUS 'undergraduate programs strive for a healthy balance that would satisfy both the specialisation needed for a subject major and the broader expectations of University education';

- major curriculum reform is underway at the University of Hong Kong, including a common core curriculum. 'By 2012, when the new curriculum comes into force, all students will be expected to take six general education modules in their first two years. These modules will reflect and explore "common human experiences". Students may select from a range of modules, but they must take at least one on each of the following topics: scientific and technological literacy, the humanities, China, and global issues';* and

- likewise, for example, the University of Brunei Darussalam

---

* HKU – Fearn, op. cit. See, e.g., http://tl.hku.hk/undergraduate–curriculum–reform – accessed 25 February 2010.

is undertaking significant curriculum reform in the direction of liberal education.

It is often said that employers want graduates who have undertaken vocational rather than liberal education. This, of course, is sometimes true, and it depends on the employer and the type of work. But many employers, it seems to me increasing numbers of employers, are actually interested in graduates who have been more broadly as well as deeply educated; who can see their specialty in its context; who have the skills, perhaps most especially the skills of analysis and communication, which are needed in their work and which a liberal education is most likely to help develop; who can adapt to change; who can work in teams as well as individually; and who have integrity. These themes came through the consultations we undertook as part of the Review of Course Structures at the University of Western Australia, and are reflected in surveys of employers and other studies.

If they employ graduates who have the capacity to think for themselves, to master new bodies of knowledge, and to be flexible in their thinking and their working with others, then the employer can help them get whatever vocationally-specific training or education they need.

Robert Hagstrom is a close associate of Charlie Munger, the close colleague of 'the oracle of Omaha', one of the world's greatest investors, Warren Buffett. Hagstrom has written a book expounding a key aspect of their investment philosophy. It is called *Investing: The last liberal art.*[*] It argues that investors can and should draw and apply insights from a wide range of disciplines – from physics, biology, the social sciences, psychology, philosophy, and literature. This is a powerful argument for liberal education.

One could make a comparable argument about what

---

[*] Robert Hagstrom, *Investing: The last liberal art*, Texere, 2002.

is needed in management education – for example, that outstanding managers can or should learn about leadership from the study of history and of psychology, about ethics from the study of moral reasoning, about the context of what they are managing and the forces that might change it from a diversity of disciplines, and so on. Similarly, a greater shared intellectual understanding between research scientists and venture capitalists – who very often do not understand each other, I suspect, coming as they tend to do from two very different cultures – should considerably increase the likelihood of successful commercial development and application of research, for example in such fields as biotechnology.

As I have suggested, liberal education has at its heart the goals of encouraging skills of critical and creative thinking, and of communication. These skills are clearly highly valued by employers, and much sought after today. The need to improve them is clearly a powerful reason for the increased focus in East Asia on liberal education as an antidote to overly specialised and formulaic and narrow technical education.

There are further reasons why I believe that liberal education is even more relevant today than it has ever been. We live in an age of global forces and of rapid change, including change driven by scientific and technological development. To be able to understand our global world and to engage effectively with it requires wide international knowledge and, ideally, experience. This is, of course, why in many places there have been efforts at 'internationalisation' of the curriculum and student experience, including in some places efforts to fight a drift away from language study, and in many institutions much increased emphasis on study abroad or student exchange.

To be able to engage effectively with rapid change requires understanding more than simply one area of specialisation: as I have suggested, it requires understanding the broad context within which that specialisation is situated, and the areas not within your specialisation that might well lead to change within it. To understand and engage with change driven by science and technology requires some understanding of that science and technology as well as other – social, human, economic, or other – factors. It is for this reason that many advocates of liberal education place increasing emphasis on including the study of various sciences and technology within it, and why it makes so much sense, as advocated by Edward Nell and others, that mathematics education be given strong emphasis within liberal curriculum.

It is increasingly commonplace to say that in a world marked by rapid change of many sorts – scientific, technological, economic, legal, social, and other – knowledge changes so quickly that, while students must acquire a great deal of knowledge as undergraduates and in other education and training, what they need more than specific knowledge – which will soon be out-dated – are the intellectual and personal skills which enable them to come to a fresh body of knowledge and master it for themselves – identify its essence and key issues, think it through for themselves, and apply it to the often-novel problems with which they have to deal.

We live in an age when many issues can only be understood and solved by bringing together the perspectives of various disciplines. From stem cell research to neuroscience to the study of global poverty to non-traditional security and beyond, expertise is needed from across a range of sciences, and social sciences and humanities, including ethics.

Moreover, various events of the last decade have highlighted to many people the need for areas of study previously neglected, and thus for a broader education if one is to be able to engage fully in the world as it is becoming. For example: the terrorist attacks of September 11, 2001 and subsequent events have highlighted the importance of understanding world religions and cultural diversity if current international conflicts are to be understood; some of the corporate collapses of the last decade, such as Enron, have highlighted the importance of education in ethics or values; and the global financial crisis has highlighted the need for a greater understanding of economic history, and of broader understanding of economic theory and policy.

This leads me to two aspects of this world of change to which I would especially like to draw attention. The first is that our current lifestyle often, perhaps overwhelmingly, involves pressures for instant action rather than sustained reflection. A liberal undergraduate education should provide graduates with some period of reflection in their lives that will equip them with values and orientations that are helpful under such pressures later, and also with a capacity for reflection that they are not likely otherwise to develop.

Secondly, we live in an age of division in which we witness, both domestically and internationally, polarisation of opinion and inadequate tolerance and humility. Perhaps this is true of all ages, but it is certainly, in my view, true of today. Liberal education, which exposes students to contrasting ideas and debates in their historical or social context, should develop greater capacity for reasoning, tolerance of opposing views, humility about one's own, and a greater sense of nuance rather than dogma. More liberal education would make extremism less likely both domestically and internationally.

One, perhaps unexpected, advocate of this view died in the last few weeks. He was Abdurrahman Wahid, the Islamic scholar who was for a time president of the world's largest Muslim country, Indonesia. It was my great privilege to host President Wahid for a discussion of education and inter-faith understanding in Melbourne when I was head of a college there.* His argument, made just over six months after the 9/11 attacks, is worth quoting at length:†

Most Muslims are strongly opposed to acts of violence in any form, undertaken in the name of religion. Consequently, it hurts

---

* See 'A large and liberal education': higher education for the 21st century, pp. 216-17.
† Abdurrahman Wahid quoted from ibid., pp. 35-6.

us to constantly see the name of Islam, "the religion of peace", linked with international terrorism. ...

We face a dangerously schizophrenic approach to educating our young people. At present, tens of thousands of Muslim students, mostly from impoverished developing nations that comprise the bulk of the Islamic world, are sent abroad to study in technologically more advanced societies in order that they may bring back home and apply to their own societies an understanding of modern science and technology.

And so it is that every year thousands of young Muslims from developing nations such as Indonesia come of age while studying as strangers in foreign lands. Their education provides for them an understanding of modern technology and science but it is, of course, left to them to reconcile this newly gained knowledge with the faith that, as foreign students in the West, they increasingly come to feel to be at the core of their identity.

Because they have not been trained in the rich disciplines of Islamic scholarship, they tend to bring to their reflection on their faith the same sort of modelling and formulistic thinking that they learnt as students of engineering or other applied sciences. Students studying liberal arts are rather better served when it comes to reflect on the place of Islam in the modern world. But precious few young Muslims from developing nations have the privilege of undertaking liberal arts courses in Western universities.

This might seem but a small matter, but the ramifications are far reaching. Left to themselves, these future leaders of Muslim societies apply the same intellectual principles they have learned in the classrooms to understanding the place of Islam in the modern society.

Many end up going down a familiar path, taking a more or less literalistic approach to the textual sources of Islam: The Koran and the traditions of the Prophet... Grabbing a few verses out of context, they seek to find answers to the challenges facing Muslim society today. The result is that they use these texts in literalistic and reductionistic fashion without being able to undertake, or even appreciate, the subtly nuanced task of interpretation required of them if they are to understand how documents from the 7th and 8th centuries, from the alien world of tribal Arab society among the desert sands, are to be correctly applied to the very different world that we live in today.

Analysing problems in a reductionistic fashion and rigorously applying simple formulas may be an appropriate approach to building a bridge, or even erecting a skyscraper, but it is grossly inappropriate and inadequate to the task of building modern Muslim society.

Sadly, without at all intending it to be so, we take the best of our young people and school them in such a way that, in the face of alienation, loneliness and the search for identity, they are unable to approach their faith with the intellectual sophistication that the demands of the modern world require of them.

Until we begin to value a broad education for our young and face up to the nature of the intellectual challenges that face them, we are unwittingly condemning ourselves to forever struggle with the very forces of violent radicalism that we regard as being anathema to our faith.

What a powerful statement for liberal education that is. I think President Wahid's argument for liberal education as a protection against extremism applies to liberal education as protection against extremism of all kinds, not simply the Islamic extremism which he mentioned and so strongly opposed.

President Wahid's argument about liberal education helping us to understand religious texts aright perhaps reminds us that, as people with a capacity for religious, political, and other beliefs, we need an education that prepares us for our lives simply as human beings, and our lives as citizens. The world needs people of humanity and it needs active citizens as much today as it ever did, and this will, I think, forever remain a powerful argument for liberal education.

A consultation process for curriculum reform: the Review of Course Structures at UWA

The Australian Financial Review
Higher Education conference, Sydney
14 March 2008

As this morning's token non-Victorian – and one of very few speakers at this conference from outside the Sydney-Canberra-Brisbane-Melbourne quadrilateral – I hope I can be forgiven some subversive remarks. This session is billed as being about 'initiatives to create diversity and differentiation', and I have been asked to speak about the University of Western Australia's Review of Course Structures.

But the UWA Review is not specifically 'an initiative to create diversity and differentiation', and, although it is possible, such an outcome cannot be taken for granted. The Review aims instead to deal with a different question: how can UWA structure its degrees to offer its students the best education it can to equip them for lives and careers in the 21st century? We are two-thirds of the way through a 20-month or longer careful consultative review process, which is likely to report in August this year with recommendations that are far from determined.

I hope that some description of and reflection on our Review will be of interest and perhaps stimulus to you in casting some light on *process* if not on outcomes. This is, if you like, a progress report on an unfinished process within one university – a process that has attracted considerable interest nationally and also internationally. I will discuss it under five headings:

- first, why are we undertaking this review, and what do we hope to achieve?

- second, what is the review process?
- third, what are the key ideas and options we are considering for reform?
- fourth, how might we evaluate them and decide what to recommend?
- fifth, what reflections arise from this that may be of interest?

First: why are we undertaking the Review, and what do we hope to achieve?

The decision to undertake a Review had various drivers. One was administrative – the sense that the courses of the University were so many, complex, and untidy that there needed to be a significant spring clean. Secondly, at a time of workload pressures, a desire for efficiency – to find a way to enhance the educational offering of the University but with considerable reduction of what some believe to be over-teaching – for example, through the elimination of excess units – and the freeing up of academics' time for research, and of administrative time for other pressing demands.

But the most profound and important driver is the desire to press the refresh button on courses so as to maximise the chances of their equipping our students for the needs of an era of rapid change, of global forces, of growth of knowledge, of new and often unexpected linkages between previously distinct bodies of knowledge, and so on. Universities and colleges – for example, liberal arts colleges – in many countries have been reviewing their curriculum and their course structures because of a sense that the needs of the 21st century might not be met by the courses of the 20th century.

This is, of course, in a context where there has been a growing focus in many countries, including Australia, in recent years on how to improve teaching, learning, and the overall student learning experience – on which, by the way, I especially encourage you to look on the University of Manchester website at their current review of these things.

It has been a world also in which efforts to facilitate mobility of students and of graduates, for study and later for work, have seen (as you know) renewed attention to how Australian degrees compare with degrees in Europe under the Bologna process, in the US with its top-end model of four-year liberal arts degrees preceding professional postgraduate education, and in various Asian countries, many of whose universities are actively learning from what they see as the world's best, especially in the US and UK.

We too have high international aspirations for our university, within the context of high aspirations for Australian higher education generally, and are keen to learn from the experience of universities nationally and internationally.

What we hope to get out of our Review is a structure for our degrees that offers students the kind of education they need, remembering that we at UWA attract one of Australia's youngest undergraduate cohorts, with the highest proportion straight from school, and of very high prior academic attainment. We also aim at courses to provide the communities we serve with well-educated graduates, and, of course, to enhance UWA's strategic position – locally, nationally, and internationally.

Though we welcome greater diversity among higher education institutions, and our Review may help to differentiate us, we are not seeking diversity or differentiation for their own sake. We must also be careful not to differentiate ourselves in a way that makes us less attractive to prospective students.

My second question is: what is our review process?

Our consultative process has involved:

- formation of a Steering Group, chaired by the Deputy Vice-Chancellor (Education), representing much of the senior leadership of the University, including Academic Board and student leaders, but – whether rightly or not – not including representation from faculties;

- the distribution in December 2006 of a detailed discussion paper, within and beyond the University community, inviting written responses by 30 April 2007;

- the appointment of a Senior Academic Reviewer, Professor Ian Reid, who is leading much of the discussion and other work on this Review, and of other staff for the Review;

- the holding in early 2007 of various forums and consultation meetings, and articles in university publications, for staff, students, and alumni, to encourage input to the process;

- the creation of working parties of academics from around the University on key topics such as breadth and depth in education, the teaching-research nexus, Honours, and postgraduate coursework;

- the undertaking of research, including with the help of the Australian Council for Educational Research – including, for example, receiving information from some dozens of universities around the world on their course initiatives; and

- consideration by the Steering Group of the 160 written submissions, working group reports, and research, and preparation of an issues and options paper, *Courses for Tomorrow's World*, which was released in October 2007.

Courses for Tomorrow's World discussed context, and educational principles, and set out seven options for reform of course structures. Following its release, we held some 30 consultation meetings between October and December – in every faculty, for all students, for all staff, for Academic Board, University Senate, and so on. Written responses to the paper were encouraged by the end of January this year, and we received around 90 submissions. Consideration is now underway on these by the Steering Group, which has commenced preparation of an analysis of the implications of each option, preparation for market research, and so on, prior to the making of recommendations in about August this year, which will go to our Academic Board and Senate for deliberation and decision.

It goes without saying that the attitude of our Vice-Chancellor and Executive will be enormously influential. Any change will be implemented in a realistic timeframe, with ample advance notice and preparation time – perhaps not until, say, 2011 if the change is major.*

The third question is: what are the key ideas and options we are considering?

The paper discusses some key issues or principles: the importance of giving effect to the graduate attributes UWA has already identified as those it wants to develop (what UWA calls its 'Educational Principles'); the challenge of achieving an appropriate balance between breadth and depth of knowledge, sometimes expressed as a need to include both 'general' and 'special' elements, with many people arguing for – and some against – some form of broadening of undergraduate education; and the importance of developing research skills as a key to lifelong learning, an international and inter-cultural focus, enriching the learning environment in others ways, simplifying course administration and nomenclature, and achieving the optimal relationship between undergraduate and postgraduate courses.

The seven options we set out and are considering are (in extremely brief description):

- option 1: better embedding our UWA Education Principles, or graduate attributes, in every course. This is generally accepted as the bare minimum that should be done, and is included in every other option;

---

* In the event, the proposals – made in September 2008, further refined, and then adopted by the University in late 2008 and early 2009 – were implemented as 'New Courses 2012'.

- options 2, 3, and 4 are different forms of building into every course one semester, or a distributed equivalent of a semester, of general foundational units or other broadening material also aimed at developing key generic skills;
- option 5 would make a four-year Honours degree the standard UWA undergraduate program, giving ample room for common, general or broadening units as in options 2, 3 and 4, along with a research capstone and/or practicum and/or Study Abroad;
- option 6 would see UWA replace its 129 or so undergraduate programs with a few general undergraduate degrees, with expanded provision of postgraduate degrees, a bachelors and masters being typically secured in five years: clearly, the 'Melbourne model' is one form – but far from the only form – of this basic model;
- option 7 would massively simplify our courses into one or two comprehensive undergraduate degrees – either simply a Bachelor of Arts and Sciences, or a Bachelor of Arts and a Bachelor of Sciences – plus a variant (perhaps called a BPhil) for especially high achievers, with expanded provision of postgraduate degrees.

There is much more detail and argument in our paper, but that gives you a quick overview.

Almost simultaneously with this central issues and options paper, our Review has also issued a discussion paper on the need to expand postgraduate coursework within the University, and some ideas for a coherent University-wide framework for such degrees. The 30-odd recommendations of this working party have now been accepted by our Academic Council, and this may prove to be a significant, if unsung, achievement of the Review.

Meanwhile, there has been much discussion across the University about the seven options for more fundamental reform.

So my fourth question is: how to evaluate these seven options?

In considering the 90 submissions and roughly 30 consultation meetings, our Steering Group is also preparing for detailed modelling of some options, market research, discussion in key overseas markets, and further consultations. We are also undertaking a kind of SWOT analysis for each option – considering each option in the light of strengths in the University which we wish to preserve, problems we hope to solve, opportunities we want to pursue, and risks that we need to mitigate.

The strengths to preserve include the high quality of the student body and academic staff, a comprehensive range of courses, depth in every field of study, the nexus with a research-intensive culture, a rich all-round learning environment, including the Guild, student clubs and societies, colleges, etc, and international standards of excellence as a frame of reference.

The problems to solve include unduly complicated, inconsistent, and untidy course structures, what many staff perceive – as no doubt in all universities – as excessive workload pressures on them, pressures on students to choose a career pathway too early, what many regard as some lack of student maturity in professional programs, inequitable aspects of admission to professional programs, a gap between rhetoric and reality on graduate attributes, over-specialised undergraduate courses, and what some regard as, despite our existing efforts, insufficient preparation to participate in a globalised and culturally diverse environment.

Opportunities to pursue include expansion of exemplary existing UWA practices – such as a strong research focus throughout some courses, including from first year; inter-disciplinary project work in some courses; discipline-focussed communication skill development in some courses; and some programs which are particularly good at stretching outstanding students. Other opportunities include, of course, selective adaptation of quality-enhancing structures from elsewhere.

The risks we need to mitigate include, for example, the risks of stagnation, risk of loss of enrolments (either by making bad changes or by failing to make necessary changes), risks to reputation, and under-estimating the costs of structural change.

We will be evaluating each of our options in the light of these and other considerations, and making recommendations in about August.

So, finally, what reflections arise from this that may be of interest?

Our process has been ambitious, consultative, and with no predetermined outcome. We are exploring the implications of options before deciding what to do. This consultative process has many pros, and some cons.

On the positive side, it creates the possibility of buy-in, a sense of ownership, around the campus community and beyond, including in the alumni, business, professional, governmental, and other areas we consult. It means the University takes into account the wisdom and expertise of such people before deciding what to do, and how to do whatever it decides to do. Some of this buy-in, for example from business leaders, raises the possibility of philanthropic and other support in implementing whatever we do.

It has been gratifying to have public and private statements endorsing the process even from people with very different hopes and fears about its outcomes. The goodwill of deans has been important to gain, and much appreciated.

On the other hand, such an open process can create amongst some colleagues a sense of threat: the fear of change, as we all know, can be a powerful force. An open process can enable the forces against change to mobilise, strategise, resist, and lie in wait. This may create some real bias to the status quo.

However, it can also raise expectations beyond what can

ever realistically be in prospect of achievement. I have been in too many meetings where it has been said or implied that 'the Review of Course Structures' will solve this or that problem which, in reality, it has little prospect of solving. It has also been necessary to say that good ideas for course development should not be held up because of the Review: life must go on while the Review takes place, and if need be, matters can be revisited when the Review is completed.

The Review has encouraged discussion around the University about the courses we offer, the way we teach, and how we enrich the student learning experience generally. Such discussion is, in my view, highly desirable, and creates the possibility of other positive change.

Some people find the discussion of big educational ideas, and drawing from the experience of leading universities around the world, stimulating, even liberating. Others find it difficult to handle, even threatening. To set our focus firmly on educational reform that positions the University for our goal of being genuinely one of the top 50 universities in the world within a few decades is not easy – but is important, and exciting for many.

With mixed but generally good results, we deliberately encouraged responses to the seven options in our paper to be based on their educational merits, urging focus on what will enable us to offer the best education we can, rather than the first conversation-stopping response being to focus on resource constraints or logistical difficulties.

The discussion of the equity and access aspects of some of our options has, I think, helped to encourage focus on UWA's equity, diversity, and access initiatives generally, and on our desire to develop the next wave of initiatives in this area. This is very positive.

In a highly successful university with proud traditions, it is natural that some people will think that things aren't broken, and so don't need to be fixed. It is interesting how conservative some radicals can be. Others, however, will focus on how we can make a very good university into a great one, and how we can make good courses into the best that we can offer. This is the ambitious spirit of our Review.

The responses to the Review overwhelmingly welcome it as a timely and appropriate process, and I have no doubt that this is right. Whether the UWA Review of Course Structures leads to radical change or to little change, it will have given our University community a real chance to debate what the purposes of a university education are and how best these purposes are met in the 21st century. I believe that in the process we will also have contributed something to discussion of these matters in other universities, both nationally and internationally. I very much hope that this is so.

Curriculum reform: law and breadth

Award Ceremony for the Faculty of Law
The University of Western Australia
13 May 2009

It is the tradition of the University to acknowledge that this campus is situated on Noongar land, and that Noongar people remain the spiritual and cultural custodians of their land, and continue to practise their values, languages, beliefs, and knowledge.

Tonight's ceremony is also about acknowledgement – acknowledgement and celebration of the outstanding achievements of students of the Law School; and acknowledgement and expression of profound gratitude for the generosity of donors, whose prizes and scholarships recognise, encourage, and support the pursuit of excellence by our students.

Tonight also provides the University with an opportunity to acknowledge other outstanding achievements of Law School students, staff, and alumni, under the leadership of my good friend, the Dean, Professor Bill Ford – achievements such as the silver medal won by UWA law student Hayden Teo at the Jessup International Law Moot competition in Washington, DC; other successes for UWA law students, such as in the Fulbright Scholarships and WA Youth Awards; the legal research work of a range of UWA Law School staff, with books and articles on diverse topics, from the harmonisation of Australian consumer law, to native title and legal issues relating to the stolen generations, to sports law, and much else besides; the Premier's Book Award to UWA senior lecturer Dr Antonio Buti for his biography of Sir Ronald Wilson; the appointment of UWA law graduates to high office, including Justice Robert French as Chief Justice of Australia, and Christian Porter as Attorney-General of Western Australia; and much else.

For example, while sorry to see Professor Neil Morgan move from being a full-time staff member to an adjunct member of staff, we were delighted that his outstanding talents were recognised with his appointment as Inspector of Custodial Services, and the University is nominating him to the Australian Learning and Teaching Council for recognition by them of his outstanding contributions to student learning. I am delighted that two members of our Law School staff will be honoured tonight for their outstanding teaching. These, and much more, are achievements to be acknowledged and celebrated.

As someone who will soon be leaving UWA, with much sadness of farewell I might say, to take up the Wardenship of Rhodes House, Oxford, with responsibility for running the Rhodes Scholarships, I am very conscious of the extraordinary number and quality of UWA law students who have gone on Rhodes Scholarships to Oxford. These include – to date – one Prime Minister of Australia, Bob Hawke (I hope, Bill, the Law School has another one in the pipeline), at least two Attorney-Generals of Australia, Peter Durack and Daryl Williams, and several judges as well as other distinguished lawyers, past and present. UWA law graduates have continued to do very well in Rhodes selection in recent years also, and do very well in other highly competitive scholarships, such as the Fulbright, that make possible postgraduate study in some of the world's leading universities.

One of the great advantages of study in Oxford – at least when it is for two or more years – is that, as well as enabling an extraordinary intellectual honing, it exposes students to the broadening experience of living and studying alongside students of very diverse disciplines in their colleges, and to taking part in a rich diversity of extra-curricular activities of a broadening kind.

I would like to speak briefly about the value of educational breadth for lawyers by brief reference to three remarkable lawyers who believed in its importance.

When I was a law student for some three years at the University of Queensland 30 years ago (one of my tutors, by the way, was Quentin Bryce), it would have been taken for granted by most law students, I think, that the greatest lawyer Australia had produced was Sir Owen Dixon, a High Court judge for 35 years and Chief Justice of the High Court of Australia from 1952 to 1964. It is clear from reading Philip Ayres's splendid biography of Dixon that Dixon greatly valued his education in classics for the contribution that it made to his work in the law. Ayres wrote:

> From his studies in classics Dixon learned to value precision in thought, clarity of expression, and logical sequence in the parts of a composition, and these qualities mark everything he ever wrote. In his 1961 obituary for his friend and brother High Court judge, Sir Wilfred Fullagar, he could have been speaking of himself when he praised Fullagar's 'classical scholarship which did not desert him as the years advanced. His style of writing, formed doubtless by his classical training, gave an added distinction to his writings. No one sensitive to language can fail to perceive that his judgments not only were masterly embodiments of judicial

reasoning but contained a singularly apt and felicitous use of English in the expression of a legal subject'.

Another distinguished Australian lawyer, who pursued an academic legal career, including as a long-time law school dean, before becoming a Vice-Chancellor and then Governor-General of Australia, is Sir Zelman Cowen. I had the privilege of working with Sir Zelman as he prepared his memoirs, *A Public Life*. In them, Sir Zelman tells of how much he later valued, though he slightly resented it at the time, being guided by the head of his university college to study arts and law, rather than simply law. Sir Zelman writes of the benefits in education and personal development of having opened up for him 'a learning and cultural experience' which was much richer and more stimulating than simply studying law alone.

Sir Zelman this year will be celebrating his 90th birthday. One of the advantages of such longevity with a life of such rich opportunities is that one can meet just about anyone. Sir Zelman knew Sir Owen Dixon well, and he also knew the third remarkable lawyer to whom I will briefly refer, an American, Robert Maynard Hutchins. In 1927, Hutchins became Dean of the Yale Law School at the age of 28. Two years later, at the age of 30, he became President of the University of Chicago, which he was to lead for over 20 years. To over-simplify his thinking and his many reform proposals, Hutchins believed that, prior to the study of law, students should have a liberal education, preferably exposing all students to the so-called 'great books' – a general education which equipped them with intellectual breadth and intellectual skills, all the better to be both good citizens and to be ready for professional education.

Of course, the model of general undergraduate education prior to postgraduate legal education is the very model of legal education in the great universities in the United States.

There are many people who believe that the classical arguments for breadth are even more powerful in the world today – where specialised knowledge needs to be understood in context, and all of us need the capacity to adapt to rapid changes in knowledge and in so many aspects of the world around us. Clearly we live today in an age of rapid change and of global forces, not all of them benign, including of scientific and technological forces which many of us barely understand, and with ever-changing linkages between topics – say, national security and religion, or the climate and economics – which linkages were barely considered just a few years ago.

As part of their renewed efforts to improve the quality of the student learning experience they offer, universities around the world are increasingly asking the question – what structure and content of university courses will best equip students for lives and careers in this world of the 21st century? UWA has been a leader in this international process of reviewing and refreshing courses.

In 2007 and 2008, the University of Western Australia undertook a highly consultative review of the structure of our courses. Many members of the Law School, staff and students, and other lawyers took part in this consultative review, and the University has decided to implement its recommendations, most likely from 2012. This is the so-called 'UWA Future Framework' for degrees. At the risk of over-simplifying, the essential elements of this Future Framework are, as I said probably from 2012:

- a radical simplification of our undergraduate degrees, in which students will have a high degree of choice of what they can study as undergraduates within the framework of one of four three-year degrees, a Bachelor of Arts, Bachelor of Science, Bachelor of Commerce, Bachelor of Design, and a four-year degree, the research-intensive Bachelor of Philosophy (Hons);
- the introduction into undergraduate degrees of requirements for breadth, research skills and communication skills development, and community service;

- the moving of most of our professional courses – law, medicine, dentistry, and engineering – to postgraduate entry only, with a three-year JD replacing the current LLB; and

- with pathways from the point of entry to the University guaranteeing a significant proportion of students that, subject to satisfactory undergraduate results, they can progress from a more general undergraduate degree into postgraduate law, while leaving a significant proportion of postgraduate law places open to competition on the basis of good performance as undergraduates – something which we believe will make for the most equitable entry to law study.

While this will lengthen the time of university study for some, many of our law students will not study for longer, or not for much longer, than at present. But, as has long been the case in the United States, and is coming in some other parts of Australia, it will be necessary for them to complete an undergraduate degree in some other field prior to commencing law.

Following the two-year consultative Review, the University believes that law and other professional fields will be best undertaken as postgraduate study. It is no reflection on the existing profession – I know that many practitioners agree with this – to argue that a better professional education is possible if students come to it with greater breadth both of knowledge and of experience, and with already well-developed intellectual skills, including of research and communication.

It is agreed by many, not only that students will be better equipped for legal study if they have additional personal growth and breadth of knowledge before commencing it, but that it is better for students not to be as strongly pressured as they are now to make this crucial life decision – whether to go into law or medicine or some other professional course – in year 12, at the age of 17 or even 16. It seems to make much sense to be able to enter the University, test out various capabilities and fields of interest, and then to come to law, ideally as a passion.

Similarly, for law to be able to attract students from the widest diversity of backgrounds, intellectual and social – including more readily to attract students who have proven greater capacity at university than, for whatever reason, they were able to at secondary school – should be good for the students themselves, for the legal profession, and for the community.

Moving law to the postgraduate level creates a great opportunity for the Law School to reform and refresh the legal curriculum, and much good work along these lines has already been done in the Law School, which I heartily applaud.

The UWA Law School has a very proud record. Its alumni and its current students and its staff – all so superbly represented here tonight – have achieved outstandingly. But this is a University that does not rest on its laurels. We cannot do so as the world around us changes. We believe that the UWA Future Framework will help to ensure that future generations of UWA law graduates are as well prepared for lives and careers in this century as we can equip them to be.

Let me again congratulate tonight's prize-winners on your outstanding achievements, and again thank the donors of your prizes. As well as supporting the crucial work of the Law School and encouraging and supporting our students, your presence tonight embodies the links between the University and the wider profession and community which we are always keen to encourage, and which we value and appreciate deeply. Let me also thank the parents and friends whose support helps make possible the success of our students: your contribution is deeply valued. And let me thank my colleagues on the staff of the Law School for your dedication and your achievement.

It is a great privilege to be here with you all.

The teaching-research nexus

Seminar on 'Achieving Teaching-Research Connections'
Currie Hall, The University of Western Australia
16 June 2008

The website that has just been launched (www.trnexus.edu. au) provides materials which I think can be of very great value to all of us interested in the teaching-research nexus. I would like to congratulate the team who have undertaken this project, produced this impressive and useful website, and arranged today's seminar. Thank you very much indeed.

I have been asked to speak about the teaching-research nexus from the policy-maker's perspective. Please forgive me if I speak with particular reference to this University. I hope that this will provide some thoughts of interest for colleagues from other universities also – whom I am delighted to see here at UWA. A very warm welcome. But my paper will be, at best, the perspective of one policy-maker in one university. Perhaps I should also say that I am not wholly comfortable with the implicit assumption that someone like a DVC (Education) is best described as a 'policy-maker'. He or she is, at least in a university such as this, at best one voice – albeit an influential and perhaps even leading voice – in the shaping of institutional policy, and one pair of eyes in the monitoring of its implementation and performance. Moreover, I think that the role of a person in a position such as this is not simply to make policy, as though at a distance from the reality with which that policy is concerned, but to try to influence, through a variety of aspects of human leadership (and not simply policy-making and management), the way colleagues think about their priorities and how they go about them. I see the encouragement of discussion such as today, of conversation, of debate as important to this.

I also think it important that so-called policy-makers about education or teaching and learning be continually reminded that the importance of what they do ultimately depends upon its impact for good on the actual experience of students. Perhaps, rather than endlessly reiterate the phrase 'teaching-research nexus', we should in fact occasionally rephrase it as the 'research-student learning nexus', with teaching seen clearly as the intermediary means to an end – a good student learning experience – rather than an end in itself.

Having said that, however, I also want to emphasise that it seems to me that the importance of the teaching-research nexus should be, not only the benefit that it has for student learning (important though that this), but also the positive effects it can have for research that is enhanced by its interaction with the teaching of students. Speaking as someone who has encouraged and supervised much undergraduate research work, some of which has been published, I also know, for example, that some of my own research has been greatly enriched by years of discussing the underlying material with undergraduate as well as postgraduate students. And yet it seems that the emphasis on the teaching-research nexus tends to come from those concerned with the promotion of good teaching rather than those concerned with the promotion of good research. So perhaps one of the first points for the policy-maker to note on the teaching-research nexus is the importance of engaging his or her colleagues in *both* the teaching *and* the research 'sides' of university policy-making and performance management, and indeed of trying – as we try here at UWA – to overcome the sense that there are 'sides' at all.

One of the reasons the emphasis on the teaching-research nexus appears to come more from those of us on the teaching 'side' than those on the research 'side' may be because, at least in research-intensive universities, talk of the teaching-research nexus is partly a way of claiming space and attention for teaching in a culture in which research has often seemed more greatly valued. In some universities, on the other hand, it may be partly to claim space for research in a teaching-focussed culture. UWA is a university which has traditionally placed strong emphasis on research. In the last ten to 15 years, it has admirably placed a renewed emphasis on improving the quality of teaching, learning, and the student experience. This has required raising the profile of teaching and learning, and seeking to balance the research-intensive culture with a focus on teaching and learning.

Getting the balance right between teaching and research seems to many people to remain a continual issue or challenge. This reflects the fact that it cannot be taken for granted that the interaction between teaching and research will invariably be positive. Indeed, it may well be negative. Teaching and research compete for time. They may reflect competing priorities. For example, in teaching we may think it important to help students develop an overview of a discipline, including inter-disciplinary perspectives and the broader context of knowledge in which the disciplinary specialisation can best be understood; research may encourage ever-greater specialisation within a discipline or sub-sub-discipline (though I would also point out that there has in recent years been increasing emphasis again on the importance of inter-disciplinary approaches in research as well as teaching). Discussion of a teaching-research nexus may be an attempt to square the circle – to reconcile the otherwise-competing approaches or demands of teaching and research; to turn a negative relationship into a positive one. While seeking a positive nexus as an aspiration and a strategy is highly desirable, our talk of a teaching-research nexus does not of itself make the relationship a positive one. To pursue the example I just gave: it would only be positive if the emphasis on research-led teaching was combined with an emphasis on the kind of breadth that is also educationally desirable.

A university such as this is strongly committed to a positive interaction between research and teaching. In 1998, in the wake of the Boyer Commission Report, *Reinventing undergraduate education: a blueprint for America's research universities,* with its stress on 'learning as inquiry', UWA's Teaching and Learning Committee created a working party on the teaching-research nexus, chaired by the then Deputy Vice-Chancellor and now Vice-Chancellor, Alan Robson; and in 2001 UWA took part in a joint study of practice and policy with Curtin and Ballarat universities, published by the federal education department under the title *Strengthening the Nexus Between Teaching and Research.* This University might not have adopted a stand-alone policy such as the University of Melbourne has under the title 'The Teaching-Research Nexus: How research informs and enhances learning and teaching in the University of Melbourne', nor a 'Teaching-Research Nexus Plan' such as Swinburne plan to develop. But the teaching-research nexus is nonetheless very prominent in policy documents, as well as in practice, at UWA.

In its strategic plan, this University lists nine 'defining characteristics' of itself. One of these is simply: 'research-intensive, with a strong teaching and research nexus across all our disciplines'. This may be thought to be a classic case of a rhetorical claim or aspiration to a teaching-research nexus. But there is more to it than that. A good deal flows from this statement.

Within the University, this claim is followed through in a variety of ways in the processes of planning, reporting, review, and accountability, that provide the structure and processes through which university policy is articulated and its implementation overseen. It may truly be said that the desire positively to combine research and teaching *flavours* a great deal of what the University does, and how it does it – staff recruitment, development and promotion; student mix; approaches to curriculum and teaching methods; resource allocation; publicity materials; and on and on. It is also possible to point to many good, even exceptional, instances of positive teaching-research nexus – including the disciplines in which from first semester of first year, the subject is approached through a research focus, and the field in which the faculty dean personally oversees the research-focussed work of outstanding undergraduates from first year on.

More specifically at a university policy level:

- the broad strategic plan leads into what we call an 'Operational Priorities Plan', and to management plans in particular areas. UWA's Operational Priorities Plan for 2006-08 contains a section, under teaching and learning, which sets out an 'operational objective' 'to further develop the links between teaching, learning and research'. It sets out strategies and specific actions to implement this, and assigns operational responsibility to a range of officers of the University, including deans of faculties;

- the University's management plans for teaching and learning, and also for research, both refer to giving effect to the teaching-research nexus;

- in the cycle of review of courses – e.g. the BA or the BSc– a report is required on the 'functionality and visibility of [the] teaching-research nexus';

- in the cycle of reviews of schools within the university (our equivalent of academic departments), a report is required on 'the coordination and collaboration in curriculum development and research (including graduate output) achieved between teaching and research areas in the school' and the 'extent of [the] teaching-research nexus';

- the University's 'Guidelines for the Establishment and Review of UWA Research and Training Centres' say that 'a centre should enhance the teaching-research nexus in clearly identifiable ways' and 'In particular, research staff in centres should be encouraged to contribute to teaching and/or supervision of students enrolled in cognate schools.' Proposals for the creation of centres require an account of how they will enhance the teaching-research nexus in the University;

- the description of the role of the University's informal 'discipline groups' says: 'Discipline Groups are likely to have their roots in research but, through the teaching-research nexus, will have an influence on teaching'; and

- academic staff are required to prepare an 'Academic Portfolio' for promotion, tenure and annual Performance Development Reviews. The portfolio covers teaching, research, and service, and in the teaching and learning section staff are asked to 'Outline how your curricula promotes the teaching-research nexus and encourages student engagement with the discipline and its emerging issues/directions.'

So there are a variety of ways in which the teaching-research nexus is reflected in University planning, approval, and review processes. It may be evident to you, and unsurprising, that there are different notions here of the ways in which research and teaching do and should positively interact.

This University's efforts to produce a positive interaction between teaching and research is reflected in such strategies as expanding opportunities for research-based learning in undergraduate courses, including the introduction of fully-funded research projects for undergraduate students; expanding the Postgraduate Teaching Internship Scheme, which gives selected 'higher degree by research' students supported teaching experience while undertaking their research; revising human resource policies and school management policies to reduce barriers between career research staff and 'teaching and research' staff; and promoting teaching opportunities for career research staff.

We see one intended outcome of our 'Foundations of Teaching and Learning' program as being that new, or newish, academic staff 'demonstrate the relationship between teaching, research and scholarship in your own teaching practices'; and we see a growing recognition of the value and legitimacy of 'the scholarship of teaching and learning'.

Encouragement of linkages between teaching and research

will come indirectly in other ways. For example, under the theme of encouraging 'student engagement' in the out-of-classroom life of the University, we should be encouraging students to attend, say, special public lectures or research seminars by outstanding scholars. This aspect of emphasis on 'student engagement' should encourage the teaching-research nexus.

No doubt the graduate attributes we seek to encourage – or, as UWA calls them, 'educational principles' we seek to apply – are encouraged by teaching-research linkages. But we – like, I am sure, most universities – do not really know how well those attributes are developed, let alone what contribution the teaching-research nexus makes to them.

And so the question remains: how much impact do the teaching-research nexus and our policies about it actually have on the teaching and the research our academics undertake; and, above all, how much impact do they have on the real learning experience of students? Is there a *co-incidence* of research and of teaching, rather than a concerted and positive *interaction* between the two? How, indeed, do we know that the negative effects of the competing demands of research and teaching do not overwhelm the positive effects of their interaction?

Here at UWA, we know, for example, that our Student Guild is in principle supportive of the importance of the teaching-research nexus; but we do not know what impact students actually think it has on them. The principal teaching and learning indicators which this University uses – for example, for operational targets for faculties, and for performance review purposes – are the Course Experience Questionnaire (CEQ) and our internal student evaluations of units, SURF, which stands for Student Unit Reflective Feedback. Yet there is no question on the CEQ which relates directly to the teaching-research nexus. This is important. The student evaluation used across the country to measure institutional performance in teaching and learning has no direct reference to the teaching-research nexus. If that nexus is to be taken seriously across all institutions, perhaps it should. I will come back briefly to the question of whether it will be taken seriously in all institutions. Students are able to make comments about their course on the CEQ form, and these comments are analysed using the CEQuery software package. None of the over-25 categories under which comments can be categorised relates to the teaching-research nexus. Our internal SURF survey, which only has six questions, also has none that refers directly to the connection between teaching and research.

More encouragingly, the bank of questions which individual teaching staff can choose to use for their confidential SPOT – Student Perception of Teaching – surveys, does include questions that staff can choose to use relating to research skills, use of recent research findings, and so on. But SPOT surveys are for the use of individual staff only, for their own self-reflection, and are not used by the institution to monitor what, or how, we are doing.

It is commonly said that 'what gets measured gets done'. The absence of any connection between the teaching-research nexus and the standard teaching and learning indicators seems to me to make it less likely than it would otherwise be for the teaching-research nexus to be taken seriously by all of us – including deans of faculties, heads of schools, unit coordinators, and individual academic staff members.

Another way of saying this is that we do not measure the extent of teaching-research interaction, nor the effects (benefits and costs) of this; and, although we have policies and strategies aimed at encouraging this in various ways, our incentives towards this – for faculties and schools, and individual academics – are few and blunt. It would be good if the combined effect of this teaching-research nexus project and the Teaching Quality Indicators project[*] were to make it straightforward to change this.

Given that research is very unevenly spread across Australian

---

[*] Projects funded by the Australian Learning and Teaching Council, previously the Carrick Institute for Teaching and Learning in Higher Education.

universities, and therefore that the teaching-research nexus is liable to be variously interpreted and unevenly valued, I wonder whether there would also be very uneven interest between universities in any CEQ question that asks students about the links in their courses between teaching and research.

There are other ways in which the strategic commitment to the teaching-research nexus is followed through. In the first round of Australian Universities Quality Agency (AUQA)* audits, some of those universities that especially value the teaching-research nexus will have referred to it in their performance portfolio. In some cases – though from quick examination of AUQA audit reports, surprisingly few – this resulted in commentary and even a recommendation from AUQA related to the teaching-research nexus. Where there was a recommendation, in line with AUQA processes this will have led to a follow-up report, and the expectation of more being said in the second-round AUQA audits now underway. In some universities, this will have provided some impetus to greater focus on the teaching-research nexus.

Here at UWA, there are a number of special projects and reviews underway which are important for long-term policy-making, and have implications for the teaching-research nexus here. These include our Review of Course Structures, a working party on what UWA needs to do in its educational activities to become one of the top 50 universities in the world within 50 years, and our involvement in the Teaching Quality Indicators project, and reviews of student evaluation surveys.

Our Review of Course Structures, which will report in about three months' time, has been informed by a working party on the teaching-research nexus. That working party argued that 'It is important that we articulate "research" as the essential survival skill of the 21st Century, enabling graduates to access, interpret and use new knowledge throughout their lives, rather than

---

* AUQA was succeeded by the Tertiary Education Quality and Standards Agency (TEQSA): of the making of acronyms there is no end.

conceiving research as an elitist engagement in essentially very esoteric knowledge'. Responding to this, the Review's issues and options paper says that:

> While there are certainly challenges to be overcome, the creation of a research culture at all levels of tertiary study is increasingly important. In the information age, it is research skills that will enable graduates to become familiar with new fields, and that will equip them to respond to changes in the underlying base of knowledge within their discipline.

Various of the options for structural change at UWA which are currently being analysed further, before the Steering Group makes recommendations to the University, involve embedding research skills development into more, if not all, undergraduate degree courses. The Course Structures Review is thus providing an excellent opportunity to revisit the teaching-research nexus explicitly and directly.

Another process underway at UWA with potential for long-term policy impact is discussion of the educational attributes of the world's 'top 50' universities. The discussion paper on this, while reflecting some ambivalence about the reality of a beneficial teaching-research nexus in some instances, draws particular attention to the fact that many leading universities are providing undergraduates with opportunities to participate in research themselves. We are engaged in a university-wide discussion of what we can learn from the educational attributes of 'top 50' universities for what we at UWA should do, and one important manifestation of this will be the priorities and strategies we choose for our next Operational Priorities Plan covering the five years from 2009 to 2013 – what is likely to be the most important planning document for UWA for the next five years.

It would be premature to predict what these processes of discussion at UWA will lead to, but it would be startling and disappointing if it did not produce further clarity regarding and emphasis on ensuring the reality of positive interaction between research and teaching.

Institutional planning and policy-making takes places within the framework of government policy. This too can have significant impact on the teaching-research nexus. It is possible that the current Bradley review of higher education will result in policies which encourage greater diversification of the missions and roles of universities. Some may over time become more comfortable to be essentially teaching, rather than teaching and research, institutions. If this is so, it may further diversify approaches to the teaching-research nexus between universities. Similarly, it is quite possible that in the development of compacts between universities and the government – compacts related to the particular missions of individual institutions – there will be further emphasis on the teaching-research nexus in the case of some universities.

However this may turn out, as a so-called university 'policy-maker' really interested in what actually happens for students both in and outside the classroom, I again warmly welcome this project on the teaching-research nexus or, as I am tempted to rephrase it, 'generating positive interaction between research and student learning'. I especially welcome the encouragement and help this project gives to individual academics to develop further the various links between research and teaching, and the encouragement and help it gives to policy-makers in encouraging and supporting our colleagues in doing so.

Assuring academic quality: what makes an effective Academic Board?

Conference of Chairs of Academic Boards
Perth, Western Australia
22 October 2007

As my remarks today will make clear, in my view an effective, independent Academic Board focussed on academic quality assurance is no less an essential element of the running of a successful university in the increasingly competitive environment of today and tomorrow than it has ever been.

I ought to begin by making clear that what I want to say is by way of personal reflections based principally on my own experience in a small number of Australian universities. I am conscious that there are many different sizes, roles, powers and other characteristics of Academic Boards, but – rather than attempt a sophisticated taxonomy – I will make broad statements that I believe should (and I hope will) apply generally. If my statements are too broad-brush, they may nonetheless act as a provocation to debate.

The question 'what makes an effective Academic Board?' depends on what the purpose of an Academic Board is. In my view, the central purpose of an Academic Board in an Australian university is academic quality assurance. Other roles are attributed to Academic Boards – such as communication, a forum for debate, and so forth – and these have real value. But it seems to me that the role for which an Academic Board is essential – which a university needs and which a Board is likely to be uniquely capable of providing – is the maintenance of the academic standards of the institution.

In his paper for the Australian Universities Quality Agency

(AUQA), 'The Role of Academic Boards in University Governance', Anthony Dooley says that 'The Board should be the engine room of the university'.* I find this a puzzling image. In my mind, it is the role of those with executive responsibility – such as deans and their teams, and Vice-Chancellors and theirs – to *initiate* new activities by the faculty or university; for example, to initiate the creation of new academic programs. It is the role of the Academic Board to ensure that these initiatives are undertaken within an appropriate framework of academic standards, policies, and processes, and to test these initiatives against them.

As we know, Lord Acton famously wrote that 'power tends to corrupt, and absolute power corrupts absolutely'. Power is apt, sooner or later, to be misused. Constitutional structures of states must balance the need to have sufficient concentration of power for effective action to be possible, and sufficient checks and balances against the excessive concentration of power to ensure, if possible, that it is not abused or misused, or that abuse is identified and rectified. It seems to me that in the constitutional structure of a university, the Academic Board plays a crucial role as a form of check or balance.

In a modern university, there is the executive or management function, which is exercised by deans, Vice-Chancellors, and the administrative apparatus of the university; the governance function of the University Council or Senate, which gives formal approval to the strategy and highest level policies and key decisions of the university; and there is also an academic quality assurance mechanism, the Academic Board. You will notice that this characterisation is itself an over-simplification: for example, in some universities, and in many at some time, the most important line of cleavage is between the deans and the central leadership of the institution. But I think the tripartite distinction between functions and arms of the university –

---

* Anthony Dooley, 'The Role of Academic Boards in University Governance', Australian Universities Quality Agency (AUQA), 2007, p. 20.

executive, institutional governance, and academic quality assurance – remains.

The relationship between these three functions and arms of the university changes over time. It is commonly imagined, I think, that it has changed considerably in the last decade or more as universities have had to respond to the increasing need to position themselves in a competitive market – for example, for international students, for Australian postgraduate students, and increasingly for Australian undergraduate students, and for other sources of revenue – and have become what Simon Marginson and Mark Considine call 'the enterprise university'. There is no doubt that the challenges and opportunities of the last decade or so, including the growth of university reliance on international student fees, have in many cases affected the relationship between executive officer-holders and Boards. But a glimpse at the histories of older Australian universities would also show that there was no 'golden age' of perfect equipoise between these bodies either – instead, many instances of competition for power and of discord. If you seek an example, why not read A P Rowe's book, *If the Gown Fits*, arising from his decade as Vice-Chancellor of Adelaide from 1948?

In my view, the increasingly competitive market environment in which universities have to operate means both that Academic Boards need to be conscious of the strategic imperatives of their institution, and constructively engaged with the university's strategy for its future, *and* that Academic Boards need to be as rigorous as ever in their upholding of academic standards.

To illustrate my emphasis on the continued need for rigorous, even unrelenting, focus on academic standards, let me take up an area which is of major interest to AUQA, and which features in your agenda for this meeting. Martin Carroll and David Woodhouse, in their discussion of 'Quality Assurance

Issues in Transnational Higher Education", have noted the growth of senior executives with specifically 'international' responsibilities; the growth of committees responsible for approving and reviewing transnational operations, which committees are often weighted towards a business rather than an academic focus; the use of private corporate arms to manage universities' transnational activities in a commercial manner; and partnerships with private operators managed through trusts and private commercial entities.

As Carroll and Woodhouse write:[†]

The core characteristic of transnational operations is that they are means of helping students learn and achieve success at standards recognised in higher education. This means that there is a leadership role for academic boards or similar committees charged with primary responsibility for the academic affairs of the institution. In some cases, the concern for financial and corporate aspects, while essential, has worked to diminish effective academic input to the governance of transnational higher education operations.

As they later write:[‡]

...in some cases transnational higher education operations are run primarily as a "commercial" activity rather than an "academic" activity. This can mean a less central role for entities such as the academic board that have been charged with maintenance of academic governance and quality assurance. This in turn can place the maintenance of academic standards under strain, and the quality assurance arrangements for transnational activities in Australian universities range from excellent to poor.

---

* Martin Carroll & David Woodhouse, 'Quality Assurance Issues in Transnational Higher Education', in Jeannette Baird (ed.), *Quality Audit and Assurance for Transnational Higher Education*, AUQA, 2006.

† Ibid., pp. 67-8.

‡ Ibid., pp. 84-5.

I agree with the 2005 statement about 'The Purpose and Function of Academic Boards and Senates' that emerged from the National Conference of Chairs of Academic Boards and Senates:*

> The Board and its standing committee carry responsibility for quality in all academic activities… The Board should hold authority for approval, accreditation and review of new and existing academic programs, including those offered by commercial entities owned or partially owned by the university. The Board has ultimate oversight of all programs, onshore and offshore, and its processes play a key role in ensuring comparability of standards both within the institution and externally.

In my view, failure to uphold academic standards, offshore or onshore, is bad from an academic perspective *and* is bad business: sooner or later, it will damage the reputation – if you like, the 'brand' – of the institution, and potentially of Australian higher education as a whole. Academic quality assurance is an essential element of, and is not antagonistic to, the commercial and any other strategic imperatives in the conduct of profit-generating programs.

Or to take another area – the temptation to those responsible for the admission of students, in particular international students, to relax the declared admission requirements (for example, the English language requirements) of the institution so as to admit fee-paying students who do not meet the requirements but who will boost enrolments and fee income. This is one form of the temptation, to which some institutions have at times inappropriately succumbed, to lower their entrance standards. My experience leads me to the strong belief that high academic standards are good marketing: the harder it is to get

---

* See Dooley, op. cit., p. 27.

in, the more people want to get in, or, if you like, in the words of the old advertisement, 'it's the fish John West reject that makes John West the best'.

The greater the temptation to disregard academic standards, the more important is the safeguard of those standards – and thus, in my view, is the Academic Board.

Academic standards, of course, need to be considered in the context not only of universities seeking to generate revenue, or more accurately, surplus or profit from activities. Universities also seek to promote equity, access, and diversity; and an Academic Board will need to concern itself with how these crucially important objectives are to be achieved consistently with the appropriate academic values of the institution.

And so, for me, the question becomes – what enables an Academic Board to be an effective mechanism for academic quality assurance? What enables it effectively to uphold the academic standards of the institution?

First, it needs to exist. To state the obvious, a peak academic body focussed on academic quality assurance needs to have been created, and not to have been abolished. Typically, institutions which did not have a professorial board which 'morphed' into an Academic Board have had to create an Academic Board or similar body.

The idea that Academic Boards should be abolished, or neutered through being merged with some other body or by subsuming roles that compromise their central quality assurance purpose, seems to me highly dangerous.

As you will have seen, David Woodhouse and Jeanette Baird have written:*

> Is a separate academic "peak body" really needed? … wouldn't a more sensible structure have no academic board, but a governing

---

* David Woodhouse & Jeanette Baird, 'The Central Role of Academic Boards in Quality and Standards', 2006, p. 2.

body that contains a reasonable number of people who know about an educational enterprise, ie academics? Such a governing body/council could have about 20 people, including 7 academics, 2 administrators, 3 students, 3 senior managers, and 6 external members. The academic staff on a council need not necessarily be staff of that institution. Internal academic quality assurance for learning and teaching could be strengthened through the replacement of a central academic board by a small committee of acknowledged leaders in learning and teaching across the institution. This committee might be responsible for university-wide review of standards, including external comparisons, and ensuring good practice in curriculum and assessment design.

This seems to me to raise many problems. First, it implicitly invites the governing body of the institution to focus on and decide on academic matters on which I would prefer that it generally defers to a more traditional Academic Board. Secondly, it replaces a large and in some sense representative body with a small committee of learning and teaching experts – a category, incidentally, about which I have some scepticism, even suspicion. And who will guard these guardians? Who will protect us against the protectors? The existence of a more traditional Academic Board may be, I would argue is, important for academics around the institution having an appropriate sense of ownership of the academic enterprise, and for communication within the institution.

There may be better ways of organising the academic quality assurance function than the presently constituted Academic Boards, Academic Senates or Academic Councils of our universities – but let us be very careful that in well-meant change we do not undermine that quality assurance, and raise fresh problems. Every Australian higher education institution needs some form of Academic Board.

Secondly, it needs to be independent of the management of the institution. This seems to me axiomatic as a necessary element of effective quality assurance, as it would be of, say, effective audit. The statement in the 2005 paper on 'The Purpose and Function of Academic Boards and Senates' states it well: The Board 'is independent of, but shares membership with, senior executive, senior management and Council'.[*]

My personal view is that this independence is in danger of being fatally compromised if the Vice-Chancellor or a deputy Vice-Chancellor chairs the Academic Board. But I agree with the 2005 statement that 'frequent and full communication between the Chair [and] Deputy Chairs [of the Academic Board] and Vice-Chancellor [and I would add, deputy Vice-Chancellors] is necessary to implement the Board's mission'.[†]

Thirdly, the Academic Board needs to have a clear and resolute focus on academic quality assurance. This involves not simply declaring policy, but ensuring that the policy is actually carried out. As Anthony Dooley has pointed out, some audit panels have divided quality assurance into two parts – 'development of appropriate policy; and monitoring its implementation'. He also points out that AUQA 'audit panels question the extent to which policy is implemented and systematically monitored'.[‡] Tony Pollock, the head of IDP, made this point at the national symposium in Sydney in August on the English language skills of international students: the problem, he said, was not the admissions policies of institutions; it was the instances when these policies were not implemented in practice.

Anthony Dooley's paper also says that 'Boards' roles as forums for collegial discussion are often at odds with their perceived roles as policemen'.[§] He also points out that 'the tension between a community of scholars and the meeting of an enforced standard is one which is felt in many aspects of

---

[*] See Dooley, op. cit., p. 26.
[†] See ibid., p. 26.
[‡] Ibid., p. 10.
[§] Ibid., p. 13.

university governance'.* I respond to this by saying two things. First, we should encourage collegial communities of scholars in which it is accepted that the upholding of standards is an essential activity, important to the integrity of that community of scholars, and – so far as possible – to be welcomed rather than resisted. Secondly, to compromise the upholding of standards for fear of undermining collegiality is to make the wrong bargain: better some period of frosty relations, even of unpopularity, than to risk the standards and reputation of what the institution stands for.

Fourthly, the Academic Board needs to combine that clear focus on academic quality assurance with a constructive engagement with the strategy of the institution's executive leaders.

Universities have multiple objectives, and operate in complex and highly competitive strategic environments. The Academic Board needs, in my view, to remember that it is the executive leadership of the institution, under the ultimate governance body, that must determine the strategy for the institution. The role of academic quality assurance is not to stymie the strategy of the university, but to ensure that it is chosen and implemented consistently with the appropriate academic standards of the institution.

Audits of some universities have referred to 'aligning academic governance and executive management', and 'an effective partnership between Academic Board and the executive'.† There are different ways of achieving this. But at their heart will be a relationship between Board and executive management which is, ideally, mutually respectful; in which the Board will be co-operative and constructive but also uncompromising on standards.

Balanced against my urging to Board officers to be

---

* Ibid., p. 17.

† Ibid., p. 12.

courageous, I should also observe that a Board that establishes itself simply as an obstacle to change regarded as important by the executive management and the governing body is unlikely to prolong its own effective life.

Fifthly, the Academic Board needs effective leaders. It follows from what I have already said that I think such leaders need to combine a rigorous commitment to quality assurance with an understanding of institutional strategy and imperatives, and also a capacity for communication and ideally skills of diplomacy. They must be able to command the respect, however grudging, of institutional executives and academic staff alike.

How to ensure a steady supply of such paragons may, of course, be a problem, especially if the position of the Board is not well-entrenched and respected within the culture of the institution. I therefore think that the position of chair or president of the Academic Board should be established and treated within the university as one of importance and authority, neither at loggerheads with nor subservient to the executive leadership. Individuals who have had experience in Board committees and in other leadership roles within the institution will generally be best. Personally, I like very much the model that has Board officers, carefully identified, serving for a run of years in increasingly senior roles – say, as Deputy Vice-President, then as Vice-President, and then as President of the Board – coming to that last role with considerable experience.

It is important that Board leaders should be neither subservient to, nor beholden to, nor needlessly hostile to those with executive responsibility. This raises sometimes-hard questions for institutions and individuals. Should Board officers be included in executive groups or not? Should the pattern be established, or carefully avoided, of Board officers going on to hold executive positions – of the Board presidency being a stepping stone to a deputy Vice-Chancellorship or deanship?

As in most things in life, Board leadership requires a balance – of clarity of purpose, resolution, courage and fearlessness on the one hand, and humility, willingness to listen, and willingness to contemplate the possibility of being wrong, on the other.

There are various types of perversion of Board leadership that need to be guarded against. Let me mention three types I have imagined myself to have observed over the years. The first is the person whose independence, even integrity, may be compromised by personal ambition to high executive office. The second is the demagogue, one who (perhaps with ambition to make a name for themselves as a slayer of executive dragons) imagines him- or herself to be the voice of the people – 'the voice of the academy', as if there was only one voice in what one would expect and want to be a diverse range of voices. The third is the over-enthusiastic Board officer who takes on the role of executive officers of the university – for example, themself designing and enthusiastically promoting entrance programs for the university which leads them into the same temptations, to compromise standards, into which other designers and promoters of pathway programs can too readily be led. Leadership that avoids these and other traps is what we need.

Sixthly, the Board also needs a membership that will also effectively balance understanding of institutional needs with commitment to upholding standards.

Of course one of the recurrent issues for Academic Boards in many universities is that they become too large to be effective – though, as I will go on to touch on, a large body may work effectively through committees that report to its plenary meetings. There is also a danger in a Board that has too small a membership.

There is a risk in some bodies that too many members are too concerned not to have their own proposals questioned that they are reluctant to question the proposals of others. A P Rowe in *If the Gown Fits* wrote:[*]

> In the University of Adelaide [this was in the 1950s] the main academic committee dealt well enough with small matters, though at a considerable expenditure of time; but in large matters I found it to be a kind of mutual protection society in which no breath of criticism of any department might be heard. ... In my experience, fear of change dominated the massive academic committee of which I write.

One safeguard against the problem that, say, no dean dares criticise a proposal put forward by another dean, lest his or her own proposals be criticised later, is to have a number of elected members, beholden to no one, and encouraged in their role as questioners.

So is having a Board secretariat that ensures that the procedures required for proposals to come to the Board have been fulfilled: for example, without being mindlessly bureaucratic, that the documentation required to support a proposal for a new academic program has been properly completed.

Seventhly, the Academic Board needs an effective committee structure.

David Woodhouse and Jeannette Baird, in their somewhat dismissive paper on 'The Central Role of Academic Boards in Quality and Standards', say: 'As a group, usually large, of academics from across the institution, the academic board also faces difficulties in discharging its critical quality assurance responsibilities'. They argue that it is too likely to defer to the expertise of disciplinary specialists, and unlikely to have sufficient 'professional expertise in the design and quality assurance of higher education curricula and assessment methods'.[†]

---

[*] A P Rowe, *If the Gown Fits*, Melbourne University Press, 1960, pp. 25-6.
[†] Woodhouse & Baird, op. cit., p. 2.

It seems to me that the answer to this is to have an effective committee structure; small enough and continuous enough to be focussed, but large, diverse, and sufficiently rapidly changing not to become cliques; involving – and helping to train – colleagues from around the university; drawing in specialist expertise as it is needed; and developing its own expertise and that of its support staff over time in the fields with which it is concerned.

Eighthly, all this should be embodied – I think the modern word is 'embedded' – in the culture of the university. Many political scientists have said that the political culture of a community will determine how the institutions created by formal legal documents actually function in practice. This is certainly true of universities.

Cultures can be created, and they can be changed. Indeed, cultures are the creations of countless acts of individuals over time. I think it is desirable for those who value the kind of Academic Board I have sketched to work to encourage a culture within our institutions which will uphold this.

And so, in short, my answer to the question 'what makes an effective Academic Board?' is that there needs to exist an independent body with a clear and resolute focus on academic quality assurance, combining that with positive understanding of the institution's broader strategy; led effectively, fearlessly but constructively, and with a membership that ensures thorough though constructive scrutiny; with an effective committee system; and all this embedded in the culture of the institution – a culture that both gets things done, and does so with full respect and regard for the high academic standards which, in my view, should be at the heart of any academic institution.

Supporting the best student experience for the 21st century

Asia Pacific Student Services Association (APSSA) Conference
Queensland University of Technology
7 July 2010

It is a great pleasure to be with you here today at this 12th international conference of the Asia Pacific Student Services Association. I greet you warmly as fellow educators of the generations who will shape the future of this region of the world, and indeed of the global community to which we all belong; and I am delighted that we have so many students with us to help us explore the issues of student engagement, support, and building graduate capability.

Actions, they say, speak louder than words; and a good example drawn from your own experience can illuminate much larger issues. So I thought that the best thing I could do this morning might be to describe to you the issues I have been personally dealing with in that most rewarding part of my role as Warden of Rhodes House, Oxford, which is concerned with supporting in Oxford some 200 or so of what it is no exaggeration to describe as some of the finest postgraduate students in the world, the current Rhodes Scholars studying in Oxford. While in some respects this may seem far removed from the realities of student services in, say, large non-residential universities, I hope it will become evident why I believe that this experience, which I will describe in some detail, illuminates issues of importance for Asia Pacific student services colleagues, and that this experience involves so many elements of the student support activities with which we are all concerned, and, I think, has relevance to many of the global trends and challenges so many of us face.

As you may know, the Rhodes Scholarships were founded under the will of Cecil Rhodes, an Englishman who rose to immense wealth and power in southern Africa in the late 19th century, and died in 1902, leaving his estate primarily to endow the world's first great international scholarships program – what came rapidly to be known as the Rhodes Scholarships. This was truly one of the greatest drivers of the internationalisation of Oxford University in the 20th century, and thus a driver of internationalisation in higher education more generally, and a forerunner of many subsequent programs of student mobility.

Rhodes's vision was that by bringing from many countries around the world outstanding young people into the collegiate environment of Oxford, his scholarship could encourage them to do something with their lives to promote the public good; and also that by the intermixing in Oxford of young people who would go on to be leaders in their nations, he could promote international understanding and, indeed, peace. He aimed no less than, in his words, to help 'render war impossible'.

This was and remains a noble vision, as relevant in the 21st century as it was in the late 19th and very early 20th centuries when he articulated it. As Warden of Rhodes House, Oxford, I am responsible, under the Rhodes Trustees and working with colleagues, for the running of the Rhodes Scholarships today, and thus for helping to ensure that Rhodes's noble vision is given the best effect it can be in the 21st century. Since 1903, when the first Rhodes Scholars came to Oxford, the bequest of Cecil Rhodes, today being supplemented by the generous support of other donors, has fully funded over 7,000 Rhodes Scholars in Oxford. They include Scholars who went on to be presidents and prime ministers of several countries, and other leaders in politics, public service, universities, the professions, business, not-for-profit and international organisations, the media, and much else besides.

Today, some 83 Rhodes Scholars are selected each year to come to Oxford from 14 different countries or groupings of countries around the world. The calibre of Rhodes Scholars studying in Oxford today, all (or almost all) aged between their early and their late 20s, is extremely high. Rhodes's original vision was of bringing together exceptional young people from the three great powers of his day – the British Empire, as it then was, now the Commonwealth; the United States; and Germany. This has shaped the countries from which Rhodes Scholars are currently chosen, which include in our region Hong Kong, India, Pakistan, New Zealand, and Australia. One part of the strategic dialogue now underway in the global Rhodes community is how to refresh this geographic spread to reflect the evolving realities of the 21st century, and there is great interest in creating, with sufficient philanthropic support, Rhodes Scholarships from other countries in this region and beyond.

Rhodes Scholars are chosen, according to the Rhodes criteria – intellect, character, leadership, and service – by selection committees in their home countries comprising Rhodes alumni and distinguished members of the business, academic, and professional communities there. Rhodes Scholars today come to Oxford as graduates of universities around the world, and almost all of them now undertake postgraduate degrees – Masters or doctoral degrees – in Oxford, though some still gain great benefit from undertaking the more traditional 'second BA', tapping in to one of the greatest strengths of Oxford, which is undergraduate tutorial teaching in the colleges. Traditionally, the Rhodes Scholarship has encouraged intellectual and personal breadth, and while many Rhodes Scholars use their extraordinary opportunity in Oxford to deepen their professional or specialist knowledge and skills, many also use it to broaden their academic as well as personal horizons.

At any one time, the Rhodes Trust is supporting around 200 or more Rhodes Scholars studying in Oxford. All become members of Oxford colleges, and we encourage them to take an active role in the life of their colleges and of the wider University. Almost all live for their first year in college accommodation, something we strongly encourage, and many live throughout all their time in Oxford in college accommodation, while others move into private accommodation, including shared houses and flats.

One part of my role is to support the current Rhodes Scholars in their time in Oxford, and I do this with the help of colleagues at Rhodes House, Oxford, the home of the Rhodes Scholarships. How do we do this?

Once they are chosen in their home countries, and with help from the Rhodes National Secretary in their country, we (especially the Registrar, her assistant, and I) work closely with our new Scholars to place them in appropriate courses and colleges in Oxford. This means that we have close contact with them prior to their coming to Oxford, including providing pre-departure information that will help them prepare for the unfamiliar environment of Oxford. On coming to Oxford, as well as taking part in welcome, or orientation, activities in their colleges, their academic departments, and for university-wide activities, there is a 'welcome day' or orientation day at Rhodes House, and other welcome activities organised by Rhodes Scholars.

This introduces the new Scholars to the range of extra-curricular and social activities in the Rhodes community in Oxford, which today includes at least three parties each term at Rhodes House for all Rhodes Scholars, small lunches and dinners for all in the Warden's home, other events – from recitals to mock talent shows to speaker meetings with distinguished visiting speakers – and the activities of the Rhodes Scholars' own groups, in particular the Rhodes Scholars' Southern Africa Forum, the Rhodes Women group, the Black Association of Rhodes Scholars, and the LGBT – lesbian, gay, bisexual, and transgender – group. The new Scholars are also, for example, introduced to the email list* through which Rhodes Scholars

---

* Now also Facebook group.

communicate with each other quite independently of what is officially provided. Thus, while Rhodes Scholars are typically very active in their colleges, departments, and university-wide activities – from sport to music to drama to politics to religious and community service activities and much else – there is also today a strong sense of engagement in a Rhodes community in Oxford which aims to supplement, but not replace, their other communities of belonging and engagement within the University.

On the day that I became Warden of Rhodes House last July, I emailed all the then-current Rhodes Scholars and gave them three invitations – to a party the next week (I thought I might as well start as I meant to go on), to come and see me individually if they had any matters they wished to discuss with me, and to be in touch with their thoughts about the Scholarship and how to improve it. As well as profoundly affirming how deeply the Scholars value the life-transforming opportunity they are given, their many dozens of emails, letters, and conversations had certain themes and suggestions. The most frequently recurring was the desire for more opportunities to mix with Rhodes Scholars of other countries, so that they truly benefitted from the opportunity to engage with fellow students from around the world. This has been a central theme of our subsequent efforts. As there are no British Rhodes Scholars, all Rhodes Scholars share the experience of coming to Oxford and England from abroad; and their mixing with British students must come, if it comes much at all, in their colleges, departments, and university activities.

Another theme of our activities has been regular communication with our Scholars, including through email 'updates' from the Warden and through our continually evolving website. As well as academic advising, mentoring, and pastoral care of various kinds offered within their colleges, departments, and university services, such as the counselling service, we at Rhodes House seek to offer personal support for Rhodes

Scholars – from discussing with them their choices regarding courses and careers, to supporting them through personal journeys which, while overwhelmingly positive, naturally involve many bumps and even traumas. As well as engaging with them at our many social and other activities, I meet individually for at least half an hour each with all Rhodes Scholars each year – with the first-year Scholars during their first, most exciting but also dauntingly transitional, term, and with later-year Scholars later in the year, and with each of them for as long as it takes when they have particular issues, such as supervision issues or personal dilemmas, which they wish to discuss.

There being patterns to human behaviour, there are, of course, patterns to these discussions, and I have particular questions to which I revert. Many years ago I asked the then Vice-Chancellor of Oxford, Sir Richard Southwood, for advice on a career matter. He replied, 'There's no vice like advice', and continued the discussion, not as the giving of advice, but the probing of an issue which I was appropriately left to decide. Influenced by this, I seek, not to give advice, but to ask questions – questions which I hope help Scholars to identify and reflect on and, as necessary, resolve the matters before them. In particular, I encourage them to think about how what they are doing in Oxford – in their studies, but also in their other activities – can best help them become the people they want to be – how it can best open up that range of career options they want to have, and how it can best equip them to make that positive difference in the world they want to make. Cecil Rhodes said that he wanted his Scholars to fight 'the world's fight' – to make a difference for good in the world – and Rhodes Scholars are encouraged to seek to do this. They are encouraged, not by prescribing what this means, but by asking them to think about what it means for them. My role is to nudge but not to proselytise.

I encourage Rhodes Scholars to reflect on their own strengths and weaknesses, but perhaps above all on identifying their positive passions – on what they feel driven or perhaps called to do; what they do, not because they have to, but because they almost cannot help doing it. It seems to me that the greatest chance of impact and ultimate satisfaction comes from living a life in which you are fulfilling your positive passions, developing those strengths and dealing with those weaknesses which enable you to do what your inner drivers most powerfully and positively compel you to do. I ask them to think about what they would like to be doing 20 or 25 years from now. I also ask them to consider this question: what do you need to do in your life that will enable you, when you are old and grey, sitting on the verandah looking back over your life, to be contented and happy that you have lived your life the way you wanted and the best way you could? There is, of course, no easy or definitive answer for these questions, but the point is to encourage Scholars to think about their ultimate aspirations, and how their more immediate actions might, or might not, help them towards those deeper goals.

There are, of course, at times more urgently pressing issues. To those undertaking research degrees, I speak of the loneliness of the long distance researcher – the inevitable psychological isolation that is experienced by individuals, however sociable and socially supported they may be, who are undertaking a major research project on which their Masters or doctoral degree depends. I speak also of the near-inevitable emotional roller-coaster ride which doctoral study involves, and encourage them to consider how for doctoral students – as for all students, as perhaps for all human beings – it is necessary to think about that range of strategies which work for you as an individual to manage the unavoidable stresses and anxieties of life, to which examined research work and impending exams give particular piquancy. For those about to face exams, despite my vow against giving advice, as well as discussing strategies for managing stress, I give the best (and simplest) advice I can: answer the question the examiners set. As examiners of students' work know, it is surprising how often those sitting exams do not give a direct answer to the specific question set, but simply dump the information they can remember that somehow connects with the topic.

For those about to leave Oxford and become our alumni, I ask them to think about how to maintain the extraordinary connections they have made in Oxford, how to stay involved with us and with their fellow alumni, and also to think about how they can, from wherever in the world they are working, contribute the lessons of their experience to global conversations about the issues with which they are involved. The internet, of course, provides one opportunity for this.

When Rhodes Scholars come, or as it is expressed in the language of Oxford 'come up', to Oxford, one part of the welcome to them is a formal dinner called the 'Coming Up Dinner'. When they leave or, in Oxfordese, 'go down', there is, unsurprisingly, a formal 'Going Down Dinner'. These traditional rites of passage are moments of significance for many, markers of turning points in their lives, and events we go to some trouble to try to make special for them. Increasingly, we are working to help those leaving Oxford to connect with fellow Rhodes alumni in the places around the world to which they are returning or going, as well as to stay connected with the global community of Rhodes Scholars; and there is more that we can and will do.

We have this year introduced an online Scholar Experience Survey, in which we ask our current Rhodes Scholars to evaluate and give comments on their courses, their colleges, and the support they have received from Rhodes House. The results are both encouraging and helpful, both affirming our efforts but also providing useful pointers for improvement – for example, pointing us towards doing more to help Scholars in their preparations for Oxford, including in their course choices. Our ability to provide help is, of course, limited by the available resources, both our own and those within the University of Oxford – a university which, like almost all British public institutions, is being affected and will be more so by the ever-tightening public finances of the age of austerity that is descending upon the UK and many other countries.

There is, of course, much else that I could describe about the experience of Rhodes Scholars in Oxford, but this, I hope, provides some sense of what we do. Though the context may seem very different from where you work, I suspect that some at least of the content will seem very familiar. The themes of this conference are 'supporting', 'engaging', and 'building graduate capabilities', and that is precisely what we are aiming to do also.

You will have recognised many familiar themes in what I have described:

- the fact that, though there are patterns, each individual experience is distinctive, each individual has their own potential which they must be encouraged to identify, develop, and fulfil towards goals and values which are their own, and each individual has their own problems which they must be supported in seeking to handle;

- the importance of support in the transition from one environment to another, support in the form of appropriate welcome and orientation activities but sustained support beginning before students come and continuing throughout their time with us, and in fact beyond;

- the importance of community and a sense of belonging, and of social and extra-curricular activities which promote this;

- the fact that no category of people is exempt from depression, anxiety, and other mental health issues, and that for all students assistance in developing resilience and an emphasis on positive wellbeing is important;

- the desire of international students to mix more with students of other countries, and not only with their own – important though some mixing with their own undoubtedly is;

- the growth of postgraduate student numbers within many universities, and the uneven adjustments many universities are making from an almost exclusively undergraduate focus to one more balanced between undergraduates and postgraduates;

- the ways in which, however imperfectly, new technologies are being used to supplement and help shape the community and the support provided to students;
- the inescapable issue of resources; and much else.

But there are broader points I wish to make. The Rhodes Scholarships reflect a philosophy of education that emphasises the identification and development of academic knowledge and skills, crucially important as they are, *alongside and in the context of* the development of other qualities and values. The Rhodes Scholarships are an example, I like to think an exemplar, of this broad view of education. This broad view competes against alternative views of higher education which, on the one hand, focus narrowly on the development of academic skills and knowledge alone, and on the other hand, focus purely on higher education as being to train people for doing particular jobs. Against these narrowly academic and narrowly vocational views of education, the Rhodes philosophy is to seek to nurture people who will be strong, indeed exceptional, in intellectual, including academic, attainment but also strong in character and values, in their capacity as leaders, and in their commitment to service to the community, in whatever form that service might take. Indeed, the Rhodes Scholarships explicitly aim to identify and develop people who will be, in a phrase we use, 'leaders for the world's future'. The Rhodes educational philosophy thus has much in common with, say, ideals of liberal education – what in the 19th century was quite often referred to as 'large and liberal education', a phrase I borrowed shamelessly for the title of a book in which I develop some of the ideas I am expressing this morning.*

---

* Donald Markwell, *'A large and liberal education': higher education for the 21st century*, Australian Scholarly Publishing & Trinity College, University of Melbourne, 2007.

It is my view that, in these early years of the 21st century, as universities around the world, including many around the Asia Pacific region, have been re-assessing their educational purposes and programs to seek to ensure they are as relevant as possible to the new century, there has been a resurgence in the recognition of the importance of broad education of the kind embodied in the Rhodes ideal and in the ideals of liberal education. This is evident in universities from the US Ivy League to Manchester and Aberdeen in Britain to many in Asia – certainly some in China, Korea, Singapore, Hong Kong, and Brunei – to such Australian universities as the Universities of Melbourne and of Western Australia. Universities in many countries have been reviewing and refreshing their curriculums, in many cases placing greater emphasis on intellectual breadth and fundamental transferable skills – for example, inter-cultural, international, and inter-faith understanding; communications skills; research skills, so as to be able to solve unfamiliar problems requiring the identification and application of unfamiliar knowledge; and community engagement, so as to be connected more closely with the world around us. Richard Conant* gave us the example this morning of the necessity of inter-disciplinary approaches to the environment, and to understanding and dealing with all aspects of climate change.

The Rhodes philosophy has it also that intellectual skills and personal qualities are developed not only in the classroom, but in extra-curricular activities and in colleges and in other communities to which students belong and in which they engage. Leadership in extra-curricular activities should be one of the hallmarks of those chosen for the Rhodes Scholarship; and Cecil Rhodes explicitly provided for his Scholars to go to Oxford because of what he saw as the benefits of its colleges. Over the last decade or so, universities around the world have, for a variety of reasons, again been considering the best educational experience they can offer to students. In this broad

* Ecosystem ecologist and professor at Queensland University of Technology.

process of reassessment of quality of education, I believe there has been a renewed recognition by many university leaders of the importance of student engagement, of extra-curricular activities, of a sense of belonging to a community within the university, of supporting students throughout their university life-cycle, and of residential colleges as providing, when they are operating well, arguably the richest immersive environment in which to be a fully engaged student.

The value of residential colleges in encouraging student engagement has been supported, for example, by results of the Australasian Survey of Student Engagement, and renewed emphasis on residential colleges is seen in universities from Yale and Princeton in the US to Fudan in China, and many others in several countries, including Australia. While many universities will not be residential, or not for more than a small proportion of their students, they can nonetheless, as the retiring Vice-Chancellor of the University of Manchester, Alan Gilbert, has said, seek to develop the attributes, such as of community and inter-mingling of students of diverse disciplines, that best approximate to the benefits of residential college life. Partnerships between universities and private providers of accommodation to create genuine 'living learning communities' can be one important form of this. It has again come to be widely recognised among university leaders that students learn a great deal both from each other and from their involvement in extra-curricular activities. It has become clearer than ever that what can be conveyed in the classroom cannot of itself be sufficient to equip graduates for the world in which they will live and work: so, for example, study abroad and exchange programs and other forms of student mobility, and programs of experiential learning of various kinds, have emerged to greater prominence.

The significance of all this for student service professionals seems to me profound. It means that your role – our role – is not only more important than ever; it means that it needs to be conceptualised more than ever as being an educational, and not simply a service delivery, role. How we conceptualise our roles will significantly help to determine how, and how well, we fulfil our roles. If the out-of-classroom aspects of the student experience are recognised as crucial to the quality of students' education, then we will best serve the education of our students precisely by conceptualising our role as being to contribute to their education. And we must prepare ourselves well to make that educational contribution.

Let me give an example close to my own heart as the former head of a college at the University of Melbourne. It is possible to think of a university residential college as being an 'accommodation provider', and so it is. But if that is all it is, then it is a hostel, not a college. A college, properly so called, must be a provider not merely of accommodation but above all of education – education that is all the richer for being in a residential context; education that is offered through academic support and challenge, through mentoring and pastoral care, through extra-curricular activities, through the friendships and belonging that the college community offers, and through the focus, balance, and purposeful motivation that college leaders should bring. If those running a college think of themselves merely as accommodation providers, rather than as providers of education in a residential context, they will miss many of the important opportunities they have to contribute to the education of their students, and their college will truly not be worthy of that name.

What I am saying, of course, has been said by others before, and more eloquently and persuasively. For example, you are probably familiar with the important paper *Learning Reconsidered: A Campus-wide Focus on the Student Experience*, published in the United States in 2004 by the National Association of Student Personnel Administrators and the

American College Personnel Association. Let me quote its conclusion:[*]

> This document asserts that learning must be reconsidered – that new research, changing times, and the needs of today's emerging generations of students require that our traditionally distinct categories of academic learning and student development be fused in an integrated, comprehensive vision of learning as a transformative process that is centered in and responsive to the whole student. Every resource on every campus should be used to achieve transformative liberal education for all students, and all colleges and universities are accountable for establishing and assessing specific student outcomes that reflect this integrated view of learning. There will be extensive and appropriate variation in the specific student outcomes each institution emphasizes and in the administrative structures, division of responsibilities, and assessment methods used. But a common and central theme, regardless of institutional type, student demographics, or campus culture, will be the establishment of vibrant educational partnerships among members of the academic faculty and student affairs professionals in which all campus educators share broad responsibility for achieving defined student outcomes.

While I do not wish to defend all the big and bold claims in *Learning Reconsidered*, I do wish especially to argue that its conception, if not its precise language, of student affairs professionals as student affairs *educators* is essential for the best student learning experience in the 21st century. It is certainly as an educator that I conceive my role, and I hope that it is as an educator that you conceive your role.

In saying this, I am conscious that academic faculty members are highly variable in their willingness to act as partners in the educational process. Many are outstanding; many are not. Quite apart from professional jealousies, there is, of course, the

---

[*] *Learning Reconsidered*, p. 35.

fact that academic faculty members are highly variable in their commitment to the education of students in the first place, partly – but not only – because of the intense competing demands of research. To my mind, this unevenness of academic faculty members' commitment to the education of students makes the educational role of student affairs professionals all the more important.

One of the reasons for the renewed focus over the last decade in the quality of student experience has been the increased competition between institutions within countries and between countries for students – competition for students partly as sources of the talent which institutions and countries need in the so-called 'knowledge economy' of our day; partly as the sources of the diversity of student cohort which increasingly educators believe will benefit all; and partly, let us be frank, as sources of revenue. Enlightened institutional leaders recognise the importance of student affairs professionals in the attraction and retention of students – students who bring talent, diversity, and money. They recognise, for example, that all those things done to promote interaction between so-called 'international students' and domestic students, within the university as a community containing many opportunities for engagement in sub-communities, will help to make the university more attractive to students from abroad. Yet, as has been manifest clearly in Australia over the last year, institutions have varied widely in their attentiveness to the needs of international students. Too many practices in universities, including the use of the term 'international students', separate international students from domestic students, where the emphasis should wherever possible be to bring them together.

As institutions increasingly focus on the challenge of retaining the students they attract, and on the problem of student attrition, they should recognise the importance of the work of student affairs professionals in helping to create and nurture that sense of belonging to a cohort and a community which appears so important to student retention. This is all the more important as institutions in many countries engage seriously with the challenge, posed especially vigorously by governments in some countries, to attract and retain students from low socio-economic status backgrounds. In Australia and New Zealand, as in a number of other countries, this involves particular and very important challenges of being supportive to Indigenous students, and encouraging among them, as among other students, a sense of belonging to the community.

Perhaps partly because my own life, which began in the outback of Queensland, was shaped by the unfolding of unexpected educational opportunities, including being awarded the scholarship which I now administer from Oxford, I am acutely conscious of the importance of education as a life-changing opportunity, and of the responsibility of institutions to reach out to potential students of all backgrounds, to seek to ensure that students of potential aspire to and take these opportunities regardless of the disadvantages which they have suffered. This is a matter both of fairness to individuals and of ensuring the best use of talent within the community. Student affairs professionals in many universities have a significant role to play in the outreach of their institutions to students from disadvantaged backgrounds, of making them feel they will belong if they come, and helping them to feel they belong and helping them to succeed when they do come.

This sense of belonging is important also to another of the great global trends of our time – the increasing and essential emphasis on the engagement of alumni to support an institution. Alumni who have felt engaged while in the university or college are much more likely to be receptive to engagement with it, and generous in support for it, after they have graduated. In some cases, of course, their generosity comes in the form of support for student activities – a student centre, or support for sporting or musical or theatrical facilities, or other support.

It is my privilege to work in the magnificent surroundings

of Rhodes House, Oxford, in the centre of Oxford, itself one of the most beautiful university towns in the world. Rhodes House provides a superb venue for many of the student activities in which we are engaged. You will be aware that recent years have seen an increased emphasis in many institutions on the provision of suitable physical spaces for student activities and student services. This has come alongside a renewed emphasis on optimising physical spaces for other aspects of teaching and learning, including the integration of libraries with other student facilities, the provision of spaces which make student discussion and engagement easier and even enticing, and the integration of previously dispersed student services in more convenient unified hubs. Increasingly, of course, thought is given to how to integrate the provision of services on campus with the provision of services online: including, of course, considering the challenge of how to engage students in all that the on-campus experience can offer when so many are so tempted to regard campus as optional in the online age, and in the age of increasing off-campus work.

In the spirit of *Learning Reconsidered*, but also in the spirit of earlier traditions of education of which the Rhodes ideal is one exemplar, I have implicitly depicted the best student experience for the 21st century as being one in which the various elements of the student learning experience – curricular and extra-curricular, in and out of classroom, and ideally in a residential environment – are all regarded as being important, and being complementary to each other. This philosophy is easier to express than it is to implement. The professional divides between academic faculty members and student affairs professionals are one example of the difficulties. There are other divides. The reference I have just made to the importance of physical spaces and to technological aids to education reminds us of the importance, in university planning and in the execution of those plans, of bringing together those academic leaders responsible for leading the university's thinking on its educational activities, those professionals responsible for campus and building planning, and those professionals responsible for information technology, so that productive conversation between them can lead to a shared sense of the best spaces and best use of technology within those spaces to support the best student learning experience. I have had the fortunate experience of working in various universities and colleges with campus and building planners and IT experts who were keen to learn and engage with the educational philosophy of the institution; they, like others, look to institutional leaders to facilitate and lead such potentially fruitful conversations, and such leadership is not always forthcoming.

This vision of the best student learning experience, while increasingly attractive to many educational leaders, is also at variance with the reality on many campuses. Surveys of the first-year experience in Australian universities, for example, have shown – and I quote a summary of the comparison of 2004 and 2009 surveys:[*]

> First year students are spending fewer days and less time on campus. Fewer are involved in extra-curricular activities around campus. Fewer say they have made close friends. More indicate they keep to themselves at university. Yet, in apparent contradiction, the students of 2009 report more involvement in group work for study purposes, both in and out of class. ... The trend towards part-time work during semester continues. ... Predictably, there have been dramatic rises in the use of various forms of ICTs for study-related purposes and students are embracing these opportunities and are highly positive about the benefits. One consequence is the on-campus, face-to-face experience is taking on less significance and students are having less direct contact with academic staff.

The authors of this study, Richard James, Kerri-Lee Krause,

---

[*] Richard James, Kerri-Lee Krause & Claire Jennings, *The First Year Experience in Australian Universities: Findings from 1994 to 2009*, March 2010, pp. 1-2.

and Claire Jennings, suggest as one of the responses to this:*

> During the next few years attention might be given to ways in
> which students are informed of the kind of engagement that
> effective higher education requires. In other words, universities
> will need to do more to spell out their expectations for student
> involvement in learning.

I would say that it is important for educational leaders to
articulate and sell to students a vision of their engagement
in a rich campus life, actively engaged both in and outside
the classroom, as the best student experience they can have. I
agree with these authors of the Australian first-year experience
study that the spelling out of expectations, and I would say the
persuasive articulation of this vision of the best student learning
experience, will be increasingly important as more students enter
'higher education unfamiliar with its character and with lower
levels of achievement in their previous educational experience'.
This will require leadership.

Writers and speakers on leadership increasingly tell us that,
not least because of new information and communication
technologies, institutions are less hierarchical than once they
were, so that leadership needs to be more collaborative, more
open, and more based on influence and less on the blunt exercise
of power than once it was. There is much truth in this, and this is
important for those of us whose roles include the identification
and encouragement of future leaders. While the growth of
managerialism in many universities also provides examples of
more old-fashioned models of leadership, I think of leadership,
not as the holding of a position, but – as someone once defined it
– as doing what is necessary to challenge or lead a group of people
effectively to confront their real issues. It is possible, indeed it is
highly desirable, for student affairs professionals to be leaders in
this sense: for example, helping by their voices and their actions

---

* Ibid., p. 9.

to influence the discussion within their university on the shape of the student learning experience it offers. It is also, of course, highly desirable to have champions, not least to have champions in the senior executive of a university, and the cultivation and education of such champions is itself an act of leadership by student affairs professionals. Having champions at the highest levels of the institution committed to the educational importance of the work of students affairs professionals is important not least in the politics of resource allocation within an institution.

Please do not imagine that in my discussion of some of the trends and challenges I see that I believe these are uniform within and across all countries. Of course they are not. Resources, to which I have just referred, is one important area of divergence. I referred earlier to the age of austerity that is descending in the UK and some other countries, most especially in Europe and North America. The reduction of resources available for higher education in some countries – especially through reduced government funding, and the decline of endowments during the global financial crisis of these last two years or so – contrasts sharply with the vigorous commitment of governments and donors in some countries, especially in Asia, to ensure that the leading higher education institutions of their countries are continually and rapidly increasing in quality. If this divergence between tightness in some countries and expansion in others continues significantly for a long period of time, the consequences will be profound, including for the relative attractiveness of institutions in those countries to the most talented academic and professional staff, and to students, undergraduate and postgraduate.

Whether in an area of tightness or an area of expansion, it seems to me that an important leadership role for student affairs professionals is to help to shape, to articulate, and to implement the educational philosophy of your institution. The role you play – the role we play – in the student learning experience has never been more important. There are major obstacles to our being able to support the best possible student experience: but the rewards, to our students and indeed to ourselves as educators, of our working to do so make it very much worth the effort.

Welcoming new Rhodes Scholars: intellect, character, leadership, and service

Each year, the Association of American Rhodes Scholars (AARS) hosts a 'Bon Voyage Weekend' (BVW) in Washington, DC, to farewell US, Caribbean, and Bermudan Rhodes Scholars about to go to Oxford. On the arrival of Rhodes Scholars from around the world in Oxford, a 'Welcome Day' each year at Rhodes House includes an address of welcome from the Warden.

Rhodes Scholars' departure from Washington, DC

Departure lunch for US, Bermuda, and Caribbean Rhodes Scholars
Cosmos Club, Washington, DC
29 September 2010

What an enormous personal pleasure it is for me to be with you here in Washington – with the Scholars of the class of 2010 from the US, Jamaica and the Commonwealth Caribbean, and Bermuda, and with Rhodes alumni of many generations. Many thanks to Steve Crown, George Keys, Nick and Marla Allard, and so many other friends in the Association of American Rhodes Scholars for making me – but more importantly, our new Scholars – so welcome during this Bon Voyage Weekend, and many thanks also to Elliot Gerson, our US National Secretary, for his tireless work.

I would also like to take this opportunity to thank Joyce Knight and Beth Maslowsky in the Washington office for their support for Scholars from election on, their miracle-working

---

* This speech was first published as 'Liberal education and international understanding', *The American Oxonian*, Fall 2010.

with visas, their saintliness and patience with online applications, and so much more. We are all immensely grateful.

I look forward very much to welcoming our new Scholars at Rhodes House, Oxford, on Saturday – unless the Supreme Court finds in the meantime, as I suspect it will, that enduring two speeches from me in under 72 hours is 'cruel and unusual punishment'. I will of course be welcoming you with nearly 50 other Scholars from a dozen other countries around the world, lifelong friends waiting to be met and made.

As part of the superb and inspiring BVW program, the 2010 Scholars yesterday heard a fascinating presentation from Jack Zoeller on Alain Locke (Rhodes Scholar for Pennsylvania & Hertford 1907). Locke was, as you will know, the first African-American Rhodes Scholar, and the last African-American Scholar until 1963, even as many black Rhodes Scholars were elected from other countries over the intervening decades. Locke was the victim of racial discrimination by his fellow Scholars, amongst many others. This is not an episode of which we can be proud, but it is one from which we can learn – including about the risks of discrimination even by people apparently chosen on the basis of character, and the importance of standing up against it whenever it may be found. Is this not relevant to various forms of discrimination, including on the basis of religion, today?

After yesterday's session on Locke, a 2010 Scholar said to me that a lesson he drew from Locke's experience was the importance of connecting in Oxford with Scholars and students of other countries. I couldn't agree more. There is an episode related to this that may be of interest.

Locke went up to Oxford in 1907. In 1910, a London *Daily Mail* article entitled 'The Americans at Oxford' attacked US Rhodes Scholars for keeping themselves to themselves and not engaging their English surroundings and fellow Oxford students. The writer said:

... the American Rhodes scholar makes friends only with his compatriots... After the first week in Oxford the words "British insularity" are murmured with an accompanying shrug of the shoulders, and the American retires into his shell – the [American] club – where he reads American papers, discusses American politics, sings American songs, and might, indeed, just as well be back in America for all the good he does to himself or to Oxford.

The *Daily Mail*'s writer, simply called 'An Oxford Man', argued that this was directly contrary to the purpose of the Rhodes Scholarship. In recent decades we have often spoken primarily of the purpose of the Rhodes Scholarship as being to develop future leaders who will fight 'the world's fight' and come 'to esteem the performance of public duties as [their] highest goal'. This is certainly an important, a very important, goal of the Scholarship: public spiritedness, active citizenship, public service, public leadership. This was brilliantly displayed for our new Scholars yesterday by Senator Sarbanes and Senator Lugar. But this was not the only purpose, and in the early years of the Scholarship many people were probably more aware of another of Cecil Rhodes's goals – nothing less than nurturing international understanding and peace. Rhodes apparently understood that the development of such understanding took time, and despite the outbreak of war in 1914 and 1939, the goal – through educational relations to promote peace – has endured, and (for example) after both world wars the Rhodes Scholarships for Germany, abolished or suspended during the wars, were ultimately created afresh, in 1930 and again in 1970. Last Friday at Rhodes House we marked the 40th anniversary of the creation again in 1970 of the Rhodes Scholarships for Germany, and the retirement of Thomas Böcking, German National Secretary for the last 31 years, and of Silvia Böcking.

The *Daily Mail* article of 1910 criticising American Rhodes

Scholars as keeping to themselves and not getting to know other students, and so defeating this purpose of the Rhodes Scholarships, caused considerable controversy on both sides of the Atlantic. For example, *The New York Times* ran a large article headed 'Rhodes Scholars resent "An Oxford Man's" attack', saying that the criticisms made in the London *Daily Mail* misrepresented them, and they 'do not avoid close association and friendship with Englishmen'. Alain Locke also drafted a response. He began: 'The Rhodes bequest is a huge and unique educational experiment…' He argued that 'the Rhodes idea, in its original and [deep] intention, was that the Rhodes Scholar should' seek 'to confront national bias, eradicate national prejudice, and educate nations to mutual good will and understanding' by what he did back 'in his home country and as a result of his training and experience as a Rhodes scholar'. He also noted that unexpected differences in temperament and values between the English and Americans led to misunderstanding, and he tried to explain some of these. Locke concluded that the 'primary aim and obligation' of a Rhodes Scholar 'is to acquire at Oxford and abroad generally a liberal education, and to continue subsequently the Rhodes mission [of international understanding] throughout life and in his own country. If once more it should prove impossible for nations to understand one another as nations, then, as Goethe said, they must learn to tolerate each other as individuals.'

Tolerance and understanding are helped, I think, if we heed the prayer of the great poet of Scotland, Robbie Burns – to be able to see ourselves as others see us. Consider whether your behaviour will be seen by others as extending the hand of friendship, or as sticking only to your own nationality.

This also means stepping outside the expectations and assumptions formed by our own upbringing and life experience to date, and finding what we can of value in the new environment. One US Rhodes Scholar wrote to me recently: 'letting go of US-centric expectations … means, at least: not expecting a huge amount of coddling from advisors, accepting (and even revelling in!) the odd formalities of certain Oxford traditions, giving cricket, rugby and rowing a chance, and learning to laugh at cold rain. My two most rewarding extra-curricular experiences at Oxford', he wrote, 'were learning (and later obsessing over) competitive cricket and renting [and] tending an allotment garden… These are experiences that simply do not exist in the US, much less at US universities. It would have been easier to stick with my hobbies from [college back home], but much less rewarding'.

You are joining a community, in Oxford and globally, of outstanding people drawn from 14 countries or groupings of countries around the world. Seizing every chance to get to know fellow Rhodes Scholars and other students from other countries is one of the most valuable aspects of the remarkable opportunity that lies before you. On my first day as Warden in July last year, I emailed all of the then-current Scholars and asked them for ideas about improving the Scholarship. The most powerfully recurrent theme in responses from Scholars from the US and many other countries was the desire for more opportunities to mix with Scholars of other countries, and our parties and meals and other events at Rhodes House aim to help provide such opportunities. Please always come when you can, and engage with Scholars of other countries!

One of the most important figures in the history of the Rhodes Scholarships – anywhere, anytime – was the first American National Secretary to the Rhodes Trust, Frank Aydelotte, who served in that role from 1918 to 1952, also serving as President of Swarthmore for nearly 20 years during that period. In referring to Frank Aydelotte, I wish to pay a tribute of admiration and gratitude to all the American National Secretaries – Frank Aydelotte, Courtney Smith, Bill Barber, David Alexander, and Elliot Gerson. I am grateful that Elliot was able to represent us all at the memorial service for David Alexander at Pomona College on Saturday, as we are all grateful to David for 17 years of outstanding service to the Rhodes Scholarships as US National Secretary.*

Frank Aydelotte's charming book of 1946, *The American Rhodes Scholarships: A Review of the First Forty Years*, shows that the issues I'm discussing now were equally relevant then. In a chapter entitled 'What the American Rhodes Scholar gets from Oxford', Aydelotte notes that coursework is prescribed in less detail than many American students are used to, and that there is a greater stress on individual initiative and independent work, and thus a greater challenge of managing your own time, including so as to balance the academic work that is essential in vacations with the travel that is also desirable. Even after several decades, Aydelotte's is an excellent introduction, and I encourage you to find it and read it.

Frank Aydelotte, like Alain Locke, had much to say about American Scholars engaging with the British and with Scholars of other countries. Writing at the end of World War II, and explicitly describing Rhodes's purpose as overcoming 'the scourge of war and anarchy', Aydelotte's image is of continual conversation between students from the US, the UK, Commonwealth and other countries, and travel well-chosen and well-balanced with academic work, leading to American Rhodes Scholars developing what he calls 'an internationalist point of view'. Amongst much else, he said, the American Scholar comes no longer to speak of 'the English' but to understand and appreciate the diversity of the English, liking some and not liking others, as with individuals at home. Aydelotte believed that time in Oxford as a Rhodes Scholar makes you both 'a better American', your pride in your country better grounded than before, and also 'a citizen of the world'.

Frank Aydelotte may have described the US Rhodes Scholar in different language from Alain Locke years before, but both well understood the mission of the Scholarship to promote

---

* See 'David Alexander: the Rhodes ideal and liberal education' in the section of this book 'On leaders'.

international understanding, and the need for Scholars of all nations to interact.

Locke, as we all know, was the victim of racial discrimination. As we also know, one of the most powerful cries against discrimination rang forth from the Lincoln Memorial in this city in 1963, when Dr King dreamt that his children would 'not be judged by the colour of their skin but by the content of their character.'

'The content of their character'. If the promotion of international understanding is a primary goal of the Rhodes Scholarships, then a criterion of selection has always been and always will be the content of your character. Cecil Rhodes said not only that he wanted Scholars with 'moral force of character and … instincts to lead', but specified many of the qualities of character he sought: 'truth, courage, devotion to duty, sympathy for and protection of the weak, kindliness, unselfishness and fellowship'. The winning of a Rhodes Scholarship is not a certificate to say you have such character; it is a lifelong challenge to you to show that you do. It is a challenge to live a life of integrity and authenticity.

As you may know, Groucho Marx is said to have said: 'what people want these days is sincerity. If you can fake that, you've really got it made'. In a slightly more useful vein, Frank Aydelotte wrote:

> It is interesting to note that Rhodes evidently regarded leadership as founded upon moral courage and public spirit, concern for the common welfare, as much as upon more aggressive qualities… The go-getter, who covets for himself the largest number of undergraduate offices, the big man of the campus, is not so likely to be a leader in middle life as the [student] whose concern is the common good rather than personal kudos, and who seeks to relate his college studies to some aspect of the public welfare in the present or the future.

Aydelotte wrote that the choice of Rhodes Scholars was hard, and the members of selection committees must be 'good judges of human nature ...free from prejudice ... gifted with intuition and imagination', and with experience. Aren't you lucky to have faced such selection committees last November! But your work is not done yet. Your character will continue to be judged by your fellow Rhodes Scholars and by the communities you serve over the years and decades ahead.*

President Kennedy once misquoted Dante as saying that the hottest places in hell are reserved for those who in moments of great moral crisis maintain their neutrality. Even if Dante didn't say that, it is a good sentiment. In this Cosmos Club last December, I met with several Rhodes alumni who have worked in the public and non-profit sectors, and we discussed the values of the Scholarship. A retired general asked how a selection committee could identify the young person who, when all was said and done, had the courage to stand and fight, not cut and run. It is a good question, and another challenge to us all.

I have been talking about some of the great values on which this Scholarship is founded. Today the Rhodes community has an opportunity to think afresh about how we give the best effect we can to these great values. Last Saturday in Oxford about 125 or more Rhodes Scholars of many countries and years took part in a forum on big issues about 'The Rhodes Scholarships for the 21st century'. As at some previous discussions, we looked at such questions as: How do we make the Scholarship equally attractive to outstanding young women as to outstanding young men and to outstanding young people from all parts of the community in all Rhodes countries? This is an important question which has not yet received the full attention it merits in the global Rhodes

---

* It is interesting to see the works of Rhodes Scholars on the connection between leadership and character, and related issues – for example, Joseph L Badaracco, Jnr, *Questions of Character: Illuminating the Heart of Leadership Through Literature*, Harvard Business School Press, 2006. See also Clayton Christensen, James Allworth, and Karen Dillon, *How Will You Measure Your Life?*, HarperCollins, 2012.

community. From what countries should Rhodes Scholars be drawn over the decades ahead? How do we respond best to the profound challenge of reduced resources and increased costs? And several more.

These questions are part of a broader process of consultation over the last 15 months, which has already produced many results:

- the creation I have already mentioned of more opportunities for Scholars in Oxford to engage with each other, including with Scholars of other countries;

- governance protocols which provide that from now on between half and two-thirds of Rhodes Trustees will be Rhodes Scholars;

- the appointment, after consultation, of eight new Trustees from several countries around the world, five of them Scholars passionately committed to the Scholarship;

- the creation of new Trustee committees, including the Scholarship Committee with the task of advising on what needs to be done to ensure that the Rhodes Scholarship remains the world's leading scholarship in perpetuity;

- a growing openness to creating, if funds can be found from new sources, Scholarships for new countries, including from countries once served by Rhodes Scholarships, to refresh the Scholarship's geographic footprint for the realities of this century;

- the distribution just a few weeks ago of details of Scholars going down; and

- the creation of additional opportunities for alumni engagement and connectivity, including a refreshed website and a task force of Scholars now working on how we best develop an online Rhodes community. We are in some ways, which I am sure will evolve in dialogue over the years ahead, hoping to build upon, and perhaps take global, the fine work which the AARS has been and is doing, for which I know I am far from alone in being very grateful.

I mention the outcome of consultations to date to encourage you to take part in the future in helping to shape the Scholarship to help give the best effect we can to its great values in the 21st century.

The 110th anniversary reunion in Oxford in 2013 will provide an opportunity for Scholars of all countries and all generations to meet – in Cecil Rhodes's phrase, 'meeting and discussing their experiences and prospects' – and help to shape its future. Many members of the class of 2010 will still be in Oxford then, and I hope that others will return for the reunion.

I am also, of course, deeply – daily – conscious that we face a significant financial challenge – an unsustainable rate of drawdown on our endowment in the wake of international financial storms and increasing costs – and I am extremely grateful to all Scholars who have already stepped forward through annual giving, through bequest pledges, and through major gifts. But that, you will be pleased to know, is a topic for another day.

Today, it is a delight, a luxury, to be here with you celebrating the values that make this Scholarship so special in this country, in the Caribbean and Bermuda, and globally. To all of you, many thanks. To the class of 2010: congratulations, good luck, bon voyage, and welcome!

Welcoming Scholars to the Rhodes community in Oxford

Welcome to the Rhodes Scholar class of 2010*
Rhodes House, Oxford
2 October 2010

Scholars:

It is so good to see you here today at this important and exciting, if in some ways slightly daunting, moment in your life's journey.

When, last Monday morning, with Bob Wyllie, Krista Slade, and two later-year Scholars, I met the Canadian and Indian Scholars at Heathrow, one of the newly-arrived Scholars, astonishingly alert after a long flight, did what the *Unofficial Guide* suggested always worked with me, and started a conversation by reference to the pet kangaroo my family had when I was a little boy in the outback of Australia a long time ago.

This got me thinking – thinking about the journey through life that by some route has brought each of us, from some far corner of the globe that we call home, to this home of the Rhodes Scholarships today. Let me say what cannot be stressed enough – how warmly welcome you are, how delighted my colleagues and I are that you are here, how keen we all are to get to know you, to encourage you in your progress and to encourage and support you even more when things are down.

Few Rhodes Scholars doubt that their time in Oxford is life-transforming. A world of new opportunities is now opening to you – a world of potential friendships and experiences you have probably not imagined; and neither you nor I know in what ways this experience will transform you. But being open to opportunity and change requires a willingness to try out new

---

* The texts of the welcome speeches for 2009 and 2011, which have slightly different emphases, are on the Rhodes House website. My 2009 speech of welcome was also published in *The American Oxonian*, Fall 2009.

things and to take risks. Rhodes Scholars, though often rightly seeking self-improvement, are often also risk-averse, and often, having never had to practise the fine art of coming back after failure, have not yet developed the skills of resilience we all need. I hope that in your time here you will take risks, and think about how to improve your skills of overcoming the inevitable stumbles and even traumas life will unavoidably bring.

Your time in Oxford is not only a chance to try new things, and to embrace rather than judge or repel what is unfamiliar; it is also a chance to pause. You are here because you have been exceptionally successful in your studies and in extra-curricular activities. While we of course want you to remain successful in these ways, now is also a chance to pause, take stock, reflect, and consider where you want to go in life's journey, and how you will along the way make the most valuable contribution you can to the lives of others. Think about your development as a person in all its aspects. By this I do not mean planning furiously for the next urgent step in your breathless progress to exalted office. I do mean thinking about the things that really matter to you in life, the deep passions or inner drivers, the aspirations or the callings, that will motivate you in a life of leadership and service; the aptitudes you have and how to give them best play; and the weaknesses you have and how to overcome or at least manage them.

When I ask you, as I will, what you want to be doing in 25 years' time, or what you think you need to do to be ultimately satisfied that you have lived a good life, I am not trying to encourage obsessive careerism or a Soviet-style five-year plan for your life: I am trying to encourage you to reflect on how you can make the greatest difference in the areas that matter most to you. I am also trying to encourage you to think about how you can best use your time in Oxford to prepare yourself for your life and career beyond. Consider the deep purposes of your life, and how and when you will give best expression to them.

This is a paradox: in the intense, sometimes exhaustingly intense, busy-ness of Oxford nonetheless to 'smell the roses' and reflect on the things that matter most. As with so many things in life, this requires balance. Another paradox is that this time in Oxford is one of the great experiences of your life – I never doubted that for myself, and I doubt if you will doubt it for yourself – but at times it may also feel like one of the hardest, most homesick, or loneliest times. When this happens, aided by the descent into long grey wet winter, remember that you are not alone. Many others have felt this way before – 'Oxford blues' is a familiar phrase – and many others will be feeling it at the same time as you. Experience suggests that the sixth week of every term, and the third week of Hilary term, are the deepest moments for many – though sadness and depression do not necessarily obey any timetable. You are also not alone because there are people here to help – your fellow Rhodes Scholars, other students, college nurses and doctors and other advisors, staff of the university counselling service, and many of us here at Rhodes House. Do not hesitate to seek help, even just to talk. Please do read the advice from later-year Scholars, born of their experience, on 'Oxford blues' in your welcome pack.

We at Rhodes House cannot promise to solve all problems for you – academic, personal, financial, or other – but two things are certain: one, that we will do everything we can; and two, that the only problems we definitely cannot help with are the ones we don't know about. Please do let us know early of problems you see coming – for example, talk early with the Registrar, Mary Eaton – and enable us to do what we can to help. More generally, of course, try to stay ahead of difficulties: plan ahead, deal early with problems, discuss them with your friends, other advisors and us; think in advance about your strategies for minimising and managing stress.

All of this is also an indirect way of saying that as a Rhodes Scholar you are a member of a community – a Rhodes community in Oxford, and a global Rhodes community of Scholars from many nations and generations around the world. I hope that you will be active in the Rhodes community here and, once you leave Oxford, as a Rhodes alumnus over the decades ahead.

One of the most valuable opportunities you have in the Rhodes community is the opportunity to get to know exceptional people from many countries, including people who will be leaders in all sorts of fields around the world over the decades ahead. You can develop a community of friends from many countries – a global network of future leaders who are your friends – but only by extending the hand of friendship, and by taking it when it is offered to you. Remember also that this is a community and not a clique; and please do not let your nationality or other group of Rhodes Scholars be seen as a clique within the Rhodes community.

While you are a member of the Rhodes community, you are – importantly and simultaneously – a member of several other Oxford communities as well: your college, your course or department, the communities associated with your extra-curricular activities, for many a faith community, and perhaps others. Our Rhodes activities seek to supplement, not to supplant, the other communities of belonging and engagement to which you belong, and we hope you will take an active involvement in them, including most especially in your college.

With an educational philosophy that emphasised the development of 'breadth' and engagement with fellow students from different backgrounds, including of course British students, Cecil Rhodes was keen that Scholars have all the benefits of college life in Oxford, including that they be based in colleges all around Oxford and not clustered in a few. Whatever your college, throw yourself into it and make the most of it.

There will be many aspects of Oxford that may seem puzzling at first, old-fashioned, inefficient, mysterious. Once you have become familiar with them, many of them will come to seem charming; others you will realise are part of the unfathomable genius of one of the world's greatest and most distinctive universities; and others you will, I hope, develop the wisdom simply to accept without judgement.

You are here because you applied for and accepted a scholarship based on a vision and on values. Rhodes's vision was that, by bringing exceptional all-round students into the collegiate environment of Oxford, you – we – could be broadened in perspective and encouraged to see public duties as our highest goal, and that by the mixing of Scholars and other students of this and many other countries international understanding and indeed peace would be promoted. The values are inherent in this vision and in the criteria on which Rhodes Scholars are chosen – criteria of excellence in intellect, character, capacity for leadership, and commitment to service. Let me say a little about each of these in turn.

Intellect. You were chosen as a strong student and admitted to a course because you were judged to be academically well suited and motivated for it. If you are like I was when I first came to Oxford, you will be quietly fearing that now you will be found out – now it will at last come out that you aren't really up to it, or as good as all these other students. Don't believe a word of it. You were chosen for a Rhodes Scholarship and admitted to Oxford because you *are* up to it. But don't go to the other extreme. You will only do well by working hard – working hard combined, I hope, also with a rich and balanced life of extra-curricular activities, including the purposeless enjoyment of friendships and many moments of idle reflection. During this year, many Scholars will make applications and receive offers for second or third year programs – most commonly the DPhil – which depend on meeting academic conditions. Do not take those conditions for granted. It will be important to discuss your second and third year options with Mary Eaton and with me; and essential also that, if you have doubts about your current course, you talk with Mary also. Please do not lift a finger without talking with Mary!

Oxford should be a period of further intellectual growth for you. It is especially good at helping you develop greater capacity for clarity of thought, for rigorous analysis, and for clarity of expression. It places a strong emphasis on thinking, writing, and speaking with precision. It often does this through a strong emphasis on questions. 'What exactly do you mean?' and 'Why do you say this?' are two. In many fields of life – certainly in leadership in any field – one of the keys to achievement is the art of asking the right questions – fundamental questions that penetrate to the core of what is at stake. Oxford is the home of good, if hard, questions. Your thesis, if you write one, will probably best be conceived as answering a very precise question. If you sit exams, the best advice I can give you, far more important than it probably sounds, is 'answer the question': answer the specific question that is set. When you come to see me, what you may think is my giving you advice will actually most often be my trying to help you identify the right questions for you to ask yourself, and suggesting some possible ways for you to answer them for yourself.

Your Oxford studies are in a context where you have the opportunity both to pursue one or more fields of specialisation, and importantly to develop further the breadth of knowledge needed to understand your specialisation in context, to see the often ever-evolving links between apparently separate fields of study, to be able to respond well to a changing world, and to be an educated person. You can develop breadth through, for example, going to almost any lecture or seminar on any lecture list in the University, to special lectures, to clubs and societies, to the cultural activities with which Oxford and London are so rich, and through friendships with students, including Rhodes Scholars, of disciplines, of countries, and of backgrounds different from your own.

Not only is postgraduate study, which most of you are now entering for the first time, usually less prescriptive – for example, about precisely what to read – than undergraduate study, but

Oxford is traditionally particularly unprescriptive about what you need to study. The traditional Oxford doctrine is that you are expected to master a field of study, not a narrow topic, and to have your own well-considered lines of interpretation on the issues that count, not just to have read and recycled particular chapters or articles. All this requires a greater degree of individual initiative and capacity for independent study than many students are used to. This – and all the immense array of enriching extra-curricular activities – requires careful attention to the management of time.

In all of this, though you are likely to receive more individual attention, you are also likely to receive less prescriptive guidance and less affirmation from those who teach or supervise you than you may be accustomed to. Oxford may be the home of piercing questions, but it is not the home of personal or academic affirmation. Do not expect anyone to fall at your feet. That stopped when you ceased to be an undergraduate, perhaps when you hopped on the plane. It is quite likely that the invaluable intellectual challenge and stretching you will face, perhaps combined with less affirmation than you may be used to or (being human) need, will shake your confidence for a while, perhaps a long while. But experience shows that the chances are very high that you will emerge sharper and stronger, including with well-justified confidence about what you are good at and well-founded modesty about what others are better at.

Character. Cecil Rhodes was very clear about attributes he wanted to see in his Scholars. Some Scholars have heard me speak about this earlier in the week. As well as referring to 'moral force of character and … instincts to lead', Rhodes specified attributes wanted: 'qualities of … truth, courage, devotion to duty, sympathy for and protection of the weak, kindliness, unselfishness, and fellowship'. As some have heard me say before, the winning of a Rhodes Scholarship is not a certificate to say that you have such character; it is a lifelong challenge to you to show that you do. It is a challenge to live a life of integrity and authenticity. Your character will continue to be judged by your fellow Rhodes Scholars and by the communities you serve over the years and decades ahead.

One part of character is the courage to stand up to authority when justice demands that. Another is not believing that the rules don't apply to you. The Rhodes Scholarship has very few rules, set out in the Handbook which you have and should read carefully; I hope that none of you will need reminding of them. Wilful or wilfully ignorant breach of the rules will not bring forth from me the kindliness which was another of Rhodes's desired attributes of character.

One of the important questions for Rhodes Scholars is how to combine the apparently saintly qualities of unselfishness that are sought with the more assertive qualities and the relentless ambition often considered necessary for success in many fields of public and business life. The answer lies in part in the first two attributes I quoted from Cecil Rhodes: truth and courage; living a life of integrity and showing moral courage; knowing what you believe and standing firmly – fighting – for it.

This leads us to the connection between character and **leadership**. Rhodes Scholars should be leaders, in whatever fields, whose leadership is grounded in ethics and integrity. Goodness knows how much all our countries need excellent leadership, and ethical leadership. I hope that one of the topics on which you will reflect while you are in Oxford and over the years beyond is on the nature of leadership, and how you can be the best leader you can be. My own favourite definition of good leadership is that it is doing what is needed to get a community or organisation to deal effectively with its real issues.

Two attributes of excellent leadership that are much spoken of today are humility, and emotional intelligence. The business writer Jim Collins is well known for his notion of 'level 5' leadership, the most effective form of leadership, which combines personal humility with resolute professional focus and will.

Humility is not a quality that comes naturally to all Rhodes Scholars, but it is worth working at.

A few months ago we had at Rhodes House a talk on leadership from Rhodes Scholar Joseph Nye, author of, amongst much else, a book called *The Powers to Lead*. Joe Nye lists six skills needed for leadership, and one of these is emotional intelligence. This too is worth working at. For example, as you engage with British people both in and out of Oxford, as you develop friendships with Rhodes Scholars and other students from other countries, seek to develop your capacity for empathy. Try to understand them, and do not rush to judgement. The development of empathy will increase your capacity to understand, appreciate, and get the most from whatever new environments you enter, whatever new people you encounter, and it will increase your capacity to lead effectively.

One of the phrases you will often hear in the Rhodes community is that Rhodes Scholars should fight 'the world's fight'. This is one way of expressing the idea that the purpose of leadership should be **service**. While all Rhodes Scholars are called to do something with their lives that will make the world better than it would otherwise be, our tradition has never been to be prescriptive about what form this service should take. The lives of so many Rhodes Scholars, good people making a difference for good in so many corners of the world, reflect diverse pathways. Each person and each path is unique. Part, I hope, of what you will reflect on over your time in Oxford is what your unique form of service will be; what you will do with your life that will make the greatest difference you can for good in the world. As you reflect on this large and crucial question, there are many opportunities as a Rhodes Scholar to serve communities near and far, including through Rhodes activities such as – just to name one – the Rhodes Scholars' Southern Africa Forum, and through activities in the wider community.

Without becoming insular, one community that requires service is the Rhodes community itself. All of us have been given a life-transforming opportunity through what a Scholar in the year above you described as 'this incredible gift' of a Rhodes Scholarship. It is my hope that both in Oxford and over the decades beyond you will do all you can to help ensure that 'this incredible gift', of which you are now a beneficiary, is equally available to future generations of exceptional young people like you – young people who, as you will do, will make a difference for good in the world. If I did not believe in the importance of this, I would not be standing here today.

Today it is my immense privilege and pleasure to welcome you – to Britain (which it feels odd for an Australian to do!), to Oxford, to postgraduate study, to the Rhodes community in Oxford, to the global community of Rhodes Scholars. You have multiple transitions to manage, and multiple opportunities to seize. All of us here at Rhodes House will do all we can to help. We are delighted that you are here – and I hope that you are too.

Welcoming Rhodes alumni

Luncheon to mark the 50th anniversary of 'coming up'
of the Rhodes Scholar class of 1960
Rhodes House, Oxford, 25 September 2010

A very warm welcome to this lunch to mark the 50th anniversary of the 'coming up' to Oxford in 1960 of the Rhodes Scholars elected around the world in 1959 – the year of my birth!

I am delighted to welcome my dear friend Lady Williams, who with elegance and grace helped make Rhodes House so welcoming for the 28 years that she and Bill, Sir Edgar, Williams were here. And I am delighted to welcome members of the class of 1960, including John Price, who will respond to this toast on behalf of his class. We think also of other members of this class, all of whose names are listed on the menu card; including those who have passed away, but who are not forgotten.

It is fitting especially to remember Bill Williams, wise and legendary Warden, who was legendary also for serving during the war as Chief of Intelligence to Montgomery, playing a key role in the defeat of Rommel at the Battle of El Alamein.

In 1978, 15 years after going down from Oxford, one member of the class of 1960 wrote warmly and charmingly from his office in New York to 'E. T. Williams, Esq. Warden of Rhodes House Oxford, England':

Dear Mr. Williams:

In all likelihood you have completely forgotten the name and other attributes of the undersigned, but I am the undergraduate whom you very gracefully suffered through a meeting with in the late fall of 1960 when I was discoursing freely about Correlli Barnett's book on the Desert Generals, being completely unaware of your prior life as the Fox who outfoxed the Desert Fox.

Despite that intriguing beginning of a relationship, I must say that I came to enjoy immensely the occasions on which I had an opportunity to spend some time with you during my stay at Oxford and I remain very much in your debt. I can truly say that I look back on my days at Oxford, and especially the afternoons and evenings at Rhodes House, with the greatest of pleasurable memories.

I am sure that all Scholars of 1960, and of so many other years, share that sense of gratitude to Bill and Gill Williams for all they did – just as we all share in gratitude to this remarkable Scholarship for the opportunities we have been given, a Scholarship which makes such a difference in the lives of people who make such a difference.

Members of the class of 1960 have made good use of those opportunities, and gone on to positions of leadership and service, making a difference in many fields in many countries: good people doing good.

As an avid reader of the, of course, compelling and unputdownable *Register of Rhodes Scholars 1903-1995*, who has studied the several pages devoted to the year of 1960, I have wondered how best to capture the achievements and contributions of this Rhodes class. Many have worked in government service in their countries – in Canada, and Ghana, and several other countries. More than one worked in the White House; one became Director of the US Peace Corps, Governor of Ohio, and later a college president; at least two served at high level in the World Bank, more than one as an ambassador, at least one as a chief justice. One member of the class of 1960 became a much-honoured Indian film-maker; at least one a novelist; many worked – and some continue to serve – with distinction in law, medicine, engineering, as physicists and economists, in industry and commerce. Many became leaders in higher education, in teaching and research; one a general who became a headmaster –

not the only school principal of the year; one the editor of *Foreign Policy* magazine; and much else.

But it occurred to me that one way to convey the impact of members of the class of 1960 is through the titles of just some of the dozens of books published by them:

- *Constitutional Change in South Africa*
- *Macroeconomic Policies in an Interdependent World*
- *The Great Cat Massacre and Other Episodes in French Cultural History*
- *Excitations in Liquid and Solid Helium*
- *The Spread of Current in Excitable Cells* – there seems a lot of excitement in the class of 1960
- *Strategies and Saints: fighting drugs in subsidized housing*
- *Winning Trial Advocacy: how to avoid mistakes made by master trial lawyers*
- *Canada's Changing Defense Policy 1957-63*
- *The Bible in Dialogue with Modern Man*
- *Exile and tradition: studies in African and Caribbean literature*
- *Newman* [the *Blessed* John Henry Newman*]: *the contemplation of mind*
- *A New Case for the Liberal Arts*
- *Computers in the Guidance and Control of Aero Space Vehicles*

And many, many more.

This is just part, just one slice, of what this remarkable cohort of Rhodes Scholars has contributed to the world – providing many fine examples to current and future generations, many different models of fighting 'the world's fight'. As we reflect on the achievements of the Rhodes class of 1960, we draw

---

* Newman had the previous month been beatified by Pope Benedict XVI, thus becoming the Blessed John Henry Newman.

inspiration for the future of what this Scholarship can do for and through further generations of exceptional young people such as those who first came to Oxford in the autumn of 1960.

John Price (Iowa & Queen's 1960), who will respond to this toast, has – like many other Scholars – combined service in the public and the private sectors. After reading Philosophy, Politics, and Economics (PPE) in Oxford, John went to Harvard Law School. After working on the Rockefeller presidential campaign in 1968, he served in the White House from 1969 to 1971, including as Special Assistant to the President for Urban Affairs at a time of very important work in that and related fields, working closely with Daniel Patrick Moynihan. He then returned to the private sector, first briefly in the law and then in banking and finance, with a strong interest in foreign trade. Throughout, he has also, in Cecil Rhodes's words, 'esteemed the performance of public duties': for example, serving on the executive panel advising the Chief of Naval Operations from 1972 to 1979; with the Council on Foreign Relations; as a trustee of his Iowa alma mater, Grinnell College; and serving *this* alma mater as founding Chairman of Americans for Oxford, providing pioneering leadership in encouraging support for this great University, for which leadership and support we are especially grateful.

It will very soon be my pleasure to call on John Price to respond. But first, ladies and gentlemen, in recognition of this 50th anniversary, I ask you please to toast with me – 'The class of 1960'.

> *Luncheon to mark the 50th anniversary of 'coming up'*
> *of the Rhodes Scholar class of 1961*
> *Rhodes House, Oxford, 17 September 2011*

What a remarkable class of Rhodes Scholars it was who were chosen around the world in the weeks just before and just after the election of President Kennedy in November 1960, and who first arrived in Oxford – who first came to this building, perhaps to get your first stipend cheque – in the autumn of 1961!

It is a great pleasure to welcome members of that class and their partners back to Oxford today, and to welcome everyone who joins in celebrating the 50th anniversary of their coming up. I am grateful to Arthur Scace (Ontario & Corpus Christi 1961), who will respond to this toast on behalf of his fellow members of the class of 1961. Until this morning, my dear friend – our dear friend – Lady (Gill) Williams had intended to come, but she has what I gather is the flu and just cannot make it. It is fitting especially also to think of Bill Williams today, whose photograph – pipe in hand – is in the booklet you have. I am sure that all Scholars of 1961, and of so many other years, share in deep gratitude to Bill and Gill Williams for all they did.

The youthful faces of the Rhodes class of 1961 as they were in 1960-61 may also be seen in the celebration booklet you have. Later in this lunch, I will be presenting each of the members of the class of 1961 here today with a framed copy of their own photograph – a small memento of this celebration.

Sadly, the list of Scholars in our booklet includes a surprising number of names and youthful faces of Scholars who have passed away. We honour their memory.

The recent reflections of several 1961 Scholars about their experiences are in that celebration booklet also. Those reflections refer to the great kindness of Bill and Gill Williams, to the adjustments needed in coming to Oxford and the benefits of this, to experiences shared and friendships formed – many of which friendships are lasting a lifetime – and to the impact of the Rhodes Scholarship on their lives.

In his reflection, Baruch Knei-Paz, who is here today, writes: 'Oxford made me? Well, actually, the Rhodes Scholarship made me.' And Brian Tulloch, also here today, writes: 'There will be many examples of the great changes that Rhodes' generous idea of time at Oxford brought about to its recipients.' And so there are. I love that phrase 'Rhodes' generous idea of time at Oxford'. I am sure we all share in gratitude for the generous gift to us of our life-changing time at Oxford.

Just as the Scholarship had great impact on the remarkable individuals of 1961, so they have had great impact on others in their turn. Members of the class of 1961 have contributed to communities and professions around the world in many ways: as doctors, engineers, professors of many disciplines, soldiers, lawyers, Christian priests and a historian of Jewish experience, bankers, business people of various kinds, public servants – national and international, and more. Your class includes, just to take a few examples, a legal adviser to the British Foreign and Commonwealth Office; a Superintendent of the US Military Academy, West Point, and the head of a defence intelligence college; a senior executive in Anglo-American and director of De Beers; a minister in the Singapore government; a judge of the US Supreme Court, and a special counsel to the US Senate Watergate Committee; a Chichele Professor of the History of War in Oxford, Bob O'Neill, who has been a close friend of mine for nearly 30 years; Scholars who have worked for various international organisations, including the World Bank and the International Labour Organisation.

There were also three Olympians, whom I will name. Graham Bond (Queensland & Balliol 1961) represented Australia in gymnastics at the 1956, 1960, and 1964 Olympics. Graham, by the way, sat on the selection committee in Queensland in 1980 that elected me as a Scholar – so he has a lot to answer for! (Roger Scott, who is here today, and whom I have known since my undergraduate days when he was Professor of Public Administration at the University of Queensland, does not share in that culpability.) Our other Olympians of the class of 1961 are Murray (Tich) McLachlan (Natal & Wadham 1961), who swam for South Africa at the 1960 Olympics, and Eng-Liang Tan (Singapore & Balliol 1961), who had represented Singapore in water polo at the 1956 Olympics.

This is just part, just one slice, of what this remarkable cohort of Rhodes Scholars has achieved and contributed to the world – providing many fine examples to current and future generations, and inspiring us to think with optimism and hope about how much more the Rhodes Scholarship can do through nurturing the talents of future generations, as it did for those who first came to Oxford in the autumn of 1961.

Arthur Scace (Ontario & Corpus Christi), who will respond to this toast, came to Oxford after five years studying economics at Toronto and Harvard. He wrote to Warden Williams from Harvard in February 1961, as the question of what he would read where in Oxford was being determined: 'After 5 years of economics, my mind has become dulled, and it would be foolish to continue this line of study.' So Art read law, and he has never looked back. He also captained Oxford in ice hockey against Cambridge, and rowed and played squash for Corpus. After Oxford, Arthur continued his legal studies at Osgoode Hall in Toronto, and went into legal practice – ultimately, as a Queen's Counsel, becoming the national head of a very major Canadian legal practice, recognised as a leading authority on Canadian tax law and author of an authoritative work on income tax law in Canada, a leader in professional bodies, in business (for example, as chairman of Scotiabank), a leader in community activities (for example, as chair of the Canadian Opera Company), and with Susie a generous philanthropist.

Most especially, we are grateful that from 1973 to 2009 Art served with dedication and distinction as the Canadian Secretary to the Rhodes Trust, responsible through all those years for the selection process for the Scholarships in Canada. For this, and for so much more, we are profoundly grateful to Art, and also very much to Susie. Art has continued to be a great friend and supporter, including in his advice for and his commitment to the fundraising efforts on which the future of the Rhodes Scholarship depends.

On 1 November 1961, Arthur Scace wrote this note from Corpus Christi:

Dear Mr and Mrs Williams. I have just returned from your party, and having enjoyed myself so much, thought a note was in order. Your hospitality tonight was greatly appreciated as until tonight, I had only met the Canadian and Rhodesian delegations of Rhodes Scholars. Thank you very much for a most pleasant evening. Sincerely, Arthur Scace

On 12 June 1962, Susan Kernohan wrote this note:

Dear Mrs Williams, Thank you very much for giving me the opportunity to hear [tonight's] concert. I enjoyed it immensely. It was also a great pleasure to meet you and Mr Williams as I have been hearing a great deal about you from Arthur. …

Thank you again for a delightful evening.

Sincerely, Susan Kernohan

At the bottom of this note, Bill Williams annotated: 'Art Scace's girl'. Susie and Art were married in August 1963, and we are delighted that they are both here today along with other Scholars of 1961 and what Bill, in the long-gone style of those days, would have called 'their girls'.*

You are extremely welcome.

---

* There were no women Rhodes Scholars in 1961. The first women came to Oxford as Rhodes Scholars in 1977 after equality legislation in the UK made it possible for Cecil Rhodes's will of 1899 to be amended to provide for this.

'Still for ever, fare thee well!'

Farewell dinner hosted by the Rhodes Trustees
Malmaison Hotel, Oxford
6 December 2012

I would like to begin by paying tribute to Jakes Gerwel.[*] On the one occasion that I met Nelson Mandela, Jakes's name arose, and Mr Mandela said simply: 'He is a very wise man'. So true. Like others, I am profoundly grateful for Jakes's remarkable life, for his influence for good in the new South Africa and beyond, and for his superb Chairmanship of the Mandela Rhodes Foundation; and like so many others, I deeply mourn his passing.

I would also like to acknowledge with deep sadness the passing yesterday of a dear friend of mine, Dame Elisabeth Murdoch, at the age of 103.[†] She was, for me, a kind of angel, and I with countless others also deeply mourn her passing.

Many thanks to Don Gogel for your kind words, and to you and the Trustees for hosting tonight's dinner – just as I am grateful to John Hood and to Andrew Graham for hosting such a moving farewell event with current Scholars at Rhodes House on Sunday, and for their kind words then.

It has been a unique and inspiring privilege and an exhausting challenge to serve as Warden of Rhodes House from July 2009. I would like to thank the Trustees for this opportunity, and to thank them and others for the support which has been given to me in my time as Warden.

---

[*] Professor Gert Johannes ('Jakes') Gerwel (18 January 1946-28 November 2012): Amongst many other roles, Jakes served as Vice-Chancellor of the University of the Western Cape (1987-94), Director-General in the Office of President Nelson Mandela and Secretary of the Cabinet (1994-99), Chancellor of Rhodes University (1999-2012), and Chair of the Mandela Rhodes Foundation (2003-12).

[†] There are a number of references to Dame Elisabeth Murdoch (8 February 1909-5 December 2012) in '*A large and liberal education': higher education for the 21st century*.

It seems oddly appropriate to be here at the Malmaison Hotel, the former Oxford prison, where in a sense my Wardenship began. When in February 2009 – in the dark days of the global financial crisis, when markets were still collapsing around the world – I came over from Australia to be interviewed for the Wardenship, I stayed here, and it was probably in the old prison cell that was my hotel room here that I made the decision that, whatever the nature and scope of the challenges of the Trust, they had to be met, and that – as a grateful Rhodes Scholar who had devoted his career to education, including to the messy business of leading change in educational institutions – I was, perhaps naively but irresistibly, willing to take on that challenge.

It seemed then that we would need to raise about £50 million. When I started as Warden four months later, it was soon clear that we would need to raise, over the decade, at least twice that much. I did not know when I was interviewed just how great a change to the governance of the Trust or to the staff capacity at Rhodes House was needed to be able to meet that challenge.

Chief among the positive discoveries when I came to Rhodes House was the high quality of the current Scholars, and the willingness – when invited in – of so many Scholars of all generations, grateful for what the Scholarship has done for them, to be part of the response to the challenges we faced. Colin Lucas, to whom the Trust and I owe special thanks, said to me 'it's the kids [the current Scholars] who make it worthwhile', and he was right; it has been an inspiration and a delight to deal with them. My own passionate commitment to do all that was needed for the future of the Rhodes Scholarships was sustained by the remarkable encouragement given by Rhodes Scholars of all generations around the world, including the current Scholars in Oxford.

Everything which I have done has been motivated by the desire to help to give the best effect in our time and for the future to the great and enduring vision which Cecil Rhodes left of a uniquely special scholarship program that would promote both civic-minded leadership and, as we have reminded ourselves of late, harmonious connections – even peace – between nations. To uphold this vision in challenging times, it was necessary simultaneously to try to do more things than one would ideally have chosen. This included:

- to expand our communication and outreach to Rhodes alumni, which for me involved – amongst other things – between 90 and 100 alumni events in 17 countries in three years;

- to consult our alumni if we were to engage their help, and to take many other steps in the light of that consultation, including...

- to transform the governance and transparency of the Trust if we were to have any chance of mustering the support we needed;

- to expand the activities for Scholars within Oxford if they were to be able to make the most of their time in Oxford, and if their vital support for the Scholarship now and over the decades ahead was to be ensured;

- to refresh and modernise many other aspects of the Trust's operations, including to make it equally attractive to outstanding young women as to outstanding young men;

- actually to go out and ask for financial support, through annual giving and bequests as well as major gifts; and

- to begin to develop plans and to seek the resources for expanding rather than contracting the Scholarship to give renewed effect to the global vision of Cecil Rhodes in the geopolitical realities of the 21st century.

Many people – Trustees; Rhodes Scholars of all generations within Oxford and around the world; Rhodes Trust staff, a number of whom have been truly magnificent; and many friends of the Scholarship – many people contributed to this turnaround in the affairs of the Trust. I am proud to have played some part in this historic effort, and would like again to express gratitude to all those – Trustees, staff, Scholars, and others – who provided support to me in the role that I was playing.

I think that together we focussed on the core purposes of the Rhodes Trust and the Rhodes Scholarships. Together, we learnt the immense power of engaging Rhodes Scholars in contributing to the self-renewal of our community and heritage. And in the process, I think that together we rediscovered the importance of what the early Wardens seem, rightly I think, to have regarded as essential to achieving Cecil Rhodes's vision – engaging the Scholars in a community in Oxford when they are here, and keeping them connected through the decades afterwards. I think that we can together be quietly proud that some £33 million was raised in three years, while current Scholar satisfaction with their support from Rhodes House on a 1 to 5 scale, with 5 the maximum, registered at 4.88.

Of course, while inspiring, rewarding, and productive, it was also an exhausting and demanding time, as anyone understanding the scale of the challenge, the remorseless workload needed, and the practical reality of turnaround and change management would realise. I very much hope that, with the thoughtful, caring, and effective support of the Trustees, my successor will maintain and build the momentum that is needed to make the Rhodes community in Oxford and globally as vibrant as it should be, and to ensure that the Scholarships not contract and be diminished. I am sure that the Rhodes community wishes to build on what has been achieved, not to retreat, and that it hopes even, as I do, that the best is yet to come.

Christmas and the New Year are good times for looking ahead to even better things to come, and I wish you and your families happy times together in this holiday season. My own children are glad to have their Dad back, and we will have a summer Christmas together in Australia for the first time in four years. 'In all the world so wonderful, there's no place like home.'

Since my stepping down as Warden to return to Australia was announced and, soon after, my appointment to run the Menzies Research Centre, I have received many, many hundreds of very warm, generous, and affirming messages from around the world. One of these is from a Scholar in his 90s who came up in 1946.[*] He concluded his very moving message with a line from Byron with which I will conclude, as it encapsulates what I want most of all to say:

> Fare thee well! And if for ever,
>
> Still for ever, fare thee well!

---

[*] George Cawkwell (New Zealand & Christ Church 1946).

Part V:
'Love is stronger than death'

'Love is stronger than death'

Choral Evensong for the Feast of St Frideswide
St George's Cathedral, Perth, Western Australia
28 October 2007

As we mark this feast of St Frideswide, the 8th century princess and nun who is patron saint of Oxford, and with friends and colleagues from the Oxford Society here this afternoon, it is fitting to reflect on the bonds – historical and contemporary – which link the Anglican Church in this diocese and specifically this Cathedral, with Oxford and especially with the University of Oxford.

There is in this Cathedral a tablet in memory of the Revd John Burdett Wittenoom, MA, Colonial Chaplain here in Western Australia from January 1830 until his death in January 1855, aged 66. The tablet was, in its own words, 'erected by members of the flock of which he was so long the respected pastor', and says – I quote again – that 'under [his] ministry, amidst the struggle and privation of an infant colony, a scion of the Church of England was planted in a remote wilderness'.

I wonder how often Wittenoom contrasted his life in this 'remote wilderness', as it then was, with the Oxford of his youth. For Wittenoom was a member of Brasenose College, an Oxford graduate who brought to this 'infant colony' the liturgical and theological approaches of the Oxford of his day. Wittenoom shows, not least, Oxford as an intellectual resource for the wider world, which it very much remains.

If I may be permitted a personal note: my own journey, 150 years after Wittenoom came to Western Australia, was very different. I was born and was a young boy in what was certainly still in some sense 'a remote wilderness' in far outback Queensland, and sometimes reflected on the contrast with it when I was, as an adult, for 14 years an Oxford postgraduate student and then an Oxford don.

Wittenoom's legacy was not only in the Anglican Church here in Western Australia. Some of it was personal. There is in this Cathedral a plaque in memory of his grand-daughter, Edith Cowan, social reformer, prominent Anglican, and the first Australian woman Member of Parliament, whose name has been given to another university, here in this city, and whose image appears on our $50 notes.

Those who enjoy the rivalry, friendly or otherwise, between Oxford and Cambridge may be interested to know that John Tonkin in his history of this Cathedral writes of the early decades of Anglicans in 19th century Western Australia: 'The difference between Oxford and Cambridge clerical backgrounds in these early years was not without significance, for their traditions ran deep."

Oxford partisans will be pleased to hear that the index of Professor Tonkin's book shows 18 references to Oxford, and only five to Cambridge – and that is not counting the 13 references to the 19th century Oxford Movement, the Anglo-Catholic movement which so profoundly affected the Anglican Church, and the three references to the Oxford Group, the Moral Rearmament Movement, which had some modest influence here, as we have been reminded in recently reflecting on the life of the late Kim Beazley, Senior.[†]

The impact of Oxford is, I am not the first to suggest, evident in this Cathedral even today. Thanks not least to the vision and leadership of the Dean, himself a former chaplain of Christ Church, Oxford, the best of Oxford is reflected here: in the encouragement to intellectual thought and discussion, which

---

* John Tonkin, *Cathedral and Community: A History of St George's Cathedral, Perth*, University of Western Australia Press, p. 14. I regret that some other sources for quotations in this sermon are unknown.

† Kim Edward Beazley, AO (30 September 1917-12 October 2007): Member of the Australian Parliament, 1946-77; Minister for Education, 1972-75.

can support and illuminate faith; in the magnificent and often inspiring way that scripture, tradition, choral music, and liturgy blend together, as they do in some at least of the chapels of Oxford, and not only though perhaps especially at New College, Magdalen, and Christ Church, with their magnificent choirs; in the sense of community and belonging which Oxford nurtures in its colleges, and which is an important and deliberate part of the life of this Cathedral congregation as a 'loving, exploring community'.

If Oxford Society members like the sound of this – remember that this Cathedral very warmly welcomes you throughout the year, and not only to celebrate the Feast of St Frideswide.

I was fortunate in May this year to be back in Oxford and, knowing that I would be standing here today, revisited Christ Church Cathedral to see the simple tablet on the floor, between other more elaborate memorials and tombs from centuries past, which bears one word: 'Frideswide'.

There is as well the shrine of St Frideswide, most recently reconstructed in 2002; a tapestry banner dedicated to St Frideswide; a medieval stained glass window of her; and the beautiful St Frideswide window of Edward Burne-Jones from 1858, with its many bright-coloured panels telling the story of St Frideswide – her entry to a nunnery; the pursuit of her, despite her monastic vows, by the love-struck or dynastically-minded or perhaps merely lecherous King Algar; her hiding in bushes and in a pigsty; her establishing a new nunnery at Binsey; her healing the sick; Algar struck blind by a bolt of lightning; Frideswide on her death-bed; and a ship of souls transporting her to heaven. The truth is that different accounts exist of Frideswide's life, and only a little is really known for certain.

Moved as I was by seeing again Christ Church's tributes to St Frideswide, who had founded a monastic church where Christ Church Cathedral now stands, and whose earthly remains are buried there, something else also struck me powerfully on that visit. As I was leaving the Cathedral, I noticed a plaque in the cloister, in memory of a chorister, Jeremy Angus Sebastian Clement Kitchen, born in 1967 and died in 1985 – obviously at the age of 17 or 18; which is every parent's nightmare. This also-simple plaque contained these words: 'Love is stronger than death'. Our Dean here at St George's Cathedral, the Very Revd John Shepherd, was Chaplain of Christ Church from 1980 to 1988, and knew this young man and his family.

These words – 'love is stronger than death' – have, of course, been used by others – as a chapter title by the theologian Paul Tillich, as the title of at least two different books, in the lyrics of songs, and no doubt elsewhere.

I can only imagine what led the grieving family to choose these words. Perhaps part of it is simply the sense, important to so many of us, that those whom we have loved and who have died live on in our loving memory. But it seems to me that those words – 'love is stronger than death' – in some sense encapsulate much, perhaps indeed the essence, of the Christian faith.

Certainly these words came again to mind in reflecting on today's Gospel reading. This reading from the 14th chapter of John's Gospel is part of Jesus's farewell to his disciples, in the long night before his death. He has told them that he would soon die, betrayed by one of them, and denied by Peter; and then come these words of comfort, reassurance, consolation, for this small band of no doubt confused and distressed disciples.

Jesus's words remain words of comfort still. When he was dying, the historical novelist and poet Sir Walter Scott had this – the 14th chapter of John's Gospel – read to him on his deathbed. I cannot read or hear this passage from John without thinking of Thomas Tallis's beautiful, certainly comforting (I am tempted to say 'divine') musical setting of them:

> If ye love me,
> keep my commandment,
> and I will pray the Father,
> and he shall give you another comforter,

that he may 'bide with you forever,

e'en the spirit of truth.

In these words and those that follow, Jesus links love for him with obedience to his commandments. That same night he has said to the disciples:*

A new commandment I give unto you, That ye love one another; as I have loved you, that ye also love one another.

By this shall all men know that ye are my disciples, if ye have love one to another.

So love for Christ, and keeping his commandments, includes loving one another, and through this love showing the world that ye – that we – are his disciples.

In this passage for the first time Jesus says that, to those who love him, and keep his commandments, God will send the Holy Spirit – the spirit of truth, advocate or Paraclete, counsellor, comforter – who will enable believers to understand the words of Jesus which before his death they may not have understood. Jesus has already described himself as the Truth. The Spirit of Truth will bring to the disciples' remembrance all that Jesus said and did. The Holy Spirit, or Paraclete, is sent by the Father, at Jesus's request, and in Jesus's name; and teaches and leads believers into truth.

And so Jesus's disciples are assured that his departure through the death which he is soon to undergo will in fact presage a return – his going almost a form of coming. In fact, 'the return of Jesus is conceived in this passage in different ways: he returns to the disciples shortly after his crucifixion in the resurrection appearances (vv. 18ff.); he comes in the person of the Holy Spirit, the Paraclete (vv. 15ff.); he comes together with the Father to make his abode with those who love him (v. 23).'

---

* John 13: 34.

Those who love me will keep my word, and my Father will love them, and we will come to them and make our home with them.*

The emphasis in John's Gospel on love is very powerful. We all recall the passage in John 3:16:

For God so loved the world, that he gave his only begotten Son, that whosoever believeth in him should not perish, but have everlasting life.

Love indeed is stronger than death.

As well as God's love for the world, John emphasises the Father's love for the Son, the Son's love for his disciples, and the disciples' love for one another. 'By this shall all men know that ye are my disciples, if ye have love one to another.'

Our other reading for today, from the First Book of Maccabees, is from the Apocrypha – the 'hidden works' – of the Old Testament, books contained in some but not in other versions of the Bible, but from which – within the Anglican tradition – 'the lectionary attached to the Book of Common Prayer, from 1549 onwards, has always contained prescribed lessons'.†

Today's reading from the First Book of Maccabees is part of an account of the struggle for Jewish independence and the reassertion of the Jewish law and culture in the second century before Christ, against those who had replaced Jewish culture with Greek culture. As 'in earlier phases of Jewish history, [an] increase in the attraction of heathen cultures among Jews evoked equally strong anti-foreign reactions.' Our reading includes an account of Mattathias's revolt to 'rescue the [Jewish] law out of the hands of the Gentiles'. In this reading we see Mattathias's long final speech before his death – the kind of long final speech

---

* John 14: 23.
† *New Oxford Annotated Bible*, Oxford University Press, 2006.

before death which other great Israelites of the past, such as Jacob, Moses, and Samuel, have had. 'In it he described how Israel's past heroes were rewarded for their loyalty to the law and covenant.'

Our reading from John's Gospel is from Jesus's long final speech before *his* death – his farewell to his disciples – in which the focus is, not on the law, but on love – and on the keeping of commandments at the heart of which are the commandments to love God, and to love one another.

Today – as I think of the memorials in Oxford's Christ Church Cathedral to St Frideswide, patron of Oxford, and to a chorister who died long before his time; and of the memorials in this Cathedral to John Burdett Wittenoom, who brought something of Oxford to what was then 'a remote wilderness', and to his grand-daughter, Edith Cowan – I think above all of Jesus's call *to us* to be a loving community, and I think of those haunting words that seem to me to say so much: that 'love is stronger than death'.

INDEX